ROMAN DRAMA

The Library of Liberal Arts
OSKAR PIEST, FOUNDER

ROMAN DRAMA

THE PLAYS OF PLAUTUS AND TERENCE

Translated by
FRANK O. COPLEY

THE PLAYS OF SENECA

Translated by
MOSES HADAS

With an Introduction by
MOSES HADAS

The Library of Liberal Arts
published by

Bobbs-Merrill Educational Publishing
Indianapolis

Titus Maccius Plautus: *ca.* 255 - 184 B.C.

Publius Terentius Afer: *ca.* 195 - 159 B.C.

Lucius Annaeus Seneca: 4 B.C. - A.D. 65

• • • • • • • • • • • • • • • • • • •

The Bobbs-Merrill Company, Inc.
4300 West 62nd Street
Indianapolis, Indiana 46268

First Edition
Eighth Printing — 1977

Library of Congress Catalog Card Number 64-66074
ISBN 0-672-60455-8 (pbk.)
ISBN 0-672-51095-0

CONTENTS

INTRODUCTION

Drama, like other amenities of civilized life, the Romans learned from the Greeks. Centuries before Rome reached a level of wealth and sophistication which could afford and require cultivation of the fine arts, Greece had already attained a literature and art and philosophy as mature as any the world has seen. If the Romans had remained insulated from the Greeks they might have achieved an original art and literature independent of Greek models; but it would be absurd to expect them to rise from the primitive by laborious stages when the perfected art of the Greeks was available to copy or adapt. Politically, Greece was under Roman domination; culturally, as Horace put it, captive Greece captivated its captors.

The first considerable literary production in Latin was a translation of a Greek classic—a version of the *Odyssey* by Livius Andronicus (*ca.* 284–204 B.C.). There was a practical motivation for this work: Roman schoolboys needed a piece of literature to study. And there was practical motivation for drama also, which Livius proceeded to translate. State festivals included performances of various sorts, and as festivals became more elaborate and the expectations of spectators were raised, it was natural for dramatic performances to be included, as they were in Greek festivals; the obvious way to supply texts was to translate them from the Greek. For the so-called Roman Games of 240 B.C., Livius Andronicus composed and acted in the first Latin comedy and the first Latin tragedy, and so set Roman drama on its way. Livius' tragedies were all adaptations of Greek models, with plots and dramatis personae drawn from Greek myth. Those connected with the Trojan War (which comprise the larger number) may have had a special interest for the Romans because the story of the Trojan connection with the foundation of Rome, familiar to us from the *Aeneid*, had already been promulgated.

Naevius (*ca.* 270–201 B.C.), Livius' immediate successor, did apparently try to introduce genuinely Roman themes, but the playwrights who followed, whether in tragedy or comedy, reverted to purely Greek models. Besides Plautus and Terence, whose works survive and can be described more fully, these dramatists were Ennius (239–169 B.C.), who was a pioneer in several genres, his nephew Pacuvius (220–130 B.C.), and Accius (170–86 B.C.). Of the works of these men no complete specimen survives; we have only some titles and short quotations or allusions in later writers. On the basis of these scanty fragments, we can judge that early Roman tragedy was highly rhetorical and filled with intense passion and that it exploited sensational spectacle. In the performance of Accius' *Clutemestra*, for example, we are told that two hundred richly caparisoned mules carrying the loot of fallen Troy paraded across the stage.

It is no accident, but a true index of the relative vogue of the two forms, that surviving Roman comedy so far predominates over tragedy. Even in Greek lands, when Romans could know them, drama meant comedy, not tragedy; comedy is what Romans who kept abreast of Greek literature could read, comedy is what tourists or soldiers serving in Greek-speaking areas could see. The great days of classical tragedy had ended with the fifth century B.C. Plays written in succeeding centuries tend to be mere literary exercises; revivals of Aeschylus, Sophocles, and Euripides, mere museum pieces. Euripides himself marks a transition from the remote and heroic to the immediate and familiar. His plots and personages are still drawn from the heroic world of myth, but their problems and aspirations are those of ordinary humanity. Slaves and children and ragged figures appear on the stage; love stories become prominent; there are complicated intrigues, separations, and recognitions; and the objective is generally a happy, not a "tragic," ending. It is the theater of Euripides that is the spiritual ancestor of Greek New Comedy, of which all our Roman comedies are adaptations.

The lineal ancestor of New Comedy is the Old Comedy of Aristophanes and his rivals, from which New Comedy derived its invented plots and its characters of familiar contemporary types. Although Old Comedy is filled with serious political and social criticism, its method is farce, and its characters seldom engage our sympathies as human beings. As in tragedy, they tend to resemble mathematical symbols that facilitate discussion of an abstract problem; we do not agonize with them as individuals and yearn for their vindication. It is here that New Comedy made its great innovation. The only complete play of Menander which has so far come to light is his *Dyskolos*, or *The Bad Tempered Man*, first published, in modern times, in 1959. The slightness of this piece is hard to reconcile with the high reputation of its author; the turning point comes when a city youth pacifies the sour father of the country girl he wishes to marry by helping him out of a well. But the very blandness of the story and its homespun characters must have delighted audiences wearied by heroics grown empty. The *Dyskolos* is one of Menander's earliest efforts; some of his maturer plays, of which we have considerable fragments, are much richer in character and plot, but the dramatis personae and their problems and aspirations remain universally recognizable middle-class types. It was because of its universal intelligibility that New Comedy was exportable to non-Greek audiences.

Unpretentious as New Comedy is, like all formal Greek literature it is careful to preserve traditional forms. Not only is the composition all in verse, but the casts of characters and even the plots seem to be repeated with only minor changes from play to play. In one after another, a young man is in love with a girl owned by a white slaver who is about to dispose of her elsewhere; his cunning servant defrauds the young man's father of the necessary sum; the girl is discovered to be of good birth (having been kidnaped or exposed in infancy) and hence an eligible bride. But as in the case of Greek tragedies or of Doric temples, so in comedy the artist secures his special effects through significant variations and refinements of an established pattern. These are usually so extensive and striking as to make each play a novel creation. In some the pattern is blurred altogether. *Amphitryon,* for example, has such Plautine characteristics as mistaken identities and a comic slave; its plot, however, is not a free invention but derives from a traditional myth on the birth of Hercules, which it travesties. It is therefore thought to derive not from New but from Middle Comedy, of which little is known except that it often did travesty myth. Thus, gradations in affections and loyalty and wit give even such stock characters as slaves and parasites and forlorn maidens individual reality. Nor are the free-born children brought up in slavery merely a dramatic convention; in the Hellenistic world poverty and war were endemic; many infants were, in fact, exposed, and many persons displaced. Another theme whose regular recurrence may puzzle the modern reader is that of the irregular sexual liaison. Here it must be remembered that ancient society recognized the double standard: respectable young men were allowed latitude; respectable young women were not. Girls involved in relationships that we should regard as illicit are not of the sort whom their lovers could marry; respectable girls eligible for marriage are never involved in such relationships. Far from being demoralizing, the plays are often lessons in propriety.

The Romans made no effort to dissemble their indebtedness to their Greek models; rather, they advertised it by retaining Greek costumes and background and even Greek names of persons and places. In a genre addressed to a large and undiscriminating audience, such fidelity to literary tradition may seem to be unnecessary pedantry, but there are parallels in other civilizations; the Japanese plays of Chikamatsu, which are strikingly like New Comedy in several respects and enjoyed very wide popularity, are even more scrupulous in observing traditions of form. Possibly Greek backgrounds and persons were retained for much the same reasons that English literature long represented frivolous or raffish characters as being French or of French descent. To show respectable gentlemen being ridiculed or defrauded by impudent slaves, as they frequently were in Greek plays, might be damaging to the image of ideal Roman behavior. Plautus, however, does occasionally introduce an allusion to some Roman usage or event, and both Plautus and Terence use episodes from more than one Greek play in constructing a single Latin one.

The scanty record of the life of Titus Maccius Plautus (ca. 255–184 B.C.) was reconstructed centuries after his death and probably rests on nothing more substantial than deductions from his writings. According to the traditional account, he was born at Sarsina in northern Italy, became a stage carpenter or possibly an actor, traveled abroad on business, in which he lost his savings but perhaps learned Greek, was reduced to menial labor in a flour mill, and wrote plays successful enough to enable him to devote full time to writing. His reputation was such that imitations were passed off under his name; by the first century B.C., 130 plays were attributed to Plautus. The learned Varro, who was Julius Caesar's librarian, drew up a list of twenty-one which he considered authentic, acknowledging that others might be also. These are probably, but not certainly, the twenty-one (counting the fragmentary *Vidularia*) which we have. Plautus surely wrote more than these twenty-one; on the other hand, some of the twenty-one may not be his. Evidence for dating is available for only a few of the plays. On the basis of these few, it would appear that the earlier plays are metrically simple, the later ones metrically ornate; but this criterion is inadequate for constructing a chronology, and therefore the plays are normally arranged not by date but alphabetically according to their Latin titles. They are *Amphitryon* (the basis of Giraudoux's *Amphitryon 38*); *Asinaria*; *Aulularia* or *Pot of Gold* (the basis of Molière's *L'Avare*); *Bacchides,* which rests on mistaken identity; *Captivi* (with *Aulularia,* the basis of Ben Jonson's *The Case Is Altered*); *Casina; Cistellaria; Curculio; Epidicus; Menaechmi* (the basis of Shakespeare's *Comedy of Errors*); *Mercator; Miles Gloriosus* or *Braggart Soldier; Mostellaria* or *The Haunted House*; *Persa* or *The Girl from Persia; Poenulus* or *The Carthaginian*; *Pseudolus*; *Rudens* or *The Rope*; *Stichus*; *Trinummus*; *Truculentus*; and *Vidularia*.

Plautus' comedy is ebullient and robust; his primary object is to evoke the greatest possible volume of hearty laughter, and he will sometimes descend to clowning in order to gain his end. His characters belong to a familiar and limited cast, like those in the *commedia dell' arte* or in a good comic strip, and the plots in which they are involved are similarly limited in range. But underneath the superficial sameness (enhanced by stock masks), the type characters are individualized, not only in pronounced cases like the miser in *Aulularia,* the father in *Captivi,* and the white slaver in *Rudens,* but also in the ordinary men and women who are victimized by life and then come to terms with it. Men want, by and large, to establish their identity, marry the right girl, and live happily ever after; and this, in most of the plays, is what they do. Unlike the more bookish Terence, Plautus was a practical man of the theater and also knew life at first hand. Not only do his plays show a sophisticated sense of theater, but even so romantic a piece as *Rudens* communicates a sense of reality. Unlike his Greek models (and his Latin successor, Terence, who copied them more closely) Plautus makes frequent use of lyric measures. The Greeks inserted choral interludes between the episodes of their plays, but these were impractical on the Roman stage. For the musical element, Plautus substituted many solos and duets, and thus produced the effect of musical comedy or Italian operetta.

Caecilius Statius, active between Plautus and Terence, was ranked as their peer by ancient critics, but his works have not survived. All of the six plays written by Terence (195–159 B.C.) have survived. Terence was born in Africa, brought to Rome as a slave, educated by his owner, the senator Terentius Lucanus, and upon liberation took the name of Publius Terentius Afer ("the African"). He was befriended by Scipio Africanus the Younger, and became one of the coterie of wits known as the Scipionic Circle. In the prologues of his plays, Terence speaks of himself and his work and refutes criticisms —that he received help from his noble friends in composing his plays, that he plagiarized, that he "contaminated," that is, used characters or scenes from two Greek plays in a single Latin one. Actually, this "contamination" shows his skill in construction and his ethical objectives. By introducing two sets of lovers, perhaps drawn from different originals, and interweaving their stories, he not only enriches the plot but also affords illuminating contrasts of character and motivation. The skill with which the parallel plots, whether from the same or different originals, are fused, and their moral implications illustrated, improves from play to play. Terence is a literary artist, quiet and refined in tone and polished in language. His neat aphorisms have become part of common speech: "A word to the wise"; "Fortune favors the brave"; "While there's life there's hope"; "Many men, many minds"; and, most characteristic of Terence himself, "I am a man; whatever pertains to man concerns me" ("Homo sum, humani nihil a me alienum puto"). In the order of their production, Terence's plays are: *Andria, Heautontimorumenos* or *The Self-Tormentor, Eunuchus, Phormio* (the basis of Molière's *Les Fourberies de Scapin*), *Hecyra* or *The Mother-in-Law*, and *Adelphoe* or *The Brothers.*

In the two centuries that elapsed between Terence and Seneca, Rome changed from republic to empire and the political transformation affected society and literature as well. Because participation in public life was restricted, men turned to literature; and because free expression of original ideas was discouraged, they turned to the practice of pure belles-lettres. Subjects from Greek mythology were favored because they were safely remote and offered scope for literary virtuosity; and because publication was by public readings (*recitationes*) to invited audiences, a premium was placed on elaborate rhetorical devices and quotable gems calculated to elicit bursts of applause. The philosophy of the age was Stoicism, not the revolutionary teaching of the brotherhood of man preached by the founders of the school, but pale lessons of forbearance, inward self-sufficiency, and avoidance of passions.

Through the influence of his philosophical essays upon

Montaigne and of his tragedies upon Shakespeare, Seneca (4 B.C.–A.D. 65) is the main vehicle for the transmission of the intellectual climate of his age to the modern world. He was born at Cordova of a cultivated family. His father was a distinguished rhetor; one of his brothers was Gallio, the procurator of Achaea mentioned in the Book of Acts; the other was the father of the gifted epic poet Lucan. Seneca himself was a highly successful lawyer until, at the age of forty-five, he was banished to Corsica on the improbable charge of adultery with Claudius' wife, Messalina. In the year 49 he was recalled to become tutor, with the praetorian prefect Afranius Burrus, to the youthful Nero. Because of Seneca's tutelage, the first five years of Nero's reign (54–59) were regarded as a golden age; but then Nero asserted his authority and relations with Seneca grew strained. In 65 he was charged with complicity in a conspiracy against the emperor and ordered to take his own life.

The larger portion of Seneca's literary output comprises his philosophical essays, which are highly rhetorical in form and teach a placid kind of Stoicism. Rhetoric and Stoicism characterize his tragedies also. So prominent and pervasive is the rhetoric, so unlike ordinary speech, that it becomes a kind of music, and the tragedies, hence, a species of opera; strained passions and hyperbolic expressions that would be ludicrous in ordinary speech become appropriate and effective in opera. The obvious Stoic elements in the plays are numerous isolated passages praising life lived according to nature, indifference to worldly blessings, the ideal of kingship as ministry rather than mastery—the last probably intended for Nero's instruction. But the plays as a whole may be intended to promote Stoic "apathy" or avoidance of passion, for each is a demonstration of disaster resulting from ambition, vengeance, love, or the like.

Except for the *Octavia,* which deals with a Roman subject and is probably not by Seneca, all the plays in the Senecan corpus are derived from Greek originals, many still extant and available for comparison. In modern times (but not in the Age of Humanism), the inevitable comparison with the Greeks has been most damaging to Seneca's reputation. To the Greeks' probing into the mysteries of man's relations to external forces, and to the precariousness of human existence, Seneca seems indifferent. He is concerned instead with lurid exhibitions of human potentialities in overreaching and agonizing passion. But although he is using Greek models, Seneca is not writing Greek tragedy; it is fairer to judge him not as a degenerate Greek, but rather as an embryonic Elizabethan. If moral issues are simplified to a confrontation between spotless whites and unrelieved blacks, at least there is a satisfying demonstration of man's enormous capacities to inflict and suffer anguish in a style befitting tragic heroes.

Whether Seneca's tragedies were actually performed is questionable. They are written, indeed, with expert attention to effectiveness of presentation; scenes like those of Andromache sparring with Odysseus over the whereabouts of Astyanax in the *Trojan Women,* or of Atreus gloating unseen over Thyestes feasting, in the *Thyestes,* would be immeasurably enhanced by performance. On the other hand, the choruses which set the episodes off from one another are written not in strophes suitable for singing and dancing in the Greek manner, but in long successions of metrically identical lines not suitable for stage performance. Probably, then, the plays were not acted out but perhaps recited by a cast of readers, who may have worn costumes.

The ten plays in the Senecan corpus are: *Hercules (Mad), Trojan Women, Phoenician Women* (apparently incomplete), *Medea, Phaedra* (based on Euripides' *Hippolytus), Oedipus, Agamemnon, Thyestes, Hercules (on Oetaea),* and *Octavia.* As this list seems to indicate, and as we should surmise, Seneca's favorite among the Greek tragedians was Euripides. The *Hercules (on Oetaea),* which is almost twice as long as the average, contains much material that is un-Greek as well as un-Senecan. The only play besides the *Octavia* for which no Greek model is extant is the *Thyestes,* which is therefore valuable not only as being the most informative example of Seneca's dramaturgy, but also as filling a gaping lacuna in extant treatments of the Argive legend.

Until 55 B.C., when Pompey built Rome's first permanent theater of stone, plays seem to have been given in makeshift temporary structures, probably in the Forum. The theaters that we know, from extant remains and from Vitruvius' book on architecture, were enclosed by massive walls but had no roofs, partly because the space was too great to span without central supports and partly in order to provide light, since artificial illumination was impractical. Sometimes awnings were used. There was a curtain, which was raised from the floor rather than lowered from above. The Greek theater's open, circular orchestra, in which the chorus performed, was rather U-shaped in the Roman theater and was occupied by spectators, the first fourteen rows being reserved for the nobility. The stage was high, narrow, and very long. Characters could occupy different parts of the stage simultaneously without noticing one another, and "asides" could come naturally. The backdrop was a permanent structure of three house façades, in ornate architectural style, separated by narrow alleys; the hero of *Menaechmi* was obliged to keep his wife and mistress in adjoining houses. There was no means of showing an interior; in order to have a heart-to-heart talk with the maid dressing her hair, a lady trundled her dressing table out into the street. Acting companies were owned by a manager, with whom the donor of the plays or the official called "aedile" made his arrangements. The use of stock masks and costumes enabled audiences to identify with ease the slave, the courtesan, the gallant, and the like. Because plays were given as part of a gay festival, the audience was apt to be boisterous; but they must have been perceptive as well, to have appreciated the artistry of the performances.

MOSES HADAS

NOTE ON THE TRANSLATIONS

THE COMEDIES

For the translations of the comedies of Plautus, the following Latin texts were used:

The Menaechmi: Edition of Moseley and Hammond (Cambridge: Harvard University Press, 1933).

Mostellaria (*The Haunted House*): Editions of E. H. Sturtevant (New Haven: Yale University Press, 1925) and E. A. Sonnenschein (Oxford: Oxford University Press, 1961).

Rudens (*The Rope*): Edition of E. A. Sonnenschein (Oxford: Oxford University Press, 1950).

These texts were constantly compared with the Oxford Classical Text edition of W. M. Lindsay.

For the comedies of Terence, the text used was S. G. Ashmore, *The Comedies of Terence* (Oxford: Oxford University Press, 1908); again, the Oxford Classical Text edition, by Kauer and Lindsay, was consulted.

The translations included in this edition have been extensively revised from the individual editions published in The Library of Liberal Arts. In these versions, as in the earlier ones, I have attempted to translate ideas and situations rather than words. I kept one question constantly before me: If this character were speaking contemporary American English, how would he have expressed the idea he has in mind? It will be immediately obvious that this principle is bound, on occasion, to lead to an English version that bears little resemblance, on the purely verbal level, to the original Latin. In these revised translations, however, I have sought to avoid slang expressions or colloquialisms that are regional or apt to become outdated. I trust that however much the words of Plautus and Terence may suffer, their ideas and the general tone and tenor of their manner of expression will emerge with clarity and with as much precision as is possible in a translation.

F. O. C.

THE TRAGEDIES

The translations of the tragedies of Seneca have been prepared from the Latin texts of F. Leo (1879), Peiper-Richter (1902), and F. J. Miller (Loeb Classical Library, 1917).

The present translations, which have been published as separate editions in The Library of Liberal Arts, do not attempt to make Seneca a contemporary but deliberately seek to reflect his own rhetorical virtuosity in vocabulary and syntax. Rhetoric is as important in Senecan tragedy as music is in operatic libretto, and to efface it would strip the plays of what makes them moving and meaningful, and leave only a bare framework of frightfulness.

M. H.

Plautus

THE MENAECHMI

Introductory Note

Of all Plautus' plays, the one best known in modern times is *The Menaechmi* ("The Menaechmus Twins"). It is a simple farce, based on the device of mistaken identity. The play consists of nothing but a series of scenes in which one twin is mistaken for the other by different characters and in different ways, the whole strung loosely around a central plot, the search of one brother for the other. The play was imitated by Shakespeare in *The Comedy of Errors* and has been revived, imitated, and adapted many times by lesser playwrights.

It is not known when *The Menaechmi* was first produced. Some say as early as 215 B.C., some as late as 186 B.C. Neither the author nor the title of the Greek original is known.

The scene is a street in Epidamnus (Dyrrhachium, modern Durazzo) on the coast of the Adriatic; as the Prologue tells us, the characters are not Athenians, but Sicilians, from Syracuse. The stage setting shows the usual two house fronts with doors opening on the street. The Prologue, which includes a thick interlarding of puns and other obvious laugh-getters, tells us what we need to know in order to be ready to follow the story when it begins.

CHARACTERS

THE PROLOGUE

PENICULUS ("WHISK BROOM"), a sponger

MENAECHMUS I, a young man, married, living in Epidamnus

MENAECHMUS II (also known as SOSICLES), his twin brother, living in Syracuse

EROTIUM, a courtesan

CYLINDRUS, a cook

MESSENIO, slave to MENAECHMUS II

A SLAVE GIRL from EROTIUM's house

MATRONA, MENAECHMUS I's wife

SENEX, MENAECHMUS I's father-in-law

MEDICUS, a doctor

SCENE: *A street in Epidamnus, with two house fronts upstage.* MENAECHMUS I's *house is stage left;* EROTIUM's *is stage right. There is an altar at the center of the stage.*

4

THE MENAECHMI

Prologue

(As the curtain rises, the Prologue steps to the footlights with hand outstretched. He grins and addresses the audience.)

Well! How do you do! I want to start off by extending good wishes—to myself and to you, my friends! I bring you Plautus —not in person, of course, but it's his script I'm using. Please be nice and listen.

Now here's our story. Attention, please! I'll make it as short as I can.

Oh, yes; you know what our writers do nowadays in their plays: "Scene: A street in Athens"—every time!—just so you'll think they've caught more of the true Greek spirit. You'll not catch me doing that—unless it's the truth. I'll have to admit that there is something of the Greek in this story, but after all, it isn't Attic, just Sicilian.

Well, that was by way of prologue to the story. Now I'll give you the story itself, in full measure—and no cups, or pints, either—no, sir, the whole jugful! When it comes to telling a story, I'm very big-hearted.

Once there was a businessman in Syracuse, quite an old fellow. He had twin sons, two of them. The boys looked so much alike that their nurse couldn't tell them apart. For that matter, neither could their mother. At least, that's what a fellow who saw the boys told me. I haven't seen them—so don't any of you go imagining I have.

Now when the boys were seven years old, their father loaded a great big boat with boxes and bales and put one of the twins on board, and took him with him to Tarentum to sell the stuff. The other twin he left at home with his mother. It so happened that there was a fair going on at Tarentum when he got there. Lots of people had come to town, as they do to fairs. Among them was a businessman from Epidamnus. He picked up the boy and took him off to Epidamnus. As for the father, after he'd lost the boy he was brokenhearted and got so heartsick over it that a few days later he died, right there in Tarentum.

After the news got back to Syracuse to the boys' grandfather that the one twin had been kidnaped and that the father had died at Tarentum, the grandfather changed the name of the other twin. He was so fond of the one that had been kidnaped that he gave his name to the one who stayed home—the name Menaechmus, the same name that the first twin had. As a matter of fact, it was the grandfather's name, too. I remember his name very well, because I once heard his creditors shouting at his heels. Just so you won't make any mistakes later on, I'm telling you now ahead of time: both twin brothers have the same name.

Now I've got to take my feet back to Epidamnus, so that I can give you the story exactly measured off. If any of you has anything he'd like me to get for him in Epidamnus, please speak right up and let me know. Only one reservation: he's got to give me the wherewithal to pay for it. "Cash on the barrelhead, or you're wasting your time!"—that's me! ("Cash on the barrelhead" to *me,* and you'll waste a lot more than your time!)

But I'll go back to where I started and stick to my subject. That fellow from Epidamnus whom I mentioned a minute ago, the one who kidnaped the first twin, had never begotten chick nor child—unless you want to call his wealth his "children"—and that was misbegotten. He adopted the boy he'd kidnaped, made him his son, got him a wife with a good dowry, and named him his heir when he died. For it so happened that just after there had been a cloudburst he was going out to his country place. He started to ford a river not so very far from the city, but the current was too strong and swept his feet from under him—in fact, you might say that the river kidnaped the kidnaper—and carried him off to the place where such people belong. As for the adopted son, he inherited a large fortune. That's his house there *(points)*—I mean, of course, the kidnaped twin's.

Now that other twin, the one who lives in Syracuse, has just arrived today in Epidamnus, accompanied by his slave. He has come to look for this very own twin brother of his. This city is Epidamnus, as long as this play is on the stage. We'll call it something else when we do another play. The cast of characters often changes, too, the same way: sometimes a pimp lives here, sometimes a young man, sometimes an old man—rich man, poor man, beggar man, sponger, priest.

Act One

Scene I

(Enter PENICULUS, *stage left.)*

PENICULUS: The young fellows call me Peniculus—means "Whisk Broom," you know—because when I come to dinner I sweep the table clean.

People who put chains on prisoners and leg irons on runaway slaves are being very stupid, in my opinion. Here's a poor fellow, already miserable; you add new grief to the grief he already has; naturally, he's all the more anxious to run away and cause you trouble. They get out of their chains one way or another. Put leg irons on them, and they file off the ring that holds them together, or they knock out a rivet with a rock. You're just wasting your time! If you want to do a good job of keeping a prisoner, so that he won't run away, you ought to tie him down with food and drink. Load up a table, and hold his nose over that! See that he has things to eat and drink, what *he* thinks is enough, every day: he'll never run away; no, sir, not even if his life's at stake! You'll have no trouble keeping him, so long as you use that kind of bond on him. These food-and-drink chains are very elastic: the more you stretch them, the tighter they bind. Just look at me. I'm going to Menaechmus' house, where I've been bound over for some time now; I'm going quite freely, so that he can lock me up. You see, he doesn't just feed people; he builds them up and gives them a new lease on life. There isn't a better doctor in town! Just to show you what the young man is like: he's a great eater himself, and every meal is a feast. The way he heaps up the tables, the kind of platter piles he gets together—why! You've got to stand on your couch, if you want something from the top!

But I've been on furlough these many, many days. I've been domiciled at home with my own dear ones—"dear ones": that's the most expensive food and drink on the market, for I won't have anything less dear than that. And now on top of that, my "dear ones"—those neat rows of them—are running out on me.

I'll go in to see Menaechmus now—but the door is opening. Look! It's Menaechmus himself. He's coming out.

SCENE II

(MENAECHMUS I *enters from his own house. He stumbles down the steps, and then turns back, shaking his fist toward the door.*)

MENAECHMUS I: You're a pretty poor wife, you are! And you're stupid and mean and bad-tempered; for if you weren't, you'd show some sympathy for your husband's likes and dislikes! And furthermore, if you do anything like that to me again, I'll throw you out! I'll get a divorce! You can go home to your father! Every time I want to go out you hang onto me, you call me back, you keep asking questions: "Where am I going? What am I going to do? What's my business? What am I going after? What'll I bring home? What have I been doing while I was away?" Wife? I married no wife! I married a custom's inspector: I have to declare everything, past, present, and future!

The trouble with you is that I've spoiled you. But now I'll tell you what I'm going to do. I see to it that you have plenty of household help, plenty of food and clothes, even fancy ones, and jewelry. There isn't a thing you need that you don't have. And so, if you're smart, you'll keep out of trouble: you'll stop spying on your husband.

And furthermore, just to make it worth your while to spy on me, I'm going to find a girl to go out and have dinner with me tonight.

PENICULUS (*aside*): Our friend there is putting on a great show of scolding his wife, but I'm really the one who's getting the benefit of it. If he goes out to dinner, he'll be hurting me, not his wife.

MENAECHMUS I (*turns to audience*): Hooray! That was telling her! That finally chased her away from the door! Where are all the wandering husbands? Why don't they hurry up and buy me a present, and congratulate me on my brave battle with the enemy? (*He pulls a woman's dress from under his coat.*) Not more than a minute ago, I stole this from my wife in there, and I'm going to give it to the girl next door. That's how you do it: a slick trick for a sly spy! Now this was a fine stunt, this was *good,* this was neat, this was really *engineered.* I got this away from her, the old witch! It's going to cost me something to take it over here (*motions toward* EROTIUM's *house*), but we'll charge it up to good will. I grabbed this souvenir from the "Enemy" herself—and not a man on our side got a scratch!

PENICULUS (*steps toward* MENAECHMUS): Say, my friend, are you going to share that souvenir with me?

MENAECHMUS I: Damnation! I've stepped into a trap!

PENICULUS: No, no! You stepped right into headquarters. Don't be afraid!

MENAECHMUS I: Who is it?

PENICULUS: It's me!

MENAECHMUS I (*turns around*): Oh! Am I glad to see you! What good luck! How are you? (*They shake hands.*)

PENICULUS: How are *you?*

MENAECHMUS I (*still shaking hands*): What's on your mind?

PENICULUS: Nothing—but I've got my hand on the best friend a man ever had.

MENAECHMUS I: For my purposes, you couldn't have timed your coming here better than you did.

PENICULUS: That's me! There's nothing about timing I don't know.

MENAECHMUS I (*with a leer*): Want to see something worth looking at?

PENICULUS: What chef prepared it? I'll know by looking at what's left on the platter whether he got the seasoning right.

MENAECHMUS I (*drapes dress over his shoulders*): Tell me, did you ever see one of those pictures painted on a wall, where an eagle was carrying off Ganymede, or Venus was— you know, Venus and Adonis——?

PENICULUS: Sure, lots of times, but what have those pictures got to do with me?

MENAECHMUS I: Well, look at me: anything about me that reminds you of them? (*He assumes a girlish pose and simpers.*)

PENICULUS (*disgusted*): What kind of a getup is that you're wearing?

MENAECHMUS I (*titters*): Tell me I'm the *sweetest* boy!

PENICULUS: Sweet! Eat! Say, when do we eat?

MENAECHMUS I: Just say what I tell you to.

PENICULUS: All right, all right; you're the *sweetest* boy.

MENAECHMUS I (*pouts*): Wouldn't you like to add something to that on your own?

PENICULUS: Oh, perfectly darling!

MENAECHMUS I: Go on, go on!

PENICULUS: Nothing doing, unless I know what's in it for me. You and your wife are having a quarrel, so I'm going to be very careful about getting involved with you.

MENAECHMUS I: She doesn't know where our party is going to be; we've got the whole day to burn. Let's make it good and hot!

PENICULUS: Well, that's better! How soon can I set fire to it? The day's half gone already, you know.

MENAECHMUS I: You're the one who's holding things up with all your talk.

PENICULUS: Dig my eye out by the roots, Menaechmus, if I say one word unless you tell me to.

MENAECHMUS I (*thinking he hears a noise at his house door, whispers*): Come away from the door. Over here!

PENICULUS: All right.

MENAECHMUS I: A little farther! Over here!

PENICULUS: All right!

MENAECHMUS I (*aloud*): Now we're safe. Come on away from that lion's den.

PENICULUS (*laughs*): Well, well! You would make a good chariot racer.

MENAECHMUS I: What do you mean?

PENICULUS: You keep looking back over your shoulder, to see if your wife is catching up with you.

MENAECHMUS I: Say, what do you think!

PENICULUS: What do *I* think? I think whatever you think. If it's "Yes" with you, it's "Yes" with me; if "No" with you, then "No" with me.

MENAECHMUS I: How are you on smells? If you smell something, can you tell what it is?

PENICULUS: Nobody better!

MENAECHMUS I: All right! Take a whiff of this dress I've got: what's it smell like?

PENICULUS (*sniffs*): Thievery! (*Sniffs again*) Women! (*Sniffs again*) Dinner!

MENAECHMUS I: Blessings on you, my boy. You got it right every time. Yes, I stole this dress from my wife; now I'm going to take it to this girl next door, Erotium; and I'm going to order a dinner for me, for you, and for her, right away.

PENICULUS: Fine!

MENAECHMUS I: And then we'll drink right through the night "till Phoebus doth arise!"

PENICULUS: Good. That's making it short and to the point. Shall I knock on the door now? (*He raises his fist as if to knock.*)

MENAECHMUS I: Yes—or no, wait a minute.

PENICULUS (*disgusted*): You've held up the party a solid hour.

MENAECHMUS I: Knock *gently*!

PENICULUS: What are you afraid of? Think the doors are made of glass?

(*Knocks. A girl's head appears through the partly opened half door.* PENICULUS *continues knocking on the other half.*)

MENAECHMUS I: Stop! Stop! Please! Please! See, she's coming out herself! Just look at the sun! Compared to her fair charms, it's a mere shadow.

SCENE III

(*Enter* EROTIUM.)

EROTIUM: Why, darling! Menaechmus! Hello! (*She turns her back on* PENICULUS.)

PENICULUS: What about me?

EROTIUM (*looks over her shoulder, contemptuously*): To me, you just don't count.

PENICULUS (*aside*): Don't count, don't I? Well, in the army even the fellows who don't count still eat.

MENAECHMUS I: I've asked them to prepare a dinner at your house for me today—

PENICULUS: "Dinner?" You mean "contest." That's what it'll be today. In this contest, you and I will both—drink. Whichever of us turns out to be the better contestant—with the wine jug—he's your man. You decide which one you'll spend the night with.

MENAECHMUS I (*calf-eyed*): Oh, you're wonderful! How I hate my wife when I see you!

PENICULUS (*smirks*): Meanwhile, you've got to put on something of hers.

(*He takes the dress from* MENAECHMUS *and starts to drape*

it over MENAECHMUS' *shoulders.* MENAECHMUS *seizes it angrily, and holds it out to* EROTIUM.)

EROTIUM: What's this?

MENAECHMUS I: Your gain and my wife's loss, my sweet.

EROTIUM (*fingers the dress*): You win, hands down! I like you better than any of the others who come to me.

PENICULUS (*sneers*): That's a woman for you! All sweet talk, so long as she sees something to grab. (*Turns to* EROTIUM) Why, if you really loved him, you'd have nipped his nose off with kisses by now.

MENAECHMUS I: Here, Peniculus, take it. I want to perform the ceremony of dedication that I promised.

PENICULUS: Give it here. (*Snatches it and throws it over his own shoulders*) But please, please! dance like this with the dress afterward. (*He does a pirouette.*)

MENAECHMUS I (*embarrassed*): Who, me? Dance? You're crazy.

PENICULUS: Who's crazy, you or me? If you're not going to dance, get rid of it, then.

MENAECHMUS I (*steps forward, holding the dress across his outspread arms*): I risked my life today to steal this!

PENICULUS (*aside*): Yes, in my opinion Hercules never ran so great a risk when he stole the girdle from Hippolyta.

MENAECHMUS I (*holds dress up to* EROTIUM): Take it. It's yours, for you're the only woman who understands me.

EROTIUM (*takes dress*): That's the right spirit. Good lovers should always feel like that.

PENICULUS (*aside*): Yes, especially if they're in a hurry to get to the poorhouse.

MENAECHMUS I: Four minae I paid for that when I bought it for my wife a year ago.

PENICULUS (*aside*): Four minae down the drain, as your accounts will show!

MENAECHMUS I: Know what I'd like you to do?

EROTIUM: Yes, I know, and I'll do anything you want.

MENAECHMUS I: Well, then, have dinner prepared for the three of us at your house.

PENICULUS (*all eagerness*): And go get something fancy from downtown: Piglet, daughter of Meat Ball; Bacon, son of Ham, or some split pigs' heads, or something like that! When those appear on the table in their gravy, they make me feel like a hungry hawk!

MENAECHMUS I: As soon as you can.

EROTIUM: Why, of course.

MENAECHMUS I: We'll just step downtown. We'll be right back. While dinner's cooking, we'll have a drink or two.

EROTIUM: Come whenever you like; things will be ready.

MENAECHMUS I: Hurry it up, won't you? (*To* PENICULUS) Come on. (*He starts off, stage left.*)

PENICULUS (*with a leap*): You bet I'll come on. I'll keep my eye on you! I'll be right at your heels! I wouldn't lose you today for the wealth of the gods! (*Exit with* MENAECHMUS.)

EROTIUM (*turns to house*): Somebody in there! Send Cylindrus, the cook, out here to me right away!

SCENE IV

(*Enter* CYLINDRUS.)

EROTIUM: Get a basket and some money—oh, here; here's six drachmae. Take that.

CYLINDRUS: Right!

EROTIUM: Go along now and buy things to eat. See that you get just enough for three, not too little, not too much.

CYLINDRUS: Who is coming?

EROTIUM: I'll be there, and Menaechmus and Peniculus.

CYLINDRUS: Hah! That's *ten* you've named! Peniculus easily takes the place of eight.

EROTIUM: Well, I've told you who's coming: you take care of the rest.

CYLINDRUS: All right. Dinner is practically ready. Tell them to go take their places.

EROTIUM: Hurry up.

CYLINDRUS: I'll be right back. (*Exit* CYLINDRUS.)

Act Two

Scene I

(*Enter* Menaechmus II, *stage right, followed by* Messenio, *carrying a small sea chest. Behind* Menaechmus *come several sailors carrying boxes and baskets.*)

Menaechmus II: Sailors are never happier, Messenio, in my opinion, than when, out at sea, they catch their first sight of land in the distance.

Messenio (*grumbles*): You're happier, to be perfectly frank, if when you get to the land you see it is your own. Now I ask you: Why have we come to Epidamnus? Or are we going to run in on all the islands, like the tide?

Menaechmus II: We're looking for my brother—my own twin brother.

Messenio: Yes, but when are we going to get through looking for him? It's six years now since we started spending our time this way. We've been to Istria, Spain, Marseilles, Illyria, all over the Adriatic and Magna Graecia, up and down the whole Italian Coast, anywhere you can get by sea. If you were looking for a needle, you'd have found it by now, if there were any needle. We're looking for a dead man among the living; we'd have found him long ago, if he were alive.

Menaechmus II: That's exactly what I'm looking for, someone who can tell me for sure, who can say that he knows my brother is dead. Once I've found that out I won't spend another minute looking for him. But until I do, as long as I live I'll never stop looking. I know very well how much he means to me.

Messenio: You're picking flaws in an open-and-shut case. Why don't we go home—or are we going to write a book called "Around the World with Menaechmus"?

Menaechmus II: Do as you're told! Take what you're given!

Watch your step! Don't you bother me. We're not doing this to suit you.

MESSENIO (*aside*): Hm! What he said there put me in my place—short and to the point! A long lecture couldn't have told me more. Just the same, I can't help speaking. (*To* MEN-AECHMUS) Excuse me, Menaechmus, but when I check our funds, we're traveling very, very light. Yes, sir, I think that if you don't go home, you will run out of money looking for your brother, and then you'll be sorry. You know how these people here are: In Epidamnus they all like their fun, and they're the greatest drinkers in the world. Besides that, a lot of shysters and swindlers live here. Besides that, they say the girls here are the smoothest lot you can find. Why, they call the town Epidamnus because it's a damn bad deal for prac-tically everybody who stops here.

MENAECHMUS II: I'll take care of that. Just give me the money.

MESSENIO: What do you want with it?

MENAECHMUS II: I'm worried about what you just said.

MESSENIO: Worried? Why?

MENAECHMUS II: I'm afraid you may make Epidamnus a damn bad deal for me. You're very, very fond of the ladies, Messenio. And I get angry pretty easily; I've got a damned bad temper! If I've got the money, I'll keep us safe on both counts; you won't do anything you shouldn't do, and I won't lose my temper at you.

MESSENIO (*hands him the purse*): Take it and keep it. I don't care what you do.

SCENE II

(*Enter* CYLINDRUS, *with a basket full of food.*)

CYLINDRUS: I've got some nice things—just what I wanted. I'll put a good dinner on the table tonight. But look! There's Menaechmus! Here's where I catch it! The company's coming already, and I'm not back from market yet. I'll go up and speak to them. Hello, Menaechmus!

MENAECHMUS II (*surprised*): How do you do? But I don't think we've met.

CYLINDRUS: Don't think we've met? Don't you know who I am, Menaechmus?

MENAECHMUS II: No, I really don't.

CYLINDRUS: Where's the rest of the company?

MENAECHMUS II: What company are you talking about?

CYLINDRUS: Why, that sponger friend of yours.

MENAECHMUS II: Sponger friend of mine? (*To* MESSENIO) The fellow's crazy.

MESSENIO (*aside to* MENAECHMUS): Didn't I tell you there were a lot of swindlers here?

MENAECHMUS II: What sponger are you looking for, my friend? Do I know him?

CYLINDRUS: Peniculus—you know, "Whisk Broom."

MESSENIO: Oh! I've got that right here with our things. (*Starts to open the sea chest, but gives up when he sees no one is paying attention to him.*)

CYLINDRUS: Menaechmus, you're a little early for dinner. I'm just getting back from market.

MENAECHMUS II: Say, tell me, my friend: How much do pigs cost here—the pure white ones that they use for sacrifices?

CYLINDRUS (*puzzled*): Two drachmae.

MENAECHMUS II (*offers him a coin*): Here, take this two-drachma piece from me. Go have yourself purified at my expense. I'm sure you're not quite right in the head, making a nuisance of yourself like this to a perfect stranger, you—whoever you are.

CYLINDRUS: I'm Cylindrus. Don't you know my name?

MENAECHMUS II (*impatiently*): Cylindrus or Coriendrus, damn you either way! I don't know you and I don't even want to know you!

CYLINDRUS: But your name *is* Menaechmus.

MENAECHMUS II: As far as I know. You show good sense when you use my name. But where did you ever meet me?

CYLINDRUS: Where did I meet you? Why, the girl who lives here is the one you're in love with—Erotium. I'm her slave.

MENAECHMUS II: I am not in love with her, and I haven't the slightest idea who you are.

CYLINDRUS: You don't know who I am? Why, many's the time I've served drinks to you at our house!

MESSENIO: Oh, my! not a thing here to dent this fellow's head with!

MENAECHMUS II: You served drinks to *me*? Look: I've never been to Epidamnus before today, never even seen the place!

CYLINDRUS: You say you haven't?

MENAECHMUS II: I most certainly do.

CYLINDRUS (*points to* MENAECHMUS I's *house*): Don't you live in that house there?

MENAECHMUS II: Damn the people who live there!

CYLINDRUS (*aside*): He *is* crazy, talking like that about himself! (*Aloud*) I beg your pardon, Menaechmus.

MENAECHMUS II: What *do* you want!

CYLINDRUS: If you ask me—that two-drachma piece you promised me a while ago—(MENAECHMUS *threatens him, and he shrinks back*) for really, you know, you can't be feeling quite well, Menaechmus, talking like that about yourself and all—if you're smart you'd order a sacrificial pig (MENAECHMUS *threatens again*)—a *small* one—for yourself.

MENAECHMUS II (*turns away in disgust*): What a lot of nonsense! You make me tired!

CYLINDRUS (*aside to audience*): He often jokes with me like that. He's the funniest fellow, when his wife's not around! (*Turns to* MENAECHMUS) I beg your pardon.

MENAECHMUS II: What *do* you want?

CYLINDRUS (*points to his basket*): See what I've got here: have I bought enough for the three of you, or should I go get some more—(MENAECHMUS *threatens him again*) I mean for *you* and the *sponger* and the *girl*.

MENAECHMUS II: *What* girls, *what* spongers are you talking about?

MESSENIO: What the devil's the matter with you? Why do you keep pestering him?

CYLINDRUS: What business is it of yours? I don't know you. I'm talking to this man. I know him.

MESSENIO: Well, believe me, you're out of your head. I'm sure of that.

CYLINDRUS (*to* MENAECHMUS): I'll go get dinner ready. It won't take long, so don't go too far away. Nothing else you want, is there?

MENAECHMUS II: Yes, go get lost!

CYLINDRUS (*growls under his breath*): Be better if you'd go yourself (*stops as he realizes* MENAECHMUS *has heard him, turns with a silly grin on his face*)—I mean, go in and take your place, while I put these things by Vulcan's fiery flame. (*Backs toward door*) I'll go in and tell Erotium you're waiting out here, so she can ask you to come in. You shouldn't have to wait around out here. (*Exit, stumbling, into house.*)

MENAECHMUS II: Has he gone? Yes, he has. Well, Messenio, that was no lie you told me about this place. I'm finding *that* out!

MESSENIO (*sagely*): Just you watch! I think the woman who lives there is a bad one, to judge by what that crazy fellow who just went in told us.

MENAECHMUS II (*puzzled*): But I wonder how he knew my name?

MESSENIO: Oh, there's nothing wonderful about that. What these girls do is this: They send their slaves to the waterfront, if a foreign ship comes in. They try to find out where a fellow comes from, what his name is. Then they grab onto him and stick to him like glue. If they manage to sell him their bill of goods, they take him for all he's got and then send him packing. Now, you're the harbor, see? And she (*pointing to* EROTIUM's *house*)—she's a pirate ship, standing in on you. I really think we'd better watch out for her.

MENAECHMUS II: Yes, that's good advice.

MESSENIO: I won't be sure you think it's good advice unless you watch your step very carefully.

MENAECHMUS II: Quiet a minute! The door squeaked. Let's see who's coming out.

MESSENIO: I'll just put this down. (*He turns to sailors.*) Keep an eye on the baggage, will you, boys?

SCENE III

(*Enter* EROTIUM. *She talks through door to slaves within, and, meanwhile, wedges the door open.*)

EROTIUM: Leave the door like this. Go along, now. I don't want it shut. You in there, get ready! Careful, now! Don't forget anything. Put the covers on the couches; light the incense. We want to have things nice. That's the way you catch your man. This comfort—the men will show a loss for it; to us, it's clear profit. (*She turns.*) But where's Menaechmus? The cook said he was out here. Oh, there he is! I see him. I find him very handy. Yes, he's a real help to me. Naturally that makes him star boarder in my house. Now I'd better get over there and say "hello" to him. (*She turns on her smile, and runs toward* MENAECHMUS *with outstretched arms.* MENAECHMUS *steps back, startled.*) Why, honey boy, I'm surprised! Why are you waiting out here? The door's wide open to you. My house is more yours than your own is. (*No response from* MENAECHMUS *except a blank stare*) Everything's ready, just what you asked for and just what you wanted. You won't have to wait at all. (*Still no response*) The dinner—you ordered it, you know—it's all ready. You can go in and take your place any time you like.

MENAECHMUS II (*to* MESSENIO): Who's this girl talking to?

EROTIUM: Me? Why, I'm talking to you, of course.

MENAECHMUS II: Have we ever met before? Do we know each other?

EROTIUM: Why, of course! Venus has told me to be especially nice to you, and that's enough for me. It's no more than you deserve, either. Yes, sir! You're so generous to me, you're making me a rich woman all by yourself.

MENAECHMUS II: Messenio, this girl is either crazy or drunk. I'm a complete stranger, and she talks to me as if she'd known me for years.

MESSENIO: Didn't I tell you that's what always happens here? These are just leaves floating down now. Stay here three days, and the tree will fall on our heads. That's the way these women are: nothing but traps for your money, all of them. But just let me talk to her. (*Turns to* EROTIUM) I beg your pardon. May I have a word with you?

EROTIUM: What is it?

MESSENIO: Where did you meet this gentleman?

EROTIUM: Where? Right here. We've known each other for a long time. Right here in Epidamnus.

MESSENIO: Right here in Epidamnus? Why, he's never set foot in this town before!

EROTIUM: Ha-ha-ha! Aren't you funny! Menaechmus, dear, why don't you go in, please? It'll be much nicer in there.

MENAECHMUS II: Well, the girl calls me by the right name, sure enough. I can't help wondering what this is all about.

MESSENIO: She got a whiff of the money you've got there.

MENAECHMUS II: Yes, that's it. Thanks for the warning. Here, you take it. *Now* I'll find out whether she is more interested in me or my money.

EROTIUM: Let's go in and have dinner.

MENAECHMUS II: That's nice of you, but no, thanks.

EROTIUM (*surprised*): Then why did you ask me to fix dinner for you a while ago?

MENAECHMUS II: Who, me? I asked you to?

EROTIUM: Yes, of course—for you and your friend, the sponger.

MENAECHMUS II: What the devil sponger? This girl is out of her head, for sure.

EROTIUM: Peniculus, you know—"Whisk Broom."

MENAECHMUS II: Who is this "Whisk Broom" you keep talking about? The one you brush up with?

EROTIUM: Silly! The one that came with you a while ago, when you brought me the dress that you stole from your wife.

MENAECHMUS II: *What?* I gave *you* a dress that I stole from my wife? Are you crazy? This girl's asleep on her feet, like a horse.

EROTIUM (*pouts*): Why do you want to make fun of me and go saying you didn't do what you did?

MENAECHMUS II: Now what is it I say I didn't do, that I did?

EROTIUM: That you gave me your wife's dress.

MENAECHMUS II: I still say I didn't. Me? I haven't ever had a wife and haven't got one now, and since the day I was born, I've never been inside this town before. I had breakfast on the ship; then I came out here and ran into you.

EROTIUM: Oh, for goodness' sake! What ship are you talking about? What's this, now?

MENAECHMUS II: Why, a plain, old, wooden ship, been used so long and repaired so often—it's as full of plugged holes as a pegboard.

EROTIUM: Please, now, stop being funny and come on in with me.

MENAECHMUS II: Really, my dear girl, you're looking for somebody else, not me.

EROTIUM: Don't I know you? You're Menaechmus. Your father's name was Moschus. You're supposed to have been born at Syracuse, in Sicily—where King Agathocles was ruler, and next Phintias, and next Liparo. When he died, he handed the throne on to Hiero, and now it's Hiero.

MENAECHMUS II: Everything you say there is right enough.

MESSENIO (*aside to* MENAECHMUS): Say! You don't suppose she comes from there? She certainly knows all about you.

MENAECHMUS II (*aside to* MESSENIO): Yes! You know, I don't think I can go on refusing her invitation.

MESSENIO: Don't you do it! You're finished if you step inside that door!

MENAECHMUS II: Oh, just be quiet. Everything's all right. I'll agree with anything the girl says, if I can get free entertainment out of it. (*Turns to* EROTIUM) Say, when I kept saying "no" to you a while ago, I had a reason for it: I was worried about my friend here, for fear he'd tell my wife about the dress and the dinner. Shall we go in now, if you're ready?

EROTIUM: Are you going to wait for Peniculus?

MENAECHMUS II: I certainly am not! I don't care a bit for him, and if he comes, I don't want him let in.

EROTIUM: Ha! That will suit me very well! (*They start toward door, arm in arm.*) But do you know what I'd like you to do—please?

MENAECHMUS II (*expansively*): Just give me your order, madam!

EROTIUM: That dress you gave me just now—would you take it to the embroiderer's, and get it fixed up and have him add some fancywork that I want?

MENAECHMUS II: Say, that's a good idea! Kill two birds with one stone. It'll look different, so my wife won't recognize it, if she should see you on the street.

EROTIUM: Well, take it with you later, when you go.

MENAECHMUS II: Certainly.

EROTIUM: Let's go in. (*She enters house.* MENAECHMUS *turns back to speak to* MESSENIO.)

MENAECHMUS II: I'll be right with you. I just want to tell this fellow one more thing. Hey, Messenio, come here.

MESSENIO (*turns, but doesn't move*): What do you want?

MENAECHMUS II: Jump!

MESSENIO: What for?

MENAECHMUS II: For just because. (MESSENIO *comes over toward him, dragging his feet.*) I know what you're going to call me.

MESSENIO: That makes you twice as bad.

MENAECHMUS II: It's all settled! I've got her where I want her! Go on now, as quick as you can, take those boys to a rooming house. *You* see that you get back here to meet me before dark.

MESSENIO: But, sir, you don't know those girls.

MENAECHMUS II: Quiet, I tell you! Mind your own business! I'm the one who will get hurt, not you, if I've made any mistakes. This girl is stupid, *simple!* From the way things looked just now, we've got some easy pickings here! (*Exit into* EROTIUM'S *house.*)

MESSENIO: Oh, God. You're not going, are you? It's the

end for him, all right. He's the dinghy; she's the pirate ship;
she's got a line aboard him, and she's dragging him off. She'll
roll him, for sure! But I'm a fool, asking myself to keep my
master in line. He bought me to obey his orders, not to be
his commanding officer. (*Heaves a sigh, turns to sailors*) Come
on, boys, so that I can get back here on time, as he told me to.

(*Exeunt.*)

ACT THREE

SCENE I

(*Enter* PENICULUS, *stage left.*)

PENICULUS: More than thirty years old I am, and in all that
time I've never made a worse move—never committed more
of a downright crime—than I did today: I let myself get stuck
for jury duty. There I sat, yawning my head off, and Menaechmus sneaked out on me and went to Erotium's house,
probably. Didn't want to take me along. Damn the man who
invented this jury business to take up busy men's time! Why
don't they pick men who have nothing to do for that job?
And if they aren't there when the roll is called, slap a fine
on them, right away. There are lots of people who eat only
one meal a day; they've got nothing to do. They don't eat,
themselves, and they never invite anybody to eat with them.
They're the ones who ought to give their time to juries and
meetings! If that's the way things were, I wouldn't have missed
a dinner today. So help me, I'm sure he meant me to have it.
I'll go anyway. Maybe there are some scraps left—that's a
thought! Makes me feel better already. (*Enter* MENAECHMUS
from EROTIUM's *house. He is obviously drunk.*) But what's
this I see? It's Menaechmus. He's got a garland! He's coming
out! Dinner's all over. Yes, I certainly came on time. I'll watch
what he does, and go up later and speak to him. (*He slips
into the alleyway.*)

SCENE II

(MENAECHMUS II *stumbles down the steps, talking back through the open door. He has the dress over one arm.*)

MENAECHMUS II: Forget it, will you? I'll get this fixed up real nice and pretty and bring it back right away. You won't know it's the same one, it'll look so different.

PENICULUS (*aside*): The dress! He's taking it to the embroidery shop. He's cleaned up the dinner! He's drunk up the wine—and me, his friend, I've been shut out. Believe you me, I'm not the man I am if I don't make him pay for that! I'll get back at him! Just watch what I'll give him!

MENAECHMUS II (*turns toward audience*): Ye gods in heaven, did you ever give any man more good luck on one day, when he had less reason to expect it? I've had a dinner, and drinks, and a girl. I've got this (*holds up dress*)—fallen heir to it, you might say, and this is the last time that will ever happen to it.

PENICULUS (*aside*): I can't hear very well what he's saying from my corner here. But he's had his dinner, and he's talking about me and my share in it.

MENAECHMUS II: She said I gave this to her and stole it from my wife. I could see she was making some kind of mistake, but I jumped right in, just as if I did know something about it, and started "yessing" her. Whatever she said, I agreed to it. Why make a long story of it? I've never had a better time at less expense.

PENICULUS (*aside*): I'll go to him. I'm just itching to stir him up. (*He starts toward* MENAECHMUS, *shaking his fist.*)

MENAECHMUS II: Who's this? What's he coming this way for?

PENICULUS: Well! How *do* you do? Steady as a feather, aren't you? Call yourself a friend! Traitor! Cheap sneak! What did I ever do to you? Any reason why you should spoil everything for me? Ran out on me a while ago downtown, didn't you? Polished off the dinner without me, didn't you? What's the idea of doing that? Fallen heir, have you? Well, I was just as much heir as you.

MENAECHMUS II (*elaborately polite*): Please, please, my friend, what have I to do with you? What do you mean by talking like that to me? You don't know me; I'm a stranger here. (*Suddenly angry*) Or how'd you like *me* to give *you* some trouble—you and your tough talk!

PENICULUS: Huh! You've given me that already, I'd say.

MENAECHMUS II (*polite again*): Tell me, my friend, if you don't mind, what's your name?

PENICULUS: Going to make fun of me now, are you? As if you didn't know my name.

MENAECHMUS II: But I don't! As far as I know, I've never seen you before. I haven't ever met you. Anyway, whoever you are, leave me alone. (*Starts to walk away*)

PENICULUS: Menaechmus! Wake up!

MENAECHMUS II: I'm awake—at least I think I am.

PENICULUS: Don't you know me?

MENAECHMUS II: Wouldn't say I didn't if I did.

PENICULUS: Don't you know your old friend?

MENAECHMUS II: You aren't right in the head, my friend. I can see that.

PENICULUS: Now listen: Did you steal that dress there from your wife and give it to Erotium?

MENAECHMUS II: No! I tell you I haven't got a wife. I didn't give a dress to Erotium, and I didn't steal one. Are you crazy?

PENICULUS: This is the end! Didn't I see you come out with that dress on? (*He takes a few mincing steps, in imitation of* MENAECHMUS I.)

MENAECHMUS II: You go to the devil. Think everybody's a pansy, just because you are? You mean to say you saw *me* wearing this dress?

PENICULUS: I certainly do.

MENAECHMUS II: There's a place for fellows like you. Why don't you go there? Or get yourself purified; you're completely crazy.

PENICULUS: By God, nobody'll ever get me not to tell your wife the whole story now, exactly what happened. Talk like that to me, will you? Well, it'll all come home to roost. You'll pay for eating that dinner; I'll see to that! (*Exit into* MENAECHMUS I's *house.*)

MENAECHMUS II (*shakes his head, as if to clear it*): What is all this? Is everybody I see trying to make a fool of me? But the door squeaked. (*Looks around as* SLAVE GIRL *enters from* EROTIUM's *house*)

SCENE III

(SLAVE GIRL *enters. She is carrying a large gold bracelet. She runs up to* MENAECHMUS II *and holds the bracelet out to him.*)

SLAVE GIRL: Menaechmus, Erotium says, pretty please, will you take this along with you to the goldsmith? She'd like an ounce of gold added to it, and to have it all done over.

MENAECHMUS II (*makes a grab for bracelet;* SLAVE GIRL *pulls it back out of reach*): Sure, sure! I'll do that! And anything else she wants done, tell her I'll do it—anything she likes.

SLAVE GIRL: You know what bracelet this is?

MENAECHMUS II: No. Gold one, I guess. (*He succeeds in grabbing bracelet.*)

SLAVE GIRL: This is the one that you once told us you stole from your wife's jewel box.

MENAECHMUS II: Not I! No, sir!

SLAVE GIRL: What, you don't remember? Well, then, give me back the bracelet, if you don't remember it. (*She tries to grab it, but* MENAECHMUS *holds her off.*)

MENAECHMUS II: Wait a minute. (*Pretends to examine it carefully*) Why, yes, of course! I remember! Yes, this is the one I gave her. This is it. Say, where are the arm bands that I gave her along with it?

SLAVE GIRL: You never gave her any arm bands.

MENAECHMUS II: Oh, yes, of course. This was all I gave her.

SLAVE GIRL: Shall I tell her you'll take care of it?

MENAECHMUS II: Yes, I will. I'll see that she gets the dress and bracelet both back at the same time.

SLAVE GIRL (*coyly*): Menaechmus, dear, please have some earrings made for me, about two drams weight, the kind with pendants, so I'll be glad to see you when you come to our house.

MENAECHMUS II: All right. Give me the gold; I'll pay for the work.

SLAVE GIRL: Please, you give the gold! I'll pay you back later.

MENAECHMUS II: No, no; you give it; I'll pay you back double—later.

SLAVE GIRL: But I don't have it.

MENAECHMUS II: Well, I tell you—when you get it, give it to me.

SLAVE GIRL: Nothing else you want, is there?

MENAECHMUS II: Yes—just tell Erotium I'll take care of these things. (*Exit* SLAVE GIRL *into* EROTIUM'S *house*) Yes—I'll take care of them, all right; I'll sell them as quickly as I can for whatever I can get. Has that girl gone in yet? Yes, she has, and she's shut the door. All the gods are helping me, that's a fact! They're making me rich! They *love* me! But why am I staying here, when I've got the chance to get away from this sink of iniquity? Hurry up, Menaechmus! Get along! Step out! I'll take off this garland and throw it over to the left. Then, if they come after me, they'll think I went that way. I'll go and find my slave, if I can. I want to tell *him* about my good luck. (*Exit, stage right.*)

ACT FOUR

SCENE I

(*Enter* MENAECHMUS I's *wife* (MATRONA) *and* PENICULUS, *from* MENAECHMUS I's *house.*)

MATRONA: I just won't stand for it! Married to him, and

he cheats on me! My husband! Sneaks out all the things in the house and takes them to—to *that woman!*

PENICULUS: Oh, stop it, will you? You'll catch him in the act pretty soon; I'll fix that. Just come along this way. (*He starts to go away from the house toward stage left.*) He was taking your dress to the embroidery shop. He had a garland on, and he was drunk—yes, your dress, the one he stole from you earlier today. (*He sees garland.*) Look! There's the garland he had on; was I right, or wasn't I? Yes, he went this way, if you want to follow him. (MENAECHMUS I *appears, stage left.*) Say, look! What luck! He's coming back! And he hasn't got the dress, either.

MATRONA: What'll I do to him now?

PENICULUS: What you always do. Give him a tongue-lashing; that's my vote. Let's get back here. (*Motions toward the alleyway*) Shoot him from a blind!

SCENE II

(MENAECHMUS I *walks slowly across stage.*)

MENAECHMUS I: This is a silly way we have of doing business, and a nuisance, too! And the more important a man is, the more he feels he's got to do business this way. Everybody wants to have lots of clients. Nobody asks whether they're honest or dishonest. It's more a question of how much money they have than of how honest they may be. If a man's poor and tries to do the right thing, he's just no good. But if he's rich and dishonest, he's a "fine man." People who don't care what's legal or fair dealing are the ones who keep their patrons really interested. Lend them money, and they'll swear you didn't. Lawsuits? They've got lots of them! Pirates! Robbers! They have committed perjury and broken the law for every drachma they've got. Sue them? They love it! When they're told to appear in court, their patrons have to be there, too. It's our job to defend them, whatever they've done, whether it's a criminal or a civil case. Take me today: one of my clients had me considerably worried. I couldn't make the plea I wanted to or move for a change of venue; he kept hanging on to me and getting in my way. I filed a brief with the aediles in defense of some of the things he'd done—there were lots of them, and they were pretty bad! I offered a lot of confused stipulations mixed up all kinds of ways, presented my case either at greater length or more briefly than the truth required —all of this, just to get a postponement. And what did he do? Why, it was all I could do to get him to post bail for the later date! And I've never seen a man caught more red-handed: there were three unimpeachable witnesses for every dishonest trick he'd pulled.

Damn him, anyway! He's completely ruined my day. And damn me, too, for not having better sense than to go downtown. I had a fine day planned, and I've spoiled it. I ordered a dinner; Erotium's waiting for me, I'm sure. The minute I could, I got away from court. She's angry with me now, I suppose. The dress I gave her—that ought to calm her down. Yes—stole it from my wife and gave it to Erotium (*He has now arrived in front of* EROTIUM'S *house and is about to knock on the door.*)

PENICULUS (*aside, to* MATRONA): What do you say to that?

MATRONA: He's a pretty poor husband, and I made a mistake in marrying him.

PENICULUS: Can you hear what he's saying?

MATRONA: Yes.

MENAECHMUS I: If I were smart, I'd go in here, where I can enjoy myself.

PENICULUS (*steps out, seizes* MENAECHMUS *by the sleeve*): Wait a minute! You have some trouble coming first.

MATRONA: Yes, sir! You'll pay plenty for taking that!

PENICULUS (*aside to* MATRONA): That's giving it to him!

MATRONA: Did you think you could do mean things like that without getting caught?

MENAECHMUS I: What *is* all this about, my dear?

MATRONA: You're asking *me?*

MENAECHMUS I: Well, want me to ask *him?* (*Nods toward* PENICULUS. MENAECHMUS *comes up to* MATRONA *and puts his arm around her shoulders.*)

MATRONA: Take your hands off me!

PENICULUS (*to* MATRONA): Go to it!

MENAECHMUS I (*to* MATRONA): Why are you cross with me?

MATRONA: You ought to know.

PENICULUS: He knows. He's just pretending he doesn't, the good-for-nothing.

MENAECHMUS I: What *is* the matter?

MATRONA (*bursts into tears*): My dress—

MENAECHMUS I (*startled*): Your dress?

MATRONA: Somebody—my dress!—(MENAECHMUS *starts to tremble, tries to appear nonchalant.*)

PENICULUS (*to* MENAECHMUS): What are you scared of?

MENAECHMUS I: Who, me? Why, I'm not scared of anything.

PENICULUS: Nothing but one thing: the dress. That made you turn pale. Yes, you! You shouldn't have eaten the dinner behind my back. (*To* MATRONA) Go after him!

MENAECHMUS I (*whispers to* PENICULUS): Keep quiet, won't you? (*He shakes his head at* PENICULUS.)

PENICULUS: No, sir, I won't keep quiet. (*To* MATRONA) He's shaking his head at me not to talk.

MENAECHMUS I: Why, I did not! I never shook my head at you and I didn't wink at you, either. (*Gives* PENICULUS *an exaggerated wink.*)

PENICULUS: You've got plenty of nerve, haven't you? Insisting you didn't do what anybody can see.

MENAECHMUS I: By Jupiter and all the gods I swear, my dear—is that enough for you?—that I didn't shake my head at him.

PENICULUS: You've convinced her on that point. Now go on back.

MENAECHMUS I: Back where?

PENICULUS: To the embroidery shop, I'd say. Go on! Go get the dress!

MENAECHMUS I: What is this dress you're talking about? (MATRONA, *instead of taking* PENICULUS' *cue, bursts into tears and starts to walk away.*)

PENICULUS (*disgusted*): I give up! She can't keep her mind on her own property.

MATRONA: O-o-o-oh! I'm *so* unhappy!

MENAECHMUS I (*follows her, puts arm around her shoulders*): Why are you unhappy? Tell me all about it. One of the slaves been acting up? (*More sobs*) Has one of the slaves been talking back to you—the girls?—the boys? (*More sobs*) Tell me about it. They won't get away with that.

MATRONA: Ridiculous! (*She jerks away from him.*)

MENAECHMUS I: You're awfully cross; that makes me feel bad.

MATRONA: Ridiculous!

MENAECHMUS I: It must be one of the slaves you're cross at.

MATRONA: Ridiculous!

MENAECHMUS I: You're not cross at *me*, then, are you?

MATRONA: Now—that's *not* ridiculous.

MENAECHMUS I: Why! I haven't done anything wrong!

MATRONA: There you go! Ridiculous again!

MENAECHMUS I (*tries to comfort her. She keeps pushing him away*): Tell me, my dear, what's the matter with you?

PENICULUS: Fine man! Sweet-talking you!

MENAECHMUS I (*angrily, to* PENICULUS): Can't you stop bothering me? I'm not talking to you, am I?

MATRONA: Take your hands off me!

PENICULUS: That's the stuff! (*To* MENAECHMUS) Go on, now! Eat the dinner when I'm not there! Then afterward come out with your garland on and make fun of me—drunk, too!

MENAECHMUS I: Now, look here! I tell you I haven't had any dinner and haven't set foot inside that house today. (*Points to* EROTIUM's *house*)

PENICULUS: You say you haven't, do you?

MENAECHMUS I: I most certainly do!

PENICULUS: Of all the nerve! I've never seen anything like it! Didn't I see you a while ago right here in front of the house? Standing there with your garland on? Saying I wasn't right in the head? Saying you didn't know me? Insisting you were a stranger here?

MENAECHMUS I: Why—why, no! This is the first time I've been home since I left you some time ago.

PENICULUS: Yes, I know you! You didn't think I had any way to get back at you. All right. I've told your wife everything.

MENAECHMUS I: What did you tell her?

PENICULUS (airily): Oh, I don't know. Ask her.

MENAECHMUS I: What is this, my dear? What in the world has he been telling you? (She turns away.) What is it? Why don't you say something? Won't you tell me what it is?

MATRONA: As if you didn't know! Asking me!

MENAECHMUS I: Well, really, I wouldn't be asking you if I knew.

PENICULUS: Fine fellow he is! Look at him, pretending he doesn't know! (To MENAECHMUS) You can't keep it quiet. She knows all about it. Yes, sir, I told her the whole story.

MENAECHMUS I: What is this?

MATRONA: Since you haven't any sense of decency at all and aren't willing to admit what you did, just be quiet and listen. You'll find out why I'm cross and what he's been telling me, I guarantee that. Somebody stole a dress from me.

MENAECHMUS I: Somebody stole a dress from me?

PENICULUS: See! He's trying to trip you up! He'll do anything! It was stolen from her, not from you. For if it had been stolen from you, we wouldn't know where it was.

MENAECHMUS I (angrily): Mind your own business! (To MATRONA) What were you saying?

MATRONA: My dress, I tell you! It's gone!

MENAECHMUS I: Who stole it?

MATRONA: Hah! The one who took it can tell you that.

MENAECHMUS I: Who was it?

MATRONA: A man called Menaechmus.

MENAECHMUS I: Well! That was a mean thing to do! Who is this Menaechmus?

MATRONA: You're "this Menaechmus"—so there!

MENAECHMUS I: Who, me?

MATRONA: Yes, you.

MENAECHMUS I: Who says so?

MATRONA: I do.

PENICULUS: And so do I. And you gave it to this woman, Erotium, here.

MENAECHMUS I: I did that?

MATRONA: Yes, you, you, you, I say!

PENICULUS: Want us to go get an owl to say, "you, you," at you? We're getting tired.

MENAECHMUS I: By Jupiter and all the gods I swear, my dear (is that enough for you?) that I didn't give—

PENICULUS: Oh, no, no, no!—that what we're saying is the truth.

MENAECHMUS I (*realizes he is beaten*): Well, but I didn't exactly *give* it to her. I just, uh—uh—you know!—I just lent it to her.

MATRONA: Well, after all, I don't lend your clothes to any-body. Women should lend women's clothes, and men, men's. Now you go and bring that dress back.

MENAECHMUS I: I'll see that it's brought back.

MATRONA: Well, you'd better, I think. You'll not get into the house unless you've got the dress with you. I'm going in. (*She starts toward house.*)

PENICULUS: Hey! What about me? I put a lot of time on this for you.

MATRONA: You'll be paid back for your time when some-body steals something of yours. (*Exit.*)

PENICULUS (*disgusted*): Hah! That will be never. I haven't got anything anybody'd steal. Damn you, anyway, both of you! I'm going on downtown. I can see quite clearly that I've lost my place in this house. (*Exit, stage left.*)

MENAECHMUS I (*as soon as he sees that stage is clear*): My wife thought she was hurting me when she shut me out! As if I didn't have another place, and a nicer one, too, where I can get in. (*Turns toward his house*) If you don't like me, that's just too bad! Erotium likes me. She won't shut me out; she'll shut me in with her. Now, I'll go and ask her to give me back the dress I gave her. I'll buy her another one, a nicer one. (*He goes to her door and knocks.*) Hello! Anybody home? Open the door, somebody, and ask Erotium to come out here a minute.

Scene III

(*Enter* Erotium.)

Erotium: Who's asking for me?

Menaechmus I: Somebody who thinks he isn't much compared to you.

Erotium: Why, Menaechmus, dear! Why are you waiting out here? Come on in.

Menaechmus I: Wait a minute. Do you know why I've come to your house?

Erotium: Yes—the usual reason.

Menaechmus I: No, no. Say—uh, that dress—please, honey —the one I just gave you—will you give it back to me? My wife has found out all about it, exactly what I did. I'll buy you another one worth twice as much—you just pick it out.

Erotium: Why! I gave you that dress to take to the embroidery shop, just a few minutes ago. Yes, and the bracelet too, to take to the goldsmith's to be made over.

Menaechmus I: To *me*? You gave the dress and a bracelet to *me*? No, you didn't, and I can prove it. I gave it to you a while ago, didn't I, and went downtown? Well, I'm just coming back now, and this is the first I've seen of you since then.

Erotium: I see what you're up to. Just because I trusted you, you're thinking up a little scheme to cheat me.

Menaechmus I: No, really! I'm not asking for it because I want to cheat you. No! I tell you, my wife's found out about it.

Erotium: Well, I didn't ask you to give it to me, either. You brought it to me yourself, you gave it to me—said it was a gift. Now you want it back. All right! Keep it! Take it! Wear it, you or your wife, either one! Put it away in your cedar chest, if you want! You! You'll not set foot in here from now on, don't you fool yourself! Here I was so nice to you, and that's the way you treat me. Just for that, it's cash in advance from now on. You can't lead me around by the nose, and then cheat on me! Just go find somebody else to cheat! (*Starts toward her house*)

MENAECHMUS I: Oh, now! Wait! Don't be so cross! Please! Wait a minute! Please come back. Wait, won't you? Please come back, just for my sake! (*She slams door in his face.*) There she goes. (*Rattles door*) She's locked the door. Now I'm really locked out! Nobody believes a word I say, either at home or at Erotium's. I'll go and talk to my friends about this, and see what they think I'd better do. (*Exit, stage left.*)

ACT FIVE

SCENE I

(*Enter* MENAECHMUS II, *stage right, and* MATRONA *from* MENAECHMUS I's *house. They do not see each other.*)

MENAECHMUS II: I was awfully foolish when I gave the purse and the money to Messenio. I suppose he's three fathoms under in a dive somewhere.

MATRONA: I'll go out. I want to see how soon my husband is coming home. Oh, look! I see him. Thank heaven, he's got the dress!

MENAECHMUS II: I wonder where Messenio is wandering around now.

MATRONA: I'll go up to him and give him the reception he deserves. (*To* MENAECHMUS) Aren't you ashamed to show your face here, you disgraceful thing, with that dress you've got there?

MENAECHMUS II: What's this? What's the matter with you, madam?

MATRONA: Shame on you! How dare you even whisper? How dare you say a word to me?

MENAECHMUS II: Now just what have I done? Why shouldn't I dare to say anything?

MATRONA: You ask *me* that? Of all the insolence!

MENAECHMUS II: Madam, don't you know why the Greeks always said that Hecuba was a "bitch"?

MATRONA: No, I do not!

MENAECHMUS II: Because Hecuba used to do exactly what you're doing. Anybody she saw, she started snarling at him. And so, quite properly, they started calling her a "bitch." (*He starts to walk away.*)

MATRONA: You've insulted me! I will not stand for it. I'll get a divorce and live alone the rest of my life rather than sit back and let you insult me the way you do.

MENAECHMUS II: What's it to me whether you can put up with your husband or are going to leave him? Say, do people always do this sort of thing here—start telling wild yarns to a stranger the minute he gets here?

MATRONA: What "wild yarns"? No, I tell you: I won't stand for it any longer. No, sir! I'll get a divorce rather than put up with the way you act.

MENAECHMUS II (*shrugs*): Heavens! As far as I'm concerned, go get a divorce and live by yourself as long as God is on his throne!

MATRONA: But you told me over and over that you didn't steal this. (*Points to dress*) Now you're holding it right under my nose; aren't you ashamed?

MENAECHMUS II (*sighs*): Really, madam, you're being very impolite and very unpleasant. You mean to say that somebody stole this dress from you? Why! Another woman gave it to me, to have some alterations made on it!

MATRONA: Now, really, that's the—! All right! I'm going to get my father and tell him the awful things you've been saying and doing. (*Calls into house*) Decio! Go find my father and tell him to come back to my house with you. Tell him there's a terrible mess! (*A slave leaves the house and goes off, stage left.*) (*To* MENAECHMUS) When he gets here, I'm going to tell him everything you did.

MENAECHMUS II: Are you crazy? What did I do?

MATRONA: You took my dress and my jewelry—your own wife's!—and gave them to—*that woman!* Is my story right, or isn't it?

MENAECHMUS II: Oh, come now, madam—please, tell me, if you don't mind, what's your favorite prescription for nerve strain? I need a little, if I have to listen to you. I'm sure I don't know who you think I am. I met you the day I met Hercules' wife's grandfather.

MATRONA: You can laugh me off, but you can't laugh *him* off, my father. Here he comes. Just look around. Do you know *him?*

MENAECHMUS II: Sure! Sure! Met him the same day I met Calchas the prophet. This is the first time I've ever seen either of you.

MATRONA: You say you don't know me? Don't know my father?

MENAECHMUS II: Yes, and I'll say I don't know your grandfather, too, if you want to bring him on.

MATRONA: Oh, you! You're acting just the way you always do.

Scene II

(*Enter* SENEX, *hobbling with cane.*)

SENEX: I'm an old man, but this seems to be important, so I'll get along and hurry as much as I can. But it isn't easy for me; I'm not fooling myself about that. Not as spry as I used to be! You know what people say: "Full of years!" That's me—so full I can feel them pressing me down. (*He stops and rests on his cane.*) My strength is gone. Bad business, being old! Yes, *very* bad. Troubles, troubles, troubles! All the troubles you have when you get old! Why, if I should just *list* them all—(*he starts to count them off on his fingers, then stops, shakes his head*). No, no! Makes my speech too long. (*He hobbles off again toward stage center.*) But this business has got me really worried. What do you suppose it is? Why should my daughter all of a sudden ask me to come to her house? And didn't tell me what it was, either—what she wanted or why she'd sent for me. Well, I think I know just about what it is, anyway. I expect she and her husband have been having a little argument. That's the way these women always are. Think they have to make slaves of their husbands! Think they have a right to because *they* brought the dowry! Uncivilized, that's what they are! And the husbands, too—they aren't always pure as lilies. Just the same, there's a certain amount a wife has to put up with. And, you know, a married daughter never invites her father to her house unless she's got a reason: her husband's done something, or they've had a spat. Well, whatever it is, I'll soon find out. Oh! There she is! I see her—right in front of the house—and her husband, too. Grim! It's just what I suspected. I'll call her.

MATRONA: I'll run to meet him. Hello, father dear! How are you?

SENEX: I'm all right. How are you? (*She bursts into tears.*) I hope you're not having any trouble. You're not having any trouble, are you? That's not why you asked me to come? (*No answer*) What are you crying about? Why is he angry? What's he doing 'way over there? Had a little skirmish, the two of you—haven't you? Now come on, tell me which of you started it. And make it short—no long orations.

MATRONA: I never did anything wrong at all. You can put that out of your mind right now, father. But I just can't stay on here! I can't stand it, not in any way, shape, or fashion! So take me away, please.

SENEX: Now what is all this?

MATRONA: He's just making me a laughingstock, father.

SENEX: Who is?

MATRONA: *He* is, the man you gave me away to, my husband.

SENEX: Aha! There's your quarrel! How many times have I

told you, both of you, not to come to me with your fault-finding?

MATRONA: How could I help it, father?

SENEX: You want *me* to tell *you?*

MATRONA: Yes, if you don't mind.

SENEX: How many times have I made it clear that you should be patient with your husband, that you shouldn't always be watching his comings and goings, and that you shouldn't pry into his affairs.

MATRONA: Yes, but he's carrying on with *that woman* there next door.

SENEX: Well, he shows good taste. You just keep sticking your nose into his business, and I have no doubt he'll carry on with her even more.

MATRONA: And he goes over there for drinks.

SENEX: Well, is he going to go for drinks any the less because of *you,* whether he gets them there or somewhere else? Haven't you any sense of fitness, girl? Do you think you can stop him from going out any more than you can stop him from inviting people in? Do you expect your husband to be your slave? If you do, why not be consistent about it: Assign daily jobs to him, tell him to go find a chair with the slave girls, and card wool?

MATRONA: Well! I seem to have hired you to be lawyer for my husband, not for me. You're standing beside me, but you're standing up for him.

SENEX: If he's done anything wrong, I'll call him down for it much more sternly than I did you. Now see here: He sees that you have plenty of clothes and jewelry; he gives you all the household help you need, and all the food. It would be better, my girl, to be sensible about all this.

MATRONA: But he's been stealing my jewelry and dresses—and I had them put away, too. He robs me! He takes my pretty things when I'm not looking and gives them to women like—like *her!* (*Points to* EROTIUM's *house*)

SENEX: He's wrong, if he does what you say. But if he

doesn't, you're wrong in accusing an innocent man of something he didn't do.

MATRONA: Why, no! He's got the dress right now, father, and the bracelet, too, that he'd taken to her. He's bringing them back because I found out.

SENEX: I'm going to find out right now from him what happened. I'll go over and speak to him. Tell me, what's the trouble, Menaechmus? What are you two quarreling about? I'd like to know. What are you cross about? Why is she angry? What's she doing 'way over there?

MENAECHMUS II: I don't know who you are or what your name is, sir, but I swear by Jupiter on high and all the gods—

SENEX: Swear? About what? Swear to what, for heaven's sake?

MENAECHMUS II: That I've done absolutely nothing to that lady, the one who's been accusing me of stealing this (*points to dress*) and taking it away from her.

MATRONA: Liar!

MENAECHMUS II: If I've ever set foot inside that house where she lives, I pray heaven that I may be the unluckiest of all the unlucky men in the world!

SENEX: Are you crazy, to say a thing like that, or to say you never set foot inside your own home? You must be completely out of your mind!

MENAECHMUS II: Do you, sir, say that that is my house, there?

SENEX: Do you say it isn't?

MENAECHMUS II: I do indeed say it isn't. That's right.

SENEX: No, indeed, it's not right, to say it isn't—unless you moved out yesterday. (*To* MATRONA) Come here, dear. (*Whispers*) What about it? You haven't moved out, have you?

MATRONA: Now where would we go, or why would we do that?

SENEX: I'm sure I don't know.

MATRONA: It's perfectly plain; he's making a fool of you. Don't you get it?

SENEX: All right, all right, Menaechmus. You've had your fun. Now let's get down to brass tacks.

MENAECHMUS II: Pardon me, but what have I to do with you? Where did you come from? Who are you? How am I obligated to you, or to her, either? She's making me sick and tired.

MATRONA (*whispers to* SENEX): Look! Don't his eyes look funny? He's turning pale in the face, too! His eyes are awfully bright. Look!

MENAECHMUS II (*aside*): What could be better? They say I'm crazy: why don't I pretend I am? That'll scare them away.

MATRONA: Look, the way his arms hang! Look at his mouth! (*Runs to* SENEX) What'll I do now, father?

SENEX: Come on over here, dear, as far away from him as you can. (*He puts* MATRONA *behind him and stands firm, brandishing his cane at* MENAECHMUS.)

MENAECHMUS II (*charges between them; they run to opposite sides of stage*): Evoe, and again, Evoe! Bacchus! Whither callest thou me to the wildwood, and to the hunt? (*He turns and faces stage front.*) I hear thee, but I cannot depart from here, for on my left a rabid female hound keeps watch upon me, and behind me a stinking goat, who many a time in his long life hath damned an innocent man with false witness.

SENEX: Why you—!

MENAECHMUS II (*turns toward* MATRONA, *rushes at her, and brandishes his fists under her face*): Lo! Apollo from his oracle doth bid me burn out her eyes with flaming brands!

MATRONA (*she retreats slowly, hands held over her face*): Oh, father! Help! He's threatening to burn my eyes out!

MENAECHMUS II (*gives up pursuit of* MATRONA *when he sees she is not going to leave stage*): Ah, me! They say I'm crazy, when they're the ones who are crazy.

SENEX: Sst! My dear!

MATRONA (*goes over to* SENEX): What is it?

SENEX: What had we better do? Do you think I'd better call the slaves out? Yes, I will. I'll go and get some men to take him away and tie him up inside, before he makes any more trouble.

MENAECHMUS II (*aside*): Oh-oh! I'm stuck! If I don't figure out something, they'll take me into their house. (*He starts toward* MATRONA *again.*) Dost thou bid me not spare my fists at all upon her face, if she departs not from my sight to the depths of death? I shall do thy bidding, Apollo! (*He rushes at* MATRONA, *fists clenched.*)

SENEX (*to* MATRONA): Run in the house as quick as you can, or he may really hurt you!

MATRONA (*to* SENEX): I'm running! (*Stops at door*) You keep an eye on him, father! Don't let him get away! (*Turns to open door, bursts into tears*) Oh dear, oh dear! To think I should live to see a thing like this! (*Exit into house.*)

MENAECHMUS II (*aside*): Got her out of the way, all right! (*Aloud*) Now for this foul, filthy, fuzzy-faced, trembling Tithonus, born son of Cygnus—thus thou biddest me, Apollo, to smash his limbs and bones and joints to bits with the very staff that he holds in his hands! (*He makes a grab for* SENEX's *cane, but* SENEX *stands firm and brandishes the cane at him.*)

SENEX: You'll get into trouble if you touch me or come one step closer to me!

MENAECHMUS II (*drops back, pretends to get a new inspiration*): I'll do thy bidding! I'll take an axe and I'll—(*he starts toward* SENEX *again, swinging an imaginary axe*)—I'll chop out his gizzard, clean to his backbone, chip, chop, chip!

SENEX (*aside*): Well, now, I'll have to watch out; I'll have to be careful. Yes! I'm getting a little uneasy about him, the way he's acting. He may really hurt me! (*He takes a firm stand, cane upraised.*)

MENAECHMUS II (*defeated again, withdraws, pretends still another inspiration*): Many are thy commands, Apollo! Now thou biddest me to take a team of wild, unbroken horses, and climb into my chariot, and run down this little, old, stinking, toothless lion. Now I'm in my chariot! Now I have the reins! Now the whip's in my hand! Get up, my steeds! Let us hear the clatter of your hoofs! In quickened course be bent your nimble knees! (*He gallops toward* SENEX.)

SENEX (*raises his cane, brandishes it at* MENAECHMUS): Try to scare me with a team of horses, will you?

MENAECHMUS II (*slides to a stop*): Lo, Apollo! Once more thou biddest me charge that man, who standeth there, and kill him! (*Again* SENEX *brandishes cane.* MENAECHMUS *again comes to a sliding stop, and pretends to stumble backward out of chariot.*) But who is this, who seizeth my hair and draggeth me from my car? Thy bidding, Apollo, and thy order he doth change!

SENEX (*aside*): For heaven's sake, the poor man is in a bad way! (*Shakes his head*) Why, he's gone completely insane, and a little while ago he was perfectly all right. It's a terrible attack he's had—and so sudden, too. I'll go and get the doctor as fast as I can. (*Exit, stage left.*)

MENAECHMUS II (*peers around stage*): Well! Are they finally out of my sight? Why! They made me pretend to be insane! But what am I wating for? Why don't I get off to the ship, while I still can safely? (*To audience*) Please, all of you, if the old gentleman comes back, don't tell him which way I went, will you? (*Exit stage right.*)

SCENE III

(*Re-enter* SENEX.)

SENEX: My backsides ache from sitting, my eyes ache from looking, all from waiting for the doctor to get back from his calls. Tiresome old fool! He finally dragged himself away from his patients and came. Said he'd had to set a broken leg for Aesculapius and a broken arm for Apollo. I wonder now—what have I got here? A doctor or bronze-foundryman? (*He looks back. The doctor enters, stage left.*) Ah, here he comes. Would you hurry up a bit, please?

Scene IV

MEDICUS: What did you say was wrong with him? Tell me, sir: Is he suffering from hallucinations? Would you say that he had a comatose hysteria? Or perhaps hydrocephaly?

SENEX: Now see here: I asked you to come here so that *you* could tell *me* and could cure him.

MEDICUS: Oh, that's no problem. He'll be all right. I give you my word of honor on that.

SENEX: Well, you take care of him—and care about it, too.

MEDICUS: Care about it? Why, I'll worry, worry, worry, all day long! That's how much I'll care about taking care of him. (MENAECHMUS I *enters, stage left.*)

SENEX: Well, there he is. Let's watch what he does.

Scene V

MENAECHMUS I: Good God! What a run of bad luck I've had today. I thought I'd kept everything quiet, and then my dear friend Peniculus let out the whole story—disgraced me, scared the life out of me. My Mr. Fixit: all the trouble he made for me, after all I've done for him! I swear I'll have his life for it. *His* life? What do I mean, "*his* life"? It isn't his; it's mine. It's my food and my money that have kept him alive. I'll separate him from his immortal soul! And Erotium here—acted just the way you might expect, being what she is. Because I ask her to give me the dress to take back to my wife, she says she already gave it to me. I feel just awful!

SENEX (*to* MEDICUS): Hear what he's saying?

MEDICUS: Yes. Says he feels awful.

SENEX: Would you talk to him, please?

MEDICUS: Good afternoon, Menaechmus. (MENAECHMUS, *startled and angry, bares his arm and threatens to punch* MEDICUS.) Oh, come now! Mustn't leave your arm bare! Don't you know you may make yourself a lot worse?

MENAECHMUS I (*jerks away*): Oh, go hang, will you?

SENEX (*whispers*): Notice anything?

MEDICUS (*whispers*): Notice anything! Why, an acre of se-
dato-purgative herbs won't even check it! (*Turns to* MENAECH-
MUS) Pardon me, Menaechmus.

MENAECHMUS I: What do you want?

MEDICUS: Would you mind answering a question or two?
Do you prefer white or red wine?

MENAECHMUS I: Oh, go to the devil, will you?

MEDICUS (*to* SENEX): See! There's the first, tiny indication of
psychosis! (*To* MENAECHMUS) Won't you please answer the
question I asked?

MENAECHMUS I: Why don't you ask me whether I like my
bread purple—or red, or yellow? Whether I like scales on my
birds and feathers on my fish?

SENEX: Oh, my! Hear that? He doesn't make sense at all!
Why don't you hurry up and give him something, before it's
too late?

MEDICUS: No, wait a minute. I have a few more questions
to ask him.

SENEX: You'll kill the man with all your talk!

MEDICUS: Now, tell me: Do your eyes often seem fixed and
staring?

MENAECHMUS I: What? What do you think I am, a lobster?
Of all the—!

MEDICUS: Tell me: Do your bowels ever rumble, as far as
you've noticed?

MENAECHMUS I: When I've had plenty to eat, they don't;
when I'm hungry, they do.

MEDICUS (*to* SENEX): Well, now, there's nothing abnormal
about that answer. (*To* MENAECHMUS) Do you sleep soundly?
Have any trouble getting to sleep?

MENAECHMUS I: I sleep soundly, if I've paid my debts—say,
Jupiter and all the gods damn you, you and your questions!

MEDICUS (*to* SENEX): Now he's beginning to show the first
signs of instability: hear what he said then? Better watch out!

SENEX (*to* MEDICUS): Instability? Why, he's Wisdom personified from what he's saying, compared to what he was a while ago. For then he kept calling his own wife a mad bitch.

MENAECHMUS I (*overhears*): What did I call her?

SENEX: You're a sick man, I tell you.

MENAECHMUS I: Who, me?

SENEX: Yes, you. You even threatened to run me down with a four-horse team. Oh, yes, you did: I saw you do it, myself; I say you did, myself.

MENAECHMUS I (*furious*): Yes, and *you* stole Jupiter's holy crown; I know that. And they threw you into jail for it; I know that. And when they let you out, they tied you up and gave you a whipping; I know that. And you murdered your father and sold your mother into slavery; I know that, too. Accuse me of things, will you? How do you like my answers; do they make sense or not?

SENEX (*to* MEDICUS): For heaven's sake, doctor, hurry, please! Whatever you're going to do, do it! Don't you see the man is delirious?

MEDICUS (*solemnly*): You know what I think you'd better do? Have him brought to my clinic.

SENEX: Is that your opinion?

MEDICUS: Yes, it is. In there, I'll be able to take care of him the way I think is best.

SENEX: All right, just as you like.

MEDICUS (*to* MENAECHMUS, *soothingly*): I'll give you a twenty-day course of sedato-cathartic treatments.

MENAECHMUS I: Oh, you will, will you? Well, I'll string you up and give you a thirty-day course of treatments with a bull whip.

MEDICUS (*to* SENEX): Go get some slaves to take him to my clinic.

SENEX: How many do we need?

MEDICUS: Judging from the severity of his illness, I'd say no less than four.

SENEX: I'll have them here right away. (*Starts toward* ME-NAECHMUS' *house*) You keep an eye on him, doctor.

MEDICUS: N-n-no, I'll go along home, so that I can prepare what I need. You tell the slaves to bring him to the clinic.

SENEX: I'll get him there right away.

MEDICUS: Well—see you later. (*Backs off stage, keeping eye on* MENAECHMUS *all the time*)

SENEX: Yes, good-by. (*Exit into* MENAECHMUS' *house.*)

MENAECHMUS I: My father-in-law—gone! The doctor—gone! Alone at last! Ye gods, what does this mean, these people saying I'm crazy? Why, I haven't been sick a single day since I was born. I'm not crazy! I'm not starting any fights or quarrels! I'm perfectly sane, and so is everybody else; I can see that. I recognize people; I talk to people. Say! Maybe they're wrong: they say I'm crazy; maybe they're the ones who are crazy. What am I going to do now? I'd like to go home, but my wife won't let me in, and nobody'll let me in here (*indicates* EROTIUM's *house*) either. What a mess this has turned out to be! (*He goes to his own doorstep and sits down.*) I guess I'll stay right here. When it gets dark, at least, I think she'll let me in.

SCENE VI

(*Enter* MESSENIO, *stage right.*)

MESSENIO: Want a pattern for a good slave? Here it is: He takes care of his master's affairs, sees to them, keeps them in order, keeps his mind on them, and when his master is away he minds his master's business just as thoroughly as if the man were there—or even better. He thinks more about the lash on his back than about the food in his craw, and more about the whip on his shanks than about the state of his belly, if he's got his wits about him. Let them stop and think a minute, those good-for-nothing fellows—stop and think what they've got coming from their masters. Lazy good-for-nothings! The lash, the leg irons, the mill; weariness, hunger, cold! No fun, that. But that's what they get for being shiftless. And that kind of trouble troubles me.

So I've decided to be a good slave, not a bad one. That's

my principle, and I stick to it. Doing all right for myself, too! Other men can do as they please. Me—I'll do my duty. I'll be respectful, keep out of trouble; no matter what happens, master will know I'm right behind him. Slaves who keep out of trouble and are respectful are the ones their masters think highly of. Those that aren't respectful will show plenty of respect for the beating they'll get. Well, it won't be long, now. Pretty soon master's going to pay me back for all I've done. I do my slave's job with just this one thing in mind: How will it affect my back?

I took the baggage and the sailors to the rooming house, as Master told me, and now I'm coming to meet him. I'll go knock on the door, so that he'll know I'm here—and get the man out of that sink of iniquity. (*Sees* MENAECHMUS I, *sitting on steps*) But I'm afraid I've come too late. Looks as if the battle's over.

SCENE VII

(*Enter* SENEX *from* MENAECHMUS' *house, followed by four* LORARII. *They are huge, brawny men, the "whippers" of the household.*)

SENEX: Now for heaven's sake, do as I tell you! Think! Think! Be careful! Do exactly what I told you. Pick that man up (*points to* MENAECHMUS) and take him to the clinic (*they hang back;* SENEX *advances on them, cane upraised*)—or maybe you don't care what happens to you! (*They start toward* ME-NAECHMUS. MENAECHMUS *gets up, starts to back away.*) Now, don't you pay any attention—not a one of you—to anything he says. What are you waiting for? Why the hesitation? You ought to have grabbed him by now. I'm going to the doctor's; I'll be there when you get there. (*Exit, stage left.*)

MENAECHMUS I: Hey! What's all this? What are these fellows coming after me for? (*To* LORARII) What do you want? What are you after? (*The* LORARII *surround him.*) What's the idea of blocking me off? (*They seize him, hoist him to their shoulders.*) Where are you taking me? Where are you going

with me? Help! For heaven's sake, somebody! Help! Help!
(*To* LORARII) Let me go, will you?

MESSENIO: What am I seeing! It's my master! Of all the
nerve! Some men are picking him up and carrying him off!

MENAECHMUS I: Won't anybody *please* help me?

MESSENIO: I will, master. I'm not afraid. What a shame!
What a disgrace, you people! My master is being kidnaped
here in broad daylight, right on the open street, in a peaceful, law-abiding town! He's a free man—came here of his own
free will. (*He dances around the* LORARII, *pounding them
with his fists.*) Let him go!

MENAECHMUS I: Please, whoever you are, help me, will you?
Don't let these fellows do this to me! Its an outrage!

MESSENIO: You bet I'll help you! I'll protect you! I'll stand
by you! Yes, sir! I won't let them kill you! I'd rather be killed
myself! That fellow there who's got you by the shoulder—
gouge his eye out, will you, sir? I'll plow up the others' faces
and plant my fists in them. (*To* LORARII) By God, you'll wish
you hadn't tried to kidnap my master! Let him go!

MENAECHMUS I: I got this fellow's eye!

MESSENIO: Let's see his empty eye socket! (*To* LORARII)
You robbers! You kidnapers! You pirates!

ONE LORARIUS: Help! Stop it, will you?

MESSENIO: Let him go, then.

MENAECHMUS I (*to* LORARII): What do you mean by laying
hands on me? (*To* MESSENIO) Beat them up! (*They drop* ME-
NAECHMUS *and start to back away.*)

MESSENIO (*pursuing them*): Go on, now, get out! Get out
of here! (*As the last one goes by,* MESSENIO *kicks him.*) There!
There's one more for you. That's what you get for being the
last to go! (*Brushes himself off, turns to* MENAECHMUS) I
gave them a good going over, all right! Suited me fine. Well,
well, sir, I certainly got here just in time to help you!

MENAECHMUS I: Yes, my friend, whoever you are. God bless
you! If it hadn't been for you, I'd never have seen the sun
set today.

MESSENIO: Yes! Well, sir, if you'd like to do the right thing—
how about setting me free?

MENAECHMUS I: Set you free? Me?

MESSENIO: Yes, sir. After all, sir, I did save your life.

MENAECHMUS I: What is this? You're making a mistake somewhere, my friend.

MESSENIO: A mistake? What do you mean?

MENAECHMUS I: I give you my word on it: I'm not your master.

MESSENIO (*smirks*): Oh, now—don't put it that way.

MENAECHMUS I: No, I mean it. No slave of mine ever did anything like that for me.

MESSENIO: Well, then, sir, since you say I'm "not yours," let me go free.

MENAECHMUS I: Why, sure! As far as I'm concerned, consider yourself free—go anywhere you like.

MESSENIO: You really mean it?

MENAECHMUS I: Of course I mean it—as far as I have any rights over you.

MESSENIO (*beams*): That makes it "patron" now, instead of "master," doesn't it? (*He shakes hands with himself.*)—Congratulations on your emancipation, Messenio! Thank, thanks! —But patron, sir, please: remember I'm at your orders just as much as when I was your slave. I'll live at your house and go home along with you, when you go.

MENAECHMUS I: Oh, no, you won't!

MESSENIO: I'll go to the rooming house now and get the baggage and the money for you. (MENAECHMUS *looks blank.*) Oh, it's all locked up in your trunk—the purse with the money, you know! I'll bring it here to you right away.

MENAECHMUS I: Well, sure—go ahead.

MESSENIO: I'll give it back to you, exactly what you gave to me. You just wait here. (*Exit, stage right.*)

MENAECHMUS I: This is the strangest business! The funniest things are happening to me today! Here these folks (*nods toward his own and* EROTIUM'S *house*) say I'm not who I am, and shut me out. And now on top of that this fellow says he is my slave, and I set him free. *He* says he's going to bring me a purse and some money. If he does that, I'll tell him he's free—to go anywhere he wants, so that when he gets his wits back he won't be asking me for the money. My father-in-law and that doctor said I was insane. What does it all mean, I wonder? Must be a dream; that's the way it looks to me. Now I'll go over here to Erotium's, even though she is angry with me. Maybe somehow I can get her to give me back the dress, so that I can take it home. (*Exit into* ERO-TIUM'S *house.*)

SCENE VIII

(*Enter* MENAECHMUS II *and* MESSENIO, *stage right.*)

MENAECHMUS II: The nerve of you! You mean to tell me you met me here today, since the time when I told you to come and meet me?

MESSENIO: Why, yes! Not more than a few minutes ago I hauled some fellows off you who were kidnaping you—four of them—right in front of this house. You were shouting to high heaven, and I ran up and saved you—beat them off by sheer brute force, and no thanks to them. And so, because I saved your life, you set me free. When I said I was going after the money and the baggage, you ran around ahead of me as fast as you could, to meet me, so that you could say you didn't do what you did.

MENAECHMUS II: I told you to go free?

MESSENIO: Certainly.

MENAECHMUS II: Oh, no, I didn't. There's one thing you can be perfectly sure of: I'll turn slave myself before I'll set you free.

SCENE IX

(*Enter* MENAECHMUS I *from* EROTIUM'S *house.*)

MENAECHMUS I: You can swear to it all you like, but that won't make it any more true that I took the dress and the bracelet from you earlier today. Damn you all, anyway!

MESSENIO: For heaven's sake! What do I see!

MENAECHMUS II: Well, what do you see?

MESSENIO: Your spit and image!

MENAECHMUS II: What *are* you talking about?

MESSENIO: It's your own face; couldn't be any more like it!

MENAECHMUS II: Hm! Is kind of like me, when I stop and think what I look like.

MENAECHMUS I (*sees* MESSENIO): Oh, there you are, my friend—what's your name—who saved my life.

MESSENIO: Excuse me, please, sir, but would you mind telling me your name?

MENAECHMUS I: Not at all! After what you did for me, I'd hardly mind doing anything for you. My name is Menaechmus.

MENAECHMUS II: Oh, no! That's *my* name.

MENAECHMUS I: I'm a Sicilian, from Syracuse.

MENAECHMUS II: My home town and my home country, too.

MENAECHMUS I: What do I hear you saying?

MENAECHMUS II: Nothing but the truth.

MESSENIO (*turns to* MENAECHMUS I): Well, I know this man; he's my master. I thought you (*indicates* MENAECHMUS I) were he. (*Nods at* MENAECHMUS II) I'm afraid I even made some trouble for him. (*Turns to* MENAECHMUS II) Please excuse me, if I said anything silly or stupid to you.

MENAECHMUS II: You must be out of your mind. Don't you remember; you came off the ship with me this morning.

MESSENIO: Why, of course! That's perfectly right. (*To* MENAECHMUS II) You're my master. (*To* MENAECHMUS I) You'll have to find another slave. (*To* MENAECHMUS II) Hello to you! (*To* MENAECHMUS I) Good-bye to you! I say that *he* (*pointing to* MENAECHMUS II) is Menaechmus.

MENAECHMUS I: But I say I am.

MENAECHMUS II: What are you trying to tell me? (*To* MENAECHMUS I) *You* are Menaechmus?

MENAECHMUS I: I certainly am. And my father's name was Moschus.

MENAECHMUS II: *You* are *my* father's son?

MENAECHMUS I: No, no, my friend, *my* father's. I have no

desire to appropriate your father. I'm not trying to take him away from you.

MESSENIO: Ye gods in heaven, answer this prayer for me! I never hoped it would come true, but I have a suspicion it might, now. If I'm not completely fooled, these are the two twin brothers. They both say their father had the same name, and they both say they came from the same place. I'll ask my master to step aside. Menaechmus!

MENAECHMUS I and MENAECHMUS II: Yes?

MESSENIO: I don't want both of you—just the one that came on the ship with me.

MENAECHMUS I: I didn't.

MENAECHMUS II: I did.

MESSENIO: You're the one I want, then. Come over here.

MENAECHMUS II: Here I am. What do you want?

MESSENIO (*whispers*): That man is either a superb actor or your own twin brother. I've never seen one man who looked more like another. Water's not more like water, or milk like milk—believe me!—than he's like you and you're like him. Besides, he says his father was the same as yours, and he says he came from the same place as you. I think we'd better go and ask him some questions.

MENAECHMUS II: Good advice! Thanks a lot. Do that, will you? You're a free man, if you can prove that he's my brother.

MESSENIO: I hope I can.

MENAECHMUS II: So do I.

MESSENIO (*to* MENAECHMUS I): I beg your pardon. I think you said your name was Menaechmus.

MENAECHMUS I: That's right.

MESSENIO: Well, his name is Menaechmus, too. You said you were born in Syracuse in Sicily; that's where he was born. You said your father's name was Moschus; so was his. Now you can both help me and yourselves at the same time.

MENAECHMUS I: After what you did for me, you couldn't ask anything that I wouldn't be glad to do. I'm a free man, but I'm at your service, just as if you'd bought me, spot cash.

MESSENIO: I'm hoping that I can prove that you are twin

brothers, born of one mother and one father, on the same day.

MENAECHMUS I: Remarkable statement! I hope you can do what you say you can.

MESSENIO: I can. But come now, both of you, answer my questions.

MENAECHMUS I: Any time you like, just ask. I'll answer; I won't keep anything back that I know about.

MESSENIO (*to* MENAECHMUS I): Your name *is* Menaechmus?

MENAECHMUS I: Right.

MESSENIO (*to* MENAECHMUS II): And yours, too?

MENAECHMUS II: Yes.

MESSENIO (*to* MENAECHMUS I): You say your father was named Moschus?

MENAECHMUS I: Yes, I do.

MENAECHMUS II: So was mine.

MESSENIO (*to* MENAECHMUS I): You're from Syracuse?

MENAECHMUS I: Certainly.

MESSENIO (*to* MENAECHMUS II): What about you?

MENAECHMUS II: Of course.

MESSENIO: So far everything agrees perfectly. Let's go on. (*To* MENAECHMUS I) Tell me! What's the earliest memory you have of your home?

MENAECHMUS I: I remember that I went to Tarentum with father on business, and that later I got lost from him and was taken away from there.

MENAECHMUS II: God bless me!

MESSENIO (*to* MENAECHMUS II): What are you shouting about? Be quiet! (*To* MENAECHMUS I) How old were you when your father took you on that trip?

MENAECHMUS I: Seven years old. Yes, I was just starting to lose my baby teeth. And I've never seen father since.

MESSENIO: How many sons did your father have then?

MENAECHMUS I: The best I remember, two.

MESSENIO: Which was the older, you or he?

MENAECHMUS I: We were both exactly the same age.

MESSENIO: How is that possible?

MENAECHMUS I: We were twins.

MENAECHMUS II: The gods are answering my prayers!

MESSENIO (*to* MENAECHMUS II): If you keep on interrupting, I won't say another word.

MENAECHMUS II: No, no, you go on; I'll keep quiet.

MESSENIO (*to* MENAECHMUS I): Did you both have the same name?

MENAECHMUS I: Of course not. I had the name I still have, Menaechmus. My twin brother was called Sosicles.

MENAECHMUS II: Everything points to it; I can't hold back any longer. (*To* MENAECHMUS I) You're my twin brother (*holds out his hand*); I'm so glad to see you! I'm Sosicles!

MENAECHMUS I (*holds back*): Well, how did you get the name Menaechmus, then?

MENAECHMUS II: Why, after we got the news that you had wandered away from father and had been kidnaped by some stranger, and that father had died, our grandfather changed my name. He gave me the name you'd had.

MENAECHMUS I: I guess that must explain it. But tell me one more thing.

MENAECHMUS II: All right.

MENAECHMUS I: What was mother's name?

MENAECHMUS II: Teuximarcha.

MENAECHMUS I: That's it! My, I'm glad to see you! After all these years, too! I'd given up all hope!

MENAECHMUS II: I'm glad, too! I've been looking for you for a long time, been through a lot of misery and trouble, and I'm delighted that I've found you at last!

MESSENIO (*to* MENAECHMUS II): This is why that woman called you by his name. She must have thought you were he, when she invited you to dinner.

MENAECHMUS I: Yes! You know, I did order a dinner for myself at her house today. My wife didn't know anything about it. (*Chuckles*) Stole a dress from her, I did, and gave it to the girl.

MENAECHMUS II (*holds out dress*): You mean this dress, Menaechmus, that I've got here?

MENAECHMUS I: That's the one! How did you get it?

MENAECHMUS II: Why, that girl took me into her house for dinner and said I'd given it to her. I had a fine dinner, some drinks, and the girl, too. And I took this dress and this piece of jewelry (*holds out bracelet*) away with me.

MENAECHMUS I: I'm really glad if you've had some good luck because of me. Yes—when she invited you in, she thought you were me!

MESSENIO: There isn't going to be any delay, is there—I mean about my being free, the way you said I would?

MENAECHMUS I: He's quite right. That's only fair, brother. Set him free, for my sake.

MENAECHMUS II (*to* MESSENIO): I declare you a free man.

MENAECHMUS I (*offers hand to* MESSENIO): Congratulations on your emancipation, Messenio.

MESSENIO: Yes. But I'll need a little better start than that, if I'm going to *stay* free. (MENAECHMUS I *and* II *walk off, paying no attention to him.*)

MENAECHMUS II: Everything has turned out just as we hoped, so let's both go back to Sicily.

MENAECHMUS I: Anything you like. I'll hold an auction here and sell everything I own. And now let's go in the house, Sosicles.

MENAECHMUS II: All right. (*They start toward* MENAECHMUS' *house;* MESSENIO *runs after them, plucks them by sleeve.*)

MESSENIO: Mind if I ask you something?

MENAECHMUS I: What is it?

MESSENIO: Let me be auctioneer.

MENAECHMUS I: All right.

MESSENIO: Well, would you like me to announce the auction right now?

MENAECHMUS I: Yes. Say that we'll hold it a week from today. (*Exeunt* MENAECHMUS I *and* II *into* MENAECHMUS' *house.*)

MESSENIO (*to audience*): Menaechmus will hold an auction a week from today, early in the morning. He'll sell his slaves, his furniture, his land, his house—everything. He'll sell them for what they'll bring, cash on the barrelhead. He'll sell his wife, too, if he can find a buyer! I expect he won't get more than five million sesterces for the lot!

Now, my friends, good-bye. Give us a good, loud hand!

FINIS

Plautus

THE HAUNTED HOUSE
(Mostellaria)

Introductory Note

Of the twenty complete comedies now extant under the name of Plautus, the one commonly known as *The Haunted House* (*Mostellaria*) might well be chosen as most nearly representative of all the author's works. Basically a simple farce consisting of a series of comic scenes loosely strung on a thin thread of plot, it yet displays well developed characters, pungent human situations, and social satire as telling as any to be found in the works of more sophisticated writers such as Molière. The slave Tranio, clever and quick-witted, adapting himself with uncanny accuracy to both the problem and the persons confronting him, fairly steps out of the pages of the play. Old Scapha, the retired courtesan, gives her young mistress Philematium caustic advice on how best to profit from their age-old trade. Philolaches, undisciplined but intelligent, delivers a drunken sermon on "Youth Faces the World—and Fails." There is rich slapstick, a hilariously alcoholic banquet, and rapid, witty dialogue. Except for the somewhat haphazard plot, the play would be a master comedy.

The setting depicts the fronts of two houses, with doors opening on the street. No provision was made on the Roman comic stage for indoor scenes; all scenes which would normally take place indoors had to be played as if on the open street. Thus, in *The Haunted House*, Philematium has her dressing table brought outside the house and sits before it there, dressing and adorning herself for her meeting with Philolaches; and their subsequent drinking party with their two friends, Callidamates and Delphium, also takes place there. The playwright does not so much as attempt to create the illusion of an indoor scene. Of this obviously unrealistic situation we can say only that it must have been accepted as a stage convention. In the center and front of the stage stands an altar, reminiscent of the earliest days of the comedy, when it was part of the worship of the god Dionysus. This altar is commonly disregarded by the playwright, but is sometimes put to excellent use, as it is in the final scenes of *The Haunted House*.

The date of the first production of *The Haunted House* is unknown. The play was adapted from a Greek play called *Phasma* ("The Ghost"), possibly by Philemon. There is no Prologue; as in several of Plautus' plays, and all of Terence's, the dialogue of the opening scene provides us with the necessary antecedent facts. In *The Haunted House,* this dialogue is carried on between Tranio and another slave, Grumio, a "protatic" character who never appears again in the play.

CHARACTERS

GRUMIO, a slave
TRANIO, a slave
PHILOLACHES, a young man
PHILEMATIUM, a courtesan
SCAPHA, her maid
CALLIDAMATES, a young man
DELPHIUM, a courtesan
SPHAERIO, a slave
THEOPROPIDES, an old man, father of PHILOLACHES
MISARGYRIDES, a moneylender
SIMO, an old man, neighbor of THEOPROPIDES
PHANISCUS ⎱ slaves
PINACIUM ⎰
OTHER SLAVES AND ATTENDANTS

SCENE: *A street in Athens. Upstage, the fronts of two houses; one belongs to* THEOPROPIDES, *the other to* SIMO. *There is an altar at stage center.*

THE HAUNTED HOUSE

ACT ONE

SCENE I

(*Enter* GRUMIO. *He goes up to* THEOPROPIDES' *house and knocks on the door.*)

GRUMIO: Come on out of the kitchen, will you! Confound you! Hiding behind your pots and pans! Getting smart with me! Come on out of the house! You'll wreck the whole place yet! By heaven, if I ever get you out on the farm, I'll take it out of you, you can bet on that. Come on out, come on out, I tell you, greaseball! What are you hiding for?

TRANIO (*pushes door open, knocking* GRUMIO *backward down steps*): Now what in thunder are you yelling about here at the front door? Think you're still on the farm? Get out of here! (*Slaps him*) There! That what you wanted?

GRUMIO: Hey! Why are you hitting me?

TRANIO: Because you're you.

GRUMIO: All right! All right! Just wait till the old man gets back! Just wait till he gets home again! He goes away, and you take him for everything he's got.

TRANIO: Now how could I do that, stupid? How could anybody take anybody when he isn't even here to be taken?

GRUMIO: Oh, smart boy, are you? Anything for laughs, is that right? To you I'm just a dumb ox from the farm, am I? Well, I think I get it, Tranio: You know very well you're headed straight for trouble. It won't be long now; you'll be just one more farmhand yourself, with a pick and shovel just like the rest of them. All right. Go ahead! Have your fun while you've got the chance! Hit the bottle, throw money around, get master's son into trouble—nice boy, too! Keep right on drinking, all day, all night! Carry on like a bunch of Greeks! Buy slave girls and set them free! Pick up the check for all those loafers you've got hanging around! Buy all that fancy stuff to eat! Is this what master told you to do when he went away? Is this how he's going to find you took care of things for him? Is this the way you think a good slave ought to act—wreck master's bank account and turn his son into a silly fool? What else can I call him when he's going in for this kind of business? Why, in the old days, there wasn't a boy in the whole place had a better reputation. He watched his money. He was a very decent fellow. Well, he'd still take first prize, but for something different. And it's you that did it; you showed him how.

TRANIO: Never you mind about me! What business is it of yours what I do? What's the matter: haven't you anything to do out on the farm—cows to take care of, maybe? I like drinking, I like women. It's my hide I'm risking, not yours.

GRUMIO: The conceit of the man!

TRANIO: Damn you anyway! Phew! You stink! Garlic, genuine slop, barnyard, billy goat, pigsty, manure pile!

GRUMIO: Well, what do you want? Everybody can't smell of imported perfume just because you do! Everybody can't sit at the head of the table or have the fine food to eat that you have! All right, you can have it—your squab and your sea food and your chicken! Thanks, I'll just eat my garlic and stay where I belong. You're rich; I'm poor. Well, I can take it. One of these days I'll get what's coming to me—and so will you.

TRANIO: Grumio, Grumio! Don't tell me you're jealous! Just because I'm having fun and you aren't! Why, that's the way it ought to be. I'm the man to make love to the girls and you're the man to chase cows. Living high suits me; living low suits you.

GRUMIO: Let me see—are those holes in your head? Well, if there aren't, there will be. They'll string you up and ride you out of town on a rail and get the pig-stickers after you, when master gets back.

TRANIO: How do you know that won't happen to you before it does to me?

GRUMIO: It won't. I haven't done anything wrong—but you have, and you still are!

TRANIO: Talk, talk, talk—stop it, will you? Or how'd you like a good punch in the nose?

GRUMIO: Look, if you fellows are going to give me that hay for the cows, let's have it. If you aren't, all right, go on, keep it up, you've made a good start. Hit the bottle, act like Greeks, eat, stuff yourself, kill the fatted calf!

TRANIO: Ah-h, shut up, you, and go on home. I'm going down to Piraeus to get some fish for this evening. I'll have somebody bring that hay out to you tomorrow. Well, what are you standing there staring at me now for, you idiot?

GRUMIO: Idiot, am I? Well, it won't be long now before you'll be the one that's the idiot.

TRANIO: So long as things are the way they are, I can't worry about what's going to happen later on.

GRUMIO: Is that so? Well, just don't forget one thing; bad luck's a lot quicker than good luck.

TRANIO: Oh, stop annoying me. Go on home. Get out. You've held me up too long already. (*Exit.*)

GRUMIO: Well, there he goes. Didn't care a bit for what I told him, did he? Dear gods, please let master come home as quick as you can. He's been gone three years now, and if he doesn't get back soon there won't be anything left. It'll all be gone, every bit of it. If he doesn't get here right away there won't be enough to keep us going for a month. Well, I guess I'll go back home. (*Enter* PHILOLACHES.) Yes, sir! Look! There he is, master's son. What a disgrace! And he used to be such a nice young man.

SCENE II

(PHILOLACHES *is drunk. He speaks as he wanders uncertainly across stage.*)

PHILOLACHES: I've done a lot of thinking and I've done a

lot of wondering; I've figured it out backward, forward, and sideways—yes, I have. I've really put my mind on it—that is, if I have a mind—turned the business over and over, talked it over a long time. You take a man when he's born, what's he like, I'd keep thinking, what's he look like? And now I've found out.

A new house, that's what I think he's like, this man, when he's born. And now I'll tell you why. No, it's true, just as I tell you. You wait: you'll see. You people out there, no doubt about it, just as I'm telling you now, you listen to what I'm going to say, and you'll agree with me absolutely. Now listen, will you, and I'll tell you why this is so. I want you all to be in on this with me.

You take a house, brand-new, all clean and shiny, built just as it's supposed to be, just the way the plans said, everybody says nice things about the builders, and tells you what a fine house it is; they all want it to be a model for their own. Everybody wants one just like it, no matter how much it costs or how much work it takes. And then who moves into it? Some good-for-nothing fellow, lazy, with a bunch of sloppy slaves, never cleans up the place, never does any work around it. Right there things start going wrong with the house. It's a good house, but they don't take care of it. And now see what happens: A storm comes along, smashes some roof-tiles, maybe a rain-gutter or two, and then the owner just can't be bothered to put up new ones. Comes the rain, runs down the walls, gets inside, beams get rotten—and there goes all the builder's work. The house isn't as good as it used to be! It isn't the builder's fault, either. It's just that most people are like that: something could be fixed for a drachma, but they keep putting it off and don't do it, and finally the walls come a-tumbling down. The whole house has to be built all over again.

So much for the house. Now I want to tell you why you ought to figure people are like houses. First place: Parents are the builders of their children. They lay the foundations for them, put up the walls, do their best to make them strong. They want them to be worth while and to look good, want everybody to think so, not just themselves, so they put the best into them. "Cost is no object," they keep saying. They try to teach them the right things, give them a good education, see that they learn a respectable trade. They pay all the bills and work hard to do it. They're anxious that other people should want to have children like theirs. Comes time for them to go into the army; they see that they're outfitted the way they ought to be. Here's where they leave the builders. When they've served their first year, then you've got a very good idea how your house is going to turn out.

Now you take me. I was a fine fellow so long as the builders had charge of me. Then I became boss of the house myself, and in no time at all the place was a complete wreck. I got lazy. That was my "storm." It came and it brought me rain and hail. They made a mess of everything I'd ever learned was right. In no time at all they ripped the roof off me, and I just couldn't be bothered to fix it up again. "Rain?" That was love. It poured down on me, ran down into my heart, soaked it through. Now my money, my credit, my reputation, my good name, my social position—all gone, all together. Now I'm surely not the man I used to be. Yes, sir, that's right. My beams are wet and rotten—why, I don't think I can fix my house now. No, it's going to fall right down in a heap, foundations and all. There isn't anybody could help me.

I could break down and cry, when I think what I am and what I used to be. There wasn't a fellow worked harder than I did or was any better in athletics. Discus, javelin, ball, racing, manual-of-arms, horseback riding, I took first prize any time I felt like it. I could live on next to nothing; there was nothing too hard for me; they used to point me out as an example to the others. All the really decent fellows used to try to get me to show them how to do it. And now that it's too late and I'm no good for anything, I've sat down and figured this out all by myself.

Scene III

(*Enter* Philematium *and* Scapha *from* Theopropides' *house.* Scapha *has a little dressing table and some boxes of cosmetics.* Philematium *sits down and starts to primp. As scene proceeds, slaves bring in two couches.* Philolaches *remains at one side, unobserved by the others.*)

Philematium: My, it's been a long time since I enjoyed my bath so much; I don't know when I've felt so nice and fresh and clean, Scapha.

Scapha: Look to the end in everything; the crop was good this year, you know.

Philematium: What has the crop got to do with my bath?

Scapha: No more than your bath has to do with the crop.

Philolaches (*aside*): Oh, you beautiful, wonderful thing! There she is. That's my "storm"; took the roof right off the principles that protected me, and let love and Cupid rain down into my heart. Don't think I'll ever be able to fix it up again. My walls are soaked through. It's all over with this house, for sure.

Philematium: Look, Scapha, please. Does this dress look nice on me? I want Philolaches to like me. My darling! He's been so good to me—set me free and all.

Scapha: You just see that you *are* nice; you *look* nice enough. It isn't a girl's clothes that men like, it's what's in them.

Philolaches (*aside*): Say, that Scapha's a nice one; she's a smart old witch, all right. She knows what men like; she knows what they think!

Philematium: How's this?

Scapha: What? What is it?

Philematium: Oh, come on now, look. See if this dress really looks nice on me.

Scapha: When a girl is as pretty as you, anything you wear looks nice on you.

Philolaches (*aside*): Good for you, Scapha! Just for that

I'll see that you get a—well, something. Can't have you getting nothing for saying nice things about my girl—not when I like her so much.

PHILEMATIUM: Now don't you go saying things just because you think I want you to.

SCAPHA: Don't be silly, dear. Would you rather have me say mean things that weren't true than nice things that were? Me, now, I'd much rather have people say nice things about me that weren't true than criticize me for things that were. I wouldn't want anybody making fun of the way I look.

PHILEMATIUM: I like the truth; I want people to tell me the truth. I don't like people who aren't honest.

SCAPHA: Oh, all right. As true as you love me, and as true as Philolaches loves you, you look very nice.

PHILOLACHES (aside): What's that, you old witch? What's that you said? "As true as Philolaches loves you"? What about "as you love Philolaches"? Why didn't you say that, too? No present for you! That took care of you. I promised you a present, but now you don't get it.

SCAPHA: Well, I just don't understand it. Smart girl like you, knowing all you know, been around as much as you have, and now acting like such a fool.

PHILEMATIUM: Why, what's the matter? Tell me what I'm doing that's wrong. Won't you, please?

SCAPHA: I'll tell you what's wrong, all right. You sit around waiting for Philolaches and nobody else; you're so specially nice to him and won't pay attention to any of the others. That's for married women. A girl like you hasn't any business dancing attendance on just one man.

PHILOLACHES (aside): Now, by heaven, isn't that something! What kind of devil is this I've got in my house? Damn me if I don't murder that old dame. I'll starve her to death! I'll put her out in the cold!

PHILEMATIUM: Now, Scapha, I don't want you teaching me things that aren't nice.

SCAPHA: You're just a plain fool, thinking he's going to go

right on liking you and being sweet to you. I'm giving you fair warning: One of these days he'll walk out on you. He'll have had enough.

PHILEMATIUM: I don't think that will happen.

SCAPHA: What you think won't happen happens a lot oftener than what you think will. Now look; if what I'm telling you can't make you believe that what I say is true, just look at a few plain facts. You see what I'm like now and what I used to be. I was every bit as pretty and charming as you are, and I had just as many men crazy about me as you do. Well, I was nice only to one of them, and what did he do? When I'd gotten a little older and picked up a gray hair or two, he left me, walked out on me. That's what will happen to you, I'm quite sure.

PHILOLACHES (aside): It's all I can do to keep from tearing her eyes out. Telling her things like that!

PHILEMATIUM: I'm the only girl he ever set free. He did it so he wouldn't have to share me with anybody else. Paid the whole price, every penny, all by himself.

PHILOLACHES (aside): Now I'm telling you! There's a really nice girl with her heart in the right place. It was well worth doing. I ought to congratulate myself that I went bankrupt for her sake.

SCAPHA: My dear, you're being just plain stupid.

PHILEMATIUM: Why? Why?

SCAPHA: Going to all this fuss, just to please Philolaches.

PHILEMATIUM: But, for heaven's sake, why shouldn't I fuss?

SCAPHA: You're free, dear, free! You've got what you wanted. It's up to him, now. If he doesn't keep up his interest in you, he's wasted what he paid for your freedom—all that money!

PHILOLACHES (aside): Damned if I don't slaughter that woman. She's going to ruin my girl. What kind of advice is that to give her? Talks like a madam.

PHILEMATIUM: I'll never be able to thank him as he deserves. Scapha, you stop trying to spoil the way I feel about him.

SCAPHA: Just you remember this one thing: If you dance

attendance on him and nobody else, while you're still so young and all, when you get old, you'll be sorry!

PHILOLACHES (*aside*): I wish I could turn into a nice case of diphtheria. I'd grab that old witch by the throat and strangle her. Damn her, anyway! Telling her things like that!

PHILEMATIUM: I haven't any business feeling any different about him, now that I've got what I wanted, than I did before I worked it out with him, when I was being very, very nice to him.

PHILOLACHES (*aside*): Well, you may lay me low, if I don't free you all over again for saying that—and break Scapha's neck!

SCAPHA: If you've got it all signed, sealed, and delivered that you've got a living for life, and that Philolaches is going to be your very own lover for always, then of course I do think you ought to be nice to him and nobody else—but see to it that you get a wedding, too.

PHILEMATIUM: Your income's as good as your reputation, you know. If I just keep my good reputation, I'll have plenty to live on.

PHILOLACHES (*aside*): If I had to sell my father, I'd do it long before I'd let you want for anything or have to go around begging. Not while I'm still alive.

SCAPHA: What about the other men who are interested in you?

PHILEMATIUM: They'll be all the more interested, because they'll see that I really show my appreciation when somebody is nice to me.

PHILOLACHES (*aside*): I wish I'd get word that my father had just died. I'd take every penny I'd get and give it to her.

SCAPHA: Well, you know, that little deal of yours with Philolaches is just about played out. Day and night, eating, drinking all the time, nobody paying any attention to expenses. It won't be long now, that's sure.

PHILOLACHES (*aside*): I think we'll just start our little experiment in economy with you. Nothing to eat, nothing to drink for you for a week!

PHILEMATIUM: If you have something nice to say about him, go ahead and say it. But just you say anything else about him, and see what happens to you.

PHILOLACHES (*aside*): By heaven, if I'd taken the money I paid for her freedom and used it to buy an ox to sacrifice to Jupiter, it wouldn't have been half as good an investment. It's easy to see that she's really in love with me. Good work, Philolaches! I just meant to set her free, but she's turned out to be my defense attorney!

SCAPHA: I can see that you've got no time for anybody but Philolaches. Why let myself in for trouble? It's easier just to agree with you.

PHILEMATIUM: Give me my mirror and my jewel box, Scapha. I want to look nice. Philolaches should be here before long, you know—my darling!

SCAPHA: A girl who's not too happy about how old she's getting is the one who needs a mirror. What do you need a mirror for? You could show a mirror a thing or two yourself.

PHILOLACHES (*aside*): Now that was nicely put, Scapha. You ought to get something for that. I think I'll give a bit of spending money to—you, Philematium, my sweet.

PHILEMATIUM: Now! How's that? Look at my hair, Scapha. Is it all right?

SCAPHA: As long as you're all right, you can be sure your hair's all right.

PHILOLACHES (*aside*): Hah! Ever see anything worse than that old girl? All sweetness now, but a few minutes ago she was against everything. The she-devil!

PHILEMATIUM: May I have my powder, please?

SCAPHA: Now what do you want powder for?

PHILEMATIUM: To put some on my face.

SCAPHA: What? Might as well try to whiten ivory with lampblack.

PHILOLACHES (*aside*): That was a good one: "Whiten ivory with lampblack"! Bravo! Good for you, Scapha!

PHILEMATIUM: Well, may I have my rouge, then, please?

SCAPHA: No, ma'am. You know better than that. Why do you want to smear paint all over that pretty face of yours? You're young, dear. You haven't any business touching cosmetics at all—rouge or powder or any of the rest of that stuff.

PHILEMATIUM (*kisses the mirror*): Well, here, take the mirror, then.

PHILOLACHES (*aside*): Oh, my! She kissed the mirror. Wish I had a rock; I'd smash that mirror's face for it!

SCAPHA (*hands* PHILEMATIUM *a towel*): Here, take this towel and wipe your hands.

PHILEMATIUM: Why, for heaven's sake?

SCAPHA: You've been holding a mirror, haven't you? I'm afraid your hands may smell of silver, and you wouldn't want Philolaches thinking you'd been taking money from somebody, would you?

PHILOLACHES (*aside*): I don't think I've ever seen a smarter old woman anywhere. That was a good one about the mirror—the old rascal.

PHILEMATIUM: What do you think? Should I put on some perfume?

SCAPHA: No. Don't you do it.

PHILEMATIUM: Why not?

SCAPHA: Because a girl smells nicest when she doesn't smell at all. You take these old girls, that soak themselves with perfume—rebuilt jobs, every one of them. Poor old things—false teeth, wrinkles all smeared over with calcimine. They get to sweating and the perfume gets mixed up with the sweat, and they smell as if the cook had poured in every flavor in the kitchen. Yon can't figure out what they smell like, but you know one thing: They don't smell good.

PHILOLACHES (*aside*): Well, well! She really knows it all! She's a smart one—don't come any smarter. (*To audience*) What she said is absolutely right. Plently of you out there know it, too—any of you that have got superannuated wives that took you into camp with their dowries.

PHILEMATIUM: All right, now, Scapha. Look at my jewelry and my dress; do they suit me?

SCAPHA: Yes—not that it's any business of mine.

PHILEMATIUM: Whose business is it, then?

SCAPHA: Why, Philolaches', of course—who else? He shouldn't buy anything for you unless he thinks it's going to suit you. A man gets a girl to be nice to him by giving her jewelry and pretty clothes. What's the point of parading in front of him a lot of stuff he meant to give away? Fancy clothes are for girls who don't want people to know how old they are, and jewelry's for the homely ones. A good-looking girl without any clothes on is a whole lot better looking than one all dressed up. If you're good-looking, you know, you're pretty enough all by yourself.

PHILOLACHES (*aside*): I've kept out of this long enough. (*To* PHILEMATIUM *and* SCAPHA) What are you two up to here?

PHILEMATIUM: Oh, just fixing up a bit for you. Do you like the way I look?

PHILOLACHES: Yes, but that's enough fussing. (*To* SCAPHA) Go on in, and take this stuff with you. (*Exit* SCAPHA.) Sweetheart, Philematium dear, how about you and me having a drink or two? I'm just in the mood for it.

PHILEMATIUM: So am I. Anything you feel like doing I feel like doing, too—darling. (*They move over to couches.*)

PHILOLACHES: "Darling," is it? I wouldn't trade that "darling" for two thousand drachmas!

PHILEMATIUM: Make it a thousand, cash, will you? Special rates on "darlings" for you!

PHILOLACHES: Now, wait a minute! I've already given you a thousand, and then some. Look, it cost me three thousand to buy you free, and then—

PHILEMATIUM: Why bring that up? Am I supposed to think it was too much?

PHILOLACHES: Too much? I'd just like to hear anybody say it was too much! Why, I've never made a better investment in all my life.

PHILEMATIUM: Well, I know this: Loving you is the best investment I ever made of my time.

PHILOLACHES: That makes it come out just about right between us, doesn't it? You love me; I love you. And we both think it's a very good arrangement.

PHILEMATIUM: Come on, sit down, then. (*Calls into house*) Boy! Bring a little water, so we can wash our hands. Get the little table and put it right here. (*Two slaves come out with basin of water and table. They put them down and step back, ready to wait on* PHILEMATIUM *and* PHILOLACHES.) Let's see, where are the dice? (*She rummages in a drawer of the table.*) Want a drop of perfume?

PHILOLACHES: Perfume? What for? I've got the sweetest thing in the world right next to me. (*Enter* CALLIDAMATES, *very drunk, leaning on* DELPHIUM.) But who's this coming? Looks like my friend Callidamates and his girl. Yes, it is. Here they come. Hello, hello, my dear old friend! The troops are mustering! They'll go after the booty, side by side!

SCENE IV

CALLIDAMATES (*to slaves*): You fellows come and meet me at Philolaches' house, right on time. Hear that? It's an order, see! That place where we were, I got out of there, but quick. What fools! What a lot of tiresome talk! Now I'm going on a party to Philolaches' house. He'll be so happy to see us, he'll give us a fine time. Say, you don't drink I'm really thunk—I mean, drunk, do you?

DELPHIUM (*sighs*): This goes on every day.

CALLIDAMATES: What say I give you a kiss and you give me a kiss?

DELPHIUM: If you feel you have to, go ahead. (*They kiss.*)

CALLIDAMATES: You're sweet. Show me the way, please.

DELPHIUM: Look out! You'll fall down. Wait a minute. (*Steadies him*)

CALLIDAMATES (*sings*): Oh, oh, oh, my darling! I'm your baby, and you're my honey.

DELPHIUM: Watch out! You're lying down in the street! The couch is over there.

CALLIDAMATES: What do I care? Just let me fall down.

DELPHIUM: Go ahead.

CALLIDAMATES: Yes, but what I got in my hand—that's got to fall down, too. (*Stumbles, makes a wild grab for* DELPHIUM)

DELPHIUM: If you fall down, I'll fall down, too, you know.

CALLIDAMATES: Sure, and then we'll lie there, and after a while somebody will come along and pick us both up!

DELPHIUM: This boy is *really* drunk!

CALLIDAMATES: What's that? You say I'm sunk—I mean, drunk?

DELPHIUM: Here, give me your hand. I don't want you to hurt yourself.

CALLIDAMATES: Fine! Hold tight! (*Heaves himself up*)

DELPHIUM: Now come on with me.

CALLIDAMATES: Come on? Where?

DELPHIUM: Have you forgotten already?

CALLIDAMATES: Oh, I know. Just remembered. Of course! Going home. Going to a party.

DELPHIUM: No, no! You're going over here. (*Leads him toward* PHILOLACHES *and* PHILEMATIUM)

CALLIDAMATES: Oh, yes. Now I remember.

PHILOLACHES (*to* PHILEMATIUM): You don't mind if I go and say hello to them, do you, darling? He's one of my very best friends. I'll be right back.

PHILEMATIUM: "Right back"? That will seem like hours to me.

CALLIDAMATES: Who's that? Somebody here?

PHILOLACHES: Yes. I am.

CALLIDAMATES: Well, well! Philolaches! Best friend I got in all the world.

PHILOLACHES: Same to you. Here, make yourself comfortable, Callidamates. Where have you been?

CALLIDAMATES: Been? (*Sings*) "Where a man can raise a thirst!"

PHILEMATIUM (*makes room on couch*): Won't you come and join us, Delphium dear?

PHILOLACHES (*to slave*): Give Callidamates a drink.

CALLIDAMATES: So-o-o sleepy! Going to go to sleep. (*Waves drink away*)

DELPHIUM: Something new and different, is it? (CALLIDAMATES *falls asleep.*)

PHILOLACHES (*to* DELPHIUM): Now what am I going to do with him?

DELPHIUM: Oh, leave him alone. Leave him the way he is.

PHILOLACHES (*to slave*): Boy, start the drinks going, will you? Serve Delphium first.

SCENE V

(*Enter* TRANIO. *During his soliloquy the party continues with no one noticing his presence.*)

TRANIO: Great Jupiter has certainly put mind and muscle behind it. I'm through, finished, done for, and so is Philolaches. "Hope"? There's no hope left! "Confidence"? Where? How? Lady Luck herself couldn't save us now, even if she wanted to. What a mountain of misery I saw just a few minutes ago down on the waterfront. Master's home again. "Well, good-bye, Tranio!" (*To audience*) Say, there isn't anybody out there, is there, who'd like to make a quick drachma or two? All he has to do is change places with me for a few hours. Well, come on! Step up! Where are all you "go-ahead-and-hit-me-one-see-if-I-care" boys? All you "stick-me-in-the-front lines-I-can-take-it" fellows? You men who go out to face our enemies for three coppers a day and get ten spears in the belly? Here's six thousand drachmas to the first man to volunteer to take the rap for me! Only one condition: He's got to be double-lashed, hand and foot, to the stake. As soon as that's done, he can demand the money. But I must be losing my grip —standing around here instead of hurrying along home. (*Moves on across stage toward the party*)

PHILOLACHES: Here comes the food; here it comes! See, Tranio's back from the waterfront.

TRANIO: Philolaches—

PHILOLACHES: Yes? What?

TRANIO: You and—well, you and I—

PHILOLACHES: What about you and me?

TRANIO: We're sunk.

PHILOLACHES: How so?

TRANIO: Your father's home.

PHILOLACHES: What do I hear you saying?

TRANIO: We're done for, I tell you! Your father is home!

PHILOLACHES: Oh, for heaven's sake! Where is he?

TRANIO: Where is he? He's home!

PHILOLACHES: Who told you? Who saw him?

TRANIO: I saw him; I did, I tell you!

PHILOLACHES: Now what do I do? (*Starts to take a drink*)

TRANIO: Why ask me that? "What do I do?" You're having some drinks, that's what you're doing.

PHILOLACHES: You mean you saw him—you?

TRANIO: Yes, I, I, I saw him.

PHILOLACHES: You're sure?

TRANIO: Yes, I'm sure.

PHILOLACHES: I'm in for it—that is—say, you're not joking, now?

TRANIO: Now just what would be the point of my joking?

PHILOLACHES: What am I going to do?

TRANIO: Well, the first thing to do is to get all this stuff out of here. (*Starts to get things together, bumps into* CALLIDAMATES) Who's this taking a nap?

PHILOLACHES: That's Callidamates. Delphium, wake him up, will you?

DELPHIUM (*shakes him*): Callidamates, Callidamates! Wake up!

CALLIDAMATES: I'm awake! Give me a drink. (*Drops back*)

DELPHIUM: Wake up! Philolaches' father is home!

CALLIDAMATES: How's your father doing?

PHILOLACHES: He's doing all right. I'm the one who's not doing so well. Might as well be dead.

CALLIDAMATES: What do you mean, "swell to be dead"?

PHILOLACHES: Oh, for heaven's sake, get up, will you? My father's coming!

CALLIDAMATES: Your father's coming? Well, tell him to go away again! What's he want to come here for?

PHILOLACHES: What am I going to do? Father will be here any minute now; he'll come in and find me drunk and the house full of strangers and women. It's a wretched business to start digging a well when you're dying of thirst, but that's what I'm doing. My father's home, and here I am trying to figure out what to do about it. Oh, my!

TRANIO (*pointing to* CALLIDAMATES): Look, he's put his head down and gone to sleep again. Wake him up.

PHILOLACHES: Will you wake up? Father's going to be here any minute now—my father!

CALLIDAMATES: What did you say? Father? Get my shoes! Where's my sword? I'll murder your father!

DELPHIUM: Will you please be quiet?

PHILOLACHES (*to slaves*): Pick him up and carry him into the house. Hurry! (*They carry him toward the house.*)

CALLIDAMATES: Listen, boys: I need to go! You better get me there quick, or you'll be sorry!

PHILOLACHES (*sits down on steps, head in hands*): It's no use. I give up.

TRANIO: Oh, cheer up. I'll take care of everything. You've got nothing to worry about.

PHILOLACHES: I can't face it.

TRANIO: Forget it, will you? I've got my plans all made. Everything's going to be all right. When your father gets here, I'll fix him not only so he won't go in the house, but so he'll get away from it as fast as he can. How does that suit you? You people just go on in. Hurry up! Clear out!

PHILOLACHES: Where am I supposed to be?

TRANIO: Where do you want to be? With her and her, that's where.

DELPHIUM: Don't you think maybe we'd better just run along?

TRANIO: No, ma'am. Don't you do it, Delphium. You go on in, fix some drinks, don't let what's going on out here bother you a bit.

PHILOLACHES: I don't know; I don't know. Sounds very simple when you say it, but where's it going to end up? I'm just plain scared.

TRANIO: For heaven's sake, will you stop fussing and do as I tell you?

PHILOLACHES: Well, all right.

TRANIO: Now, first thing: Philematium, you go on in, and you too, Delphium.

DELPHIUM: At your orders, sir! Anything you want, just let us know.

TRANIO (*leers*): Now that's not a bad idea at all. I think I'd like that! (*Pinches* DELPHIUM *as she goes by; exeunt* DELPHIUM *and* PHILEMATIUM.) Now listen: Here's what I want you to do. First of all, make sure that the doors of the house are all locked. Second, see that everybody in the house keeps absolutely quiet.

PHILOLACHES: All right.

TRANIO: And I really mean quiet—just as if there wasn't a living soul in the place.

PHILOLACHES: Sure, sure.

TRANIO: Finally, when your father knocks, nobody—nobody, understand?—is to come to the door.

PHILOLACHES: All right. Anything else?

TRANIO: No—or wait, yes: I'll lock the front door from the outside here. Have somebody in there bring the key out to me, will you?

PHILOLACHES: Yes. Well, here we go. It all depends on you, now, Tranio! (*Exit* PHILOLACHES *into house.*)

TRANIO: Depends on me, does it? Well, I expect you'll do your part of it all right. Like master, like slave! The meekest, mildest man in the world can stir up a mess in a minute without any trouble at all. But here's where the work comes in, here's where you really need brains: To take things that have been knocked to pieces and turned into a mess and straighten them all out nice and smooth and without any-body getting hurt. Don't want anybody to get all upset! That's what I'm going to do. We've made a grand mess here, and I'm going to straighten it all out as smooth as silk, and not a one of us is going to get so much as a scratch in the process. (*Enter* SPHAERIO *from* THEOPROPIDES' *house.*) What are you coming out here for, Sphaerio?

SPHAERIO: Here's the key.

TRANIO: Oh, good. That's right.

SPHAERIO: Philolaches told me to ask you please to be sure and scare his father off somehow. Don't let him come in the house.

TRANIO: Now look, you tell him this: When I get through with his father, he won't dare even look in that direction. He'll be so scared he'll throw his coat over his head and run like mad. Give me the key. Go on in now and shut the door. I'll lock it from out here. (*Exit* SPHAERIO.) All right! Bring him on! Right here and now, I'm going to stage a show for the old boy that'll beat anything he'll ever see, living or dead. (*With-draws into the space between the two houses*) I'll just step back in here where I can keep an eye out for him. Then when he gets here, I'll pin it on him for a fare-you-well, the old devil.

SCENE VI

(*Enter* THEOPROPIDES, *with two slaves carrying his baggage.*)

THEOPROPIDES (*praying*): Holy Neptune, I do give thee most humble and hearty thanks, for thou hast saved me from the perils of the deep. Yes, just did make it. But if I ever so much as put one toe in the water, you have my permission to do to me, right then and there, what you were figuring on doing yesterday. No, sir! From now on, you and I just don't know each other. I put my life in your hands once, but never again!

TRANIO (*aside*): Neptune, Neptune, Neptune! You made a big mistake. What a chance you had—and you let it go by!

THEOPROPIDES: Three years in Egypt! Home at last! I bet they'll be glad to see me.

TRANIO (*aside*): They'd have been a whole lot gladder to see somebody bringing word of your death.

THEOPROPIDES (*tries door*): H'm! That's funny. The door's locked. I wonder why? Middle of the day, too. Well, I'll knock. Hello! Anybody home? Open the door, will you?

TRANIO (*steps out of hiding*): Who's that going up to our house?

THEOPROPIDES (*turns, sees* TRANIO): Well, well, it's my slave, Tranio.

TRANIO: Theopropides, sir, how do you do? I'm glad to see you back. Did you get along all right while you were away?

THEOPROPIDES: Yes, all right up to now, as you can see.

TRANIO: Well, fine, fine!

THEOPROPIDES: What about you people? Have you all lost your minds?

TRANIO: Lost our minds? What do you mean?

THEOPROPIDES: Well, look at you—walking around in the street, not a soul on duty in the house, nobody coming to the door, nobody answering when I knocked. Pounded so hard I nearly broke the door down, too.

TRANIO: Oh, my; you mean to say you touched the house?

THEOPROPIDES: Well, why shouldn't I touch it? Touch it? I pounded on it! I nearly broke the door down, I tell you.

TRANIO: You . . . you touch . . . touched it?

THEOPROPIDES: Yes, I touched it, I tell you. I touched it and I pounded on the door.

TRANIO: Oh, brother!

THEOPROPIDES: What's the matter?

TRANIO: You shouldn't have done that.

THEOPROPIDES: Now what's this all about?

TRANIO: I just can't tell you what an awful, terrible thing you've done.

THEOPROPIDES: What? What are you talking about?

TRANIO: Please, sir, come away quick; get away from the house. No, come over here, sir; come over by me. You—you did—touch—the door? (THEOPROPIDES *moves to* TRANIO; *the two slaves remain by the door.*)

THEOPROPIDES: Now how could I pound on it without touching it?

TRANIO: Oh, this is terrible! You've killed them!

THEOPROPIDES: Killed who?

TRANIO: Your son and all the rest.

THEOPROPIDES: Don't say things like that, you idiot!

TRANIO: I'm worried. I don't know whether you can get yourself and the rest of them out of this one or not.

THEOPROPIDES: What do you mean? What's this crazy business all of a sudden?

TRANIO: Say, you'd better tell those fellows to get away from there, too, sir.

THEOPROPIDES (*to slaves*): Come on over here, you two.

TRANIO (*to slaves*): Don't touch the house, boys. Oh, my, to think that you touched it, too!

THEOPROPIDES: Well, for heaven's sake, why shouldn't they touch it?

TRANIO: Nobody has so much as set foot inside that house for seven months, sir. Not since we moved out.

THEOPROPIDES: Moved out? Seven months? Speak up! What's this all about?

TRANIO: Will you take a good look around, sir, and make sure nobody's listening in on what we're saying?

THEOPROPIDES: Oh, it's perfectly safe.

TRANIO: Will you take a look anyway, sir?

THEOPROPIDES: There's nobody here. Now, let's have it.

TRANIO: A crime was committed in that house, a bloody, bloody crime.

THEOPROPIDES: Crime? What crime? I don't know what you're talking about.

TRANIO: I'm telling you: A crime was committed there a long, long time ago; many, many years ago.

THEOPROPIDES: Many, many years ago?

TRANIO: That's right. And we just found out about it, less than a year ago.

THEOPROPIDES: What sort of crime was it? Who committed it? Tell me!

TRANIO: A man who was staying there as a guest was murdered in cold blood by the man who owned the house—I imagine it was the man who sold you the place.

THEOPROPIDES: M-m-murdered?

TRANIO: Yes. And the owner took all the man's money and buried him—just think, a poor stranger—buried him right under the house.

THEOPROPIDES: Just how did you get wind of anything like this?

TRANIO: I'm coming to that. Just pay attention. One evening your son had gone out to dinner. After he got home, we all went off to bed. Everybody went to sleep. It so happened that I had forgotten to blow out the lamp. I was getting up to take care of it, when all at once he—screamed!

THEOPROPIDES: Who did? My son?

TRANIO: Yes—but ssh! Be quiet! Listen, will you? He said he'd just dreamed that the murdered man was walking toward him.

THEOPROPIDES: Oh. You mean it was just a dream. Well!

TRANIO: Yes, it was a dream. But listen! He said that the murdered man spoke to him and said—

THEOPROPIDES: Oh, yes, yes. In a dream, right?

TRANIO: I suppose you think he ought to have spoken to him when he was awake—a man who had been murdered sixty years before! You'll pardon me, sir, but sometimes you don't seem awfully bright.

THEOPROPIDES: All right, all right. I won't say anything more.

TRANIO: Now here, sir, is what the murdered man said to your son in his dream: "I am a stranger from far across the sea. My name is Diapontius. I live here. This house has been assigned to me. Orcus wouldn't allow me to enter Acheron, because I died before my time. I trusted a man, and that's what brought me to this. My host murdered me here and buried me without funeral rites, before anybody found out, right here under the house. The villain did it for the money I carried. Now, you—you move out of here! This house has a curse on it! Nobody may live here!" The queer things that have been going on around here, it would take hours to tell about them. (*The door rattles; he hisses to those inside.*) Ssh! Ssh!

THEOPROPIDES: For heaven's sake, what happened?

TRANIO: The door rattled. (*Pretends to address ghost, points to* THEOPROPIDES) He did it; he was the one who knocked!

THEOPROPIDES: Oh, my heart! I feel faint! The ghosts are going to grab me and drag me down to hell!

TRANIO (*aside*): Those fools! They'll spoil my act yet. I don't want the old boy to catch me at it.

THEOPROPIDES: What are you muttering to yourself?

TRANIO: Come away from the house! Come on, quick, please, sir!

THEOPROPIDES: Where am I supposed to go? Why don't you go, too?

TRANIO: I have nothing to be afraid of. I haven't done anything to disturb the ghosts.

VOICE (*from within, whispers*): Hey! Tranio!

TRANIO (*whispers*): Don't call me! Haven't you any sense? (*Aloud, as if to ghost*) I didn't do anything. I didn't knock on the door.

VOICE (*whispers*): Listen, please.

TRANIO (*whispers*): Shut up, will you!

THEOPROPIDES: Now wait a minute. Who are you talking to over there?

TRANIO (*whispers*): Go away!

THEOPROPIDES: Are you crazy, Tranio? Who are you talking to?

TRANIO (*to* THEOPROPIDES): Oh, excuse me. Did you speak to me? Well, for heaven's sake! I thought it was that murdered man complaining because you banged on the door. Look, sir; are you still here? Why aren't you doing what I told you to?

THEOPROPIDES: Doing? Doing what?

TRANIO: Don't look behind you! Get out of here! Throw your coat over your head!

THEOPROPIDES: Why aren't you getting out, too?

TRANIO: I haven't done anything to disturb the ghosts.

THEOPROPIDES: Oh, is that so? What about a few minutes ago? What were you so scared of then?

TRANIO: Don't worry about me, sir. I'll take care of myself. You go on, now! Get out of here as quick as you can! Say a prayer to Hercules!

THEOPROPIDES (*praying*): Holy Hercules, I offer my prayer unto thee—(*Exit, followed by the two slaves.*)

TRANIO: Yes, and so do I—for a nice big piece of bad luck for you, you old fool. Great gods in heaven! That was really close! (*Exit into* THEOPROPIDES' *house.*)

ACT TWO

SCENE I

(*Enter* MISARGYRIDES. *While he is talking, enter* TRANIO *from* THEOPROPIDES' *house.*)

MISARGYRIDES: This year has been the worst one I've ever seen for the moneylending business. I've kept my bank open from early in the morning till late at night, and I haven't been able to make a single loan.

TRANIO (*aside*): Oh, oh! I'm really in for it now. Here comes the moneylender who loaned us the money we needed to buy Philematium and to pay our bills. He'll let the cat out of the bag, if I don't get to him right away. Don't want the old man to find out. I'll go catch him. (*Enter* THEOPROPIDES.) Great gods! Why is Theopropides back so soon? You don't suppose he's got wind of something? I'd better go meet him. Am I nervous! There's nothing worse than a guilty conscience. It's surely giving me trouble. Well, whatever has happened, I'll keep on fogging the issue. That's the only thing to do now. (*To* THEOPROPIDES) Where have you been, sir?

THEOPROPIDES: Say, I just ran across the man I bought this house from.

TRANIO: You didn't tell him anything about what I told you, did you?

THEOPROPIDES: Of course I did—the whole story.

TRANIO (*aside*): Oh, brother! I'm worried! My strategy may have failed.

THEOPROPIDES: What are you saying to yourself?

TRANIO: Who, me? Oh, nothing. Excuse me, sir; did you really tell him?

THEOPROPIDES: Yes, I told him. The whole story from beginning to end.

TRANIO: I suppose he admitted that about the murdered man?

THEOPROPIDES: He did not. He said there wasn't a word of truth in it.

TRANIO: He did? Why, the—

THEOPROPIDES: Yes, he did, I tell you.

TRANIO: Now wait: Are you sure? Think a minute. He didn't admit it?

THEOPROPIDES: If he'd admitted it, I'd have said so. Well, what do we do now?

TRANIO: What do we do now? Why, file suit against him, of course. What else, for heaven's sake? Just be sure that you file it with a judge who'll believe what I say. You'll win, hands down.

MISARGYRIDES (*aside*): Why, there's Philolaches' slave, Tranio. Those two! Haven't paid me a penny, interest or principal. (TRANIO *sees* MISARGYRIDES *coming toward him, moves away from* THEOPROPIDES *to meet him.*)

THEOPROPIDES: Where do you think you're going?

TRANIO: Who, me? Oh, nowhere. (*Aside*) Am I ever in for it! My sins are catching up with me. The day I was born, they forgot to pass out the good luck. Theopropides is here, and that fellow has to show up! What a mess! Whichever way I look, there's trouble. But I'll get to Misargyrides first.

MISARGYRIDES (aside): He's coming my way. Good! Maybe I'll get my money.

TRANIO (aside): Look at that silly grin on his face. Is he off the track! (To MISARGYRIDES) Well, how do you do, Misargyrides? So nice to meet you!

MISARGYRIDES: Yes, how-do! Got my money?

TRANIO: Now is that nice? Hardly more than met you, and you stab me to the heart.

MISARGYRIDES (aside, with gesture indicating "no brains"): Empty, that's him.

TRANIO (aside, with gesture toward his purse): You can say that again!

MISARGYRIDES: All right, cut out the funny business.

TRANIO: Well, what do you want?

MISARGYRIDES: Where's Philolaches?

TRANIO: You know, I'm awfully glad you came along just now. Suits me fine. (Takes him by arm, leads him away from THEOPROPIDES)

MISARGYRIDES: Hey! Wait! What do you mean?

TRANIO: Come on over here.

MISARGYRIDES (in a loud voice): I want my interest. Do I get it?

TRANIO: I know you've got a good voice. Don't shout so loud.

MISARGYRIDES: I'll shout as loud as I like.

TRANIO: Oh, come on now, be nice.

MISARGYRIDES: Why should I be nice?

TRANIO: Now, look: Why don't you just run along home?

MISARGYRIDES: Run along home?

TRANIO: Yes, and come back about noon.

MISARGYRIDES: Will I get my interest then?

TRANIO: Yes, sure. Just run along.

MISARGYRIDES: Why should I come all the way back here, go to all that bother and waste all that time? Why don't I just wait here till noon?

TRANIO: No, no. You go on home. Really, I mean it. Just go on home.

MISARGYRIDES: Listen, I want my interest.

TRANIO: Yes, sure, sure. Just go on now.

MISARGYRIDES: You just pay me my interest. What's going on here, anyway?

TRANIO: By God, if you don't—. Please, just go along. Please! Listen!

MISARGYRIDES: No, sir. I'm going to call Philolaches.

TRANIO: Go ahead. Make it good and loud.

MISARGYRIDES (shouts): Philolaches! Philolaches! Philolaches! Philolaches!

TRANIO: Well, are you happy now? You've yelled.

MISARGYRIDES: All I'm asking is what's coming to me. You've been putting me off like this for a good many days. If I'm getting in your hair, pay me my money, and I'll go away. Just say, "Here's your money," and you won't hear another word out of me.

TRANIO: Well, suppose you get your principal.

MISARGYRIDES: No, sir. Interest. Interest first.

TRANIO: What? Why, you—! What's the idea? Trying to see what you can get away with? You'd better take the bird in the hand, my friend. We're offering you your principal.

MISARGYRIDES: No, sir. I'm not asking for my principal. Interest first, interest. That's what you owe me now.

TRANIO: Well, he's not going to pay it. He doesn't owe you any interest.

MISARGYRIDES: Doesn't owe any?

TRANIO: Not a penny. You'll get absolutely nothing out of him on that score. What do you think he's going to do—leave the country, all because you say he owes you some interest that he doesn't choose to pay? Don't be silly. You know he's not going to pay you one penny. Go on, sue him! I suppose you have a special dispensation to lend money at interest to minors.

MISARGYRIDES: Give me my interest! My interest, you hear?

Pay me my interest, you two! I want it right now. Are you
going to pay up? Interest, understand? Am I going to get it?

TRANIO: Interest, interest, interest! That's the only word
he knows, "interest." Go on, get out! I don't think I've ever
seen a more disgusting old fool than you.

MISARGYRIDES: Say anything you want. Talk doesn't scare
me. (THEOPROPIDES *approaches* TRANIO.)

THEOPROPIDES: Tranio, what's this interest he's asking for?

TRANIO (*to* MISARGYRIDES): See, here comes Philolaches' father. He just got back from a trip. He'll pay your claim, principal and interest both. Don't you go bothering Philolaches
and me any more. You'll see. You'll get your money right
away.

MISARGYRIDES: Well, if he does any paying, I want to be
sure to get mine.

THEOPROPIDES (*to* TRANIO): What's going on here?

TRANIO: I beg pardon, sir?

THEOPROPIDES: Who is that man? What does he want? I
heard him mention Philolaches. What for? He sounded a bit
annoyed with you, too. Why? What's this debt he's talking
about?

TRANIO: Why, that dirty, low-down—. Why don't you throw
the money in his face, sir?

THEOPROPIDES: Throw it in his face?

TRANIO: Yes. Black his eye and bloody his nose with it!

MISARGYRIDES: Go right ahead. Throw all the money you
want. It won't bother me a bit.

TRANIO: Hear that, sir? Just look at him. Wouldn't you
know he was a moneylender? Dirty crooks, all of them.

THEOPROPIDES: Yes, yes, yes. Never mind about all that.
I'm not interested. I want to know just one thing—just one
thing, understand? What's this money Philolaches owes him?

TRANIO: Oh, it doesn't amount to much.

THEOPROPIDES: How much "doesn't it amount to"?

TRANIO: Oh, around four thousand drachmas. Well, surely,
sir, you don't think that's very much?

THEOPROPIDES: Not very much? And interest on top of it, as I hear.

TRANIO: The whole thing comes to forty-four hundred drachmas. That's the total debt, principal and interest together.

MISARGYRIDES: Exactly. I'm not asking for a penny more.

TRANIO: I wish you would! Go on: Try asking for one penny more! Say you'll pay him the money, sir, so we can get rid of him.

THEOPROPIDES: I should tell him I'll pay?

TRANIO: Certainly, sir.

THEOPROPIDES: Me?

TRANIO: Yes, you, sir. Listen, sir! Go ahead, tell him! Come on, give him your word on it. I guarantee it's all right.

THEOPROPIDES: Now wait a minute. Not so fast. What did you do with this money?

TRANIO: Oh, it's safe enough.

THEOPROPIDES: Well, then, if the money's safe enough, you two pay it back.

TRANIO: Um-ah-yes-uh—house. Your son bought a house with it.

THEOPROPIDES: A house?

TRANIO: That's right, a house.

THEOPROPIDES: Well, good for you, Philolaches! Taking after your father! Imagine that: Philolaches going into business!

TRANIO: Why, yes. After our house got to be—the way I told you, he went right out and bought another one.

THEOPROPIDES: Is that so? A house, eh?

TRANIO: Yes, sir, a house. And do you know what a buy he got, too?

THEOPROPIDES: No, how should I?

TRANIO: Wonderful!

THEOPROPIDES: What do you mean?

TRANIO: I just can't tell you, sir!

THEOPROPIDES: Why not?

TRANIO: It's absolutely perfect! It's a beauty!

THEOPROPIDES: That's fine, fine. Well, how much is he going to have to pay for it?

TRANIO: Only twelve thousand drachmas. The four thousand drachmas was the down payment. He borrowed that from this fellow here and paid it to the owner, see?

THEOPROPIDES: Fine, fine.

MISARGYRIDES: Listen, it's getting along toward noon.

TRANIO: Won't you please pay him off, sir? He makes me sick.

THEOPROPIDES: All right (*To* MISARGYRIDES) I'll take care of it.

MISARGYRIDES: Then I'll get it from you, is that right, sir?

THEOPROPIDES: Yes. Come around tomorrow.

MISARGYRIDES: Good. That suits me. Tomorrow will be fine. Good-by. (*Exit.*)

TRANIO (*aside*): Damn him! Damn him, anyway! He came close to making a grand mess of my plans. (*To* THEOPROPIDES) You know, sir, they're a rotten bunch, those moneylenders; nobody worse. They have no sense of decency at all.

THEOPROPIDES: Where is this house my son bought?

TRANIO (*aside*): Oh-oh! Now what do I say?

THEOPROPIDES: I asked you a question; speak up!

TRANIO: Yes, sir. I'm trying to think of the owner's name.

THEOPROPIDES: Well, hurry up and think of it.

TRANIO (*aside*): Say, why wouldn't this be a good idea: Let our neighbor here next door give me a hand with this job? I'll say it's his house Philolaches bought. "The Big Lie," you know! People say it's the smart thing to do. Well, here we go! What will be, will be!

THEOPROPIDES: Well, what about it? Have you thought of his name yet?

TRANIO: Damn him—I mean, damn his name. Your neighbor here next door is the man. It's his house your son bought.

THEOPROPIDES: How were the terms? Fair?

TRANIO: Fair enough on his side. Whether they're fair on your side depends on whether you pay up. If you do, fair enough; if you don't, not so fair. It's a very good location, don't you think?

THEOPROPIDES: Couldn't be better. Say, I'd like to have a look at the house. Knock on the door, Tranio, and see if anybody's home.

TRANIO (*aside*): Oh-oh! Here we go! Now what do I say? Heading for trouble again!

THEOPROPIDES: Well? Well?

TRANIO (*aside*): I don't know what to do. He's really got me on the spot!

THEOPROPIDES: Get a move on! Go and inquire. Ask somebody there to show me around.

TRANIO: Well-uh-well-uh—. There are ladies in the house. We'll have to see first whether they'd mind or not.

THEOPROPIDES: Naturally. Of course. Go ask them and find out. I'll wait here till you get back.

TRANIO (*aside*): You old devil! Everything I try to figure out, you keep getting in my way. What a nuisance! (*Enter* SIMO *from his house.* TRANIO *withdraws between houses.*) Well! Here's a piece of good luck! That's Simo, the owner of the house, just coming out. I'll step back in here until I can collect my wits! Then when I've figured out what to do, I'll go and have a word with him.

SCENE II

SIMO (*to audience*): Things at home haven't been this pleasant for a long time. It's been many a day, too, since I've had such a lot of good things to eat all at once. My wife really put a topnotch dinner on the table. Now she says it's bedtime. Oh, no! I thought there was some catch in it when I got an extra-nice meal! Wanted me upstairs in her room, she did. Old as she is, too! You know what they say: "Never nap after eating." Go along with you! When she wasn't looking, I sneaked out of the house. I'll bet she's fit to burst in there!

TRANIO (*aside*): Just you wait till evening; you'll catch it, you old rascal. Short rations and short sleep, both, that's for you.

SIMO (*to audience*): The more I think about it, the more I observe this fact: Men with wives whose chief attractions are their bank accounts and their gray hair are singularly uninterested in sleep. They never feel a bit like going to bed. You take me, for instance. I'm determined to get out of here and get downtown, and not to go to bed. Of course I don't know anything about your wives or how they treat you; all I know is that mine is a pain and getting worse every day.

TRANIO (*aside*): If your sneaking out causes you trouble, sir, you'll have no reason for blaming it on the gods. It will be only right to blame it on yourself. Well, it's time for me to have a word with the old boy. He's in for it! Now I've figured out how to lead Theopropides around by the nose. I've got a scheme that will keep me in the clear all around. (*He goes to* SIMO.) Good morning, good morning, Simo, sir!

SIMO: Why, hello, Tranio.

TRANIO: How've you been?

SIMO: Not bad. (*They shake hands.*) What are you doing for yourself?

TRANIO: Doing? Holding a fine gentleman by the hand; that's what I'm doing.

SIMO: Now you're being very kind. That's a nice compliment.

TRANIO: No more than you deserve, sir.

SIMO: You take me now; what I've got by the hand is not exactly a fine slave.

THEOPROPIDES (*to* TRANIO): Hey, you good-for-nothing! Come back here!

TRANIO: I'll be right with you, sir.

SIMO: Well, what time does the—

TRANIO: The what, sir?

SIMO: What's been going on every day at your place.

TRANIO: What do you mean, sir?

SIMO: You know perfectly well what I mean. No, it's all

right! Go to it. Have fun while you can. Life's short, remember.

TRANIO: What? Oh! Oh, I see what you mean. I didn't realize you were talking about our—business.

SIMO: Yes, sir, you fellows really know how to pass the time; you know what's what. Cakes and wine, sea food—good stuff, choice; that's what you live on.

TRANIO: You mean we used to live on, Simo. We don't get any of that any more.

SIMO: You don't? Why?

TRANIO: Oh, Simo! We all might as well be dead.

SIMO: Don't say things like that. You've been all right so far.

TRANIO: You're right; we have. Yes, we really lived exactly the way we wanted to. But Simo, the wind's been taken right out of our sails.

SIMO: It has? How?

TRANIO: Things couldn't be worse.

SIMO: What? Why, it always seemed to me you'd gotten safely to port.

TRANIO: Oh, no!

SIMO: Why, what's the matter?

TRANIO: I'm really in for it!

SIMO: How so?

TRANIO: Another ship came in and sank us.

SIMO: I'm sorry to hear that, Tranio. What happened? What's the trouble?

TRANIO: Just listen to this: My master is home.

SIMO: Then you're really going to catch it; a whipping, irons, and, to top it off, the cross.

TRANIO: Please, please, Simo, sir; don't give me away to my master, will you?

SIMO: As far as I'm concerned, you don't need to worry. I won't tell him anything.

TRANIO: Thanks, sir; you're a real friend.

SIMO: Don't call me friend; I'm no friend of yours, boy.

TRANIO: Now, about what my master sent me over here for—

SIMO: Wait. First of all I'm going to ask you a question, and I want an answer to it: Does your master know anything about what you people have been up to?

TRANIO: Not a thing.

SIMO: What about his son: Has your master been scolding him for anything at all?

TRANIO: No. There isn't a cloud in the sky, as far as Philolaches is concerned. Now here's what my master wanted me to ask you: He wants to know if you'll let him have a look at your house.

SIMO: Why, it's not for sale.

TRANIO: Yes, I know that. But my master wants to make some additions to his house; a sitting-room for the ladies, a bathroom, and a covered portico.

SIMO: What's he been dreaming up?

TRANIO: Well, it's like this: He wants his son to get married as soon as possible. That's why he wants the additions. And he said that the architect had told him that those parts of your house were unusually fine. Now, you see, he wants to make his like yours. You don't mind, do you? I'll tell you the special reason why he wants to copy yours: He's heard that your portico is beautifully shady all the time, even in summer.

SIMO: Why, no! When there's shade everywhere else, my portico gets the full force of the sun from morning until night. It hangs around my house like a bill-collector. I haven't got any shade at all, unless maybe down the well.

TRANIO: If you haven't got a "Shadyside," how about a "Sunshine Acres"?

SIMO: Oh! Why, you—! No, it's exactly as I've described it.

TRANIO: Well, anyway, Theopropides would like to take a look at it.

SIMO: Certainly, if he wants to. If he finds anything he likes, he's perfectly free to copy it.

TRANIO: May I tell him to come over now?

SIMO: Sure. Go ahead.

TRANIO (*aside*): They say that the two greatest generals in the world were Alexander the Great and Agathocles. How about making me the third? Singlehanded, I'm staging a campaign that will never be forgotten. I've "packed up my troubles in *two* old kit bags" and foisted one of them off on Theopropides and the other on Simo. Hey! There's a new wrinkle for you—not bad! Lots of people have pack mules, but I've got pack men. And what a load they can carry; put anything over on them, and off they trot with it! Well, I expect I'd better get along to my master. Well, Theopropides, sir?

THEOPROPIDES: What? Somebody call me? Who is it?

TRANIO: Your slave, loyal unto death, sir.

THEOPROPIDES: Where have you been?

TRANIO: You sent me over there on a job, and I just want to report "mission accomplished."

THEOPROPIDES: For heaven's sake, what took you so long?

TRANIO: The owner was busy, and I had to wait for him.

THEOPROPIDES: Up to your old tricks, aren't you? Always late.

TRANIO: Well, really, sir, think what you're asking. A man can't be two places at once, you know. I couldn't very well be over there and over here at the same time.

THEOPROPIDES: Yes. Well, what did you find out?

TRANIO: You may look at the house, go all over it, any time you like.

THEOPROPIDES: Well, come on, then. Let's go.

TRANIO: Yes, sir; right this way!

THEOPROPIDES: I'm with you. (*They move toward* SIMO's *house.*)

TRANIO: See, there's the owner waiting for you at the door. You can see he's not a bit happy about having sold his house.

THEOPROPIDES: He isn't? Well, what about it?

TRANIO: He wants me to ask Philolaches to call off the deal.

THEOPROPIDES: Oh, no! Business is business! If we'd paid too much for the place, he wouldn't have been willing to take it back. If you turn an honest penny, that's strictly for your own bank account. A man can't afford to be softhearted. If you—

TRANIO: Yes, yes, sure, sir. But I thought you were in a hurry. Come on! (*Takes him by the arm, leads him over to* SIMO)

THEOPROPIDES: What? Oh, yes—go ahead. I'm right with you.

TRANIO: This is the owner, sir. Simo, this is my master, Theopropides—the man I was telling you about.

SIMO: How do you do, Theopropides? I hear you've been abroad. Glad to see you got back safely.

THEOPROPIDES: Thank you.

SIMO: Tranio, here, was telling me you wanted to have a look at my house.

THEOPROPIDES: Why, yes, if it isn't inconvenient for you.

SIMO: Not at all, not at all. Go right in and look around.

THEOPROPIDES: But—the ladies?

SIMO: Who, her? Hah! Don't bother your head about her! Go on, look around! Feel free to go anywhere, just as if it were your own house.

THEOPROPIDES: What do you mean, "just as if"?

TRANIO (*aside to* THEOPROPIDES): Ssh! Don't throw that up to him! He feels so badly about having sold it to you. Don't you see how unhappy he looks, poor old fellow?

THEOPROPIDES (*aside to* TRANIO): Yes, I see.

TRANIO (*aside to* THEOPROPIDES): Well, you don't want it to look as if you were lording it over him or were too pleased with yourself. Don't even mention the fact that you've bought the place.

THEOPROPIDES (*aside to* TRANIO): Oh, sure. I see. Good advice. Very thoughtful of you, too. (*Aloud*) It's all right now, is it?

SIMO: Yes, certainly. Just go on in; take your time; look around all you like.

THEOPROPIDES: That's really very kind of you.

SIMO: Don't mention it.

TRANIO: Now here is the front entrance and the steps, sir. What do you think of them?

THEOPROPIDES: First-rate, yes, sir, first-rate!

TRANIO: Come here, sir; look at these pillars. See how steady and solid they are.

THEOPROPIDES: Yes. I don't think I've ever seen finer ones.

SIMO: Well, they ought to be. I paid enough for them when I got them.

TRANIO (aside to THEOPROPIDES): Did you hear that, sir: "Paid enough for them"? It breaks his heart when he realizes they aren't his any more.

THEOPROPIDES: How much did you pay for them?

SIMO: Three hundred drachmas for the two, plus freight.

THEOPROPIDES: H'm. Say, they're not nearly as nice as I thought they were at first.

SIMO: Why not?

THEOPROPIDES: Look at them both, down near the bottom; see those wormholes?

TRANIO: The lumber was probably too green; that's what's wrong with them. Why, sure! They're still perfectly good. All they need is a coat of paint. Yes, sir! This is none of your cheap, shoddy local work! Look here, sir! See how the door-posts and lintels are fitted together.

THEOPROPIDES: Yes, yes.

TRANIO (to audience): Look; perfect pair of jerks, aren't they? (Points behind their backs to the two old men, winks at audience)

THEOPROPIDES: Jerks? What do you mean?

TRANIO: What did I say? Joints, I meant; joints, of course. They suit you?

THEOPROPIDES: Yes. The more I see of the house, the better I like it.

TRANIO: How about that fresco there, with a crow chasing two turkey buzzards around in circles?

THEOPROPIDES: Fresco? I don't see any fresco.

TRANIO: Why, I do. See, there are the two turkey buzzards (business of pointing and winking again)—and right there, be-tween them, is the crow. (Points to himself) He's pulling the tail feathers out of them, first one, then the other. Here, sir, look right toward me. There's the crow; see him now?

THEOPROPIDES: I certainly do not. I don't see any crow.

TRANIO: Well, if you can't see the crow, look over toward yourselves, and maybe you can see the turkey buzzards.

THEOPROPIDES: To save my soul, I can't see any fresco of any birds anywhere.

TRANIO: Well, never mind. Forget it. Your eyes aren't as good as they used to be.

THEOPROPIDES: Everything I do see I like very, very much.

SIMO: Why don't you go in? You'll find the inside worth looking at.

THEOPROPIDES: Yes, yes. Good idea.

SIMO (*opens door, calls within*): Hey, boy! There's a gentleman here; take him around the house. Show him the rooms. (*To* THEOPROPIDES) I'd take you in myself, but I've got an appointment downtown.

THEOPROPIDES: I don't need anybody to take me in; I'm not interested in being taken in! Whatever's up, I'd rather make my own mistakes than have somebody take me in.

SIMO: What? Oh! Ha-Ha! I meant "take you in the house."

THEOPROPIDES: Ha-ha-ha; yes! Well, I'll just go in without being taken in.

SIMO: Sure. Thanks. All right.

TRANIO: Wait a minute, sir; I'll just see if the dog—

THEOPROPIDES: Yes, do.

TRANIO: Shoo! Get out, dog! Shoo! Get out of here! Damn you, get out, will you! Go on now, git! Git!

SIMO: Oh, she won't hurt you. Just go right in. She's as gentle as a puppy. Go right ahead. Well, I've got to move along downtown.

THEOPROPIDES: Thanks for your kindness. Good luck to you! (*Exit* SIMO.) Tranio, listen: You have them get that dog out of the way, even if she is as gentle as a pup.

TRANIO: Why, no, sir; look! She's sleeping there just as peacefully! You don't want to make a nuisance of yourself, do you, sir, or have them think you're afraid?

THEOPROPIDES: Well, all right. Come on in with me, then.

TRANIO: I'll be right at your heels, sir, every step of the way.

(*Exeunt.*)

ACT THREE

SCENE I

(*Enter* PHANISCUS. *He has come to fetch* CALLIDAMATES *home.*)

PHANISCUS: The slave who never does anything wrong, but is always worried for fear he'll get into trouble, is the one his master loves. The one who never worries always gets into trouble sooner or later, and then he tries all kinds of crazy stunts to get out of it. He does exercises to strengthen his legs; then he runs away, but he gets caught and does for his troubles what he couldn't do for his savings—makes them bigger: They were little ones; now he's got some really big ones. Me, now, I've decided to let other fellows catch the beatings instead of me. I want my hide to go right on being the way it's been up to now: whole. If I obey my master, I'll have myself well protected all around; then I can say, "No beating for me, sir!" Troubles are raining down on the others; I don't want them raining on me. A slave can have any kind of master he wants: If he's a good slave, he'll have a good master; if he's a bad one, his master will be a bad one, too. You take our house, now: It's full of real bad ones—waste their rations, always getting whipped. When somebody tells them to go meet master, they say, "Nothing doing. You won't stick me with it. I know why you're so eager—trying to make time with master, hoping he'll put the old horse out to pasture." Well, I got this much out of it: I got put out, at least, and I'm going all alone to meet master—just me out of the whole bunch. Tomorrow master'll find out what happened, and he'll tan their hides with what's been stripped off an ox. Anyway, I don't care what happens to them; I care what happens to me. They can wear out the leather if they want to, so long as I don't have to wear out the rope.

Scene II

(*Enter* Pinacium.)

Pinacium: Hey, wait! Stop! Phaniscus, wait, will you?

Phaniscus: Oh, go jump in the lake!

Pinacium: Look at old snooty! Smarty! Wait for me, will you, you old chiseler!

Phaniscus: Chiseler? How do you get that?

Pinacium: Simple; so long as you can wangle something for yourself, you'll do anything.

Phaniscus: Yeah? So what? What's it to you?

Pinacium: Getting tough, are you? Well, everybody knows what you and master are doing together.

Phaniscus: Ow! I'm choking to death!

Pinacium: What? Why?

Phaniscus: All the gassing going on around here.

Pinacium: Aw, go on, you old faker. Pile it up, pile it up!

Phaniscus: You won't get me to start any fights. Master knows me.

Pinacium: He ought to. You've been his mattress long enough.

Phaniscus: You must be drunk, or you wouldn't say things like that.

Pinacium: Why should I be nice to you? You aren't being nice to me. Look, you old fool, let's you and me go meet master together.

Phaniscus: Well, then, you stop talking about—those things.

Pinacium: All right. I'll go knock at the door. Hello! Anybody home? Better open up before I break the door down! Hello! Open up, somebody! H'm! Nobody coming to the

door. Well, what can you expect from that bunch of good-
for-nothings? Just the same, we must be careful. Don't want
somebody coming out and beating us up.

Scene III

(Enter Tranio *and* Theopropides *from* Simo's *house.)*

Tranio: Well, what do you think of our little deal?

Theopropides: By Heaven, I'm really delighted!

Tranio: We didn't pay too much, did we?

Theopropides: Pay too much? If this house wasn't a steal,
I've never seen one.

Tranio: Like it, do you?

Theopropides: Like it? I love it!

Tranio: What did you think of the ladies' sitting room?
The portico?

Theopropides: Out of this world! I don't think there's a
public portico as big as that one!

Tranio: That's right. You know, Philolaches and I measured every public portico in town.

Theopropides: Yes? What did you find out?

Tranio: It's much longer than any of them.

Theopropides: Wonderful! A very fine deal! Why, if he'd
come now and offer me thirty-six thousand drachmas in cash
for the place, I wouldn't take it.

Tranio: Why, if you wanted to take it, sir, I'd never let
you.

Theopropides: We made a good investment with that little
deal!

Tranio: Yes, and don't you forget that I was the one who
suggested it and urged Philolaches to make it. I was the one
who gave him the idea of borrowing the money for the down
payment from the moneylender.

Theopropides: Yes. That's what kept us from losing the
whole business. Now, let's see; it's eight thousand drachmas
we owe Simo, isn't it?

TRANIO: That's it—not a penny more.

THEOPROPIDES: I'll pay him today.

TRANIO: Good idea, sir; then he'll have no excuse for reneging. Or, say, why don't you give me the money, and I'll see that he gets it?

THEOPROPIDES: Well, now, wait; I don't know about giving it to you. How do I know you won't be pulling some sort of trick on me?

TRANIO: Who, me, sir? Pull a trick on you? Why, I wouldn't even think of such a thing, not even just as a joke.

THEOPROPIDES: And me, I wouldn't even think of trusting you with anything—just as a joke.

TRANIO: After all, sir, I've never done anything of the kind to you, not since the day you bought me.

THEOPROPIDES: I know it. I never gave you the chance.

TRANIO: Seems to me you ought to be grateful to me for being so loyal.

THEOPROPIDES: I'll do well enough, if I just manage to keep you from getting away with something.

TRANIO (*aside*): How right you are!

THEOPROPIDES: You go on out to the farm, now, and tell Philolaches I'm home.

TRANIO: Yes, sir.

THEOPROPIDES: Tell him to come back to town with you right away.

TRANIO: Right, sir. (*Aside*) I'll slip down the back way here and go join the rest of the gang. I'll tell them how nice and peaceful everything is, and how I got rid of our old gentleman!

SCENE IV

PHANISCUS: That's funny. Doesn't sound as if there was any party going on here, the way there always was. I don't hear any music or anything else.

THEOPROPIDES (*notices* PHANISCUS *and* PINACIUM): What's

all this? What are those fellows looking for at my house? What do they want? Why are they peeking in?

PINACIUM: I'll try knocking again. Hello! Open up! Hey, Tranio! Open up, will you?

THEOPROPIDES: What's this all about?

PINACIUM: Open up, will you? We've come to get Callidamates.

THEOPROPIDES: Here, here, boys, what are you doing? Are you trying to break the door in?

PINACIUM: "Here, here" yourself, sir, what's it to you? It's none of your business.

THEOPROPIDES: None of my business?

PINACIUM: No, unless maybe they've just made you chief of police, "to preserve the citizenry from damage to life, limb, and property."

THEOPROPIDES: That's my house where you are.

PHANISCUS: What?

PINACIUM: Why, has Philolaches just sold it? Either that, or this old rascal is telling us a pack of lies.

THEOPROPIDES: It's no lie. In any case, what business have you here?

PHANISCUS: Business? Why, our master's at a party here.

THEOPROPIDES: At a party? Here?

PHANISCUS: That's right.

THEOPROPIDES: Don't be funny, boy.

PHANISCUS: No. We've come to get him.

THEOPROPIDES: Come to get whom?

PHANISCUS: Our master!

PINACIUM: How many times to do we have to tell you?

THEOPROPIDES (to PHANISCUS): Now listen, boy! You seem like a good sort. That house is vacant; nobody lives there.

PHANISCUS: What? This house? You mean Philolaches doesn't live here?

THEOPROPIDES: He used to, but he moved away a long time ago.

PINACIUM (to PHANISCUS): The old man's crazy!

PHANISCUS: Why, I'm sure you're wrong, sir. Because unless

he moved away either yesterday or today, I know he lives here.

THEOPROPIDES: I tell you it's been six months since anybody lived there.

PINACIUM: You're dreaming!

THEOPROPIDES: Who? Me?

PINACIUM: Yes, you.

THEOPROPIDES: Hm! Impudent, aren't you? I'm not talking to you; I'm talking to the boy here. (*To* PHANISCUS) Nobody lives there.

PHANISCUS: Oh, yes, they do! Why, yesterday, and the day before that, and the day before that, and the day before that—ever since Philolaches' father went away—there haven't been two days running when there wasn't a party here.

THEOPROPIDES: What!

PHANISCUS: That's what I said, sir; not two days running when they weren't eating and drinking, entertaining women, having all sorts of wild goings-on, with flute-girls and everything else.

THEOPROPIDES: Who's been giving these parties?

PHANISCUS: Philolaches, sir.

THEOPROPIDES: Which Philolaches is that?

PHANISCUS: Why, I think he's the son of a man named Theopropides.

THEOPROPIDES (*aside*): I've really been taken in, if he's telling the truth. (*To* PHANISCUS) May I ask you a few more questions? You say that this Philolaches, whoever he is, has been giving parties here, and that your master's been coming to them?

PHANISCUS: Yes, right here, sir.

THEOPROPIDES: Now, now, boy! You must be more stupid than you look. See here, are you sure you didn't stop off for a quick nip somewhere, and maybe had a few more than you should?

PHANISCUS: What do you mean, sir?

THEOPROPIDES: You know what I mean: You've come to the wrong house, haven't you?

PHANISCUS: No, sir. I know my way here, and I know where

I am. Philolaches, son of Theopropides, lives here. After his father'd gone off on a business trip, he bought a flute-girl and set her free.

THEOPROPIDES: Philolaches did?

PHANISCUS: Yes, sir. And her name's Philematium.

THEOPROPIDES: What did he pay for her?

PHANISCUS: Thirty—

THEOPROPIDES: —talents?

PHANISCUS: Goodness' sake, no, sir! Thirty minae—three thousand drachmas!

THEOPROPIDES: And set her free, did he?

PHANISCUS: Yes, he did. Cost him three thousand drachmas.

THEOPROPIDES: Is that so? Three thousand drachmas for a girl for Philolaches, right?

PHANISCUS: That's right.

THEOPROPIDES: And gave her her liberty, did he?

PHANISCUS: That's right.

THEOPROPIDES: And ever since his father went off on that trip, he's been having parties here, day after day, and your master has been coming to them?

PHANISCUS: That's right.

THEOPROPIDES: Uh—have you heard anything about him buying this house here next door?

PHANISCUS: No, that's not right.

THEOPROPIDES: Maybe gave four thousand drachmas to the owner as down payment?

PHANISCUS: No, that's not right, either.

THEOPROPIDES: Oh! You're killing me!

PHANISCUS: Killing you? Killing his father, you mean.

THEOPROPIDES: You can say that again.

PHANISCUS: I'm sorry to have to tell you this, sir. You must be a friend of his father.

THEOPROPIDES: Well, his father's certainly in for some grief, that's sure.

PHANISCUS: Of course, you know, that three thousand drachmas was nothing. You ought to see the way he's been throwing the money around other places.

THEOPROPIDES: Why, he's ruined his father!

PHANISCUS: Yes. And he has one slave that's a perfect devil —fellow named Tranio. The god of thieves himself had nothing on him. You know, sir, I really feel very sorry for his father. Why! When he finds this out, it'll break his poor old heart!

THEOPROPIDES: Certainly will—that is, if all this is the truth.

PHANISCUS: Now why would I be telling any lies about it, sir? (PINACIUM *knocks again*.)

PINACIUM: Hello, hello, hello! Come on, somebody! Open the door!

PHANISCUS: What's the use of knocking on the door? There's nobody there. They all must have gone out together. Let's go along.

THEOPROPIDES: Boy!

PHANISCUS: We'll try looking somewhere else. Come on.

PINACIUM: All right.

THEOPROPIDES: Boy, are you leaving?

PHANISCUS: Yes. You're a free man, sir; your hide is safe. Me, now, if I don't obey my master and take care of him, nothing will save mine. (*Exeunt* PHANISCUS *and* PINACIUM.)

SCENE V

THEOPROPIDES: Great gods! How can I say it? From what I've just heard, I haven't just been running around Egypt; I've been given the royal run-around to the end of the world and back again. I don't know where I am. (*Enter* SIMO.) But I'm going to find out, yes I am! Here comes the fellow my son bought the house from. Hello, there! What have you been doing?

SIMO: I've been downtown and I'm just coming home.

THEOPROPIDES: Anything new happen downtown today?

SIMO: Why, yes.

THEOPROPIDES: What?

SIMO: Oh, I saw a funeral procession going by.

THEOPROPIDES: Is that supposed to be new?

SIMO: Well, they said the man had just died, so I guess that makes it new.

THEOPROPIDES: What nonsense!

SIMO: Why are you so anxious to hear the news, anyway?

THEOPROPIDES: Well, I just got home today.

SIMO: I'm sorry; I'm going out to dinner. Can't invite you to celebrate with me.

THEOPROPIDES: Nobody asked you to, for heaven's sake!

SIMO: However, tomorrow's another day, and unless I find I have another engagement, I'd be very glad to have—dinner at your house.

THEOPROPIDES: Nobody asked you to do that, either; that's sure! But if you're not too busy, could you give me a minute?

SIMO: Certainly.

THEOPROPIDES: Let's see: I think Philolaches paid you four thousand drachmas?

SIMO: He did not! He never gave me one penny, that I know of.

THEOPROPIDES: Oh! Well, maybe it was Tranio, my slave?

SIMO: Tranio? Hah! Much the less he!

THEOPROPIDES: I'm talking about the down payment he made to you.

SIMO: Down payment? You must be dreaming.

THEOPROPIDES: Me? Dreaming? You're the one that's dreaming, if you think that by pretending you never got the money you can wiggle out of the deal.

SIMO: Deal? What deal?

THEOPROPIDES: The deal my son made with you while I was away.

SIMO: He made a deal with *me,* while you were away? What deal? When did he make it?

THEOPROPIDES: In any case, I owe you eight thousand drachmas.

SIMO: You do not. Not to me. But if you do, let's have it. Must keep your credit good, you know. Don't go saying you don't owe me anything.

THEOPROPIDES: I'm not saying anything of the sort. I do

owe you the money, and I am going to pay it. But don't you go claiming you didn't get the four thousand drachmas down payment.

SIMO: Now just a minute! Look here! Listen! What do you owe me that money for? Did I sell him some land, or something?

THEOPROPIDES: No, no, no! That's the amount he owes you for the house he bought from you—this house right here.

SIMO: House? He bought this house from me?

THEOPROPIDES: Why, yes. That's why I sent Tranio over to ask you to let me look at it. Didn't he tell you?

SIMO: He did not. He said that your son was going to get married, and on account of that you wanted to build some additions to your house.

THEOPROPIDES: Me? To my house?

SIMO: That's what he said.

THEOPROPIDES: Heaven help us! Have I ever been taken in! I can't think what to say. Simo, I've had it; I've really had it!

SIMO: Tranio took you into camp, did he?

THEOPROPIDES: He certainly did—all the way. He's made an everlasting fool of me.

SIMO: You don't say!

THEOPROPIDES: Oh, but I do say. That's exactly what I say: He's made an eternal idiot of me. Simo, tell me: Would you be kind enough to give me a little help?

SIMO: Certainly. What do you want me to do?

THEOPROPIDES: Step over here with me for a minute, will you?

SIMO: All right. (*They walk toward stage center, away from the houses.*)

THEOPROPIDES: Lend me a couple of strong slaves and a horsewhip or two.

SIMO: Help yourself.

THEOPROPIDES: While we're going after them I'll tell you the whole story, and you'll see how I've been reduced to idiocy. (*Exeunt into* SIMO's *house.*)

ACT FOUR

SCENE I

(*Enter* TRANIO *from* THEOPROPIDES' *house.*)

TRANIO: A man who loses his nerve when things get difficult isn't worth a hoot—funny word, "hoot"; I wonder what it means? Anyway, Master, you know, sent me off to the farm to bring Philolaches back to town, and I slipped down the alley there to our back yard. He didn't see me. There's a gate that opens on the alley from the yard; I unlocked it, got the boys and girls together, and took my whole team out that way. After I'd gotten the group out of that tight corner, my next move was to call my little playmates to order for a meeting. Soon as I got them together, what do you suppose they did? They voted me out! That left me completely on my own, of course, so I started moving right away. I'm going to do what everybody does when he's worried and confused: Stir up some more confusion, so that nobody will be quite sure what to do next. One thing I'm sure of, the old man can't be in the dark any longer about what has been going on. I'll get to him first, beat the others to it, and make my own peace with him. What am I waiting for? Wait! What's that? I heard the door open over here next door. It's my master! I want to get an idea of what he's going to say. (*Withdraws into the space between houses*)

SCENE II

(THEOPROPIDES *enters from* SIMO's *house. He talks back through door to slaves.*)

THEOPROPIDES: You boys stay right here inside the door, so that you can jump out the minute I call you. Get the cuffs

on him right away. I'll bring him up here outside the door—
my smart boy! He'll smart, all right. I'll see to that, so help
me!

TRANIO (*aside*): Cat's out of the bag! Better figure out what
you're going to do, Tranio!

THEOPROPIDES: I'll have to watch my step and make every
move very carefully when Tranio gets here. Won't do to let
him see the hook; I'll have to pay out the line ve-e-ry gently.
I'll pretend I don't know anything at all.

TRANIO (*aside*): Shame on you, sir! There isn't a smoother
operator in all Athens! Talking him out of anything will be
like talking to a stone wall. Well, anyway, here goes!

THEOPROPIDES: All set. I wish he'd show up.

TRANIO (*coming forward*): Have you been looking for me?
Well, here I am, at your orders, sir.

THEOPROPIDES: Good, good, Tranio. How are things coming?

TRANIO: The boys have left the farm; Philolaches will be
here any minute.

THEOPROPIDES: You know, I'm awfully glad you came just
now. I'm beginning to think our neighbor here is a pretty
tough customer and none too reliable.

TRANIO: Oh? How so?

THEOPROPIDES: Well, he says he hasn't even met you people.

TRANIO: He does?

THEOPROPIDES: Yes, and that you haven't paid him a single
penny.

TRANIO: Oh, come on, sir; you're joking. I can't believe
he'd say any such thing.

THEOPROPIDES: What makes you think so?

TRANIO: Oh, I see! You nearly had me fooled for a minute. Ha-ha! "Says we never paid him anything"! Good joke,
sir!

THEOPROPIDES: No, Tranio, I'm not joking; he said just
that—said he never sold his house to Philolaches at all.

TRANIO: What's that, sir? He really said that he never got
any money from us?

THEOPROPIDES: He said he'd swear on the witness stand, if

I wanted him to, that he did not sell his house and that you did not pay him any money.

TRANIO: Witness stand, eh? Well, if he wants to sue us, let him!

THEOPROPIDES: That's exactly what I told him.

TRANIO: And what did he say then?

THEOPROPIDES: He assured me that he would bring his slaves into court and that they'd back him up.

TRANIO: His slaves? Nonsense! He wouldn't dare.

THEOPROPIDES: Oh, yes, he would.

TRANIO: Why don't you beat him to it—sue him first? I'll go find him.

THEOPROPIDES: No. Wait a minute. You know, maybe you're right. I might sue him at that. Yes, I will.

TRANIO: I don't know, sir; why don't you let me handle him? (TRANIO *begins to circle altar warily, with* THEOPROPIDES *keeping close behind.*) Or on second thought, why not just tell him to go ahead and sue, after all?

THEOPROPIDES: Well—yes—but it might be a good idea to ask his slaves a few questions first.

TRANIO: Very good plan, sir.

THEOPROPIDES: What do you think? Should I see if I can get them to come over now?

TRANIO: I can't think of a better time. (THEOPROPIDES *turns toward* SIMO's *house.* TRANIO *quickly jumps up on altar.*) While you're going after them, I'll just rest here for a bit.

THEOPROPIDES: What are you doing that for?

TRANIO: Don't be dull, sir. If you get those slaves out for questioning, you don't want them making a run for the altar, do you? I'll stay on guard here, so your investigation won't be interrupted.

THEOPROPIDES: Get off there.

TRANIO: Oh, no, sir.

THEOPROPIDES: Now please, Tranio, don't grab the altar for yourself.

TRANIO: Why not?

THEOPROPIDES: Well, you see, I particularly want the slaves

to make a run for the altar. Let them have it. It'll be that much easier for me to get a judgment against Simo for the money.

TRANIO: I'd keep to the point at issue, if I were you. You don't want to give Simo grounds for another suit. I don't think you realize how ticklish a business the law is.

THEOPROPIDES: Get down from there and come over here. There's something I want to talk over with you.

TRANIO: I can tell you what I think from where I am; I'm much smarter when I'm sitting down. Besides, this is sacred ground; any advice from here will be that much more reliable.

THEOPROPIDES: Get down! Stop the foolishness! Don't you turn your back on me!

TRANIO: All right. I'm facing you.

THEOPROPIDES: Now you see here!

TRANIO: I'm seeing all right. If anybody else joined us, he'd die of starvation.

THEOPROPIDES: How do you make that out?

TRANIO: Why, because there's no living to be made between the two of us. We're two of a kind; we'd rob him blind.

THEOPROPIDES: Damn it all, anyway!

TRANIO: What's the matter with you?

THEOPROPIDES: You've made a fool of me.

TRANIO: I have? How?

THEOPROPIDES: You really wiped my nose for me.

TRANIO: Let's see; did I do a good job? Did I get it all?

THEOPROPIDES: You certainly did; you took my wits and everything inside my head with it. I've found out all about the devilment you people have been up to, from top to bottom —no, more than that: from super-top to sub-bottom.

TRANIO: Well, I can tell you one thing: I'm not going to get down from here until I'm good and ready.

THEOPROPIDES: Oh, yes, you will! I'll have them build a fire under you, blast your hide!

TRANIO: No, no, don't do that. I'd taste a lot better stewed than roasted.

THEOPROPIDES: I'm going to make an example of you.

TRANIO: Like me that well, do you? An example for the others? My!

THEOPROPIDES: You just tell me something: What sort of man was my son when I left him in your care?

TRANIO: Oh, he was a man with feet, hands, fingers, ears, eyes, mouth.

THEOPROPIDES: That's not what I asked you.

TRANIO: That's not what I answered you, either. But look, sir; I see somebody coming. It's your son's friend, Callidamates. If you have any complaints to make against me, make them while he's here, will you?

SCENE III

(Enter CALLIDAMATES.*)*

CALLIDAMATES *(aside)*: After I'd slept it all off and gotten over my hangover, Philolaches told me that his father had come home—told me, too, how Tranio had tricked him when he got here. He said he was uneasy and embarrassed about seeing his father, so the lot of them elected me ambassador to try to make peace with father. Oh, good! There he is. How do you do, Theopropides? I'm delighted to see that you are back safe and sound. Won't you have dinner at my house tonight? Please do!

THEOPROPIDES: How do you do, Callidamates? I'm afraid I can't come to dinner. Thank you for asking me.

CALLIDAMATES: Oh, come on!

TRANIO: Say you'll go, sir. I'll go in your place, if you don't feel like it.

THEOPROPIDES: Blast your hide! Are you making fun of me again?

TRANIO: Why? Because I said you might pass up a free meal as a favor to me?

THEOPROPIDES: Well, you're not going to any dinner. I'm going to have you carried off to the cross, where you belong.

CALLIDAMATES: Come on, Theopropides; don't talk that way. Say you'll come to dinner. How about it? What? (*To* TRANIO) You, Tranio; why did you climb up on the altar?

TRANIO: That big old meany there came and scared me to death. (*To* THEOPROPIDES) Now, sir, tell him what I did. There's somebody here to represent both sides now. Go on, tell your story.

THEOPROPIDES: I claim that you corrupted my son.

TRANIO: Wait a minute, please. I admit that he did some things he shouldn't have done: that he bought a girl and freed her in your absence, that he borrowed money at interest, and that he spent it all. But did he do anything different from what the sons of some of our first citizens are doing all the time?

THEOPROPIDES: H'm! I'll have to watch you; you're a pretty sharp pleader.

CALLIDAMATES: Let me sit in the judge's seat, will you? Come on, Tranio; get down. I want to sit where you are.

THEOPROPIDES: That'll be fine. You take the case and settle it.

TRANIO: Ah-ah! Looks like a trick to me. (*To* THEOPROPIDES) Give me some proof that you and I will have equal rights and take equal risks.

THEOPROPIDES: The thing that bothers me most is the way Tranio, here, made me look like a fool. I don't care so much about the rest.

TRANIO: You bet I did—and a good job it was, too. I'm not a bit sorry I did it. A man as old as you are, been around as long as you have, ought to have brains enough not to be taken in like that.

THEOPROPIDES: Maybe so, maybe so—but what do I do now?

TRANIO: If you know Diphilus or Philemon well enough,

you might tell them how your slave made you look like a fool; it would give them some wonderful ideas for their plays!

CALLIDAMATES: All right, that's enough, Tranio. Give me a chance to talk. Listen to me.

THEOPROPIDES: I'm listening.

CALLIDAMATES: First of all, you know that I'm a good friend of your son. He approached me—he felt uncomfortable about coming to you himself because of the foolishness he's been involved in. He knows you know about that, you see. Now, please, sir, forgive him if he's been foolish and immature. He is your son, you know. And boys will be boys! If he did anything wrong, I was in on it with him, and I'm the one who's to blame. I believe there's a debt, interest and principal, involved—the money he used to buy his girl free. I'll pay the whole amount; I can get it. It will come out of my pocket, not yours.

THEOPROPIDES: If anyone in the world could win me over, you could, Callidamates. What he did doesn't bother me; I don't care about that. Why, no! He can go right ahead having fun with the girls, going to parties—anything he likes. He doesn't have to wait for me to go away! If he's really sorry that he spent all that money, that's enough for me.

CALLIDAMATES: Sorry? He's brokenhearted!

TRANIO: Well, you've forgiven Philolaches. Now what happens to me?

THEOPROPIDES: You? I'm going to string you up by the thumbs and pound you to a pulp!

TRANIO: What? Even if I'm sorry?

THEOPROPIDES: So help me, I'll murder you!

CALLIDAMATES: Now, now, sir; why don't you make it unanimous? Forgive Tranio for what he's done this time, please, just for my sake.

THEOPROPIDES: Ask me anything else you want, and you can have it. But Tranio—after what he pulled on me, I'll kill him, and neither you nor anybody else will stop me.

CALLIDAMATES: Please, Theopropides. Please forgive him.

THEOPROPIDES: Forgive him? Look at him standing there! Did you see what he did? (TRANIO *makes obscene gesture at* THEOPROPIDES.)

CALLIDAMATES: Tranio, if you have any sense, stop that.

THEOPROPIDES: You just stop asking me for this favor. I'll see that he stops it—with a horsewhip!

TRANIO: That won't be at all necessary, sir.

CALLIDAMATES: Come on, come on, Theopropides. Say you forgive him.

THEOPROPIDES: Stop asking me. I don't like it.

CALLIDAMATES: Please, sir?

THEOPROPIDES: Stop that! I don't like it, I tell you!

CALLIDAMATES: It isn't going to do you any good not to like it. Now come on, forgive him just this once, for my sake.

TRANIO: Why let it bother you, sir? You know perfectly well that I'll be in trouble again by tomorrow. Then you can do a really good job; you can take it out of me for both things at once!

CALLIDAMATES: Will you, sir? Please?

THEOPROPIDES: All right, all right. I won't punish you, Tranio. No! Don't thank me; thank Callidamates. (*To audience*) Friends, our play is over. May we have your applause, please?

FINIS

PLAUTUS

THE ROPE
(Rudens)

INTRODUCTORY NOTE

Plautus' play, *The Rope* (*Rudens*) takes its name from the scene in which one character, a fisherman, comes on stage carrying a net from which a long rope trails behind him. Although the incident itself is relatively unimportant, it is very deftly used to point up the central problem of the play, for the net contains a chest dredged up from the bottom of the sea, and in the chest is a little box containing the jewelry by which the heroine is identified as a free Athenian citizen and is thus enabled to marry her freeborn lover.

The plot here indicated was a great favorite with the writers of the New Comedy, and with their Roman followers and imitators as well. A young man of free birth and of some property falls in love with a slave girl who has been brought up in a brothel. Her owner, the pimp, makes a deal with the young man either to sell the girl to him or to reserve her attentions for him. Complications of various sorts are introduced into the story, but in the end evidence of one kind or another—usually in the form of jewelry that is identified by the girl's parents—is adduced to prove that the supposed slave girl is really freeborn. She is then released by the pimp, and very properly becomes the wife of the man whose mistress she had expected to be.

This is the story of Palaestra and Plesidippus in *The Rope*. As if to add new spice to an old and hackneyed tale, the scene of the play is changed from the almost universal "street in Athens" to the seaside, where, on a lonely, rocky shore, stands a temple of Venus; near it is the little cottage of Daemones. Placed in this setting, not only the plot but also Plautus' familiar comic tricks and routines acquire a fresh and romantic flavor, and create a play which some have compared—perhaps a bit rashly—to Shakespeare's *Tempest*.

The date of the first production of *The Rope* is unknown;

like *The Menaechmi,* it has been set as early as 215 B.C. and as late as 186 B.C. In recent years it has also been placed somewhere near 200 B.C. It has perhaps the most interesting of all the Plautine Prologues, a long, half-serious, and entirely delightful discourse put into the mouth of the star-god Arcturus.

CHARACTERS

ARCTURUS, the Prologue
SCEPARNIO, slave of DAEMONES
PLESIDIPPUS, a young Athenian, resident in Cyrene
DAEMONES, an old gentleman of Athens, resident in Cyrene
PALAESTRA, a young woman, held as slave by LABRAX
AMPELISCA, a young woman, slave of LABRAX
PTOLEMOCRATIA, priestess of the temple of Venus
FISHERMEN
TRACHALIO, slave of PLESIDIPPUS
LABRAX, a pimp
CHARMIDES, an old man, friend of LABRAX
SPARAX and TURBALIO, two "whip men," slaves of DAEMONES
GRIPUS, a fisherman, slave of DAEMONES
OFFICERS OF THE LAW

SCENE: *A stretch of ocean beach near the city of Cyrene in North Africa. Upstage, right of center, the front of a small temple, with an altar before it; left of center, the front of a small cottage, the home of* DAEMONES. *Left and right, the stage is covered with patches of rushes and scattered rocks; to the right these are sufficiently concentrated to represent the inshore end of a rocky promontory. The sea is to be imagined as before and to the right of the stage; to the left lies the road to Cyrene.*

THE ROPE

There is One who rules all peoples, seas, and lands; it is his subject that I am. I owe allegiance to heaven. I'm just what you see I am, a bright and shining star, a sign that always appears when it's supposed to, here on earth and in the sky, too. My name is Arcturus. At night I shine in the heavens and keep company with the gods; in the daytime I wander around among men. Oh, yes! There are other stars, too, that drop from heaven to earth. There's a king, you know, of gods and men—Jupiter. He assigns us, some to one country, some to another, to find out what people are doing, how they are behaving. Are they honoring their obligations? Are they keeping their word? Are they making good use of their wealth? People who bring trumped-up lawsuits and offer false testimony in support of them, people who stand up in court and swear they never got money that was paid to them—we make a list of their names and take it to Jupiter; he gets a daily report on everybody who's doing wrong down here. People who perjure themselves to establish a claim at law, the rascals who get the courts to award them things that aren't rightfully theirs— Jupiter brings them into double jeopardy, all right! He tries their cases all over again, and fines them a lot more than they ever won in the first place. As for decent, law-abiding people, he records their names in a different list. And you know, these sinners have the idea that they can buy Jupiter off with gifts and sacrifices, but they're wasting their time and money; he won't have anything to do with perjurers' conscience money. People who try to do what is right have a lot better chance of winning the indulgence of the gods through prayer than do deliberate sinners. So here's my advice to all you decent people who try to carry out your obligations and live honest lives: Keep right on, and later you will have your reward.

So much for that. Now I'll tell you about our play; after all, that's really why I came here.

First of all, our author, Diphilus, said that our scene was to be Cyrene. Daemones lives over there (*pointing*); his farm and house lie right along the seashore. He's an old gentleman who was forced to leave Athens and came here to live, but he's a perfectly decent person. It wasn't because he did anything wrong that he had to leave home; he tried to rescue other people and got himself in too deep. He had a fortune honestly earned, but he lost it all by being generous. He had a little daughter, and he lost her, too—poor little thing! She was kidnaped and sold to one of our least desirable citizens; he brought her here to Cyrene—yes, he's a pimp, and she was a nice young girl, too! A young man who lives here—he's an Athenian, actually—saw her going home from her music lessons one day and fell in love with her. He went to the pimp, arranged to buy the girl for himself for three thousand drachmas, made a down payment to clinch the deal, and executed the necessary documents. The pimp behaved as you might expect—paid absolutely no attention to his promise or to the contract he'd made with the young man. He had a fellow visiting him—just two peas in a pod, the pair of them. He was an old scoundrel from Sicily, from Agrigentum, the kind that would sell out his native land. He started telling the pimp how good-looking the girl was, and the others he had, too—trim little ladies, all of them! He told him he ought to go back to Sicily with him; that was where the men really liked their pleasures, he said; that was where he could make a fortune; that was the place where the trade in pretty girls was really flourishing. Finally the pimp agreed. They slipped down to the harbor and chartered a ship. The pimp cleaned everything out of his house one night and got it on board. He told the young man who had bought the girl from him that he had a votive offering to pay to Venus—this is Venus' temple over here (*pointing*)—and so he invited him to come out here and join him for breakfast afterward. Then in less time than it takes to tell it, he boarded ship and was off with his young ladies. Somebody got word to the young man about what was going on, that the pimp was leaving town. The young man hurried down to the harbor, but the ship was already far out to sea.

Now I saw the girl being carried off, and so I decided to see what I could do for her, and see if I couldn't do for the pimp, both at the same time. I blew up a real howler of a winter storm and stirred the waves up high. I'm Arcturus, you know, the worst weather-breeder of them all. I'm stormy when I rise, and when I set I'm even stormier. Now the pair of them, the pimp and his visitor, are sitting together on a reef—washed overboard—and their ship is a total wreck. The girl, along with another little lady, got scared and jumped off the ship into the lifeboat. Now they're being washed away from the reef toward the shore, right in the direction of the house there, where the old gentleman of Athens lives. His roof is ruined—the wind blew down a lot of tiles. (*Enter* SCEPARNIO.) That's his slave who's just coming out. Before long the young man will get here, and you'll see him—I mean, of course, the one who bought the girl from the pimp.

Good-by, good luck—and put the fear of God into your enemies! (*Exit.*)

ACT ONE

SCENE I

SCEPARNIO: Ye gods! What a storm Neptune sent us last night! The wind took the roof right off the house—what am I saying? That was no wind; that was a "Tempest," by Euripides, the way it knocked all the tiles off the roof. Well, anyway, there's more light in the house, and we have some new skylights.

(*Enter* PLESIDIPPUS *from the left, and* DAEMONES *from his house.* PLESIDIPPUS *is accompanied by three officers of the law.*)

SCENE II

PLESIDIPPUS (*to officers*): Here I've taken you fellows away from your work, and we didn't get anywhere with the thing I wanted you to do—couldn't catch the pimp at the pier. But I didn't want to give up hope just because I'd been too slow; that's why I kept you so long, my friends. Now I'm going over here and stop in at Venus' temple, where he told me he was going to pay his votive offering.

SCEPARNIO (*aside*): If I were smart, I'd—oh, my aching back! —I'd get to work mixing up this clay.

PLESIDIPPUS: I hear somebody talking—can't be very far away.

DAEMONES: Hey, there, Sceparnio!

SCEPARNIO: Who's calling me?

DAEMONES: Just the man who paid his hard cash for you.

SCEPARNIO: Sounds as if you were calling me your slave, Daemones!

DAEMONES: We need lots of clay, so dig up plenty. I can see we're going to have to put a whole new roof on the house; it has more holes in it than a sieve.

PLESIDIPPUS (*to* DAEMONES): Good morning, sir—in fact, good morning to both of you. (*Shakes hands warmly with* DAEMONES)

DAEMONES: How do you do?

SCEPARNIO (*to* PLESIDIPPUS): Say, are you male or female— Greeting him as if he were your own father?

PLESIDIPPUS: Why, I'm a man, of course.

SCEPARNIO: Well, listen, Mr. "Man," go look for a father somewhere else.

DAEMONES: You see, I had a little daughter, just the one, and I lost her. I never had any boys.

PLESIDIPPUS: Maybe you will yet. I hope so.

SCEPARNIO: And I hope you'll fall and break your neck yet, whoever you are—you and your talk! Can't you see we're busy?

PLESIDIPPUS (*pointing to the cottage*): Is that where you live?

SCEPARNIO: Why are you asking that? Getting the lay of the land, so you can come back later and rob us?

PLESIDIPPUS (*to* DAEMONES, *angrily*): You must think a lot of that slave; right in front of his master, talking that way to a free man. Manners!

SCEPARNIO: Must think a lot of himself, and have few manners himself, anybody who would come up to a stranger's house and make a nuisance of himself when he had no right to.

DAEMONES: That'll do, Sceparnio. (*To* PLESIDIPPUS) What can I do for you, my boy?

PLESIDIPPUS (*still angrily*): You've had some bad luck, there —slave who interrupts when his master's present. But if you don't mind, I'd like to ask you a question or two.

DAEMONES: Certainly, certainly; no trouble at all.

SCEPARNIO (*to* DAEMONES): Why don't you go over to the swamp and cut some reeds so we can thatch the house, while the weather's good?

DAEMONES: Quiet! (*To* PLESIDIPPUS) If there's anything you need, please let me know.

PLESIDIPPUS: I'm trying to find out—can you tell me?—have you seen a fellow with curly, gray hair, a criminal type, the kind you wouldn't trust, a smooth operator—?

DAEMONES: Oh, I've seen lots of those. It's because of people like them that I'm so poor.

PLESIDIPPUS: No, I mean right here. He would have had a couple of pretty girls with him, and he'd have been all dressed up to go to the temple. It would have been this morning or last night.

DAEMONES: Why, no, my boy. It's been quite a few days since I've seen anybody going to prayers at the temple, and they can't go without my knowing it; they're always coming over here for water, or fire, or a couple of pitchers, or a knife, or a spit, or a pan for the sacrificial meat, or something—you know how it is. Sometimes I think I furnished my kitchen and dug my well for Venus, not for myself. But I've been free of that sort of thing for a good many days.

PLESIDIPPUS: From what you say there, I've had a piece of very bad luck.

DAEMONES: I hope not. I'd much rather bring you good luck.

SCEPARNIO: Look, my friend: Are you one of those people who go around to the temples looking for a handout? You had better go home and get your dinner there.

DAEMONES: Is that what it is? Were you invited to a feast here, and the man who invited you didn't show up?

PLESIDIPPUS: That's right.

SCEPARNIO: There's no chance of your going home anything but hungry from here. You'd better go to Ceres' temple, not to Venus'. Venus' business is love; it's Ceres who takes care of the bakery.

PLESIDIPPUS: The man has made a fool of me! An utter fool!

DAEMONES: For heaven's sake! What's that over there, Sceparnio? Looks like some people down along the shore.

SCEPARNIO: They look to me as if they had made a trip and been invited to a homecoming dinner.

DAEMONES: What makes you think so?

SCEPARNIO: Well, it certainly looks as if they'd had a bath last night.

DAEMONES: Their ship is breaking up offshore there. They've been in a wreck.

SCEPARNIO: That's right. But we've been in one, too, here on land; look at our house and the roof.

DAEMONES: Oh, you poor, poor people! They've fallen overboard. See them swim!

PLESIDIPPUS: Where are these people, sir?

DAEMONES: Over this way, to the right—see? Right along the shore.

PLESIDIPPUS: Yes, I see. (*To officers*) Come with me. I hope it's the man I'm looking for, damn him! (*To* DAEMONES *and* SCEPARNIO) Excuse me. Good luck to you. (*Exit* PLESIDIPPUS.)

SCEPARNIO: If you hadn't said it, we'd have thought of it ourselves. But, O Palaemon, companion of Neptune, what's this I see?

DAEMONES: What do you see?

SCEPARNIO: Women! I see them sitting in a boat, all by themselves, two of them! Oh! Are they in a bad way, poor things! Good! Good! That's right! They just missed the reef. A big wave washed their boat away toward the shore! A professional pilot couldn't have done it better! I don't think I've ever seen higher waves. They'll be all right if they just don't get caught in the breakers. Now! Now's the bad part! Oh-oh! One of them got washed overboard! But it isn't deep there; she's swimming; she'll be all right. Good for her! See that one, Daemones? The breakers are washing her up. She got up; she's coming this way. She's safe. There's the other one, see; she's jumped out of the boat onto the shore. She must be scared to death; she can't stand up! She has fallen to her knees in the water. She's all right; she got out of the surf. She's on dry land now. But she's going off to the right, the wrong way. She's heading for trouble. Oh, my! She's got a long walk ahead of her!

DAEMONES: Why should you care?

SCEPARNIO: She's heading toward the bluff; if she falls down there, she'll cut her walk short, that's sure!

DAEMONES: Sceparnio, if those women are going to pay for your dinner tonight, I expect it's all right for you to worry about them, but if you're going to eat at my house, I'd like you to give me a little of your time.

SCEPARNIO: Fair enough.

DAEMONES: Come on along with me, then.

SCEPARNIO: Yes, sir. (*Exeunt.*)

Scene III

(*Enter* PALAESTRA. *As she speaks, she moves toward stage center.*)

PALAESTRA: When people talk about how hard life is, they don't know the half of it. Wait till they get into it and have a little of it firsthand; then they'll see how bitter it actually is. Was this really God's will? Look at my clothes! They're all I have. Where am I? What place is this? I'm so frightened! I've been marooned! Why was I ever born? Will I have to say it was for this? Is this what I get for trying as hard as I could to do what was right? It would be bad enough to get into such trouble if I'd done something wrong to my father or mother or to the gods. But I didn't! I always tried to keep from doing anything like that. So, dear gods, what you're doing to me here isn't right; it isn't fair; it just oughtn't to be! What sort of lesson is this going to be to bad people from now on, if this is the way you treat those who have done no wrong? Why, if I thought that I, or my mother or father, had broken some law, or something, I wouldn't feel so bad. I know! It's that master of mine! It's his dishonesty that is making trouble for me; that's why I'm having bad luck. He lost his ship and everything he owned in the ocean; I and what I'm wearing are all he has left; even the girl who was in the boat with me fell overboard. I'm all alone. If she'd just been saved, this wouldn't be nearly so hard to bear. She'd have helped me. But now what hope is there! What can I do? What can I even think of doing? Here I am, all alone, landed in a place where there's nobody. Over here are rocks; over there, breakers; not a single person coming my way. These clothes are all I have to my name. What will I eat? Where will I sleep? I don't know! What's the use of going on living? I don't even know where I am; I've never been here before. Oh, I wish somebody would come along and show me a road or a path out of this place! I don't know whether to go this way or that. I don't see anything around here that looks as if people lived there. I'm cold; I'm lost; I'm scared—that's all I know. Oh, my poor mother and father! You don't know anything about this; you don't have any idea what bad luck I've had. I was born free—really and truly free—but that's all the good it did me. I couldn't be any more a slave if I'd been born that way. They had me, I was their daughter, but they didn't get anything out of it, ever at all!

SCENE IV

(*Enter* AMPELISCA.)

AMPELISCA: Oh, what's the use! I can't think of anything better than just to lie down and die. I'm in such trouble! That's all I can think of: Trouble, trouble, trouble—it's enough to break your heart. In the end, what's the use of going on living? I always used to console myself by being hopeful, but where can I find any hope now? I've been running all over this place; I got down on my hands and knees and crept into every hole in the rocks, trying to find Palaestra. I called her, I looked for her, I listened for her, did everything I could to track her down. But I just can't find her anywhere, and I haven't the slightest idea where to go and look for her next. I suppose I could ask. Ask? Where's anybody to ask? I haven't run across a living soul. Talk about lonely desert sands—the Sahara itself isn't as lonely as this place. But no, no! I'm not going to stop. As long as I can draw a breath, I'm going to keep on looking for her. If she's still alive, I'll find her yet.

PALAESTRA: I hear somebody talking, and not very far away, either. Who is it?

AMPELISCA: O-o-oh! Oh, what's that? Somebody's voice—not very far off, either! Who is it?

PALAESTRA: Holy goddess of hope, help me!

AMPELISCA: Don't tell me my fears are over?

PALAESTRA: Wasn't that a woman's voice? I'm sure that's what I heard.

AMPELISCA: It's a woman! That was a woman's voice I heard.

PALAESTRA: You don't suppose—is it?—oh, it isn't Ampelisca?

AMPELISCA: Palaestra—is that you, Palaestra?

PALAESTRA: Why don't I try calling her? Maybe she'll hear me. Ampelisca! Ampelisca!

AMPELISCA: Yes! Who is it?

PALAESTRA: It's Palaestra!

AMPELISCA: Well, where are you?

PALAESTRA: Where am I? Oh, it's just awful, awful!

AMPELISCA: Well, that makes two of us. It's pretty awful over here, too. I wish I could see where you are.

PALAESTRA: So do I!

AMPELISCA: Let's keep calling and follow the sounds of our voices. Where are you?

PALAESTRA: Right here! Come over this way, toward me. Come on!

AMPELISCA: I'm coming! I'm coming! (*They meet, stage center.*)

PALAESTRA (*throws arms around* AMPELISCA): Hold me tight!

AMPELISCA: Yes, yes, darling!

PALAESTRA: Tell me; are you all right? Are you?

AMPELISCA: Yes—yes, I think maybe I could go on living, now that I've got you again. I can hardly believe that it's really you! Oh, darling, keep your arms around me! Honey, I do depend on you so! Why, you make me feel as if all my troubles were over!

PALAESTRA: You took the words right out of my mouth! Now I think we'd better get out of here, don't you?

AMPELISCA: Get out of here? Where, dear?

PALAESTRA: Let's go along the beach this way. (*Starts off, right*)

AMPELISCA: Anywhere you like. I'm with you. But we're so wet! Are we going to go gallivanting around here in wet clothes?

PALAESTRA: I guess we'll have to. There's nothing we can do about it, is there? But look! What's this, for heaven's sake?

AMPELISCA: What's what?

PALAESTRA: Don't you see, dear? There's a little temple here!

AMPELISCA: Where?

PALAESTRA: Over here to the right.

AMPELISCA: Oh, yes, I see. It does look like some sort of shrine.

PALAESTRA: There must be people not too far away. See how nice and neat the place is? I wonder what god it is? Please, dear god, whoever you are, save us! We've had such a hard time! We're scared! We've lost everything! We're cold and miserable! Please help us somehow.

SCENE V

(Enter PTOLEMOCRATIA.)

PTOLEMOCRATIA: Who's saying prayers to my Lady? I heard somebody praying, and so I came out. She's a good, kind goddess, and generous, too, my Lady is. That's what everybody says. She's glad to help.

PALAESTRA: Good morning, Mother.

PTOLEMOCRATIA: Good morning, girls. Why! Your clothes are soaking wet! Where have you been? You *are* in a bad way!

PALAESTRA: Why, we just now came along here from a little way back there. But that's not where we started. We'd made quite a trip before we got there.

PTOLEMOCRATIA: Oh, I see. You "rode the wooden steed over the blue, blue deep"—is that it?

PALAESTRA: That's right.

PTOLEMOCRATIA: Well, you know, girls, you should have put on clean clothes before you came here. And you didn't bring any offering, did you? People don't usually come to the temple looking the way you do.

PALAESTRA: But Mother, we were shipwrecked! We just managed to get ashore, both of us! You surely wouldn't expect us to bring an offering, would you? Where would we get one? Look, Mother; we're on our knees! We're absolutely helpless! We don't know where we are; we don't know what's going to happen next. Please let us come in, and let us stay with you. We've been through such a lot, the two of us. Please be kind, won't you? We haven't any place to go; we don't know what's going to happen to us. We have absolutely nothing except these clothes you see us wearing.

PTOLEMOCRATIA: Give me your hands, girls. Get up now, both of you. I'm just a softhearted old woman—nobody more so. But I can't offer you much, you know; this is a pretty poor sort of place. I hardly make enough to keep body and soul together. Half the time my own lunch money goes for the sacrifices to Venus.

AMPELISCA: Oh! Is this a temple of Venus?

PTOLEMOCRATIA: Yes, it is. I'm the regular priestess here. I haven't much, but whatever I have you're welcome to, as far as it will go. Come on in with me.

PALAESTRA: You're so kind and friendly, Mother. We do appreciate it.

PTOLEMOCRATIA: It's no more than my duty. (*Exeunt.*)

ACT TWO

SCENE I

(*Enter a troop of fishermen.*)

FISHERMAN: Any way you look at it, a poor man has a rough time in this world, especially if he hasn't any business of his own and hasn't learned any trade; he just has to get along with whatever he's got. As for us fellows, take a look at our outfits and you'll know how rich we are; these hooks and rods are our tools and our trade. Every day we leave home and go down to the shore to look for something to eat; this is the only school we ever go to and this is the only sport we ever get. We look for sea urchins, limpets, oysters, winkles, and clams, jellyfish, mussels, scallops. After that we try fishing with hook and line from the rocks. What food we get comes out of the water; sometimes the outcome just doesn't come out, and we don't catch any fish at all. All we get is a good salt-water bath; we sneak home the back way and go to bed without any dinner. And with the sea running high the way it is today, we don't feel too hopeful. Unless we can dig up a clam or two, it's no dinner for us, that's sure. Well, let's say a prayer to Venus over here; let's ask her to be kind and help us out today.

Scene II

(Enter Trachalio.*)*

Trachalio: That's funny! I've been awfully careful not to miss master on my way here. When he left the house, he said he was going to the waterfront, and he told me to come out here and meet him at the temple of Venus. Oh, good! Look! I see some people to ask. I'll just go over. Good morning, gentlemen! I believe I'm addressing the Honorable Society of Beachcombers, Sons of the Clam and the Cod? Strictly hungry, aren't you, boys? How're you doing? The starving pretty good?

Fisherman: Yes, about as you'd expect, for fishermen. We're hungry, we're thirsty, and we've had no luck.

Trachalio: You've been here for a while, haven't you? Well, tell me: You didn't see a young fellow coming this way, did you? He'd have looked as if he were in a hurry, a bit red in the face—good-looking boy—and he'd have had three big louts with him, officers, armed.

Fisherman: Nobody like that has come along here, as far as we know.

Trachalio: What about an old rounder, bald, with just a fringe of hair around his head, about ordinary size, potbellied, bushy eyebrows, disagreeable, sneaky, bad-tempered, foul-tongued—a thorough criminal type. He'd have had a couple of very attractive girls with him.

FISHERMAN: Any man with all those virtues and good works ought to be heading for jail instead of for Venus' temple.

TRACHALIO: I know, I know. But tell me if you saw him.

FISHERMAN: Not here; nobody like that has come here. Got to get along now. (*Exeunt fishermen.*)

TRACHALIO: Thanks. Good luck to you. It's turned out just the way I thought it would. That pimp pulled a fast one on master; he's skipped the country, damn him! Got on a boat, took his girls with him. That makes me a prophet! And to top it off, he invites master to a feast out here—he really thinks them up, he does! Well, I guess the best thing to do now is to wait right here until master comes. Besides, there's the priestess of Venus, here; she might know something more about this. If I see her, I'll ask her; she'll be able to tell me.

SCENE III

(*Enter* AMPELISCA, *carrying a pitcher, from temple.*)

AMPELISCA: I know; there's a house right next door to the temple, and you told me to go knock on the door and ask for some water.

TRACHALIO: Who's that? Somebody's "winged words" just came to my ears!

AMPELISCA: Well, for heaven's sake! Who's that? I heard somebody talking!

TRACHALIO: Who's that I see? Is that Ampelisca coming out of the temple?

AMPELISCA: Is that Trachalio I see there—Plesidippus' valet?

TRACHALIO: It's Ampelisca all right!

AMPELISCA: Yes, it's Trachalio! Hello, Trachalio!

TRACHALIO: Hello to you, Ampelisca! How are you?

AMPELISCA: How? Well, I'm young, but I'm not happy.

TRACHALIO: Oh, don't say things like that.

AMPELISCA: It's the truth, isn't it? Anybody with any sense likes to hear the truth and to tell it. But where's Plesidippus, your master?

TRACHALIO: Ha-ha-ha! Now that's a good one! As if he wasn't in there! (*Points to temple*)

AMPELISCA: Why, he is not. He hasn't been this way at all.

TRACHALIO: He hasn't?

AMPELISCA: That's God's truth you're telling.

TRACHALIO: Not my habit, is it, Ampelisca? But say, how soon will the feast be ready?

AMPELISCA: Feast? What feast do you mean?

TRACHALIO: Well, you've all been saying prayers and making offerings here, haven't you?

AMPELISCA: Are you dreaming? What are you talking about?

TRACHALIO: Now, look here; I know perfectly well that Labrax invited Plesidippus to a postsacrifice feast here, your master, my master.

AMPELISCA: Oh, now I see! I'm not a bit surprised at what you say. Cheated the gods and his friends, too, did he? Well, what do you expect of a pimp?

TRACHALIO: You mean you and your master haven't been making an offering here?

AMPELISCA: Are you crazy?

TRACHALIO: Then what are you doing here?

AMPELISCA: We were in trouble; we were scared to death; we were almost killed! We hadn't any way of getting help, and we didn't have a penny to our names! Just the same, the priestess of Venus here took us in—Palaestra and me.

TRACHALIO: What? Is master's girl, Palaestra, here?

AMPELISCA: She certainly is.

TRACHALIO: Now that's news to make a man happy, Ampelisca. But you said something about almost being killed. What happened to you two? Won't you tell me?

AMPELISCA: Oh, Trachalio! We were shipwrecked last night.

TRACHALIO: Shipwrecked? What? What's this you're telling me?

AMPELISCA: You mean to say you haven't heard? Why, the pimp was trying to sneak off and take us to Sicily! He'd loaded everything he owned on a ship. And now he's lost absolutely everything!

TRACHALIO: Good work, Neptune! Good for you! There isn't anybody rolls the bones better than you! That was a very neat throw! You threw that old sinner for a total loss. But where's old pimp Labrax now?

AMPELISCA: Dead, I guess. He had one drink too many. Neptune invited him in last night and really set them up.

TRACHALIO: Yes, and I'll bet he had to drink the "bottoms up"! Oh, Ampelisca, how I love you! You're such a sweetheart! You say the nicest things! But how did you and Palaestra get out of the wreck?

AMPELISCA: Hold on and you'll find out. We were afraid, so we both jumped off the deck together, into the lifeboat; we could see that the ship was being washed toward the reef. I hurried and untied the rope, while the crew just stood there and shook in their boots. The wind blew us and our boat away from them, off to the right. What with the wind and the waves we took a terrible beating—it was really awful!—all night long. Finally this morning the wind brought us in to shore; we were alive, and that was about all.

TRACHALIO: I see. Yes, that's old Neptune for you; he's a very fussy inspector. If there are any spoiled goods around, he tosses them out, every time!

AMPELISCA: Why, you . . . ! I hope you . . . !

TRACHALIO: You hope I what, Ampelisca? No, no. I knew the pimp was going to do just what he did; I said so again and again. I think I ought to grow long hair and a beard and go into business as the Seer of the East.

AMPELISCA: Is that why you and your master saw to it that the pimp didn't get away, since you knew all about it?

TRACHALIO: But what could my master have done?

AMPELISCA: You say he was in love with Palaestra, and you ask what he could have done? He could have kept an eye on the pimp night and day; he could have been on guard all the time. Well, it's easy to see just how much he cared about her; the trouble he took shows that—your fine Plesidippus!

TRACHALIO: Now why do you say things like that?

AMPELISCA: Well, it's obvious, isn't it?

TRACHALIO: You think so, do you? Why, look; when a man goes to the baths for a scrub, no matter how carefully he watches his clothes, they still get stolen. There are a lot of people bathing, and he watches the wrong one! The thief can tell whom to watch, but the one that's watching doesn't know who is the thief! Well, never mind! Where's Palaestra? Take me to her.

AMPELISCA: Just go right into the temple. She's in there. You'll find her resting—and crying her eyes out.

TRACHALIO: Crying? I'm sorry to hear that. What's she crying about?

AMPELISCA: You really want to know? Well, she's all heartbroken because the pimp took the little jewel box in which she kept the things she hoped would help her find her parents. She is afraid it's gone for good.

TRACHALIO: Where was the box?

AMPELISCA: Same place we were—on the ship. The pimp locked it up in his chest, so she wouldn't have any way of tracing her parents.

TRACHALIO: That was a dirty trick! Wanting to keep her in slavery when she has every right to be free!

AMPELISCA: Well, in any case the little box is gone now— went down with the ship. And all the pimp's money went right with it, too.

TRACHALIO: Perhaps somebody dived down and brought it up again.

AMPELISCA: Poor girl, she's all upset because she's lost her things.

TRACHALIO: All the more reason why I'd better go in and try to comfort her. Mustn't let her go all to pieces over it. Lots of times good luck comes when we least expect it, I'm sure of that.

AMPELISCA: Yes, and lots of people get their hopes up for nothing, too; I'm sure of that.

TRACHALIO: Well, she'd better keep her chin up; that's the best medicine for bad luck. I'll go in, unless you want me for something else.

AMPELISCA: No, go on. The priestess asked me to do an errand, so I'll do it. I'm to ask the people next door for some water. She told me they'd be glad to give it to me if I told them it was for her. (*Exit* TRACHALIO.) I don't think I've ever seen a nicer old lady; I think she deserves any help people can give her and any blessing she gets—nobody more. She was so kind; she was a real lady! She was very decent and not the least bit annoyed! Here we were, scared, not a penny to our names, wet, bedraggled, not more than half alive, but she took us in. She couldn't have done more if we'd been her own daughters. She tucked up her habit and heated water herself, so we could get cleaned up. I mustn't keep her waiting. I'll go get the water where she told me to. (*She knocks on* DAE-MONES' *door*.) Hello! Anybody home? Anybody open up? Anybody coming?

SCENE IV

(*Enter* SCEPARNIO.)

SCEPARNIO: What's all the hurry? What are you trying to do, knock the door down? Who is it?

AMPELISCA: It's just me.

SCEPARNIO: Oho! Here's something real nice! Mm—hmm! My! A pretty, pretty lady!

AMPELISCA: How do you do?

SCEPARNIO: How do you do—and many of them, you cute little thing!

AMPELISCA: May I come in?

SCEPARNIO: I'll make you feel right at home, if you'll come back a little later—this evening, maybe? Come just the way you are. Right now I haven't anything to pay you tomorrow morning. How about it? Cutie! Sweetie!

AMPELISCA: Here, here! Aren't you getting a bit ahead of yourself? Keep your hands off!

SCEPARNIO: Great gods! It's the statue of Venus come alive!

Those eyes; they really sparkle! What a figure! What breasts! What a kiss there'd be in those lips!

AMPELISCA: I'm no free-lunch counter. Keep your hands off me, will you?

SCEPARNIO: Can't I just—like this?—gently? You pretty thing! One pretty little pat?

AMPELISCA: Look, I'm busy now. When I've got time, I'll play games with you. Please! I was sent here for something. Are you going to give it to me, or not?

SCEPARNIO: What do you want?

AMPELISCA: You see what I've got here, don't you? Anybody with any sense would know from that what I want.

SCEPARNIO: You see what I've got, too, don't you? Anybody with any sense would know from that what *I* want!

AMPELISCA: The Queen of Hearts over here told me to ask you for some water for her.

SCEPARNIO: Yes, but I'm the King of Spades. You have to ask me pretty-please, or you don't get a drop. It's our well; we ran the risks; it was our tools we used; we dug it! Be nice now—or not a drop do you get!

AMPELISCA: Why do you object to giving me a little water? People do that much for an enemy!

SCEPARNIO: Why do you object to giving me a little—job? People do that much for a friend!

AMPELISCA: What! Object? Why, honey, you name it; I'll do it.

SCEPARNIO: Wonderful! I'm all set! She called me "honey"! You'll get your water. Wouldn't want you to think I didn't appreciate it when you're nice to me. Let's have your pitcher.

AMPELISCA: Here you are. Bring it quickly, will you, please?

SCEPARNIO: You just wait; I'll be right back . . . "honey"!

(*Exit* SCEPARNIO.)

AMPELISCA: How am I going to explain to the priestess why it took me so long here? (*Turns right, toward temple*) Oh, I still get a chill every time I lay eyes on those waves. But, oh, dear! What's that I see, way down the beach? It's my master,

the pimp, and that friend of his from Sicily. And here I was
thinking they'd both drowned. We're in for more trouble than
we'd thought. But what am I waiting for? I'd better go in the
temple and tell Palaestra about this, so we can get safe on
the altar before that pimp gets here and catches us. I'd better
hurry and get out of here, the way things are going! (*Exit*
AMPELISCA.)

SCENE V

(*Enter* SCEPARNIO.)

SCEPARNIO: Ye gods! I never thought I could get so much
pleasure out of plain water! I really enjoyed drawing this! The
well seemed a lot less deep than it used to. Hauling this up
was no work at all, if I do say it as shouldn't. Mustn't push my
luck too far, what with falling in love and all today. Here, my
pretty baby; here's your water. See, here's how I want you to
carry it, real nice, just like me, so I can see how pretty you are.
Say, where are you, darling? Come and get your water, will
you, please? Where are you? You know, I think she really
likes me! She's hiding, the little monkey! Where are you?
Here's your pitcher; aren't you going to come and get it?
Where are you? Better come and get it while the getting's
good! Hey, now, seriously, are you going to come and get this
pitcher? Where the devil are you? Well, by heaven, I don't
see her anywhere. She's making me look silly. So help me, I'm
going to put her old pitcher right down in the middle of the
road. But wait a minute; what if somebody walked off with
it, a pitcher that's temple property? That would get me in
trouble. I'm afraid that female is fixing things so I'll get
caught with a pitcher that's temple property. That's right; if
any judge saw me with this on my hands he'd slap me in irons
and string me up, and nobody would say "boo." It's marked
"Property of the Temple of Venus"; really sings out whose it
is, all by itself. Yes, sir, I'm going to call that priestess out
here to come and get her pitcher. I'll go knock on the door.
Hello! Hey, Mother Ptolemocratia, come and take your

pitcher. Some woman brought it over to our house. Well, I'll have to take it in! What a nuisance! Even have to carry the water over to them now, I guess. (*Exit* SCEPARNIO, *into temple.*)

SCENE VI

(*Enter* LABRAX *and* CHARMIDES.)

LABRAX: You want to get yourself good and sick and broke? Just turn yourself over to Neptune. If anybody gets mixed up with him in any kind of deal, he really fixes him up and sends him home, just like me. Yes sir, Liberty, you're a smart one; you wouldn't set foot on a ship with Hercules! But where's that pal of mine who got me into this mess? Ya-a-h, here he comes, taking his time.

CHARMIDES: Where the devil are you going in such a hurry, Labrax? I can't keep up with you. What's the rush?

LABRAX: I wish I'd never laid eyes on you! I wish you had died a painful death before you ever left Sicily. It's all your fault that I ran into this bad luck.

CHARMIDES: Well, I wish I'd got myself a room in the jail, the day I let you take me to your house. I pray the gods that from now on, for the rest of your life, everybody you take in is just like you.

LABRAX: I took in Lady Bad Luck herself, the day I brought you home. Damn you, anyway! Why did I listen to you? Why did I leave home? Why did I ever get on that boat? I lost everything I ever had, and then some, there.

CHARMIDES: Well, it doesn't surprise me that the boat was wrecked, what with you, you dirty crook, and your ill-gotten gains on board.

LABRAX: You and your bright ideas! You surely sent me to the bottom.

CHARMIDES: You and your dinners! What they gave to Thyestes or Tereus wasn't as bad as what I got at your house.

LABRAX: O-o-oh! I'm going to be sick! Hold my head, will you, please?

CHARMIDES: Ya-a-h! I hope you puke your guts out.

LABRAX: Oh, God! Palaestra, Ampelisca, where are you now?

CHARMIDES: Probably on the bottom, feeding the fishes.

LABRAX: You did it! You made me lose every penny I had. That's what I get for listening to you and your big talk—a pack of lies.

CHARMIDES: If you want to do what's right, you'll be grateful to me. You were completely tasteless but you're good and salty now—and I'm the man who did it.

LABRAX: Get out of here, will you? Go get lost!

CHARMIDES: Go yourself! Just what I was going to suggest.

LABRAX: Oh, God! I bet there's nobody in the world feels worse than I do.

CHARMIDES: Oh, yes there is, Labrax. I do—lots worse.

LABRAX: Why?

CHARMIDES: Because I don't deserve to feel like this, and you do.

LABRAX: Oh, you lucky thatch! I'd like to change places with you! You keep so gloriously dry!

CHARMIDES: Well, I'm practicing being a chatterbox. Every time I open my mouth I let go with some really smart chatter.

LABRAX: Oh, you Neptune! You run a cold, cold bath! After a trip to your establishment, I'm freezing even with my clothes on!

CHARMIDES: Yes, he doesn't even have a hot-drink counter. The only drinks he serves are salty and cold.

LABRAX: Blacksmiths are the lucky ones; they get to sit by a fire—always nice and hot!

CHARMIDES: I'd like to change places with a duck; then even after I'd been in the water, I'd be dry.

LABRAX: How would it be if I hired out to play the part of the big bad wolf?

CHARMIDES: What do you mean?

LABRAX: Why, I make such a racket with my teeth!

CHARMIDES: I guess I really deserve the ducking I got.

LABRAX: Why?

CHARMIDES: Because I didn't have any better sense than to

get on board a ship with you. You sure stirred up the waves for me.

LABRAX: It was your idea! You kept telling me there was all kinds of money to be made in girls in Sicily. You kept saying I'd rake in the cash there.

CHARMIDES: Look, you dirty devil; what did you think you were going to do—swallow Sicily whole?

LABRAX: Swallow? Oh, what whale has gone and swallowed my chest, with every penny I owned packed in it?

CHARMIDES: Probably the same whale that swallowed my wallet. It was full of money—had it in my bag.

LABRAX: Look at me! All I've got left is this one tunic and this miserable coat. I'm through, I tell you.

CHARMIDES: You can say that for me, too. We're tied.

LABRAX: If at least I still had my girls, it wouldn't seem so hopeless. Suppose Plesidippus catches up with me now! I took his down payment for Palaestra. Will he ever give me a rough time!

CHARMIDES: What are you crying about, stupid? You can still waggle that tongue of yours, and that's enough to get you out of anything.

SCENE VII

(*Enter* SCEPARNIO.)

SCEPARNIO: What's all this fuss, anyway? These two girls here in the temple, hanging onto the statue of Venus, crying their eyes out—scared of somebody, I guess. They certainly aren't happy. They say they rode out the storm last night and got washed up on shore here this morning.

LABRAX: Hey! Say, young man, where are these girls you're talking about?

SCEPARNIO: Right here—in the temple of Venus.

LABRAX: How many of them are there?

SCEPARNIO: Add you and me up; that's how many.

LABRAX: You're sure they're my girls?

SCEPARNIO: I'm sure I don't know.

LABRAX: What do they look like?

SCEPARNIO: Real cute. I wouldn't mind making love to either one of them—if I was good and drunk.

LABRAX: You're sure they're girls?

SCEPARNIO: I'm sure you make me tired. Go on, have a look, if you want to.

LABRAX: My girls must be in here, Charmides.

CHARMIDES: Oh, Jupiter damn you, if they are there or they aren't—either way!

LABRAX: I'm going to break right into that temple! (*Exit* LABRAX.)

CHARMIDES: It would suit me better if you'd break right into your grave. Say, stranger, can you tell me where I could find a place to sleep?

SCEPARNIO: Go to sleep right where you are, any place you like. Nobody's stopping you. It's a free country.

CHARMIDES: Yes, but look at me; my clothes are sopping wet. How about taking me to your house and lending me some clothes till mine dry out? I'll find some way to make it right with you.

SCEPARNIO: Well, here is my poncho; it's the only thing I have that's dry. You can have that, if you want. When it rains I always have a coat to wear and a roof to get under, all in one piece. Here, give me your clothes; I'll dry them for you.

CHARMIDES: What's the matter? Aren't you satisfied that I got cleaned out in the ocean? Are you going to clean me out here on land, too?

SCEPARNIO: I wouldn't give a hoot whether you get cleaned out or cleaned up. All I know is I wouldn't trust you with anything unless you had some security to give. Go on and sweat, or die of the cold, or get sick, or get—out. I don't like foreigners, anyway—don't want them around the house. The case is closed—period. (*Exit* SCEPARNIO.)

CHARMIDES: Wait a minute, will you? He's a slave driver, whoever he is—no sympathy at all. But what am I standing around here for? Doing me no good, wet like this and all. Why don't I go on into the temple here and sleep off my hangover? Drank too much—a lot more than I wanted. You'd think we were bottles of Greek wine, the way Neptune poured the sea water into us. Guess he thought he'd turn our bellies inside out by salting our drinks. A-a-h, why talk about it? If he'd set us up a few more, we'd have passed out cold, right there. As it is, he let us go home alive—but just. I'm going in now and see what the pimp's up to in there—my pal! (*Exit* CHARMIDES.)

ACT THREE

SCENE I

(*Enter* DAEMONES.)

DAEMONES: The gods play tricks on us men in the strangest ways! When we're asleep they send us the oddest dreams—won't even let a man rest when he's sleeping. Take me, for instance; just last night I had an awfully strange dream. There was this swallow's nest, and a monkey was trying to climb up to it [. . .] * but it couldn't get them out of it. Then it came over to where I was, this monkey, and asked me to lend it a ladder. I answered the monkey like this [. . .]: * I said that swallows were the daughters of Philomela and Procne, and I told the monkey not to go hurting creatures who came from Athens, just like me. Then the monkey started to get very ugly and threatened to make trouble for me—he was going to have me arrested. Somehow, that made me really furious; I grabbed the monkey by the middle and chained him up, the nasty beast. I've been trying all day, but I haven't been able to figure out what this dream is supposed to mean. (*Shouts and screams from within temple*) But what's all the noise? It's coming from next door, from the temple of Venus! What in the world!

* The Latin text has lacunae at these points.

Scene II

(Enter TRACHALIO.*)*

TRACHALIO: Hey, everybody! For heaven's sake! Anybody who lives anywhere around here, help, help! We can't stop this alone! It's the worst thing I ever saw; help me break it up! Show everybody that criminals don't have more influence around here than respectable people who've never tried to win fame by breaking the law. Make an example of lawlessness! Reward decency! Prove that it's the law, not force, that runs things here. Hurry, hurry! Come to Venus' temple, please, please! If there's anybody nearby who can hear me shouting, help, help! Some people here have turned themselves over to Venus and her priestess—you know the custom, we've had it for years—they have asylum; help them, will you? A wrong is on the way; wring its neck before it gets to you!

DAEMONES: What's the trouble here?

TRACHALIO: Look! I'm on my knees! I beg you, sir, whoever you are—

DAEMONES: For heaven's sake, get up off your knees and explain what all the yelling's about.

TRACHALIO: I beg you, I beseech you, sir, if you hope to have a good crop this year, and hope to get it safe and sound to market, and hope to—hope to—not catch a single cold—

DAEMONES: Are you out of your mind?

TRACHALIO: —and hope to have a fine stand of stubble, please, sir, don't turn me down! Help me in the way I ask.

DAEMONES: Well, I beg and beseech you, by your legs and heels and back, as you hope that the cat-o'-nine-tails will have the biggest litter on record, and that you'll reap a rich crop of beatings this year, tell me what the trouble is that you're yelling about.

TRACHALIO: Now, was that nice? I didn't wish you anything but good luck.

DAEMONES: It was nice enough. I was only asking that you get what you deserve.

TRACHALIO: Please, will you come over here, then?

DAEMONES: What's the trouble?

TRACHALIO: There are two women in here, perfectly innocent. They need your help. It's just a crying shame the way
they're being treated—and it's still going on, too—right in the
temple of Venus. And as if that wasn't enough, the priestess
herself is getting pushed around, too.

DAEMONES: Who has had the colossal nerve to touch a
priestess? Those women—who are they? What's being done to
them?

TRACHALIO: If you'll give me a chance, I'll tell you. They
had grabbed hold of the statue of Venus, and now this fellow
has the nerve to try to drag them away from it. By rights, they
ought to be free women, both of them.

DAEMONES: Who is this fellow who has no more respect for
the gods than that?

TRACHALIO: I'll tell you who he is. He's a cheater, he's a
crook, he's a murderer, he's a liar—absolutely the worst there
is. He's a lawbreaker without a conscience, he's filthy, absolutely shameless—to put it in one word, he's a pimp. Need I
say more?

DAEMONES: Well, from what you say, the fellow might ap-
propriately be presented with some bad luck.

TRACHALIO: You know what he did? Tried to choke the
priestess!

DAEMONES: He did, did he? He'll pay for that, by heaven.
Turbalio, Sparax! Come out here! Where are you? (*Enter*
TURBALIO *and* SPARAX *from* DAEMONES' *house.*)

TRACHALIO (*to* DAEMONES): Please go in and help them.

DAEMONES (*to* TURBALIO *and* SPARAX): I'm not going to tell
you again. Come along here with me.

TRACHALIO: Come on, sir; tell them to squash his eyes out,
like a cook with a squid.

DAEMONES (*to* TURBALIO *and* SPARAX): Grab that man by
the feet and haul him out of there like a stuck pig.

(*Exeunt* DAEMONES, TURBALIO, *and* SPARAX.)

TRACHALIO: What a racket! I think the pimp is getting a
going-over. I hope they knock out every tooth in the fellow's

head. Oh, look! The girls are running out of the temple. They look scared.

Scene III

(Enter Palaestra *and* Ampelisca.*)*

Palaestra: Now we're really up against it. No influence, no money, nobody to help us, nobody to protect us—absolutely helpless, that's what we are. We're not safe here, and there's no place to go where we could be safe. We don't know which way to turn; we're so scared, both of us. We've had such bad luck, and our master was so cruel to us just now in there. Why, that awful man! He even knocked down the priestess, poor old lady, and pushed and pulled her around in perfectly terrible fashion. We had our arms around the image, and he dragged us off it with his own hands. Well, the way things look for us now, we'd be better off dead. Might as well be dead when you're in as bad a state as we are.

Trachalio: What's this? What kind of talk is that? I'd better hurry and see if I can't cheer them up. Palaestra, Palaestra!

Palaestra: Who's calling?

Trachalio: Ampelisca!

Ampelisca: Oh, dear, who's calling?

Palaestra: Who's calling my name?

Trachalio: If you'll look around, you'll find out.

Palaestra: Oh! You can help me; you're my only hope!

Trachalio: Never mind that. Keep your courage up. Leave it to me.

Palaestra: If there were just some way to keep him from using force on us—the thought's enough to make me use it on myself!

Trachalio: Oh, stop it. Don't be silly.

Palaestra: Don't try to talk me into feeling better. Unless you can give us some real protection, Trachalio, it's all over for us.

Ampelisca: I'll die before I'll let that pimp manhandle me.

Just the same, I'm only a woman, and when I think about death, I go cold all over. This is certainly not my lucky day.

TRACHALIO: Come on, cheer up!

PALAESTRA: Look; where am I going to find all this cheer?

TRACHALIO: Don't be afraid, I tell you. Come here and sit on the altar.

AMPELISCA: What good will your old altar be to us? Why, here in the temple we had our arms around the image of Venus, and he grabbed us and pulled us off it. Even that didn't help us!

TRACHALIO: Never mind. Just sit here. I'll protect you just the same. Call the altar your fort, and I'll stand here and guard the walls. Under Venus' protection I'll march out against that dirty pimp.

PALAESTRA: All right; just as you say. O Venus, we both of us pray to thee! Our arms are about thine altar; our eyes are full of tears; on our knees we beg thee, take us into thy protection; guard and keep us! Those awful men who showed so little respect for thy temple—punish them, and by thy good will let us sit safely upon thine altar here. We're all washed up—Neptune took care of that last night, so please don't be offended or hold it against us if we seem to fall a bit short, here and there, of that well-scrubbed look.

TRACHALIO: Venus, it seems to me that these girls are asking for nothing more than what's fair; surely it will be right to grant their requests. Please forgive them; they're frightened; that's why they're doing this. Men say that you were born of a sea shell; please don't scorn them just because they look a bit barnacled. But good! Look! Here comes the old gentleman who's been so kind to all of us.

SCENE IV

(*Enter* DAEMONES, SPARAX, *and* TURBALIO, *dragging* LABRAX *between them.*)

DAEMONES: Get out of the temple! Of all the blasphemous,

sacrilegious . . . ! You, girls, go sit on the altar . . . but where are they?

TRACHALIO: Right behind you, sir; look around.

DAEMONES: Good, good; that's just what I wanted. Now, let him try to get near them! (*To* LABRAX) Did you think you were going to get away with starting a riot against the gods right here in front of me? (LABRAX *tries to get loose.*) Punch him in the nose!

LABRAX: This is illegal, what you're doing to me. You'll pay for it!

DAEMONES: What? Is he threatening me? The insolence!

LABRAX: I've been deprived of my rights. You're taking my girls away without my consent.

TRACHALIO: Take your case to any judge of any standing here in Cyrene, any man of property, and see if you have any right to hold them, or if by rights they shouldn't be declared free women. See if the law doesn't demand that you be thrown into jail and stay there so long that you wear out your whole cell.

LABRAX: When I got up this morning, I never expected to have to talk to trash like you. (*To* DAEMONES) You're the man I'm talking to.

DAEMONES: Take it up with him first; he knows who you are.

LABRAX: No, sir; I'm putting my case to you.

TRACHALIO: Sorry! You're going to have to put it to me. Are these women your slaves?

LABRAX: They are.

TRACHALIO: All right, then; let's see you touch either one of them with just the tip of your little finger.

LABRAX: What will happen if I do?

TRACHALIO: Faster than I can say it, I'll make a punching bag out of you, hang you up, and pound the stuffing out of your dirty carcass.

LABRAX: You mean to say I'm not to be allowed to take my girls away from Venus' altar?

DAEMONES: That's right; that's the law here.

LABRAX: I've got nothing to do with your laws. I'm going to take the two of them out of here. Listen here, sir, if you want to go to bed with them, you just put the cold cash right here. As far as that's concerned, if Venus has taken a liking to them, let her have them, if she'll pay the price.

DAEMONES: What! The gods pay money to you? Now see here—here's how I feel, and let's not have any mistake about it: You make one move to lay a hand on those girls, even just in fun, the least little wee bit, and I'll give you such a dressing-down that you won't know yourself. (*To* SPARAX *and* TUR-BALIO) And you two, if you don't knock the eyes out of his head when I give you the word, I'll wrap a cat-o'-nine-tails right around your necks.

LABRAX: This is compulsion!

TRACHALIO: What? Are you talking about compulsion, you dirty lowlife?

LABRAX: Are you, you triple jailbird, daring to use strong language to me?

TRACHALIO: Very well! I'm a triple jailbird and you're a model citizen. What has that to do with the fact that these girls are entitled to their freedom?

LABRAX: Entitled to their freedom?

TRACHALIO: By rights they ought to own you. Yes, they're real Greek girls. Why, this one here (*indicating* PALAESTRA) was born at Athens of perfectly respectable people.

DAEMONES: What? What did you say?

TRACHALIO: Just that she was born at Athens—freeborn.

DAEMONES: You mean she comes from the same place I do?

TRACHALIO: Why, aren't you from Cyrene?

DAEMONES: No, no; I'm an Athenian—born, bred, and raised in Attica.

TRACHALIO: Well, for heaven's sake, then, sir, do what you can to protect these girls; they're from your own home town.

DAEMONES: Oh, daughter, daughter! When I look at this girl here, I keep thinking of you, lost away off somewhere.

It nearly breaks my heart. She was three years old when we lost her; if she's still alive, I'm sure she'd be just about her age and height.

LABRAX: Cash, see? Cash I paid for the two of them to the man that owned them. What's it to me whether they were born at Athens or at Thebes? All I ask is that they behave themselves and be good slaves.

TRACHALIO: Oh, is that so, you dirty . . . ! Who do you think you are, anyway? Official good-girl-grabber? You think you can kidnap children right from under their parents' noses and kill them off at your filthy trade? This other girl here (*indicating* AMPELISCA), I'm sure I don't know where she comes from, but I know one thing—she's better than you are, you dirty crook.

LABRAX: Look! Do those girls belong to you?

TRACHALIO: How about making a test to see who's more reliable, you or me? If you haven't got more cat-o'-nine-tail tracks on your back than a longship has nails, then I'm the world's biggest liar. Then, after we've seen your back, let's look at mine. If it isn't so clear that a wine-bottle maker would call it a grade-A hide for his purposes—absolutely, perfectly clear—then why shouldn't I take a stick and beat you to a pulp? Why are you looking at the girls? You touch them and I'll gouge your eyes out.

LABRAX: Is that so? Just because you say I can't, I'm going to take both of them away with me, both together, see? (*He starts off toward* DAEMONES' *house.*)

DAEMONES: What do you think you're going to do?

LABRAX: I'm going to get Vulcan; he and Venus are always fighting.

TRACHALIO: Where is he going?

LABRAX (*knocks on* DAEMONES' *door*): Hello, hello! Anybody home? Hello!

DAEMONES: You touch that door, and, by God, I'll take a pitchfork to your ugly . . . face!

TURBALIO: Ha-ha! We don't have any fire. We never eat anything but dried figs.

DAEMONES: I'll give you fire, all right, if I can set it on your head.

LABRAX: Very well! I'll go find fire somewhere else.

DAEMONES: What are you going to do with it when you've found it?

LABRAX: I'm going to build a nice, big bonfire, right here. (*Points to altar*)

DAEMONES: Why don't you try burning the heartlessness out of yourself?

LABRAX: No, no. See those two girls on the altar? My idea is to burn them alive, right there.

DAEMONES: By heaven, I'll grab you by the beard and throw you in the fire, and when you're nice and crisp around the edges, I'll toss you out for buzzard meat! Say! You know—when I come to think of it—why!—he's that monkey who tried to grab the baby swallows out of their nest, despite my trying to stop him—you know, what I dreamed about!

TRACHALIO: Could I ask you to do me a favor, sir? Would you keep an eye on the girls and see that they don't get hurt, until I can go and get my master?

DAEMONES: Yes. Go get him and bring him here.

TRACHALIO: But you watch that he doesn't . . .

DAEMONES: If he touches them or even starts to, he'll wish he hadn't!

TRACHALIO: Be careful, sir!

DAEMONES: I'll be careful, all right. Run along.

TRACHALIO: Watch that he doesn't get away from here, either. Master and I put up two thousand drachmas bail at the jail to produce him there today.

DAEMONES: Just run along. I'll take care of everything.

TRACHALIO: I'll be back right away. (*Exit* TRACHALIO.)

SCENE V

DAEMONES (*to* LABRAX): Listen, you, if you had your choice, would you rather take a beating, and then keep nice and quiet, or just plain keep nice and quiet?

LABRAX: I don't give a damn what you say, sir. Those girls are mine. Even if you and Venus and Jupiter in heaven don't like it, I'm going to take them by the hair and drag them down off that altar.

DAEMONES: Go ahead. Touch them.

LABRAX: I'll touch them, all right.

DAEMONES: All right. Just go ahead.

LABRAX: Well, tell those boys of yours to get away from there, then.

DAEMONES: Oh, no; they're going to stay right with you.

LABRAX: No, sir; I move they don't.

DAEMONES: What will you do if they stay even closer?

LABRAX: I'll—I'll—just step back a bit. All right, sir. If I ever catch you in town, don't ever call me pimp again if I don't send you home looking like a complete fool.

DAEMONES: Yes, you just do that. But right now, if you touch those girls, you'll be in a lot of trouble.

LABRAX: A lot? How much?

DAEMONES: Oh, about as much as a pimp ought to be in.

LABRAX: Talk, talk, talk! I don't give a damn what you say. You like it or you don't, I'm going to drag the two of them off.

DAEMONES: Go ahead. Touch them.

LABRAX: I'll touch them, all right.

DAEMONES: I'm sure you will. But do you know what happens then? Turbalio, get in the house and bring out two clubs—run!

LABRAX: Clubs?

DAEMONES: And good, tough ones, see? Hurry up, now. (*Exit* TURBALIO. *To* LABRAX) I'm going to give you a reception, just the kind you deserve.

LABRAX: Damn! I went and lost my helmet aboard the ship. It would be handy now, if I had it. Listen, can I at least speak to them?

DAEMONES: No, you can't. (*Re-enter* TURBALIO.) Ah! Good! Here comes our clubman. See?

LABRAX: O-o-oh! I can already hear a drumming in my ears!

DAEMONES: All right, now. Sparax, you take one club. All right. Sparax, you stand on this side of him; Turbalio, you stand over here. Stay right there. That's it. Now listen to me. If he so much as touches one of those girls with one finger without her permission, if you don't entertain him with those clubs so thoroughly that he won't know which way is home, I'll have your hides, both of you. If he speaks to anybody, you answer for them. If he tries to get away, you wrap those clubs right around his legs.

LABRAX: You mean they won't even let me leave here?

DAEMONES: You heard me. (*To* SPARAX *and* TURBALIO) And when the slave gets back here with his master—you know, the one that went after his master—you come right on home. Do what I tell you, please, and be very careful about it. (*Exit* DAEMONES.)

LABRAX: Well! You certainly change temples around here in a hurry! This was Venus', but now it's Hercules'. See, the old boy stuck two statues of him up here, clubs and all. By heaven, I can't see any way out of here for me now; looks awfully stormy to me, both by land and by sea. Palaestra!

SPARAX: What do you want?

LABRAX: Go on, something's wrong here! The Palaestra that answered then wasn't mine. Ampelisca!

TURBALIO: Watch out, or you'll get into trouble.

LABRAX: Doing the best they can, for a pair of idiots, to give me fair warning. (*To* SPARAX *and* TURBALIO) Say, you two; it won't do any harm for me to go a little closer to the girls, will it?

SPARAX: No—not to us.

LABRAX: Will it do any harm to me?

SPARAX: No—not if you watch your step.

LABRAX: What should I watch my step about?

SPARAX: Oh—a nice, big piece of bad luck!

LABRAX: Look, please, let me go home, boys.

SPARAX: Go ahead, if you want to.

LABRAX: Thanks, thanks a lot. I appreciate that. (*He starts off.* SPARAX *and* TURBALIO *raise their clubs.*) Uh—no. On second thought, I guess I'd better stay.

SPARAX: Yes. Stay right where you are.

LABRAX: Well, well! I've certainly had a bad break, any way you look at it. But I'm going to sit it out! I'll beat those girls yet!

SCENE VI

(*Enter* PLESIDIPPUS *and* TRACHALIO.)

PLESIDIPPUS: My girl, was it? And that pimp wanted to use force on her, did he? And drag her away from Venus' altar?

TRACHALIO: That's right.

PLESIDIPPUS: Why didn't you murder him, right then and there?

TRACHALIO: Didn't have a sword.

PLESIDIPPUS: You could have picked up a club or a rock.

TRACHALIO: What? I should throw rocks at a man, as if he were a dog, even if he is a dirty devil?

LABRAX: Now I'm in for it. Here comes Plesidippus. He'll wipe up the ground with me and throw me out with the rest of the trash.

PLESIDIPPUS: Were the girls still sitting on the altar when you left to come for me?

TRACHALIO: Yes, and they're sitting there yet.

PLESIDIPPUS: Who's taking care of them now?

TRACHALIO: Some old gentleman who lives next door to the temple. He was a great help to us. He and his slaves are keeping an eye on them now. I asked them to.

PLESIDIPPUS: Take me straight to that pimp. Where is he?

LABRAX: H-h-h-hello!

PLESIDIPPUS: I don't want your "hello's." (*He throws a rope around* LABRAX' *neck.*) Now, take your pick. See this rope around your neck? You want to be carried off or dragged off? Better take your choice while you have got the chance.

LABRAX: I choose neither.

PLESIDIPPUS: Listen, Trachalio. You go down the beach, and hurry. Tell those fellows to get on into town and meet me at the waterfront—you know, those fellows I brought out here with me to take this man to jail. Then get back here and stand guard. I'm going to haul this dirty devil into court—filthy foreigner! Go on! This way to jail! (*Exit* TRACHALIO.)

LABRAX: What did I do?

PLESIDIPPUS: What did you do? You took my money for the girl, didn't you, and then sneaked off with her?

LABRAX: I didn't get away with her.

PLESIDIPPUS: What do you mean, you "didn't get away with her"?

LABRAX: Well, I didn't. I only got off with her; I didn't get away with her. I told you I'd meet you here at Venus' temple, didn't I? So didn't I? Am I here, or not?

PLESIDIPPUS: Tell it to the judge. I've heard enough talk. Come on.

LABRAX: Charmides, Charmides! Help, for heaven's sake! They've got a rope around my neck, and they're dragging me off!

(*Enter* CHARMIDES *from temple.*)

CHARMIDES: Who's calling me?

LABRAX: Look! Don't you see? They're dragging me off!

CHARMIDES: Yes, I do see—and I'm enjoying every minute of it.

LABRAX: Aren't you going to help me?

CHARMIDES: Who is it that's got you?

LABRAX: Plesidippus.

CHARMIDES: Well, you found him—keep him. Might as well take it good-naturedly and go along quietly. You've got what lots of people spend their lives hoping for.

LABRAX: What's that?

CHARMIDES: That they'll get what's coming to them.

LABRAX (*grabs* CHARMIDES): Come along with me, please, Charmides.

CHARMIDES: That's just like you. You have to go to jail,

so you try and get me to go, too. Let go of me, will you? (*He pulls away.*)

LABRAX: Oh, I wish I were dead!

PLESIDIPPUS: So do I. Listen, Palaestra and Ampelisca, you stay right where you are till I get back.

SPARAX: Could I make a suggestion? Why don't they come over to our house instead, until you come?

PLESIDIPPUS: Good idea. Very kind of you.

LABRAX: You're robbing me!

SPARAX: What do you mean, "robbing"? Get him out of here!

LABRAX: Palaestra, listen, please, please!

PLESIDIPPUS: Come along, you old reprobate.

LABRAX (*to* CHARMIDES): My dear friend . . . !

CHARMIDES: I'm no "dear friend" of yours. You can just strike me off your list.

LABRAX: Are you going to turn me down like this?

CHARMIDES: Yes, I am. I had one drink with you—that's enough.

LABRAX: Oh, damn your soul! (*Exeunt* LABRAX *and* PLESIDIPPUS.)

CHARMIDES: Yours, you mean. You know, I think there's something in that old idea that men turn into different kinds of animals. The pimp, there—he's turning into a ringdove, for it won't be long before he'll have a ring around his neck. And he can make a nice little nest for himself in jail. Just the same, I'll go along and see if I can help him. If I put my mind to it, maybe I can get him behind bars a little sooner. (*Exit* CHARMIDES.)

ACT FOUR

SCENE I

(*Enter* DAEMONES.)

DAEMONES: Yes, sir, I'm glad I did it; I'm really happy that I helped those poor girls this morning. Just think: they're looking up to me as their protector—and they're a pair of pretty young things, too! But my wife—blast her!—she keeps her eye on me every minute; she isn't going to let me tip the wink at any young girls. (*He looks toward the sea.*)

I wonder what my slave, Gripus, is up to? He went down to the shore this morning before it was even light, to do some fishing. Hah! He'd have been a lot smarter if he'd stayed home in bed. He's wasting his time and probably ruining his net, the way the sea's running now, and has been all night. Anything he catches today I could hold in my fingers to toast. Just look at those waves! Oh—Oh! My wife's calling me to dinner. Well, here I go—and get an earful of her scolding!
(*Exit* DAEMONES.)

SCENE II

(*Enter* GRIPUS. *He carries his net over his shoulder; in it is a small brassbound chest. From the end of the net a long rope trails behind him on the ground.*)

GRIPUS: To Neptune, who liveth and reigneth in the salty realm of the fish, I give most humble and hearty thanks for his having sent me home richly laden from his domains.—Yes! Safe home again, with so much stuff I can hardly carry it! Little old boat got through safely, too. Some seas out there! But she really led me to it—a strange kind of fish, but worth plenty. That was a funny sort of fishing—never heard of anything like it. But it turned out very nicely! Didn't catch one measly little fish, either—except the one I have here in my net.

It was still pitch-dark when I got up—nobody can call me lazy! I'd rather turn an honest penny than sleep and take it easy. It was blowing a gale, but I went out, tried my best to help my master—he's a poor man—and to make being a slave a little easier for myself. Really put my back into it, I did. Lazy people are good for nothing; I can't stand them! A man has to get up in the morning if he wants to get his jobs done on time. He has no business waiting for his master to tell him what to do. Fellows who like to sleep and take it easy make no money—they just make trouble for themselves.

Take me, now. I wasn't lazy, so now I've got a way of being lazy if I feel like it. (*He takes the chest out of the net.*) I found this in the water, whatever's in it. (*He lifts it.*) Whatever it is, it's very heavy. I'll bet there's money in it—and nobody knows I have it, either. Now's your chance, Gripus, my boy! I know what I'll do; here's my plan: I'll go to master, but I'll be smart; I'll use my head. I'll offer him a little something for my freedom, and keep raising the offer, a little at a time, until he sets me free. Then, as soon as I'm free, I'll buy a farm and a house and some slaves. I'll get hold of some big cargo ships and go into the trading business. Even the rich men will call me rich! Then I'll have some fun. I'll build a yacht and go on a world tour—go to every city I can think of. Then when I get to be famous and everybody knows about me, I'll build a big city, and I'll call that city "Gripustown." It will be a monument to me and what I've done—why, it will be the start of a whole kingdom!

Me and my big ideas! Right now I'd better hide this chest. Millionaire, are you? Well, "Millionaire," time for dinner— red wine and salt mackerel—and no sauce.

SCENE III

(*Enter* TRACHALIO.)

TRACHALIO: Hey, there, wait a minute.
GRIPUS: Why should I?

TRACHALIO: You have a rope trailing here. Wait a minute; I'll coil it up for you.

GRIPUS: Let go of it, will you?

TRACHALIO: Why, no; I'm going to help you. It's never a waste of time to be helpful, you know.

GRIPUS: Look, friend, there was a big storm last night. I haven't got a single fish, so don't go looking for any. Don't you see; all I have is a wet net, and not a single scaly beast in it.

TRACHALIO: Oh, I don't want your fish; I just need to have a word with you.

GRIPUS: You're giving me a pain, whoever you are.

TRACHALIO: I'm not going to let you go. Wait!

GRIPUS: You better watch out! What's the idea of pulling me back?

TRACHALIO: Listen.

GRIPUS: I will not listen.

TRACHALIO: Oh, yes, you will—later on.

GRIPUS: Is that so? Well, what do you want?

TRACHALIO: I tell you now; what I've got to say is worth hearing.

GRIPUS: Tell me what it is, then, will you?

TRACHALIO: Look around, is anybody following us?

GRIPUS: What you have to say—anything in it for me?

TRACHALIO: Well, naturally! But do you suppose I can trust you to keep it to yourself?

GRIPUS: Tell me what it is, first.

TRACHALIO: I'm going to, don't worry—if you'll promise not to tell anyone I told you.

GRIPUS: All right, I promise; I'll keep my mouth shut, mister.

TRACHALIO: Now listen:
I saw somebody steal something;
I knew the man he stole it from.
So I went to the thief,
And I made him an offer, like this:
"I know the man you stole from;

How about it now: You split fifty-fifty with me,
And I won't tell him what I know."
He hasn't given me his answer yet. What do you think I
ought to get for my share? I hope a half seems fair to you.

GRIPUS: Half? More than that! Because if he doesn't pay,
I vote that you tell the owner.

TRACHALIO: Thanks. I'll take your advice. Now, this all has
something to do with you.

GRIPUS: With me? What did I do?

TRACHALIO: You've got a chest there, haven't you? I know
whose it is; I've known him a long time.

GRIPUS: What?

TRACHALIO: That's right. And I know how it got lost, too.

GRIPUS: Yes, and I know how it got found, and I know
the man who found it, and I know who owns it now. And
what I'm saying is no more your business than what you were
saying is mine. I know who owns the chest now; you know
who used to own it. Nobody's going to take it away from me,
so don't you think you can.

TRACHALIO: You mean, if the owner claimed it, he wouldn't
get it?

GRIPUS: Owner? Listen, don't you fool yourself: Nobody
owns this but me. I caught it myself, fishing.

TRACHALIO: That's your story, is it?

GRIPUS: Look! There are fish in the ocean, aren't there?
Would you say any one of them is my property? Well, when I
catch them—if I do catch them—they're mine, they belong to
me, and nobody puts in a claim for them or tries to get any
part of them away from me. I take them down to the market
and sell them all, and it's my own property I'm offering for
sale. The law says the sea is the common property of all men,
no question about it.

TRACHALIO: Yes, I agree. So now tell me: Why shouldn't
that chest be the common property of you and me? You
found it in the sea, and that's common property.

GRIPUS: Well, if that doesn't beat all! Why, if the law was
as you say, we fishermen would all die of starvation. The

minute the fish were laid out on the counter, nobody'd buy any. They'd all come and want their share for nothing, saying that it was caught in the sea, and that's common property.

TRACHALIO: Talk about "beating all"! You mean to say a chest is the same thing as a fish? Come on, now; do they look the same to you?

GRIPUS: That's none of my business. I let down my net, or my hook, and anything that sticks to it, I pull up. Anything my net or my hook gets hold of is mine, and that's all there is to it.

TRACHALIO: Oh, no, it isn't, no, sir! Not if you pull up a piece of luggage!

GRIPUS: That's right; split hairs on me!

TRACHALIO: Now just wait a minute! Did you ever in your life see a fisherman catch a chest-fish or offer one for sale on the market? You can't just go grabbing onto any trade you feel like. You're trying to be a luggage-man and a fisherman at the same time. That's not fair! Either you show me how a fish can be a chest, or else keep your hands off anything that doesn't live in the sea and doesn't have scales.

GRIPUS: What? You mean to say you never heard of a chest-fish before?

TRACHALIO: Go on! There's no such thing.

GRIPUS: Oh, yes, there is. I'm a fisherman; I ought to know. Of course, you don't catch one very often; very few of them ever get brought in.

TRACHALIO: Come on! You think you can fool me, brother?

GRIPUS (*holds up chest*): See this color? Chest-fish this color are the rarest of all. Some of them are red—big ones, too—and some are black.

TRACHALIO: Yes! You know what I think? You're going to turn into a chest yourself, twice, if you don't watch out. First your hide will turn red, and then change to black later on.

GRIPUS (*aside*): What a mess this has turned out to be!

TRACHALIO: We're wasting time; it's getting late. What do you say we get somebody to arbitrate? Any suggestions?

GRIPUS: Yes, let the chest arbitrate.

TRACHALIO: What?

GRIPUS: That's right.

TRACHALIO: Idiot!

GRIPUS: Oh, pardon me, Mr. Genius.

TRACHALIO: You're not going to get that chest unless you can find somebody to judge the case or arbitrate it.

GRIPUS: Look, are you out of your mind?

TRACHALIO: Yes, I'm crazy as they come!

GRIPUS: Well, I may be insane, but I'm still hanging onto my chest.

TRACHALIO: You say just one more word, and I'll land my fists on your noggin; I'll squeeze your guts out, the way they do a raw sponge, if you don't let go of that chest.

GRIPUS: Go on, touch me! I'll pick you up and knock your brains out on the ground, the way I do a squid's. Do you want to fight?

TRACHALIO: Oh, what for? Why don't we just split what's in the chest?

GRIPUS: You'll get nothing out of that chest but trouble, so don't go looking for it. I'm going home. (*He starts off.* TRACHALIO *yanks on the rope.*)

TRACHALIO: Oh, no, you don't. Hard alee! You're not going anywhere. Hold fast!

GRIPUS: Any ships around here, you may be the crew, but I'm the captain. Slack off that line, you slob!

TRACHALIO: I'll slack off. You let go of the chest.

GRIPUS: No, sir! You aren't going to get richer by one sliver from that chest.

TRACHALIO: You aren't going to get anywhere by keeping on saying "no." Either you give me my share, or let's find somebody to arbitrate.

GRIPUS: What! A chest that I caught right out of the water?

TRACHALIO: Yes, but I was on the shore, and I saw you.

GRIPUS: I did the work; I took the chances; it was my net; it was my boat.

TRACHALIO: Say—suppose the owner of the chest should

come along. I saw you take it, didn't I? Well, doesn't that make me just as much a thief as you?

GRIPUS: Yes, it does.

TRACHALIO: All right, you crook. If I'm in it as a thief, how come I'm not in it as a partner? What have you got to say to that?

GRIPUS: I don't know. I don't know anything about your fancy laws. All I know is, this chest is mine.

TRACHALIO: Is that so? Well, I say it's mine, too.

GRIPUS: Wait! I've got it figured out so you won't be either a thief or my partner.

TRACHALIO: How?

GRIPUS: You just let me go my way, and you go yours, and keep your mouth shut. You don't tell anybody on me, and I won't give you any share. You keep your mouth shut; I'll keep quiet. That's perfectly fair and square.

TRACHALIO: Aren't you going to offer any terms?

GRIPUS: I already did; you were to go home, let go of that rope, and stop bothering me.

TRACHALIO: Now wait! I ought to offer terms, too.

GRIPUS: Just offer yourself out of here, that's all I want.

TRACHALIO: You know anybody who lives around here?

GRIPUS: I ought to. They're all neighbors of mine.

TRACHALIO: Where do you live?

GRIPUS: Oh-uh-uh—'way out along there; 'way out at the far edge of those fields.

TRACHALIO: How about the fellow that lives in this little place here (*points to* DAEMONES' *house*)—how would it be to let him arbitrate?

GRIPUS: Slack off that rope a minute. I want to go over here and think about it.

TRACHALIO: All right.

GRIPUS (*aside*): Hooray! It's in the bag! The stuff's mine for good and all. It's my own master he wants to arbitrate—right in my own backyard! He won't award a penny out of his own pocket, no, sir! Hah! That fellow doesn't know what terms he has offered me. I'll take it to an arbitrator, all right!

TRACHALIO: Well, what about it?

GRIPUS: Even though I know perfectly well I'm right, let's do it your way. I'd rather do that than get into a fight over it.

TRACHALIO: Good for you!

GRIPUS: Of course, I don't know this arbitrator you're taking me to, but just the same, if he's honest, he's my friend, even if I don't know him; if he isn't, even if he's my friend, he's no friend of mine.

SCENE IV

(*Enter* DAEMONES, PALAESTRA, *and* AMPELISCA.)

DAEMONES: Seriously now, girls, I'm just as sympathetic as I can be, but I'm afraid that all because of you my wife may push me right out of the house. She'll be saying that I've brought a couple of mistresses in, right under her nose. You better go and get on that altar before I have to.

PALAESTRA: ⎫
AMPELISCA: ⎭ Oh, dear, dear, dear!

DAEMONES: I'll see that nothing happens to you. Don't worry. (*To* SPARAX *and* TURBALIO, *who appear at door*) Why are you coming out here? I'm here; nobody's going to hurt them. Go on back in, both of you. Guard dismissed!

(*Exeunt* SPARAX *and* TURBALIO.)

GRIPUS: Hello, master.

DAEMONES: Oh, hello, Gripus. What's the matter?

TRACHALIO (*to* DAEMONES): Is this man your slave?

GRIPUS: I'm not ashamed of it.

TRACHALIO (*to* GRIPUS): I'm not interested in you.

GRIPUS: Why don't you just trot along, then?

TRACHALIO (*to* DAEMONES): I beg your pardon, sir. Is this man your slave?

DAEMONES: Yes, he's mine.

TRACHALIO: Well, now, isn't that a piece of luck. Yours, is he? This is the second time we've met today, isn't it?

DAEMONES: Yes, it is. You're the fellow, aren't you, who went off a little while ago to go after your master?

TRACHALIO: Yes. That's right.

DAEMONES: What can I do for you now?

TRACHALIO: This man here is your slave?

DAEMONES: Yes, he's mine.

TRACHALIO: That's a piece of luck. Yours, is he?

DAEMONES: What's this all about?

TRACHALIO: Why, the man's a plain thief.

DAEMONES: What did he do to you, that "plain thief," as you call him?

TRACHALIO: I'd like to hang him up by the heels.

DAEMONES: What's all this? What are you two fighting about?

TRACHALIO: I'll tell you.

GRIPUS: Oh, no, you won't; I will.

TRACHALIO: It seems to me that I'm the one who's making the claim.

GRIPUS: If you had any decency, you'd make yourself scarce.

DAEMONES: Gripus, pay attention to me. Keep quiet!

GRIPUS: Why? So he can get his story in first?

DAEMONES (to GRIPUS): Hold your tongue. (To TRACHALIO) Go ahead. Speak up.

GRIPUS: Are you going to give an outsider the chance to speak before your own man?

TRACHALIO: Isn't there any way to shut him up? As I was about to say, you know that pimp you hauled out of the temple a while ago? Well, this man here has his chest. See it?

GRIPUS (hides chest behind his back): I don't have it.

TRACHALIO: What do you mean, you don't have it? I can see it.

GRIPUS: Well, don't see it. I have it, I don't have it—what business is it of yours?

TRACHALIO: How do you have it—that's the question. Rightly or wrongly?

GRIPUS: I caught it. If I didn't, go right ahead and hang me. If I caught it in the sea with my net, how is it yours instead of mine?

TRACHALIO: He's trying to trick you. I'll tell you exactly how it happened.

GRIPUS: What are you going to tell?

TRACHALIO: Only what an honest man would tell. (*To* DAEMONES) Make him keep still, sir, if he's yours.

GRIPUS: What? You want me to get what your master's always giving you? Maybe he's always making you keep still, but my master here doesn't do that to us.

DAEMONES: Your friend won that round, Gripus. (*To* TRACHALIO) Now, what was is it you want? Speak up.

TRACHALIO: Yes, sir. Now, as far as I'm concerned, I'm not asking for any share of what's in that chest, and I never once said it was mine. But there's a little box in it that belongs to this lady here (*points to* PALAESTRA). You remember I told you a while ago that she was freeborn.

DAEMONES: Oh, you mean this girl here, the one you said came from the same town I did?

TRACHALIO: That's right. 'Way back when she was a little girl, she wore some pins and bracelets and things. They're all in the little box, and the box is in the chest. They aren't any good to him, and they'll be a big help to her. If she could get them, maybe she could find her parents.

DAEMONES: He'll give them to her. I'll see to that. (*To* GRIPUS) Hold your tongue!

GRIPUS: Now, listen! I wasn't going to say anything about that!

TRACHALIO: I don't want anything but the little box and the things in it.

GRIPUS: What if they're gold?

TRACHALIO: What difference does that make? We'll give you gold for gold, silver for silver, fair exchange.

GRIPUS: Let me see your gold; then I'll let you see the little box.

DAEMONES: Watch your step, Gripus. Keep quiet. (*To* TRACHALIO) Get on with your story.

TRACHALIO: I'm only asking you one thing: Have a little sympathy for this poor lady. That is, if the chest does belong to the pimp, as I think it does. Right now I'm only telling you what I think. I can't say anything for sure.

GRIPUS: See? He's trying to trap you, damn him!

TRACHALIO: Let me go on with my story. If the chest does

belong to the pimp I'm talking about, the girls here will recognize it. Tell him to show it to them.

GRIPUS: What? Show it to them?

DAEMONES: That seems perfectly fair, Gripus, asking you to show it to them.

GRIPUS: Oh, no, it isn't! It's absolutely downright unfair.

DAEMONES: Why?

GRIPUS: Why, if I show it to them, of course they'll say they recognize it.

TRACHALIO: Why you dirty . . . ! You think everybody's like you, you liar?

GRIPUS: Call me anything you like; I don't care, so long as master sees eye to eye with me.

TRACHALIO: Maybe he's on your side now, but he'll be hearing the evidence on my side.

DAEMONES: Gripus, be quiet. (To TRACHALIO) Let's hear your story, and make it short.

TRACHALIO: I've already told it, but if you didn't get it quite straight, I'll tell it over again. Both these girls here, as I said a while ago, by rights ought to be free. This one was kidnaped at Athens when she was a little girl.

GRIPUS: Tell me, what's it got to do with the chest whether they're slaves or free?

TRACHALIO: You shyster! You're trying to get me to go over everything twice, so my time will run out.

DAEMONES: Stop squabbling and tell me what I asked.

TRACHALIO: There ought to be a little box in the chest there—a little wooden box. It's got the things in it that would help her find her parents, the ones she was living with when she was a little girl and was kidnaped, at Athens, just as I told you before.

GRIPUS: Oh, damn you! Look, what's the matter? Can't those girls talk? Can't they tell their own story?

TRACHALIO: They're keeping quiet because a woman who doesn't talk is always more popular than one who chatters.

GRIPUS: In that case, the way things stand, you're neither a man nor a woman.

TRACHALIO: How so?

GRIPUS: Because whether you talk or keep quiet, you aren't popular either way. (*To* DAEMONES) Look, sir, am I ever going to get a chance to talk today?

DAEMONES: You say just one more word and I'll crack your skull for you.

TRACHALIO: As I was trying to say, sir, I wish you'd please tell him to give the little box back to the girls. If he wants some kind of reward for it, he'll get it. Anything else in the chest, he can keep.

GRIPUS: Well, it's about time you got around to saying that. Finally figured out what my rights are, have you? Back there you were going after a fifty-fifty split.

TRACHALIO: Yes, and I'm still going after it.

GRIPUS: I've seen hawks go after things, but they don't always get them.

DAEMONES (*to* GRIPUS): Can't I make you keep still without beating you?

GRIPUS: If he'll keep quiet, I'll keep quiet. If he's going to talk, then let me talk, too.

DAEMONES: Gripus, just hand that chest to me.

GRIPUS: All right, I'll let you have it—but if none of the things he mentioned are in it, give it back to me.

DAEMONES: You'll get it back.

GRIPUS: Here you are.

DAEMONES: Now, girls—Palaestra, Ampelisca—listen to what I'm saying. Is this the chest you say your little box is in?

PALAESTRA: Yes, that's it.

GRIPUS: Listen to that! Before she'd even taken a good look at it, she said that was it.

PALAESTRA: I'll make the whole thing nice and easy for you. There ought to be a little box—a little wooden box—in that chest you have there. I'll tell you exactly what's in it; don't show me a single thing. If I make any mistakes, I lose my case, and you can keep anything that's in it. But if I get them right, then they are my things, and please give them back to me.

DAEMONES: Good. That's a perfectly fair proposition, it seems to me.

GRIPUS: Fair? Not the way I see it, no, sir! What if she's a witch or a mind reader and gets everything that's in there right? Are you going to let a mind reader get away with it?

DAEMONES: She won't get a thing unless she has them all right. Mind reading won't do her any good. Well, open up the chest. I'd like to get at the truth as soon as I can.

GRIPUS: That did it! It's all over but the shouting.

DAEMONES: Open it up! I see a little box. Is this it?

PALAESTRA: Yes, that's it. Oh, father, mother! I've kept you locked up in here! In this little box I packed away every possibility and every hope I ever had of finding you again!

GRIPUS: Is that so? Well, I'll bet the gods are very angry with you, my fine young miss, locking your mother and father up in a cramped little box like that.

DAEMONES: Gripus, come over here; this concerns you. You, Miss, stay where you are, and tell us what's in the box, what it looks like; be sure you don't leave out anything. For I'm telling you now, if you make the least little mistake, don't try to turn around and say "you've got it right, now," for it won't do you any good whatever.

GRIPUS: That's fair enough.

TRACHALIO: Right. But who's asking you? You wouldn't know.

DAEMONES: All right, Miss, speak up. Gripus, watch this, and keep quiet.

PALAESTRA: There's some jewelry in it.

DAEMONES: Yes, there it is. I see it.

GRIPUS: Beaten in the first round! Wait! Don't let her see!

DAEMONES: What do the things look like? Take them one at a time.

PALAESTRA: There's a gold pin, shaped like a little sword, with letters engraved on it.

DAEMONES: A little sword—all right. But tell us now what the letters are.

PALAESTRA: It's my father's name. And then, a bit farther

over, there's a little double-headed ax, and it's gold, too, and has letters engraved on it. That's my mother's name on the little ax.

DAEMONES: Wait a minute. Your father's name is on the little sword, is it? What is his name?

PALAESTRA: Daemones.

DAEMONES: Great gods! What is this? Is this what I've been hoping for?

GRIPUS: Well! What about what I've been hoping for?

TRACHALIO: Please, both of you, go on!

GRIPUS (aside): Take it easy, both of you—or go and get lost.

DAEMONES: Your mother's name is here on the little ax, is it? Tell me what her name is.

PALAESTRA: Daedalis.

DAEMONES: Oh, dear gods! Thank you, thank you, thank you!

GRIPUS (aside): Yes—thank you for nothing.

DAEMONES: Gripus, this girl must be my daughter.

GRIPUS: So she's your daughter. So what? (To TRACHALIO) Damn you, anyway, for seeing me! And damn me for not looking around a hundred times to make sure nobody was watching before I pulled my net out of the water!

PALAESTRA: Then there's a tiny little silver sickle, and two little hands clasping each other, and a little pig—

GRIPUS: Go jump in the lake with your pig—and take the shoats with you while you're at it!

PALAESTRA: And there's a gold locket that my father gave me for my birthday.

DAEMONES: She's the one, all right. I can't hold back any longer. Daughter, daughter, kiss me! I'm your father, your very own father! I'm Daemones, and—look!—Daedalis, your mother, is in the house here.

PALAESTRA: Oh, father, father darling! I was beginning to think I'd never find you!

DAEMONES: Dear, dear girl! How wonderful to have you back!

TRACHALIO: I'm really delighted. You've been a good man, sir, and you've got your reward for it.

DAEMONES: Trachalio, here, take the chest, will you? Take it in the house, if you will, please.

TRACHALIO: Well, well, Gripus, you and your slippery tricks! Congratulations on your bad luck, Gripus. (*Exit* TRACHALIO.)

DAEMONES: Come on, dear, let's go in and see your mother. She'll be able to make a few more checks on this, because she had more of the care of you, and she'll recognize any distinguishing marks you may have.

PALAESTRA: Let's all go in together; then we can all help out. Come on with me, Ampelisca.

AMPELISCA: Isn't this wonderful? I'm so happy for you, dear!

(*Exeunt* DAEMONES, PALAESTRA, AMPELISCA.)

GRIPUS: Well, well, well! Am I a fool for dragging out that chest this morning! Or anyway, for not hiding it, once I'd gotten it, someplace where nobody would find it! Yes! I thought I was going to get one whopper of a catch, just because I caught it in one whopper of a storm. I'm sure there's plenty of money in that chest. Why don't I just go off somewhere and hang myself—for a while, anyway, until I don't feel quite so bad. (*Exit* GRIPUS.)

SCENE V

(*Enter* DAEMONES.)

DAEMONES: For heaven's sake! Was anybody ever any luckier than I am! I never thought it would happen, but I've found my daughter. It seems to be true, doesn't it? If the gods decide to bless somebody, their prayers get answered one way or another—if they've done their duty, that is. Look at me—I never expected it; I couldn't have believed it. Just the same, expect it or not, I found my daughter. And she's going to get married, too, to a fine boy from an excellent family, an Athenian, and even related to me! I want to get him here as soon as I can. Say, I told that slave of his to get out of here and over to town; I wonder why he hasn't come out yet? I think I'll have a look. (*He opens door, looks through.*) Would you look at that! My wife's still hugging my daughter to her. What a lot of silly sentimentality!

SCENE VI

DAEMONES (*speaks through door to wife*): Don't you think it's time to stop the kissing, my dear? How about getting things ready so that when I come in I can offer thanksgiving to the gods of the house for the blessing they've brought to our home? We've got sacrificial lambs and pigs on hand. Now why are you women holding up Trachalio? Oh! Good! Here he comes now.

(*Enter* TRACHALIO.)

TRACHALIO: I don't know where Plesidippus is, but I'll find him and bring him out here to your house.

DAEMONES: Tell him how it's all turned out about my daughter. Ask him to drop everything and come.

TRACHALIO: Yes, sir!

DAEMONES: Tell him I consent to his marrying my daughter.

TRACHALIO: Yes, sir!

DAEMONES: And tell him I know his father and he's a relative of mine.

TRACHALIO: Yes, sir!

DAEMONES: And hurry!

TRACHALIO: Yes, sir!

DAEMONES: Get him here right away, so we can start preparing dinner.

TRACHALIO: Yes, sir!

DAEMONES: Everything "yes, sir"?

TRACHALIO: Yes, sir! By the way, you know what I wish you'd do? Don't forget what you promised: I'm to be freed, right away.

DAEMONES: Yes, sir!

TRACHALIO: Please ask Plesidippus to take care of it.

DAEMONES: Yes, sir!

TRACHALIO: Have your daughter ask him; she'll have no trouble getting him to do it.

DAEMONES: Yes, sir!

TRACHALIO: And I'd like to marry Ampelisca, as soon as I'm freed.

DAEMONES: Yes, sir!

TRACHALIO: You said you were grateful for what I've done; I'd like something tangible to prove it.

DAEMONES: Yes, sir!

TRACHALIO: Everything "yes, sir"?

DAEMONES: Yes, sir! You did it for me; I want to do as much for you. But run along, now. Hurry to town right away and get back here.

TRACHALIO: Yes, sir! I'll be right with you. While I'm gone, you can make any preparations that are needed. (*Exit* TRACHALIO.)

DAEMONES (*laughing*): Yes, sir! Confound the man, anyway —him and his "yes, sir"! He really gave me an earful! Everything I said, "yes, sir"!

SCENE VII

(*Enter* GRIPUS.)

GRIPUS: When am I going to get a chance to talk to you, Daemones?

DAEMONES: Why, what is it, Gripus?

GRIPUS: About that chest; if you're smart, you'll be smart. "Gifts of the gods," you know. Better keep it.

DAEMONES: Do you think it's right to keep for myself what belongs to somebody else?

GRIPUS: I know—but I found it in the sea.

DAEMONES: So much the better for whoever lost it. That doesn't make it any more yours.

GRIPUS: That's why you're poor; you're too honest.

DAEMONES: Gripus, Gripus, Gripus! In the course of this life, a man runs across lots of traps, where he is fooled and gets caught. Yes, sir! And in lots of them there's bait. It looks good, you get greedy, and you grab for it—and get caught in the trap for your trouble. But if a man stops to think, keeps his head, and uses his brains, he keeps out of danger. What he does get, he gets honestly, and he earns long years of happiness out of it. That "catch" of yours, as you call it, looks to me as if it's going to do some "catching" on its own. It will cost us more to return it to its owner than we ever gained by "catching" it in the first place. You think I'm going to hide a piece of property that happened to come my way, when I know it belongs to somebody else? Oh, no, sir! Our good friend, Daemones, will do nothing of that kind. There's one thing that a really smart man knows he must guard against all the time, and that's being a party to any underhanded schemes on the part of his people. I have no time for profits made by shady deals.

GRIPUS: I know; I've seen that lots of times on the stage. The actors come out very solemnly with things like those you've been saying, and everybody applauds them because they've been giving us ordinary folks lessons in how to behave. But after the show's over, and the people in the audience have all scattered and gone home, not one of them acts the way they've been told to.

DAEMONES: Go on in the house! Stop bothering me! Watch how you talk! I'm not going to give you one penny, so don't fool yourself.

GRIPUS: Is that so? Well, I hope and pray that whatever's in that chest—jewelry, money, anything—turns to ashes! (*Exit* GRIPUS.)

DAEMONES: There you have it. That's the reason our slaves go bad on us. For if Gripus started to conspire with another slave, he'd have involved them both in a dishonest deal. The fellow would have thought he was on to something really hot, but actually he'd have been the "something hot" himself—his "something hot" would have put him right on the hot spot. Well, I'm going to go on in now and make my thanksgivings, and then I'll tell them to start dinner right away. (*Exit* DAEMONES.)

SCENE VIII

(*Enter* PLESIDIPPUS *and* TRACHALIO.)

PLESIDIPPUS: Tell it to me all over again, Trachalio. Good old Trachalio! Dear old Trachalio! Wonderful old Trachalio! Grand old friend Trachalio! Palaestra's really found her father and mother?

TRACHALIO: Yes, she has.

PLESIDIPPUS: And she's from Athens, same as I am.

TRACHALIO: So I'm led to believe.

PLESIDIPPUS: And she's going to marry me?

TRACHALIO: It looks that way.

PLESIDIPPUS: I move Daemones agrees to our engagement today. All in favor say "aye."

TRACHALIO: Aye.

PLESIDIPPUS: Good. I move we congratulate Daemones on finding his daughter. All in favor say "aye."

TRACHALIO: Aye.

PLESIDIPPUS: Move an amendment: her mother, too. All in favor—?

TRACHALIO: Aye.

PLESIDIPPUS: Do you have any motions to make?

TRACHALIO: No, but I'm voting "aye" on all of yours.

PLESIDIPPUS: Could you make a motion on how fine she is?

TRACHALIO: Who, me? I vote "fine."

PLESIDIPPUS: Here, here! I said "present" at roll call. Don't go "fining" me.

TRACHALIO: Aye, aye, sir.

PLESIDIPPUS: I move I hurry, All in favor—?

TRACHALIO: Aye.

PLESIDIPPUS: Amend that to read "take my time." All in favor—?

TRACHALIO: Aye.

PLESIDIPPUS: I move I shake her hand as soon as I get there. All in favor—?

TRACHALIO: Aye.

PLESIDIPPUS: Her father's, too?

TRACHALIO: Aye.

PLESIDIPPUS: Then her mother's?

TRACHALIO: Aye.

PLESIDIPPUS: What next? Move I kiss her father, too?

TRACHALIO: Nay.

PLESIDIPPUS: Her mother?

TRACHALIO: Nay.

PLESIDIPPUS: Palaestra herself?

TRACHALIO: Nay.

PLESIDIPPUS: Damn! Chair declares the meeting adjourned. The honorable member isn't voting "aye" when I want him to.

TRACHALIO: You're crazy. Come on.

PLESIDIPPUS: Lead on, milord, anywhere you want!

(*Exeunt* PLESIDIPPUS *and* TRACHALIO.)

ACT FIVE

SCENE I

(*Enter* LABRAX.)

LABRAX: Is there another man in the world who has worse luck than I do? Plesidippus just won his suit against me—got Palaestra taken away from me by court order. That just about finishes me. You know, I think we pimps must be real sons of joy, the way everybody gets so much joy out of it every time a pimp runs into trouble. Well, there's still my other girl. I guess I'll go to the temple and get her. Maybe at least I can take her away with me—she's all the property I have left.

Scene II

(Enter Gripus. *He is polishing a spit.)*

Gripus: No, sir, you won't see friend Gripus alive, come this evening, if I don't get my chest back.

Labrax: I could die every time I hear anybody mention that chest; it's like a knife in the ribs.

Gripus: And that crook, Trachalio, is free. I'm the man who pulled my net up out of the water and caught the chest, and you won't give me anything!

Labrax: Here! What's this? It sounds interesting! I'd better listen!

Gripus: Yes, sir, I ought to put signs up everywhere, with letters three feet high: "Found: One chest containing a large sum of money. Owner apply to Gripus." *(With a gesture toward house)* You people aren't going to get it, the way you think you are.

Labrax: Say! This fellow knows who has my chest, I think. I'd better go and have a word with him. O gods, help me, please!

Gripus *(to someone within house)*: Why are you calling me back in the house? I want to clean this spit out here. The fool thing's made of rust, not iron. I scrub it and it gets redder and redder and thinner and thinner. Somebody has doped it; it's getting old and feeble right in my hands.

Labrax: Oh-ah—good afternoon, my friend.

Gripus: Good afternoon yourself—Baldy.

Labrax: What are you doing?

Gripus: Scrubbing a spit.

Labrax: Oh! Er-ah-well-uh—how've you been?

Gripus: What's it to you? Are you a doctor?

Labrax: No. I'm a couple of places ahead of a doctor.

Gripus: Oh, a beggarman, is that it?

Labrax: You hit the nail on the head.

Gripus: You look as if you ought to be one. What's on your mind?

LABRAX: Just last night another fellow and I were in a shipwreck, and I lost everything I had, worse luck.

GRIPUS: What did you lose?

LABRAX: A chest with a lot of money and silverware in it.

GRIPUS: Do you remember what was in the chest?

LABRAX: What's the difference? It's gone.

GRIPUS: Yes, but just the same—

LABRAX: Forget it. Let's talk about something else.

GRIPUS: Suppose I know who found it? Can you identify it?

LABRAX: There were eight hundred gold sovereigns in a pouch, and besides that ten thousand drachmas in a wallet by itself.

GRIPUS (aside): Say! That's quite a haul! I'm in for a nice, fat reward! The gods haven't forgotten me! I'll get a pretty penny out of this. It's his chest, for sure. (To LABRAX) Go on, what next?

LABRAX: There was a whole six thousand drachmas in silver in a purse, and on top of that a bowl, a tankard, a pitcher, a jug, and a ladle.

GRIPUS: My, my! That was quite a fortune you had there!

LABRAX: Yes, "had," is right; "had," but not "have." It's enough to break your heart.

GRIPUS: What would you give to somebody if he could track that stuff down and show you where it is? Speak up quick, right off!

LABRAX: Six hundred drachmas.

GRIPUS: Don't make me laugh!

LABRAX: Eight hundred?

GRIPUS: Shavings!

LABRAX: A thousand?

GRIPUS: Nutshells!

LABRAX: Twelve hundred?

GRIPUS: You're talking little itsy-bitsy-bugs!

LABRAX: I'll pay fourteen hundred.

GRIPUS: What did you do? Burn your tongue, and trying to cool it?

LABRAX: I'll pay two thousand.

GRIPUS: Are you dreaming?

LABRAX: Not one penny more.

GRIPUS: Good-by. (*He turns away.*)

LABRAX: Wait. Listen, once I'm gone, I won't be back. How about twenty-two hundred?

GRIPUS: Are you asleep?

LABRAX: Well, tell me how much you want.

GRIPUS: As much as you wouldn't want to be asked for more than: Six thousand drachmas. Can't be a single penny less. Well, what is it: Yes or no?

LABRAX: What's the use? I'm stuck for it; I can see that. Six thousand it is.

GRIPUS: Come on over here, then, I want Venus to bind you to it.

LABRAX: Anything you like. Just give me my orders.

GRIPUS: Put your hand on Venus' altar.

LABRAX: All right; it's on.

GRIPUS: I want you to swear by Venus.

LABRAX: Swear what?

GRIPUS: What I tell you to.

LABRAX: Dictate what you want. I'll be right behind you. (*Aside*) What I'm about to say doesn't apply to my own property.

GRIPUS: Get a good hold on the altar, now.

LABRAX: I've got it.

GRIPUS: Do you solemnly swear that you will pay me the money the same day you get your chest back?

LABRAX: I do.

GRIPUS: "Venus of Cyrene, be witness to what I declare: If I find the chest that I lost at sea, with the money and silverware in it, and it shall in this condition revert to my hands, then, to Gripus here—" put your other hand on me, and say it—

LABRAX: ". . . then to Gripus, here (it is I who do declare it, and I pray, Venus, hear me) I will pay at once the sum of six thousand drachmas."

GRIPUS: And say, that if you evade your obligation Venus

should wipe out your business, destroy your standing, and put an end to your life. (*Aside*) I hope you get that to keep, oath or no oath.

LABRAX: "Venus, if I break any of the terms to which I've agreed, I beseech thee to bring misery to every pimp in the world."

GRIPUS: That will happen, even if you do keep your word. You wait here for me. I'll get my master to come out. The minute he comes, demand that he give back your chest. (*Exit* GRIPUS.)

LABRAX: I don't care how much he gives me back my chest, I don't owe that fellow a penny. I'm the one who decides what I've sworn to. Careful! Better keep quiet! Here he comes with his master.

SCENE III

(*Enter* GRIPUS *and* DAEMONES, *carrying chest.*)

GRIPUS: Come on out here.

DAEMONES: Where is your pimp?

GRIPUS (*to* LABRAX): Well, there you are. He has your chest.

DAEMONES: Yes, I have. I'm quite ready to admit I have it. If it's yours, take it. Everything, whatever was in it, will be put in your hands undamaged. Here, take it, if it's yours.

LABRAX: Wonderful! It's mine. (*He takes chest, kisses it.*) Dear chest, am I glad to see you!

DAEMONES: Yours, is it?

LABRAX: What a question! By heaven, if it was Jupiter's, it's still mine.

DAEMONES: Everything's in it, just as it was. I took out just the one little box, with the pins and things, that helped me find my daughter just now.

LABRAX: What daughter?

DAEMONES: Why, your girl—the one called Palaestra. I've found out she's my daughter.

LABRAX: Well, good, good! I'm glad that turned out happily, as you hoped it would.

DAEMONES: I'm not so sure I believe that.

LABRAX: No, no! Just to show you that I really am glad, don't you pay me a penny for her. I give her to you as a gift.

DAEMONES: My, my! You're too kind!

LABRAX: No, no, no! You are.

GRIPUS (to LABRAX): Say, there. You've got your chest.

LABRAX: That's right.

GRIPUS: Well, hurry up.

LABRAX: Hurry up? What for?

GRIPUS: To pay me my money.

LABRAX: Money? I'm not paying you any money. I don't owe you anything.

GRIPUS: What? What's this all about? You don't owe me anything?

LABRAX: I most certainly don't.

GRIPUS: Didn't you take an oath?

LABRAX: Of course I did, and I'll take another, if I feel like it. Oaths are for keeping property, not losing it.

GRIPUS: Now you look here, you liar; pay me my six thousand drachmas.

DAEMONES: Gripus, what's this six thousand drachmas you're demanding?

GRIPUS: He swore he'd give it to me.

LABRAX: Swore? I like swearing to things! So I committed perjury; who are you—my father-confessor?

DAEMONES: What did he promise you this money for?

GRIPUS: He swore that if I'd get this chest back into his hands, he'd pay me six thousand drachmas.

LABRAX: See here! You name someone who can act as arbitrator. I plead that you entered into our agreement with intent to defraud, and that—that—that I'm a minor.

GRIPUS (points to DAEMONES): There's your man. Put your case to him.

LABRAX: It must be somebody else.

DAEMONES: Now see here; if I find that one of you has done wrong, I'm not likely to take anything away from the other. (To LABRAX) Did you promise him the money?

LABRAX: Yes, I admit I did.

DAEMONES: But what you promised to my slave is mine by law. Don't you imagine that you can pull any of your pimp's tricks around here, because you can't.

GRIPUS (*to* LABRAX): Thought you'd found somebody you could swindle, did you? You've got to pay the money, legal tender, and I'll turn right around and pay it to him for my freedom.

DAEMONES (*to* LABRAX): Now then, since I've been kind to you, and since your property was saved for you by what I did—

GRIPUS: No, sir! By what *I* did. Don't you say you did it.

DAEMONES (*to* GRIPUS): If you have any sense, you'll keep quiet. (*To* LABRAX)—By what I did, you ought to be kind to me, too, and pay me back by doing me a favor.

LABRAX: Oh! You recognize my rights, do you? Is that what your question means?

DAEMONES: It would be surprising if I didn't recognize your rights, since I'm taking the risk of asking you to do something that implies that you have rights. (LABRAX *hesitates.*)

GRIPUS: I'm safe! The pimp's weakening. Liberty, here I come!

DAEMONES: Gripus, here, found your chest, and he's my slave. So that means I saved it for you, and all that money with it.

LABRAX: Thanks very much. And you can have that six thousand that I swore I'd give him.

GRIPUS: Hey, now! Give it to me, if you're smart.

DAEMONES (*to* GRIPUS): Are you going to keep still or not?

GRIPUS: You're pretending to plead my case; all you're doing is fixing things for yourself. No, sir, you're not going to cheat me out of what was promised me, even if I have lost the rest of what I found.

DAEMONES: I'll tan your hide if you say one more word.

GRIPUS: Go on, slaughter me if you want to! I'm not going

to keep quiet. The only way you can shut me up is with my six thousand drachmas.

LABRAX (*to* GRIPUS): Now, now, my friend. He's taking care of you. Keep still.

DAEMONES (*to* LABRAX): Step over here, Labrax.

LABRAX: Gladly!

GRIPUS: Hey! No secrets! I don't want to hear any mumble-mumble bumble-bumble. (DAEMONES *and* LABRAX *move aside.*)

DAEMONES (*to* LABRAX): Tell me, how much did you pay for that other girl of yours—Ampelisca?

LABRAX: She cost me two thousand drachmas.

DAEMONES: How would you like me to make you a good proposition?

LABRAX: That would suit me very well.

DAEMONES: I'll split that six thousand with you.

LABRAX: Thanks!

DAEMONES: You take three thousand for Ampelisca, and set her free, and pay me the other three thousand.

LABRAX: That's fine.

DAEMONES: I'll take my three thousand and set Gripus free, since it was through him that you found your chest and I found my daughter.

LABRAX: Thanks. I really appreciate that. (DAEMONES *and* LABRAX *turn back to* GRIPUS.)

GRIPUS: How soon am I going to get my money, then?

DAEMONES: It's all settled, Gripus. I have it.

GRIPUS: Yes, but see here, I want it myself.

DAEMONES: No, no! There's nothing here for you, make no mistake about that. I want you to release the pimp from his oath.

GRIPUS: Damn! Damn! Damn! This really finishes me! By the gods, you'll never cheat me again. This is the last time!

DAEMONES: Won't you have dinner with us, Labrax?

LABRAX: Certainly. The terms suit me very well.

DAEMONES: Come on in, then. (*To audience*) My friends, I'd invite you all to dinner, too, except that I'm not going to put a thing on the table and haven't got a bit of food in the house. And anyway, I expect you all have previous engagements for dinner. But if you'll be so kind as to give our play a good, loud hand, you can all come to my house for a real feast—sixteen years from now. (*To* LABRAX *and* GRIPUS) You two, you both have dinner with me today.

LABRAX }
GRIPUS }   Yes, sir!

DAEMONES (*to audience*): Your applause, please.

FINIS

TERENCE

THE WOMAN OF ANDROS
(Andria)

INTRODUCTORY NOTE

The *Andria* ("The Woman of Andros") has always been considered the earliest of Terence's plays. It was first produced in 166 B.C., when its author was still in his twenties. It was adapted from a play of the same name by Menander, with the addition of some scenes from his *Perinthia*. It is not Terence's most polished play, and in some ways—for example, by the introduction of the rather fatuous subplot revolving around Charinus—it shows signs of inexperience, but in psychological and sociological interest it is one of his best.

Based on a variant of the old "recognition" device, whereby the heroine, thought to be a slave and a foreigner, is discovered in the nick of time to be free and a citizen, the *Andria* is a study in the conflicting loyalties of son toward father, husband toward wife, and slave toward master. Pamphilus loves both his father and his wife; he cannot find a way in which to be loyal to both. Davus is devoted both to his young master and to his old; he cannot help the one without betraying the other. Simo loves his son and is deeply hurt by what he thinks to be a flouting of his authority and of his affection as well. He thinks that Pamphilus—and herein resides the sociological problem—has violated Athenian law and social custom by claiming to have *married* a foreign girl of unknown social status: Simo could have tolerated her as a mistress, if only a degree of discretion were preserved; a wife he cannot abide. In the most roundabout manner, he attempts to break up the marriage without exceeding a father's rights and without unduly hurting his son. Over all the story, its complications and its resolution, hangs the shadowy figure of Chrysis, the "Woman of Andros" herself, who never appears on the stage—she has died before the story opens—but whose kindness, generosity, and understanding are the element that gives life to the play.

The scene, as always in Terence, is laid on a street in

Athens; the setting shows the fronts of two houses with doors opening on the street. Front and center of the stage is an altar, a relic of the days when the drama was primarily a religious institution. (In this play, Terence cleverly incorporates it into the plot.) The Prologue is not concerned with the play itself but is Terence's reply to critics who have attacked him for inserting scenes from one play into another.

CHARACTERS

SIMO, an elderly gentleman
SOSIA, his freedman
DAVUS, his slave
MYSIS, a serving maid
PAMPHILUS, a young man, SIMO's son
CHARINUS, a young man, friend of PAMPHILUS
BYRRIA, slave of CHARINUS
LESBIA, a midwife
GLYCERIUM, a young girl
CHREMES, an elderly gentleman, friend of SIMO
CRITO, an elderly gentleman, friend of CHREMES
DROMO, slave to SIMO, and his whip handler.

THE SCENE: *A street in Athens. Upstage, the fronts of two houses, with double doors opening onto the street. Center, upstage, an altar covered with wreaths and foliage.*

THE WOMAN OF ANDROS

Prologue

When our author first turned his attention to writing, he assumed that the only task assigned to him was to turn out plays the public would enjoy. In point of fact, he has discovered that things are quite different; he is wasting his time writing prologues, not to outline a plot, but to reply to the strictures of our ill-tempered Dean of Playwrights.

Consider, if you please, what the critics see fit to call a misdemeanor. Menander wrote two plays, *The Woman of Andros* and *The Woman of Perinthos*. Anyone who knows either of them knows them both, for their plots are very nearly identical. They differ only in dialogue and in manner of treatment. Our author freely admits that he appropriated and transferred certain suitable passages from *The Woman of Perinthos* to his version of *The Woman of Andros*. And now his critics are castigating him for having done this; they argue that it is improper to insert scenes from one play into another.

But is their fine critical acumen merely convicting them of a lack of acumen? When they cavil at our author, they are also caviling at Naevius, Plautus, and Ennius, for it is they who set the precedent our author is following. He would much rather base his work on slipshod writing like theirs than on the foggy pedantry of his critics. I earnestly suggest, then, that they cease and desist, and give us no more of their strictures; otherwise, they may be brought face to face with some errors of their own.

We beg your good will and your courteous attention. Judge our case! Decide whether there is any hope for the future! Determine whether, when our author again takes to the writing of plays, they will be suitable for your viewing, or should rather be hissed off the stage.

ACT ONE

SCENE I

(*Enter* SIMO, *with several slaves carrying baskets of food, followed by* SOSIA, *dressed as a chef, from stage left.*)

SIMO: All right, boys; take those things in; run along! Sosia, come here a minute; I have a few things I want to say to you.

SOSIA: Oh, I know what you want; you want me to prepare a really fine dinner, don't you?

SIMO: No, it's something else.

SOSIA: Well, with what I know, what else could I do for you?

SIMO: It isn't what you know that I need for the plans I have in mind. No, what I need are two things I've always known I could count on from you: Loyalty and discretion.

SOSIA: This sounds interesting! What is it you want?

SIMO: You were a slave in my house for a long time. Well, ever since the day I bought you, when you were a little boy, you always had fair and kind treatment from me. You know that's so, I'm sure. I gave you freedom instead of keeping you as a slave, because even though you were a slave, you always behaved like a gentleman. I paid you the highest reward that I had in my power.

SOSIA: I haven't forgotten it.

SIMO: I don't regret what I did.

SOSIA: Simo, I'm glad, if I've ever done anything to please you or can do anything now, and it makes me happy that you haven't been disappointed in me. But now I'm worried; your reminding me of what you've done sounds like a reprimand. Do you think I've forgotten your kindness? Why don't you just tell me right out what you want me to do.

SIMO: I shall. Now, the first thing I have to say is this: You think there's going to be a wedding, don't you? Well, there isn't.

SOSIA: What's the idea, then? Why the show?

SIMO: You're going to hear the whole story, right from the beginning. That way you'll find out how my son has been behaving, and what I plan to do about it, and what I'd like you to do. Ever since he got out of his teens, Sosia, and began to manage his own affairs—for before that time how could you really get to know him or find out what was going on inside his head? He was too young; he would have been afraid to say what he really thought; in fact, his tutor would have seen that he didn't.

SOSIA: Yes, that's so.

SIMO: What almost all young fellows do—get interested in some sport like horse racing or hunting, or in studying philosophy—he wasn't especially attracted by any of these things, and still he liked them all in a moderate way. I was glad.

SOSIA: Yes, and you should have been. I think that by far the best principle in life is: Nothing too much.

SIMO: Well, that's how he behaved; he had no trouble getting along with everybody. Whatever company he was in, he did what they wanted to do. He went along with the crowd. He was always a good sport, never put his own interests ahead of theirs—the easiest way, you know, to make people think you are a good fellow and not talk behind your back, and to win friends.

SOSIA: He was wise, for nowadays it's complaisance that wins friends; honesty makes enemies.

SIMO: Meanwhile, about three years ago a woman from Andros moved into this neighborhood. She had no money; her relatives wouldn't take care of her, so she had to leave home. She was unusually good-looking; in the bloom of youth, too.

SOSIA: Oh—I'm afraid the woman from Andros means some kind of trouble!

SIMO: At first she led an honorable life: She was thrifty; she worked hard; she tried to make a living as a weaver. But pretty soon someone found her attractive and came to her with the usual promise of money. First there was one, and then another. Well, you know how we all are; we find pleasure much more attractive than hard work. She accepted their offers, and presently she took up the trade. It so happened that the young men who were her lovers at that time took my son there to keep them company—yes, my son. Right away I said to myself, "He's caught for sure; he's been hit." In the morning I used to watch for their slave boys as they came and went, and I'd ask them, "Say, boy, tell me, please: Who was with Chrysis yesterday?" For that was the Andrian's name.

SOSIA: I see.

SIMO: "Phaedria," or "Clinia," they'd say, or "Niceratus," for at that time those three were the most regular of her lovers. "Well, what about Pamphilus?" "Pamphilus? Oh, he just payed for his share of the party and had dinner with them." That relieved my mind a lot. Again on another day I'd ask the same questions; I always found that Pamphilus hadn't been in any way involved. Really, I felt that he had passed the test and was setting a fine example of good behavior, for when a man is brought up against that kind of people and his principles still aren't shaken, you may be sure that he can be trusted to run his own life. This pleased me very much, and on top of that, everybody began to congratulate me and tell me how lucky I was to have a son with a character like that. Well, why make the story any longer? When my friend Chremes heard what people were saying, he came to me himself and offered his only daughter, with a fine dowry, as a wife for my son. We reached an agreement; I made the engagement. Today was set for the wedding.

SOSIA: What's holding it up, then?

SIMO: You'll find out. Just a few days or so after our agreement was made, Chrysis, our neighbor here, died.

SOSIA: Fine! Fine! That's good news! I was worried about Chrysis.

SIMO: At that time, of course, my son was over there a good deal with those friends of his who had been Chrysis' lovers. He was helping them with the funeral arrangements. Sometimes he seemed upset. Once or twice he even burst into tears. That pleased me then. I kept thinking, "He didn't know her so very well, and yet he's taking her death as if she'd been very close to him. What if he had actually been in love with her? How will he act in my own case—his own father?" It seemed to me that his behavior was the sign of a tender heart and an indication of an affectionate disposition. But there's no need to say any more; I myself, for his sake, went to the funeral, too, for I still didn't suspect that anything was wrong.

SOSIA: Hm! What do you mean?

SIMO: You'll see. They carried out the body and the procession moved off. Meanwhile, among the women who were with us, I happened to catch sight of one girl whose appearance was . . .

SOSIA: Pretty good, perhaps?

SIMO: Yes, and whose face, Sosia, was so refined, so lovely . . . nothing could be more so. It seemed to me then that she was much more unhappy than the others, and besides, her appearance was more dignified and well-bred than theirs. So I went up to the attendants and asked who she was. They said she was Chrysis' sister. Right away it struck me—hard. Aha! That's what it was! That's where his tears came from; that's why he was so sympathetic!

SOSIA: Oh, my! I don't like the sound of that!

SIMO: All this time the funeral procession was moving on, and we with it. We came to the graveyard. They put the body on the pyre. The weeping began. While this was going on, that sister I mentioned went up to the fire rather closer than was wise—in fact, it was quite dangerous. Pamphilus was horrified, and right there he let out the secret of the love he had kept so well disguised and concealed. He ran up to her and seized her around the waist. "My dear Glycerium!" he said. "What are you doing? Do you want to kill yourself?" Then you could easily have seen that their love affair was of long standing; she threw herself back into his arms, tears streaming down her face, just as an old, old friend would do.

SOSIA: What's that you say?

SIMO: When I left there, I was angry and very much disturbed, and still I hadn't any good reason for taking him to task. He would have said, "What did I do? What was the matter with that? What was wrong, Father? That girl wanted to throw herself into the fire; I stopped her and saved her." A perfectly good story!

SOSIA: You're quite right, for if you'd take a man to task for saving a life, what would you do to one who did some damage or hurt somebody?

SIMO: The next day Chremes came to me bellowing that this was a terrible thing; that he'd discovered that Pamphilus was treating this foreign woman as his wife. I maintained that it wasn't so. He insisted that it was. When I finally left him, it was with the understanding that the offer of his daughter was withdrawn.

SOSIA: Didn't you then . . .?

SIMO: No, even this wasn't a good enough reason for calling him to account.

SOSIA: Why? I don't understand.

SIMO: "You yourself have set the limit on this sort of thing, father. The time will soon come when I'll have to arrange my life to suit somebody else. Just let me live my own way for a little while now."

SOSIA: Well, then, what grounds have you left?

SIMO: If because of his love affair he refuses to get married— that will be the first wrong he's done for which I can punish him. And now this is my plan: Through a pretended wedding I'll create a genuine excuse for taking the boy to task, if he refuses to go through with it. At the same time, if that villain Davus has any schemes, I'll let him get them off now when his tricks will do no harm. For I think he'll do everything, might and main, with all he's got, more, of course, to cause me trouble than to help out my son.

SOSIA: Why so?

SIMO: You can ask that? Evil heart, evil intent. And if I find out that he . . . but why talk about it? If it turns out the

way I want, I mean if Pamphilus doesn't put up any oppo-
sition, there remains Chremes. I'll have to clear Pamphilus to
him. And I think we can come to terms. Now it's your job to
make this wedding look good and real, scare Davus out of his
wits, keep an eye on my son and see what he's up to and what
plans he may make with Davus.

SOSIA: Good. I'll take care of it.

SIMO: Let's go in now. You go ahead; I'll be right with you.

(*Exit* SOSIA *into* SIMO's *house.* SIMO *walks about at a little
distance from the door.*)

SCENE II

(*Enter* DAVUS *from* SIMO's *house.*)

SIMO (*to himself*): No doubt of it—my son doesn't want to
get married, to judge from the fright I saw Davus was in a
little while ago when he heard that there was going to be a
wedding. But here he comes himself.

DAVUS (*to himself*): I wondered if we'd get away with it
like that, and I was afraid where master's everlasting good
humor would end up. When he heard that his son's wedding
was off, he didn't say a word to any of us and wasn't a bit
annoyed.

SIMO (*aside*): But now he will say something, and it will
mean more than a little trouble for you, I think.

DAVUS (*to himself*): This is what he wanted: We weren't to
know what was going on; we were to be misled by a false
sense of security, full of confidence and not a worry in the
world. Then we were to be caught off guard so that we
wouldn't have time to think up anything that might stop the
wedding. Smart!

SIMO (*aside*): That rascal! What's he saying?

DAVUS (*catches sight of* SIMO): It's master, and I didn't see
him!

SIMO: Davus!

DAVUS: Yes, what is it?

SIMO: All right, come here to me.

DAVUS (*aside*): Oh-oh! What's this?

SIMO: What have you got to say?

DAVUS: About what?

SIMO: "About what?" you say? I hear it said that my son is having a love affair.

DAVUS: Oh, yes! People here are really concerned about that! (*He starts to walk away.*)

SIMO: Are you listening to what I'm saying, or not?

DAVUS: Yes, I'm listening.

SIMO: Well, for me to probe into that now is something that a right-minded father doesn't do; what he's done up to now is none of my business. As long as it was the proper time for that sort of thing, I let him do as he pleased. Beginning with today, though, he'll have to lead a different kind of life and behave quite differently. And so I insist—or if you think it appropriate, I humbly beg you, Davus, to see that he comes back to the straight and narrow now. Why do I say that? Young men who are having love affairs are always upset when they have to get married.

DAVUS: So people say.

SIMO: On top of that, if he's got a tutor whose morals are questionable, he often ends up by taking a direction that makes a bad situation worse.

DAVUS: I'm sure I don't know what you mean.

SIMO: You don't? Nonsense!

DAVUS: No, I don't. I'm Davus, not Oedipus.

SIMO: I take it, then, you want me to put the rest of it plainly?

DAVUS: Yes, of course.

SIMO (*shaking his fist at him*): If I catch you today trying any tricks to keep this wedding from taking place, or trying to show us how smart you are in situations like this, I'll have you lashed and put in the mill, Davus, until it kills you, on these terms and with this warning, that if I ever take you out of there, I'll push the grindstone myself, in your place. Now, did you understand this? Or wasn't even that clear enough?

DAVUS: Oh, no; I got that all right. You explained the facts so clearly—didn't beat around the bush at all.

SIMO: I could stand your making a fool of me in any other matter better than I could in this.

DAVUS: Oh, don't say such things, please.

SIMO: Making fun of me, are you? You're not fooling me. But I'm telling you now: Don't do anything rash, and don't you say I didn't warn you. Watch your step! (*Exit* SIMO *into his house.*)

SCENE III

DAVUS: Well, well, Davus, this is no place to be slow or stupid, if I understood just now how Simo feels about the wedding. If we don't lay our plans pretty cleverly, it will mean the end of me or my master. And I'm not sure which to do, help Pamphilus or obey Simo. If I desert Pamphilus, I'm afraid for his life; but if I help him, I'm afraid of what Simo threatens to do, and it's not easy to fool him. First of all, he has already found out about this love affair. He's furious, and he's keeping an eye on me so that I won't pull any tricks over the wedding. If he catches me, it's the end for me. Or if he just feels like it, he'll find an excuse, rightly or wrongly, for throwing me headfirst into the mill. As if this weren't enough trouble, I've got another worry; this Andrian woman, whether she's his wife or his mistress—Pamphilus has gotten her pregnant. And it's really worth while to hear the nerve of them (for they're talking like people who've lost their heads, not their hearts); whatever the child may be, they've decided to recognize it as theirs. And they're dreaming up some tall tale now between themselves, that she's an Attic citizen: "Once upon a time there was an old man, a trader. He suffered shipwreck on the island of Andros; he died there." Thereupon, they say, this girl was thrown up on the beach, and Chrysis' father took her in, poor little orphan! What a yarn! It doesn't ring true to me, but they like the story. But Mysis is coming out of the Andrian's house. I'll go on downtown and find Pamphilus, so that his father won't catch him unprepared about this. (*Exit, stage left.*)

Scene IV

(*Enter* Mysis, *from* Chrysis' *house. She turns and talks back through the door.*)

Mysis: I heard you the first time, Archylis. You told me to bring Lesbia here. (*Turns to the audience*) Goodness! She's a careless old drunkard! She's nobody to trust a woman to in her first labor. (*Back through the door*) Should I really bring her, now? (*To audience*) Just see how little sense of fitness that awful old woman has—just because they're always getting drunk together! O gods, please let her have her baby easily, and let Lesbia make her mistakes somewhere else! (*Enter* Pamphilus, *stage left, running.*) But I see Pamphilus; why in the world is he so frightened? I'm afraid for what it may be. I'll wait and make sure that this doesn't mean bad news.

Scene V

Pamphilus (*to himself*): Is this a kind thing to do or to think of? Is this the way a father ought to act?

Mysis (*to herself*): What does he mean?

Pamphilus (*to himself*): By heaven! If this isn't an insult, what is? "He had decided that I was to be married today!" Oughtn't I to have known about it before this? Oughtn't he to have told me sooner?

Mysis (*to herself*): Oh, dear me, what do I hear?

Pamphilus: I can't believe it! Chremes had said he wouldn't give me his daughter as my wife; did he change his mind? He could see I hadn't changed! Why is he so stubborn? Why is he trying to drag me away from my Glycerium? If that happens, I'll die, absolutely. To think that any man should be so unlucky in love or so ill-starred as I! In the name of all that's holy! Isn't there any way that I can escape being Chremes' son-in-law? In how many different ways have I been insulted and snubbed! "Everything is all arranged." Hah! They cancel it. Now they want me back. Why? Unless—and this is what I suspect—they've been bringing up some kind of monstrous creature, and because they can't push her off onto anybody else, they come to me!

MYSIS (*to herself*): Oh, dear! What he's saying scares me out of my wits!

PAMPHILUS (*to himself*): For what am I to say about father? To think that he'd be so offhand about such an important matter! Just now he passed me downtown, and as he walked by, he said, "You're to be married today, Pamphilus. Get ready. Go on home." Sounded to me as if he'd said, "Run along quickly, and hang yourself!" I was thunderstruck! Do you think I could say one single word? Or find any excuse, even a foolish one, a dishonest one, a weak one? I was struck dumb! But if I'd considered ahead of time, "Now what would I do if somebody should put the question to me?"—I'd be doing something to keep from doing this. But what's the best move for me to make now? So many concerns trip me up and drag my mind this way and that: My love, my sympathy for her, my worry about the wedding, and besides that my respect for father, who has been so understanding up until now, and let me do just as I pleased. Should I go against his wishes? What a fix I'm in! I don't know what to do!

MYSIS (*to herself*): Oh, dear me, I'm afraid of where that "I don't know" may end! But now it's very important that he talk to her or that I talk to him about her. While he's in doubt, a little push will send him one way or the other.

PAMPHILUS: Who's that talking here? Oh, Mysis, hello.

MYSIS: Oh, hello, Pamphilus.

PAMPHILUS: How is she?

MYSIS: That's a foolish question! She's in great pain, and she's worried, poor girl, because today is the day that was originally set for the wedding. Besides that, she's afraid that you may desert her.

PAMPHILUS: What? Could I even think of such a thing? Would I let her be deceived, poor thing, because of me, after she has entrusted her heart and her whole life to me, when I've held her dearer than anybody else, just like a wife? She's been brought up and educated so well; she's so fine; would I let a person like that be forced to change because she had nothing to live on? I won't do it.

MYSIS: I shouldn't be worried if it were up to you alone, but only whether you could resist compulsion.

PAMPHILUS: Do you think I'm such a coward, or so ungrateful, besides, or so heartless or barbaric, that our having lived together, and my love for her, and my conscience wouldn't urge me—yes, force me—to keep my word?

MYSIS: All I know is this: She deserves not to be forgotten.

PAMPHILUS: Forgotten? Oh, Mysis, Mysis! Even now those words are written on my heart—what Chrysis said about Glycerium. She was at the point of death when she called me to her. I came in; you all went out. There we were, all alone. She began, "Dear Pamphilus, you see how young and pretty she is, and you know very well just how useful those qualities will be to her for protecting her honor and her property. Therefore, by your right hand and the god that guards you, by your honor, and by her unprotected state, I beseech you not to put her away from you nor desert her. If it is true that I have always loved you like a brother, and that she has always thought more of you than of anyone else, and that she has always tried to please you in everything, I make you her husband, her friend, her guardian—yes, her father. I leave all this property of mine to you and give it into your trust." She made her my lawful wife. Then, at that very moment, death seized her. I took Glycerium; I took her, and I'll keep her.

MYSIS: I certainly hope so.

PAMPHILUS: But why are you leaving her?

MYSIS: I'm going for the midwife.

PAMPHILUS: Hurry up. And do you hear? Not one word about the wedding, for fear that on top of her suffering this . . .

MYSIS: I understand. (*Exit.*)

ACT TWO

SCENE I

(Enter CHARINUS *and* BYRRIA.)

CHARINUS: What's that you say, Byrria? She's to be married to Pamphilus today?

BYRRIA: That's right.

CHARINUS: How do you know?

BYRRIA: Downtown just now I heard it from Davus.

CHARINUS: Oh! That's awful! My heart's been so strung up between hope and fear that now, with hope taken away, it's weary, worn out, worried, and lifeless.

BYRRIA: Oh, come now, Charinus, since you can't have what you want, want what you can have.

CHARINUS: I don't want anything but Philumena.

BYRRIA: How much better to put your energy into getting over your love for her, instead of coming back again and again to the thing that stirs you up and does you no good.

CHARINUS: When we're well, it's easy to give advice to the sick. If you were in my place you'd feel differently.

BYRRIA: All right, all right. Suit yourself. *(Enter* PAMPHILUS.)

CHARINUS: But I see Pamphilus. I swear I'll try everything before I give up.

BYRRIA *(aside)*: What is he going to do?

CHARINUS: I'll beg him; I'll get on my knees to him; I'll tell him how much I love her. I think I'll persuade him at least to postpone the wedding for a few days. Meanwhile, something will happen, I hope.

BYRRIA *(aside)*: That "something" is nothing.

CHARINUS: Byrria, what do you think? Shall I go to him?

BYRRIA: Why not? If you don't get anything out of him, at least you'll let him know that you're planning to be his wife's lover, if he marries her.

CHARINUS: Go to the devil with that sort of talk, confound you!

PAMPHILUS: Oh, there's Charinus. Hello.

CHARINUS: Hello, Pamphilus. I'm coming to you to ask for hope, salvation, help, and advice.

PAMPHILUS: Well! Why, I haven't the wits to give you advice nor the power to help you. But what in the world is the matter with you?

CHARINUS: You're getting married today?

PAMPHILUS: So they tell me.

CHARINUS: Pamphilus, if you do that, this is the last time you'll see me.

PAMPHILUS: Why so?

CHARINUS: Oh, my! I'm afraid to tell him. You tell him, Byrria, please.

BYRRIA: I'll tell him.

PAMPHILUS: What is it?

BYRRIA: He's in love with you fiancée.

PAMPHILUS: Hah! Well, his feelings aren't the same as mine, then. I say, tell me: You haven't had anything—*more* to do with her, have you Charinus?

CHARINUS: Oh, Pamphilus! Nothing at all!

PAMPHILUS: How I wish you had!

CHARINUS: Now in the name of our friendship and affection, I beg you, first of all, not to marry her.

PAMPHILUS: I'll do my best!

CHARINUS: But if you can't help it, or if your heart is set on this marriage . . .

PAMPHILUS: My heart *set* on it?

CHARINUS: . . . at least postpone it for a few days, until I can go away somewhere so that I won't see it.

PAMPHILUS: Listen, please! Charinus, I don't think a gentleman should ever take credit for something when he doesn't deserve it. I'm more anxious to get out of the marriage than you are to get into it.

CHARINUS: You've saved my life!

PAMPHILUS: Now if you can do anything, either you or Byrria, here, do it; think up something, invent something, arrange for her to marry you. I'll try to keep her from marrying me. (*Enter* DAVUS.)

CHARINUS: That satisfies me.

PAMPHILUS: Here's Davus, just when I want him. I rely on his advice.

CHARINUS (*to* BYRRIA): But you—you never give me any advice, unless it's something I don't want to hear. Get out of here, will you?

BYRRIA: Yes! Gladly! (*Exit* BYRRIA.)

SCENE II

DAVUS (*to himself*): Great gods! What good news have I heard? But where will I find Pamphilus, so that I can clear away his worries and fill his heart with joy?

CHARINUS: He's happy about something.

PAMPHILUS: It doesn't mean anything. He hasn't heard the bad news yet.

DAVUS (*to himself*): For I can imagine that now, if he's heard that's he's about to be married . . .

CHARINUS: Do you hear him?

DAVUS (*to himself*): . . . he's looking all over the city for me, half out of his wits. But where shall I look for him? Where shall I go first?

CHARINUS: Aren't you going to speak to him?

DAVUS (*to himself*): I've got it!

PAMPHILUS: Davus, come here! Stop!

DAVUS: Who's that . . .? Oh, Pamphilus, you're the very man, I'm looking for. Charinus, too? Fine! Both of you here! Splendid! I want you both.

PAMPHILUS: Davus, it's all over with me.

DAVUS: No, no! Just listen to this!

CHARINUS: I'm done for.

DAVUS (*to* CHARINUS): I know what you're afraid of.

PAMPHILUS: For my part, I don't think I'll survive it.

DAVUS (*to* PAMPHILUS): Yes, I know what's bothering you, too.

PAMPHILUS: My marriage. . . .

DAVUS: Even if I *know* all that?

PAMPHILUS: It's today.

DAVUS: Are you going to keep harping on that, even though I know all about it? (*To* CHARINUS) You're afraid you won't get to marry her. (*To* PAMPHILUS) You're afraid you will.

CHARINUS: You've got it.

PAMPHILUS: That's exactly right.

DAVUS: And I tell you, that "exactly right"—there's no danger of it! Leave it to me!

PAMPHILUS: Please, please! I'm miserable. Free me from this fear as fast as you can!

DAVUS: All right; I free you. Chremes isn't going to let his daughter marry you now.

PAMPHILUS: How do you know?

DAVUS: I know all right. Your father just now got hold of me. He said he was arranging the marriage for you today— and a lot of other things there's no time to tell now. Right away I hurried off and ran downtown to tell you this. When I didn't find you, I got up onto a high place and looked all around—nowhere! It so happened that I saw this fellow's man, Byrria, there. I asked him. He said he hadn't seen you. That bothered me; I wondered what I should do. Meanwhile, as I was coming back I got suspicious just because of the way things looked. "Hm," said I, "Not much food in the house; the master gloomy; all of a sudden a wedding! It doesn't hang together."

PAMPHILUS: What's the point of that?

DAVUS: So I went straight to Chremes' house. When I got there, there wasn't a soul at the door. That made me happy right away.

CHARINUS: Good, good!

PAMPHILUS: Go on!

DAVUS: I waited around. During that time, I didn't see anybody go in or come out, no matron of honor in the house, no decorations, no noise. I went up to the house and peeked in.

PAMPHILUS: Yes. That means a lot.

DAVUS: Well, that doesn't seem to go with a wedding, does it?

PAMPHILUS: I don't think so, Davus.

DAVUS: "Think so," you say? You're not getting it straight. It's certain! On top of that, as I was leaving I met one of Chremes' slaves; he had some vegetables, little bits of sardines —about a penny's worth—for the master's dinner!

CHARINUS: I'm a free man today, Davus, all because of your efforts!

DAVUS: Oh, no, you're not!

CHARINUS: Why not? After all, Chremes isn't going to give Philumena to Pamphilus, is he?.

DAVUS: Stupid! As if you'll necessarily marry her if he doesn't give her to him, if you don't keep your eyes open, and get around, and talk to her father's friends.

CHARINUS: That's good advice. I'll go, although I must say I've been deceived in that hope a good many times already. Good-by. (*Exit* CHARINUS.)

SCENE III

PAMPHILUS: What does Father mean, then? Why is he putting on a show?

DAVUS: I'll tell you. If he should fly into a rage now just because Chremes won't let his daughter marry you, and before he's found out how you feel about the marriage, he'd realize that he was not being fair to you, and he'd be right, too. But if you should refuse to marry her, at that point he'll put the blame on you. Then there'll be a fuss!

PAMPHILUS: I'll put up with anything!

DAVUS: He's your father, Pamphilus; it's not easy. Besides, this woman has no one to protect her. He'd find something she said, something she did—some excuse for forcing her to leave town.

PAMPHILUS: He'd force her to leave?

DAVUS: Yes, and in a hurry.

PAMPHILUS: Tell me: What am I to do, then, Davus?

DAVUS: Tell him you'll marry her.

PAMPHILUS: What?

DAVUS: What's the matter?

PAMPHILUS: *I* tell him *that*?

DAVUS: Why not?

PAMPHILUS: I'll never do it.

DAVUS: Don't say that.

PAMPHILUS: Don't you try to persuade me.

DAVUS: Think what will happen if you do.

PAMPHILUS: Yes. I'll be shut out from her and shut in here.
(*Points to his own house*)

DAVUS: No, that's not so. This is how I think it will go:
Your father will say, "I want you to get married today"; you'll
say, "All right." Tell me, what fault will he have to find with
you there? That way you'll ruin all his well-laid plans, and
with absolutely no risk. For there's no doubt about this:
Chremes isn't going to let his daughter marry you. But don't
let that lead you to mend your ways, or he might change his
mind. Tell your father you're willing, so that, although he'd
like to, he won't be able to attack you and still be fair. As for
your thinking, "With my behavior, I needn't worry about a
wife; nobody will offer me one"—he'll find one without a
dowry before he'll let your reputation be ruined. But if he
finds you're taking it in good spirit, you'll make him careless.
He'll take his time about finding someone else. Meantime,
we'll get a break of some kind.

PAMPHILUS: Do you think so?

DAVUS: Why, there's no doubt about it!

PAMPHILUS: Watch what you're getting me into!

DAVUS: Stop worrying, will you?

PAMPHILUS: I'll tell him I'll marry her. But I must be
careful that he doesn't find out I'm the father of Glycerium's
child, for I've promised to recognize it as my own.

DAVUS: A risky thing to do!

PAMPHILUS: She asked me to give her my word to that, so that she'd know she wouldn't be deserted. (*Enter* SIMO.)

DAVUS: It'll be taken care of. But here comes your father. Don't let him see you're upset.

SCENE IV

SIMO (*to himself*): I'll go and see what they're doing or what plans they're making.

DAVUS (*aside to* PAMPHILUS): He hasn't a doubt that you'll say you won't marry her. He's coming here with his speech all learned—he's been off in a corner by himself somewhere. He thinks he has found something to say that will put you off, so keep your wits about you.

PAMPHILUS (*aside to* DAVUS): If I just can, Davus!

DAVUS (*aside to* PAMPHILUS): I'm telling you; you can be sure of this, Pamphilus: your father won't have one word to say to you now, if you tell him you'll marry Philumena.

SCENE V

(*Enter* BYRRIA.)

BYRRIA (*to himself*): Master told me to drop everything to-day and keep an eye on Pamphilus, so that I'd know what he was doing about the wedding. That's the reason I'm following him now. Aha! There he is with Davus. I'll watch this. (*He steps into the alleyway.*)

SIMO (*to himself*): I see they're both here.

DAVUS (*to* PAMPHILUS): There! Hold it, now!

SIMO: Pamphilus!

DAVUS (*aside to* PAMPHILUS): Look around as if you hadn't seen him.

PAMPHILUS: Oh! Father!

DAVUS (*aside to* PAMPHILUS): Fine!

SIMO: I want you to get married today, as I told you.

BYRRIA (*aside*): Now I'm afraid for our side. What's he going to answer?

PAMPHILUS: I'll never oppose you, father, either in that matter or in any other.

BYRRIA (*aside*): Well!

DAVUS (*aside*): That shut him up!

BYRRIA (*aside*): What did he say?

SIMO: You're behaving as you should when you do what I ask and are pleasant about it, too.

DAVUS (*aside to* PAMPHILUS): Am I right?

BYRRIA (*aside*): From what I hear, master's lost a wife.

SIMO: Go on in now, so that you won't hold things up when we need you.

PAMPHILUS: I'm going. (*Exit* PAMPHILUS.)

BYRRIA (*aside*): You can't trust anybody in anything! The old proverb that you hear quoted so often is true: "Every man's his own best friend." I've seen that girl; I remember that she was good-looking, so I feel less critical of Pamphilus if he'd rather sleep with his arms around her than have somebody else do it. I'll go tell Charinus—and get myself in bad for my bad news. (*Exit* BYRRIA.)

SCENE VI

DAVUS (*aside*): He thinks I've got some trick up my sleeve, and that that's why I stayed here.

SIMO: What's Davus got to say? Nothing now, either? Nothing at all? Well, well!

DAVUS: No, not a thing.

SIMO: And yet I was sure you would!

DAVUS (*aside*): He's had a surprise, all right. I can see that. And he doesn't like it.

SIMO: Do you suppose you could tell me the truth?

DAVUS: Nothing easier!

SIMO: Pamphilus isn't finding this wedding the least bit unwelcome, is he, because of his relations with that foreign woman?

DAVUS: Of course not. Not at all. Or if he is, his unhappiness will last no more than two or three days. Then it'll be all over. No, really, he's thought the whole thing through and got it all straightened out.

SIMO: Good for him!

DAVUS: As long as it was considered proper, and his years allowed it, he had his love affair. He kept it quiet, too. He took care that it never got him talked about, which is what a proper man should do. Now he has to get married, so he has turned his attention to getting married.

SIMO: He seemed to me to be just the tiniest bit unhappy.

DAVUS: Not at all because of the marriage, but he is a little annoyed at you about something.

SIMO: What in the world is it?

DAVUS: It's childish.

SIMO: What is it?

DAVUS: Oh, nothing.

SIMO: Will you tell me what it is?

DAVUS: He says you certainly aren't wasting any money.

SIMO: Who, me?

DAVUS: Yes, you. "Why," he says, "he's scarcely spent ten drachmas for food. Doesn't look much as if his son were getting married! Which one," he says, "which *one* of my friends had I best invite to the wedding banquet?" And—and it'll have to be said—you haven't exactly thrown money around. Can't say I think much of it.

SIMO: Hold your tongue!

DAVUS (*aside*): I stirred him up!

SIMO: I'll see that that's properly taken care of. (*Aside*) What's this all about? What does this scoundrel mean? For if there's anything odd going on here, you can be sure he's the source of it.

ACT THREE

SCENE I

(SIMO *and* DAVUS *on the stage. Enter* MYSIS *and* LESBIA.)

MYSIS: Yes, indeed! It's just as you say, Lesbia; you'll have a hard time finding a man who's faithful to a woman.

SIMO (*to* DAVUS): Is this girl from the Andrian's?

DAVUS: What are you talking about?

SIMO: She is.

MYSIS: But Pamphilus, here, . . .

SIMO: What's she saying?

MYSIS: . . . has given his word. . . .

SIMO: Aha!

DAVUS (*aside*): I wish he'd be struck deaf, or she'd be struck dumb!

MYSIS: . . . He has said that he'll acknowledge the baby.

SIMO: What's this I hear? It's all over—that is, if she's telling the truth.

LESBIA: A goodhearted young man, from what you say.

MYSIS: Good? Excellent! But come on in with me; we mustn't be late.

LESBIA: All right. (*Exit* LESBIA *and* MYSIS *into* CHRYSIS' *house.*)

DAVUS (*aside*): Here's a mess! Now what do I do?

SIMO: What is this? Is he insane? A foreign woman's child? Oh! Now I understand! I almost didn't see it. Was I stupid!!

DAVUS (*aside*): What's this he "almost didn't see"?

SIMO: This is the first little scene Davus is staging for me; they're pretending the woman's in labor, so that they can scare off Chremes.

GLYCERIUM (*within*): Juno Lucina, help! Save me! Oh-h-h-h!! Oh-h-h-h!!

SIMO: My, my! So prompt! Ridiculous! When she heard that I was at the door, she hurried things up. Your timing is a little off in this scene, Davus.

Davus: *My* timing?

Simo: Your actors aren't forgetting their parts, are they?

Davus: I don't know what you're talking about.

Simo (*to audience*): If he'd caught me off guard when a real wedding was involved, what a fool he'd have made of me! But now the risks are his; I'm safe at home.

Scene II

(*Enter* Lesbia, *from* Chrysis' *house.*)

Lesbia (*Calling back into house*): So far, Archylis, I see she has all the symptoms they usually have and ought to have, if they're going to get well. Now first, see that she gets a bath. After that, give her the medicine I prescribed. I'll be back in a little while. (*To audience*) By heaven, Pamphilus has a cute baby boy! I pray God it'll live, since Pamphilus is such a fine young man and was so anxious to do the right thing by this dear, sweet girl. (*Exit.*)

Simo (*to* Davus): Well, well! How could anybody who knew you fail to see that this was all your idea?

Davus: What in the world do you mean?

Simo: She didn't tell them inside what they should do for the woman after she'd had her baby. No! She comes out here first, and then shouts from the street to the people in the house! Oh, Davus! Is that all you think of me? Do I really look like such an easy mark? Did you think you could fool me with such an obvious trick? You might at least put a little thought into it, so that it would look as if you were going to be worried if I caught on.

Davus (*aside*): Well! The master is leading himself astray, I'm not.

Simo: I told you, I warned you, not to do it. You paid no attention to me, did you? What good did it do you? Am I really supposed to believe, now, that she's had a baby by Pamphilus?

Davus (*aside*): Now I see where he's making his mistake, and I know what to do.

SIMO: Why don't you say something?

DAVUS: Believe it? Why would you? As if somebody didn't tell you that this was going to happen.

SIMO: Somebody tell me?

DAVUS: What? Do you mean to say that you figured out all by yourself that this was being staged?

SIMO: Mocking me, are you?

DAVUS: Somebody told you, for how could you ever have suspected?

SIMO: How? I know you, don't I?

DAVUS: Sounds as if you were saying that I planned this.

SIMO: I know you did!

DAVUS: You really don't know yet what kind of person I am, Simo.

SIMO: I don't?

DAVUS: No! The minute I open my mouth to tell you anything, you think I'm lying to you.

SIMO: And of course, I'm wrong!

DAVUS: Yes! Why—why it's gotten to the point that I don't dare even whisper!

SIMO: Well, I know one thing: They've had no babies here.

DAVUS: Yes, that's right; they haven't. But just the same they'll be bringing a baby out here before long. I'm telling you now, sir, that's what will happen, so you'll be prepared, and so that you won't be saying later on that Davus had anything to do with the scheme. I want you to get that idea completely out of your thoughts.

SIMO: How do you know they'll bring a baby out?

DAVUS: Somebody told me, and I'm sure it's right. A lot of things are happening, and they all add up. It's not hard to guess. Once before this she said that Pamphilus had gotten her pregnant; it turned out not to be true. Now, the minute she sees that we're getting ready for a wedding, she sends a girl right off to bring the midwife—and a baby along with her. Unless they bring the baby out, so that you can see him, it will have no effect on the wedding.

SIMO: What are you saying? When you saw that they were

planning something like that, why didn't you go straight to Pamphilus and tell him?

DAVUS: What makes you think I didn't? Who dragged him away from the woman, if I didn't? After all, we all know how madly in love with her he was. Now he wants to get married. Anyway, just leave that baby business to me. You go right on with your preparations for the wedding, and I wish you good luck with them.

SIMO: No, no. You go on in. Wait for me there, and see that what's needed is done. (*Exit* DAVUS *into* SIMO's *house.*) He hasn't quite convinced me to believe all this. Still, I wouldn't be surprised if everything he said was true. But I don't really care. By far the most important thing to me is the fact that my son has given me his promise. Now I'll go find Chremes and ask him to let his daughter marry Pamphilus. If I can get him to agree, then why wait? Why not have the wedding today? For since Pamphilus has given me his promise, I haven't the least doubt that if he reneges I can properly put pressure on him. And, by heaven, just at the right time, look who's coming—Chremes himself! (*Enter* CHREMES.)

SCENE III

SIMO: Hello there, Chremes!

CHREMES: Aha! You're the very man I was looking for!

SIMO: Same to you. I'm so glad you happened along!

CHREMES: People have been coming to me and telling me that they'd heard from you that my daughter was marrying your son today. I've come to find out who's crazy—they, or you.

SIMO: Now hold on a minute. Just listen and you'll find out what I want of you and also get an answer to your question.

CHREMES: All right. I'm listening. Tell me what you want.

SIMO: I beg you, Chremes, in the name of heaven and of our friendship—and it's a friendship that began when we were boys and has grown deeper and deeper as we grew older—and in the name of your only daughter and my only son—you're the

only man who can save him!—help me in this affair; let them
get married as we'd originally planned.

CHREMES: Here, here! Don't get on your knees to me! As
if it were right for you to win me over to a thing like that by
getting on your knees! Do you think I'm not the same man
that I was when I made the proposal? If getting married is for
the good of both of them, tell my daughter the ceremony is
about to begin. But if for either one of them there's going to
be more harm than good from the match, then please consider
the question from both sides: suppose you were Philumena's
father, and I, Pamphilus'.

SIMO: No, no, Chremes! That's just what I want to do. In
fact, I insist on it. I wouldn't be making this proposal to you
if the facts didn't justify it.

CHREMES: What do you mean?

SIMO: Glycerium and Pamphilus have had a quarrel.

CHREMES: Yes, so I hear!

SIMO: No, it's a serious one, so serious that I think the affair
can be broken up.

CHREMES: Nonsense!

SIMO: No, no; I tell you, it's really true!

CHREMES: Ridiculous! I'll tell you what it really means:
"Lovers' quarrels are but love's sweet renewal."

SIMO: Well, that's just what you and I, please, have got to
prevent, while we've got the chance and while his passion for
her is blocked off by what she's done to him. Before these wom-
en with their villainous schemes and their rascally crocodile
tears bring him around, all upset as he is, to feeling sorry for
the girl, let's get him married. I feel sure that once he has felt
the restraining influence of love and marriage with a nice girl,
he'll easily pull himself out of the bad habits he's developed.

CHREMES: That's what you think. But I don't think he can
—and he can't go on keeping that woman, nor would I stand
for it.

SIMO: How do you know he can't, if you don't give him a
chance?

CHREMES: Yes, but to take a chance like that in the case of a daughter is a serious matter.

SIMO: Well, but after all, it's not so terrible and it could come to nothing worse than a divorce—may the gods forbid it! Whereas, if my son should mend his ways, think of all the advantages: You'll have a steady son-in-law and your daughter will have a good husband.

CHREMES: All right, all right! If you're convinced that your plan is sound, I wouldn't want to stand in the way of any good you might get from it.

SIMO: I always did think the world of you, Chremes—and I was right.

CHREMES: M-mm—but, tell me!

SIMO: What?

CHREMES: How do you know Glycerium and Pamphilus are at outs?

SIMO: Davus himself told me. He knows all their thoughts and plans. He's the one who's been urging me to arrange the wedding as soon as possible. You don't think he'd do that, do you, if he weren't sure that that was what my son wanted? Anyway, you can hear the story from Davus himself. (*Calls in at door*) Boy! Call Davus out here. Oh! Here he comes!

SCENE IV

(*Enter* DAVUS.)

DAVUS (*to* SIMO): I was looking for you.

SIMO: Why? What is it?

DAVUS: Where's the bride? Isn't she coming? It's getting along toward evening.

SIMO (*to* CHREMES): Hear that? (*To* DAVUS): Until just now I've been a little uneasy about you, Davus, for fear you'd do the sort of thing most slaves do—try to trick me and fool me, because my son was having a love affair.

DAVUS: You thought that *I* would do *that*?

SIMO: Yes, I did. And for that reason I've been keeping from you something I'm going to tell you now.

DAVUS: What's that?

SIMO: You'll find out—for, you know, I almost trust you now!

DAVUS: Oh! You've finally found out what kind of man I am, have you?

SIMO: There wasn't going to be a wedding at all.

DAVUS: What! There wasn't?

SIMO: No. I was just pretending there was, so that I could put you to the test.

DAVUS: You don't say!

SIMO: That's absolutely right!

DAVUS: Well, what do you know! I never would have imagined such a thing! What a clever idea!

SIMO: Yes. Well, now listen to this: Just after I told you to go in, by good luck Chremes, here, came this way.

DAVUS (aside): Oh-oh! We aren't in for trouble, are we?

SIMO: I told him the story that you had just told me.

DAVUS (aside): What am I hearing?

SIMO: I asked him for his daughter's hand and finally got him to agree.

DAVUS (aside): Good God!

SIMO: Hm? What did you say?

DAVUS: Oh, I said, "Fine, fine!"

SIMO: Now, as far as he's concerned, there's no need for any further delay.

CHREMES: I'll just run along home and tell Philumena to get ready; then I'll let you know. (Exit CHREMES.)

SIMO: And now, Davus, since you've brought this marriage about all by yourself—

DAVUS (aside): "All by myself" is right!

SIMO: —will you please keep working on Pamphilus to get him to mend his ways.

DAVUS: I'll do that, all right!

SIMO: You can now, when he's all upset.

DAVUS: Just don't you worry.

SIMO: Well, then, where is the boy now?

DAVUS: Oh, probably at home.

SIMO: I'll go in and tell him just what I've told you. (*Exit* SIMO.)

DAVUS: It's all over for me! Why don't I just take the shortest way straight to the mill? There's no use in my asking any favors. I've made a complete mess of everything—deceived Simo, tossed Pamphilus right into a wedding, fixed the wedding for this very day, when Simo didn't expect it and Pamphilus didn't want it. Smart boy, I am! If I'd just kept quiet, there wouldn't have been any trouble. Oh-oh! Here comes Pamphilus! I'm in for it! Oh, for a hole to crawl into!

SCENE V

(*Enter* PAMPHILUS.)

PAMPHILUS: Where is that scoundrel who has ruined me?

DAVUS (*aside*): Oh, my!

PAMPHILUS: Still, I'll have to admit that I got just what I deserved, I was such a coward and so brainless. To think that I'd trust my life to a stupid slave! I was a fool, and I'm getting what I deserve—but he'll not get off scot-free!

DAVUS (*aside*): If I can get out of this one, I'll never have another worry in my life!

PAMPHILUS: I ask you, now: What shall I say to father? Tell him I won't marry her, when I've just promised I would? What kind of impudence would I need to do that? I don't know what to do now.

DAVUS (*aside*): Neither do I, and I'm doing it as hard as I can. I'll tell him I'll think of something, so that I can put off the evil day.

PAMPHILUS (*sees* DAVUS): Aha!

DAVUS (*aside*): He saw me!

PAMPHILUS: Well, well, my fine man, what have you got to say? Do you see how beautifully I'm trapped by your fancy schemes?

DAVUS: Well, I'll get you out.

PAMPHILUS: You'll get me out?

DAVUS: Of course, Pamphilus.

PAMPHILUS: Yes—the way you just did.

DAVUS: No, I hope I'll do better than that.

PAMPHILUS: Hah! Am I supposed to trust you, you devil? Got everything tangled up and wrecked, and now you'll straighten it all out, won't you? Look at the man I relied on! Everything was perfectly peaceful, and you took me out of the middle of it and dropped me right into a wedding. Didn't I tell you that's what would happen?

DAVUS: You did.

PAMPHILUS: What should I do to you?

DAVUS: Hang me. But just let me get my wits about me. I'll soon find a way out.

PAMPHILUS: Well, I certainly wish I had time to take it out of your hide, as I'd like to, but at the moment I'll do well if I take care of myself, and I'll have to pass you up.

ACT FOUR

SCENE I

(*Enter* CHARINUS, PAMPHILUS, DAVUS.)

CHARINUS: Can you believe it? Did you ever hear of such a thing? Could any man be so heartless as to take pleasure in somebody else's bad luck, and to use another man's misfortune to profit himself? Is this possible? No, no, I tell you; this is the worst kind of man there is, the kind that is ashamed to say "No" at the moment. Then later on, when the time comes to fulfill their agreements, they're forced to show their real intentions. Then they're completely shameless. They say, "Who are you? Who are you to me? Why should I give up my girl to you? After all, a man's his own best friend!" But still if you ask, "What about your word of honor?" they aren't ashamed then, when they should be; it's only when they shouldn't be that they are. But what shall I do? Shall I go to him and call him to account for the wrong he's done me? Shall I tell him just what I think of him? "But," you say, "you'll get nowhere." Oh, yes, I will. At least I'll make him uncomfortable and relieve my own feelings.

PAMPHILUS: Charinus, quite without meaning to, unless the gods help us somehow, I've ruined both myself and you.

CHARINUS: Oh, that's it, is it? "Without meaning to"! Found an excuse at last, have you? You broke your word.

PAMPHILUS: What do you mean, "Found an excuse at last"?

CHARINUS: Do you expect to fool me with fine speeches even now?

PAMPHILUS: What is the matter with you?

CHARINUS: After I said I was in love with Philumena, you decided you liked her. Oh, what a fool I was to judge your heart by my own!

PAMPHILUS: You're mistaken!

CHARINUS: Didn't your happiness seem complete, unless you could torment me, who loved her, and lead me on with false hopes? Keep her!

PAMPHILUS: Keep her? Ah, you don't know what a mess I'm in, and what a lot of grief Davus, here, has stirred up for me with his schemes—my personal executioner!

CHARINUS: What's so surprising about that, if he takes you for his model?

PAMPHILUS: You wouldn't say that, if you really understood either me or my feelings.

CHARINUS: Yes, I know; you had a quarrel with your father a while ago, and so he's furious with you and just couldn't force you to marry Philumena today.

PAMPHILUS: No, no, no! Just to show how little you know of my woes, there was no wedding being planned for me, and nobody was insisting on my getting married.

CHARINUS: Yes, I know; you just had to because you wanted to.

PAMPHILUS: Wait a minute. You don't understand at all!

CHARINUS: I understand this: You're going to marry Philumena.

PAMPHILUS: Why do you keep rubbing it in? Now listen! He never stopped insisting that I must tell father I'd marry her. He argued, he begged, until finally I gave in.

CHARINUS: Who's "he"?

PAMPHILUS: Davus.

CHARINUS: Davus? Why?

PAMPHILUS: I don't know. All I know is that the gods were angry with me for listening to him.

CHARINUS: Did you do that, Davus?

DAVUS: Yes, I did.

CHARINUS: Why! What do you mean? Why, you . . . ! I hope you die the death you deserve! Listen now, tell me: If everybody who hated him wanted him tossed into the middle of a wedding, what advice would they give him but that?

DAVUS: I made a mistake, but I'm not through yet.

CHARINUS: Yes! Sure!

DAVUS: We didn't succeed very well this way; we'll try another tack. Unless you think that because our scheme didn't work out very well the first time, this trouble can't still be made to turn out right.

PAMPHILUS: No, I'm sure of that! I'm quite certain that if you'll just keep your eyes open, you can find me two weddings instead of one!

DAVUS: Pamphilus, I'm your slave, and as such it's my duty to work with might and main, night and day, to risk my life, so long as I may help you. It's your duty, if things don't turn out quite as expected, to forgive me. My scheme isn't going very well, but I'm still at it. Or why don't you find a better scheme yourself, and let me out?

PAMPHILUS: Just what I'd like. Put me back where we were when you started.

DAVUS: All right, I will.

PAMPHILUS: But you've got to do it right now!

DAVUS: We-e-ll—But Glycerium's door here creaked.

PAMPHILUS: That's none of your business.

DAVUS (*to himself*): I'm thinking—

PAMPHILUS: Hm! It's about time!

DAVUS: I'll think it out and let you know about it right away.

SCENE II

(*Enter* MYSIS.)

MYSIS (*calls in through doorway*): Now, now! Wherever he is, I'll see that he's found and brought here to you, "your Pamphilus." Just don't you upset yourself, darling.

PAMPHILUS: Mysis!

MYSIS: Who's that? Oh, Pamphilus! What good luck that you came this way!

PAMPHILUS: What's the trouble?

MYSIS: She told me to beg you, if you love her—my mistress did—to come to her right away. She says she's anxious to see you.

PAMPHILUS: Oh, my! Here go our troubles, all over again! (*To* DAVUS) To think that all because of you, she and I should be so miserable and worried! She's asking for me because she's found out about the wedding plans.

CHARINUS (*to* PAMPHILUS): Yes, and how simple it would have been to have had not a word about them, if *he* had just kept quiet!

DAVUS: Go on! Go on! If he's not already crazy enough all by himself, drive him on!

MYSIS: Why, yes! That's exactly the trouble, and it's because of that that the poor girl is unhappy now.

PAMPHILUS: Mysis, I swear to you by all the gods that I'll never desert her, not if I have to make an enemy of every man on earth. I wanted her for myself, and I got her; we love each other. I disown any man who wants to separate us. Nothing but death shall take her from me.

MYSIS: Well! I feel better!

PAMPHILUS: Apollo's word is not more true than what I've said. If it's possible to arrange things so that father won't think that it was I who put a stop to this wedding, that's how I'd like it. But if it can't be fixed that way, I'll do the easy thing and let him think that I did put a stop to it. What does that make me?

CHARINUS: Unhappy, just like me.

DAVUS: I'm trying to think up a plan . . .

PAMPHILUS: Oh, yes! I'm quite certain whatever you try—

DAVUS: This one, for sure, I'll make succeed.

PAMPHILUS: It's about time!

DAVUS: Yes, sir—I've got it now!

CHARINUS: What is it?

PAMPHILUS: It's for him, not for you; don't you fool yourself.

CHARINUS: That's all right with me.

PAMPHILUS: What are you going to do? Tell me!

DAVUS: I'm afraid the day may not be long enough for *doing* it, so don't think you can make me stop now to *tell* about it. You two just chase yourselves out of here; you're in my way.

PAMPHILUS: I'll go and see Glycerium. (*Exit.*)

DAVUS: What about you? Where are you going?

CHARINUS: Want me to tell you the truth?

DAVUS: Oh, sure, of course! (*Aside*) Here begins a long, long story!

CHARINUS: What's to become of me?

DAVUS: What? You ought to be ashamed of yourself! Isn't it enough that I'm getting you a postponement for as long as I put off Pamphilus' wedding?

CHARINUS: Yes, but Davus—

DAVUS: Oh, what?

CHARINUS: I want to marry her!

DAVUS: Don't be silly!

CHARINUS: Come here to me, if you can do anything.

DAVUS: Why should I? I can't help you.

CHARINUS: Well, but still, if you can!

DAVUS: All right. I'll come, if anything turns up.

CHARINUS: I'll be at home. (*Exit.*)

DAVUS: Mysis, wait here a minute till I come out.

MYSIS: What for?

Davus: It's got to be that way.

Mysis: Well, hurry up.

Davus: I tell you I'll be right out. (*Exit.*)

(Mysis *moves to one side.*)

Scene III

Mysis (*aside*): It's certainly true that you can't be sure of anything! Heavens! I always thought that Pamphilus was a godsend to my mistress—a friend, a lover, a regular husband, ready to stand by her at any time. But what a lot of trouble he's brought her, poor thing! The bad easily outweighs the good. But here comes Davus. For heaven's sake, man, what are you up to? Where are you taking the baby?

Davus: Mysis, you've got to help me now with my scheme. I'm going to need all the sharpness and cleverness you've got.

Mysis: What *are* you going to do?

Davus: Never mind. Just take the baby from me and put him down by our door.

Mysis: What? On the bare ground?

Davus: Here, take some of these branches from the altar, and lay him on those.

Mysis: Why don't you do it yourself?

Davus: Because, uh—so that if I have to swear to my master that I didn't put him there, I can do it with clear conscience.

Mysis: Oh, I see. Getting awfully righteous all of a sudden, aren't you? Give him to me.

Davus: Hurry up, so that I can explain what's to come next—great gods!

Mysis: What's the matter?

Davus: Here comes Philumena's father! I'll have to give up my original plan.

Mysis: I don't know what you're talking about.

Davus: I'll pretend that I'm just getting here, too, from the right. You watch what I say, and follow up the cues I give you, whatever you may have to say. (*Exit.*)

Mysis: I haven't the slightest idea what you're up to, but

if you need my help in any way, you're smarter than I am, so I'll wait here for you. I wouldn't want to get in the way of any good idea you may have.

Scene IV

(*Enter* Chremes.)

Chremes: Well, here I come back! I've made the necessary preparations for my daughter's wedding, so that I could tell them to come for her. But what's this? By heaven, it's a baby! Here, young woman, did you put that baby here?

Mysis (*aside*): Where *is* Davus?

Chremes: Are you going to answer me or not?

Mysis (*aside*): I don't see him anywhere! Oh, dear, dear, dear! The fellow has gone off and left me!

Davus (*entering from right; aside*): Great gods! What a mob downtown! What a crowd of people suing each other! And how prices have gone up! (*Aside*) I don't know what else to say!

Mysis (*to* Pamphilus): Say, why did you leave me here all alone?

Davus: Well! What kind of nonsense is this? Mysis, where did this baby come from? Who brought him here?

Mysis: Are you crazy? Asking me a thing like that!

Davus: Well, who else should I ask? I don't see anybody else here.

Chremes (*aside*): I wonder where it came from?

Davus (*aside to* Mysis): Are you going to answer my question? (*Digs her with his elbow*)

Mysis: Ow!

Davus (*aside to* Mysis): Come over here. (*Moves stage right*)

Mysis (*aside to* Davus): You're crazy! Didn't you yourself—

Davus (*aside to* Mysis): If you say one word except what I ask for, I'll knock your— (*Aloud*) Call me names, will you? Where did it come from? (*Aside to* Mysis) Speak out good and loud.

MYSIS: From our house.

DAVUS: Aha! Amazing, isn't it, if a courtesan tries something dishonest.

CHREMES (*aside*): This girl comes from the Andrian's, if I'm not mistaken.

DAVUS (*to* MYSIS): Did you think we were such simple souls, that you could make fools of us like that?

CHREMES (*aside*): I got here just at the right time.

DAVUS: Hurry up, now. Take that baby away from our door. (*Aside to* MYSIS) Wait! Don't you dare move a step!

MYSIS (*aside to* DAVUS): Damn you! You're scaring me to death!

DAVUS: Am I talking to you or not?

MYSIS: What *do* you want?

DAVUS: You know what I want. Come on: Whose baby did you put here? *Tell* me!

MYSIS: Don't you know?

DAVUS (*aside to* MYSIS): Never mind what I know; answer my question!

MYSIS: It belongs to your people.

DAVUS: To which one of our people?

MYSIS: To Pamphilus.

DAVUS: What? To Pamphilus?

MYSIS: Well! Doesn't it?

CHREMES (*aside*): I was right all along in keeping clear of that wedding.

DAVUS: This is a downright crime!

MYSIS: What are you yelling about?

DAVUS: Is this the baby I saw brought to your house last night?

MYSIS: Why, of all the nerve—!

DAVUS: That's right! I saw Canthara with something stuffed under her dress.

MYSIS: Well, I'm certainly glad that there were several reliable witnesses present when the baby was born.

DAVUS: I tell you, Glycerium doesn't know the man for whose benefit she's staging these stunts: "If Chremes sees a

baby laid at their door, he'll take back the offer of marriage."
Oh, no! He'll insist on it all the more!

CHREMES (*aside*): Oh, no, he won't!

DAVUS: All right, now; I'm giving you fair warning; if you
don't take that baby away, I'll dump him in the middle of the
street, and you along with him—right in the mud!

MYSIS: You must be drunk! (*Picks up baby.*)

DAVUS: One tall tale after another: I'm hearing it whispered
around now that Glycerium is an Attic citizen.

CHREMES (*aside*): H'm-m-m!

DAVUS: They say he'll be compelled by law to marry her.

MYSIS: Well! If you please, *isn't* she a citizen?

CHREMES (*aside*): I didn't realize how close I came to making an awful fool of myself.

DAVUS: Who's that? (*Pretends to see* CHREMES *for first time*)
Oh, Chremes! You're just in time. Listen!

CHREMES: I've heard it all already.

DAVUS: You don't say? All of it?

CHREMES: I heard it, I tell you, from start to finish.

DAVUS: You did? Isn't it downright criminal? This woman
ought to be dragged right off to jail. (*To* MYSIS) That's the
man—so don't you go thinking you were just pulling tricks on
a Davus.

MYSIS: Oh, dear, dear! I didn't say a word that wasn't true,
sir.

CHREMES: I know the whole story. Is Simo in there?

DAVUS: Yes. (*Exit* CHREMES *into* SIMO's *house.*)

MYSIS: Don't you touch me, you worthless—by heaven if I
don't go and tell Glycerium everything—

DAVUS: Why, you silly girl! Don't you see what's been going
on?

MYSIS: No. How should I?

DAVUS: That's father-in-law! There wasn't any other way we
could manage to let him know what we wanted him to know.

MYSIS: Well, you might have told me ahead of time.

DAVUS: Do you think it makes no difference whether you do

things spontaneously, on the spur of the moment, or just follow a plan?

SCENE V

(Enter CRITO, *stage left.)*

CRITO: This is the street where they say Chrysis lived. She
preferred to come here and get rich dishonorably rather than
to stay at home and be respectable and poor. When she died
her property came to me by law. But I see some people to
ask. How do you do?

MYSIS: Goodness gracious! Do I see Crito, Chrysis' cousin?
I do!

CRITO: Why, Mysis, hello!

MYSIS: Hello, hello, Crito!

CRITO: So Chrysis—? Too bad!

MYSIS: Yes, and we've just felt awful about it.

CRITO: Well, what have you done? How are you getting
along? Everything all right?

MYSIS: How are we getting along? Oh, so-so. Doing the
best we can, as they say, since we can't do as we'd like.

CRITO: What about Glycerium? Has she found her parents
yet?

MYSIS: I wish she had!

CRITO: What? Not found them yet? I'm afraid I made a
mistake in coming then. By heaven, if I'd known that, I'd
never have set foot here. She was always called Chrysis' sister,
and everybody thought she was. She'll have legal possession of
Chrysis' property. Now here I am, a foreigner. I'll have to
bring suit. I know just how easy that will be, and how much
good it will do me; plenty of others have tried it. Besides, I
expect she has some friend to look out for her, for she was a
pretty big girl when she left Andros. They'd all call me a
pettifogger, a ghoul, a beggar. And anyway, I don't want to
leave her with no money.

MYSIS: You dear, good man! Crito, you haven't changed a bit!

CRITO: Take me in to her. I might as well see her, since I've come all this way.

MYSIS: Yes, of course.

DAVUS (*aside*): I'll go along with them. I don't want the master to see me right now.

ACT FIVE

SCENE I

(*Enter* CHREMES *and* SIMO.)

CHREMES: No, no, Simo; you've put my friendship to the test quite enough. I've taken enough chances. Just stop your pleading. Trying to do you a favor, I almost gambled away my daughter's happiness.

SIMO: But Chremes, I beg you and beseech you, as I never did before. You promised me a kindness; now please keep your promise.

CHREMES: Now see how unfair you are, just because of your own selfish interest: Just so you get what you want, you don't even consider that there's a limit to kindness. You don't think what you're asking of me, for if you did, you'd stop doing me all these wrongs.

SIMO: What wrongs?

CHREMES: How can you ask that? See what you've made me do: Here's a young fellow absorbed in another love affair, detesting the idea of getting married. You've made me promise him my daughter in a marriage that will lead to quarrels and can't posssibly last. By her trouble and misery, I'm to reform your son. You had your way. I went along with it, as long as it could be stood. Now it can't be stood; you stand it. They say Glycerium is an Attic citizen. She's had a baby. Just count us out.

SIMO: But for heaven's sake, don't let yourself believe those people! It's all to their advantage to make Pamphilus seem as bad as they can. It's the wedding that's made them start all this talk. When their reason for doing this has been taken away, they'll stop.

CHREMES: There's where you're wrong. I saw Davus myself quarreling with their servant girl.

SIMO: Yes, I know!

CHREMES: No, they were serious about it, and neither of them had noticed that I was there.

SIMO: Yes, yes! Davus told me that's what they'd do. Somehow I forgot to tell you that earlier—and I meant to, too.

SCENE II

(Enter DAVUS.)

DAVUS *(calls back into* GLYCERIUM's *house)*: Now I tell you; don't worry!

CHREMES: There's your fine Davus!

DAVUS: Crito and I will take care of everything.

SIMO: What is this, anyway?

DAVUS *(to audience)*: The man came just exactly when he was needed! I've never seen it done better!

SIMO: Damnation! Who is this he thinks did so well?

DAVUS: Everything's all fixed now!

SIMO: And here I stand. Why don't I speak to him?

DAVUS *(aside)*: It's master! What shall I do?

SIMO: Well, hello, my good friend!

DAVUS: Oh, hello, Simo! Hello, Chremes! Everything's all ready now.

SIMO: Yes, you've done a fine job of it.

DAVUS: Have her come any time you like.

SIMO: Yes, yes; of course, of course! That's all we need! Now you just answer me this: What business have you in there?

DAVUS: Who, me?

SIMO: Yes, you!

DAVUS: Oh, I just went in there a minute ago . . .

SIMO: I didn't ask you how long ago.

DAVUS: . . . along with Pamphilus.

SIMO: What? Is Pamphilus in there? Oh, great gods! Listen here: Didn't you tell me he and Glycerium had broken up?

DAVUS: They have.

SIMO: What's he doing in there, then?

CHREMES: What do you think he's doing? Quarreling with her, naturally!

DAVUS: No, Chremes. It's a disgraceful business. I'll tell you all about it. Insolent chap! A sharp one, too! From his looks, you'd say they don't come any finer. He has a serious, honest face, and his talk is very convincing.

SIMO: What's this tale you've got?

DAVUS: It's no tale of mine. It's just what I heard him say.

SIMO: Well, what did he say?

DAVUS: Said he knew for a fact that Glycerium was an Attic citizen.

SIMO: H'mmmm! (*Calls into his house*) Dromo! Dromo!

DAVUS: What are you going to do?

SIMO: Dromo!

DAVUS: Listen!

SIMO: If you say one more word—! Dromo!

DAVUS: Listen, please! (*Enter* DROMO.)

DROMO: What is it?

SIMO: Grab him and take him in the house, and be quick about it!

DROMO: Who?

SIMO: Davus.

DAVUS: But why?

SIMO: Because it suits me. Grab him, I tell you.

DAVUS: What did I do?

SIMO: *Grab him!*

DAVUS: If you find I've said a word that isn't true, kill me.

SIMO: I'm not listening. I'll stir you up!

DAVUS: But even if this is the truth?

SIMO: Yes, even if. (*To* DROMO) See that you keep him in

chains, and—oh, yes—listen; chain his hands and feet together. Go on, now. (*To* DAVUS) By heaven, I'll show you, as I live, what it means to deceive your master—and him to deceive his father!

CHREMES: Oh, come now! Don't be so cruel!

SIMO: Oh, Chremes! What a loyal son! Don't you think I deserve your sympathy? All the trouble I've had, and for a son like that! (*Calls into* GLYCERIUM's *house*) All right, Pamphilus! Come out, Pamphilus! Haven't you any sense of shame at all?

SCENE III

PAMPHILUS: Who wants me? Oh, great gods, it's father!

SIMO: What have you to say, you—

CHREMES: Ah, why don't you just get to the point, and stop the scolding?

SIMO: As if I could think of anything worse to say against him! Tell me, now: Is Glycerium a citizen?

PAMPHILUS: That's what they tell me.

SIMO: "That's what they tell me"? The monstrous insolence! Does he even think what he's saying? Is he sorry for what he's done? Look; does his face show the slightest sign of shame? The utter selfishness of it! It's against our Athenian customs; it's against the law; it's against his own father's wish; but still he's got to have that woman, no matter what the disgrace!

PAMPHILUS: You're making me very miserable.

SIMO: Hmph! It's about time you felt miserable, Pamphilus! Long ago, long ago, when you first decided that somehow you had to have what you wanted—that was when the word "miserable" really suited you. But what am I doing? Why am I tormenting myself? Why am I tearing myself to pieces? Why am I worrying my gray hairs with his madness? No. He can keep her. He can get out of my house. He can live with her.

PAMPHILUS: Father!

SIMO: What do you mean, "father"? As if you needed me

for a father! You've got a home, a wife, children, without your father's consent. You've bribed some people to say she's a citizen of Athens. You've won.

PAMPHILUS: Father, may I say a few words?

SIMO: What have you to say to me?

CHREMES: Oh, come, Simo. Hear what he has to say.

SIMO: I, hear? What will I hear, Chremes?

CHREMES: Well, anyway, let him say it.

SIMO: All right, let him say it. He has my permission.

PAMPHILUS: I admit that I'm in love with Glycerium. If that's doing wrong, I admit that, too. I put myself in your hands, father. Put any load you like on me. Tell me what I'm to do. Do you want me to get married? To get rid of Glycerium? I'll stand it the best I can. I just ask you one thing: Don't think that I've put the old gentleman up to anything. Let me clear myself and bring him out here to see you.

SIMO: Bring him to see me?

PAMPHILUS: Please, father.

CHREMES: That's fair enough. Let him do it.

PAMPHILUS: Let me have this one favor from you.

SIMO: All right. (*Exit* PAMPHILUS.) I'd do anything, just so I don't find out that he's been deceiving me, Chremes.

CHREMES: No matter how much wrong he's done, a little punishment is enough for a father.

SCENE IV

(*Enter* CRITO *with* PAMPHILUS.)

CRITO: You don't have to ask me. Any one of these reasons is enough to make me do it: First, you yourself; secondly, because it's true; thirdly, because I want to, for Glycerium's own sake.

CHREMES: Is this Crito of Andros that I see? It certainly is!

CRITO: Why, hello, Chremes!

CHREMES: What are you doing here? You don't often come to Athens.

CRITO: Oh, it just happened that way. But is this Simo, here?

CHREMES: Yes, this is Simo.

CRITO: Were you looking for me?

SIMO: Listen, you; do you claim that Glycerium is a citizen of Athens?

CRITO: Do you claim she isn't?

SIMO: Is that the way it is? Come with your lines all learned?

CRITO: What do you mean?

SIMO: What do I mean! Do you think you're going to get away with this sort of thing? Are you the fellow who takes young men, inexperienced, brought up like gentlemen, and gets them into traps? Gets them excited, makes them promises, and puts them in a turmoil?

CRITO: Have you lost your mind?

SIMO: And sticks commercial love affairs together with marriage glue?

PAMPHILUS (aside): Oh, dear! I'm afraid Crito may not stand up to this!

CHREMES: Simo, if you really knew Crito, you wouldn't think things like that. He's a fine man.

SIMO: He's a fine man? That's why it happened so neatly, that he came here today, on the very day of the wedding, and never before, eh? Yes, he certainly is a man to trust, Chremes.

PAMPHILUS (aside): If I weren't uneasy about father, I have a hint I could drop to Crito that would be to the point.

SIMO: You shyster!

CRITO: Well!

CHREMES: That's the way Simo is, Crito. Please overlook it.

CRITO (to CHREMES): He'd better watch the way he is. If he insists on saying anything he pleases to me, he'll hear a few things that won't please him. (To SIMO) Am I the cause of your troubles? Are they any concern of mine? Can't you bear your own misfortunes in a decent fashion? I'm telling what I heard. We can soon find out whether it's true or not. Some years ago an Athenian lost his ship near Andros. He was cast ashore, and along with him this woman we've been talking about—she was just a little girl then. He had lost everything, and he happened to turn first to Chrysis' father.

SIMO: Here he goes: Chapter One.

CHREMES (*to* SIMO): Don't! Let him alone.

CRITO: Is he going to annoy me like that?

CHREMES (*to* CRITO): Please go on.

CRITO: The man who took the Athenian in was a relative of mine. It was there that I heard from him that he was an Athenian, and it was there that he died.

CHREMES: What was his name?

CRITO: His name? Right now?

PAMPHILUS (*to* CRITO): Phania.

CHREMES: Oh, good heavens!

CRITO: Yes, sir; I do believe it was Phania. One thing I do know; he said he was from Rhamnus.

CHREMES: Great gods!

CRITO: Lots of other people heard this same story, Chremes, at the time, right in Andros.

CHREMES: If it could only mean what I hope it does! Tell me, what did he say about the girl then? Did he say she was his daughter?

CRITO: No.

CHREMES: Whose daughter did he say she was?

CRITO: His brother's.

CHREMES: She's mine, for sure!

CRITO: What's that you say?

SIMO: What are you saying?

PAMPHILUS: Prick up your ears, Pamphilus!

SIMO: What makes you think that?

CHREMES: Why, that Phania; he was my brother.

SIMO: Yes! I knew him. That's right.

CHREMES: He was a refugee from the war here and left with the intention of following me to Asia. He was afraid to leave her here then. This is the first time since then that I've had any news of him.

PAMPHILUS: I can hardly control myself, my head's in such a whirl of fear, hope, joy, and amazement at this sudden bit of good luck!

SIMO: Well, well! I'm glad in more than one way that the girl we've been talking of has been found to be your daughter.

PAMPHILUS: I'm sure you are, father.

CHREMES: But there's one small point that I'm still bothered about.

PAMPHILUS (*aside*): You would be! Fussy old man! You'd find a flaw in perfection itself.

CRITO: What do you mean?

CHREMES: The name isn't right.

CRITO: Oh, well! She was called something else when she was little.

CHREMES: What was it, Crito? I don't suppose you can remember, can you?

CRITO: I'm trying to.

PAMPHILUS: Am I going to let his bad memory stand in the way of my happiness, when I can just as well clear up the matter myself? Look, Chremes, the name you're looking for is Pasibula.

CHREMES: Pasibula? That's it!

CRITO: Yes, that's it.

PAMPHILUS: She's told me that a thousand times.

SIMO: I'm sure you know, Chremes, that we're all delighted at this news.

CHREMES: Thanks, thanks! I do, indeed!

PAMPHILUS: There's still some unfinished business, father—

SIMO: Under the circumstances, all has long since been forgiven!

PAMPHILUS: Now that's what I call a fine father! As for her being my wife, you don't want to change the present arrangements, do you, Chremes?

CHREMES: You've got an excellent case—unless your father disagrees.

PAMPHILUS: You do agree, don't you, father.

SIMO: Yes, of course.

CHREMES: Her dowry, Pamphilus, is ten talents.

PAMPHILUS: That suits me.

CHREMES: I'm going right in to my daughter. Come with me, Crito, for I think she'll scarcely know me. (*Exit* CHREMES *and* CRITO.)

SIMO: Why don't you have her moved over to our house?

PAMPHILUS: Good idea. I'll tell Davus to look to it right away.

SIMO: He can't do it.

PAMPHILUS: Why not?

SIMO: Because he has a bit of business of greater importance and of more immediate concern to himself.

PAMPHILUS: What's that?

SIMO: He's chained up.

PAMPHILUS: Oh, father! Chained up? That wasn't right!

SIMO: Who said anything about chaining him upright?

PAMPHILUS: Have him released, please.

SIMO: All right. I'll see to it.

PAMPHILUS: Hurry, please.

SIMO: I'm going in. (*Exit* SIMO.)

PAMPHILUS: What a happy, lucky day!

SCENE V

(*Enter* CHARINUS.)

CHARINUS: I wonder what Pamphilus is up to. Ah! There he is.

PAMPHILUS: Maybe somebody might think that I can't believe this is true, but I feel like having it true, just the same. I think that the gods live forever for this reason: Their pleasures are their own property forever. Why, I'll live forever myself, if no trouble spoils my present happiness. But whom would I most want to meet, to tell him my story?

CHARINUS (*aside*): What's all this happiness? (*Enter* DAVUS.)

PAMPHILUS: I see Davus. Of all men, he's the one I most want to see. For I know that he, more than anyone else, will share my joys in a real way.

DAVUS (*aside*): Now where do you suppose Pamphilus is?

PAMPHILUS: Davus!

DAVUS: Who's that?

PAMPHILUS: It's Pamphilus.

DAVUS: Oh! Pamphilus.

PAMPHILUS: You don't know what's happened to me.

DAVUS: That's right. But I know what's happened to me.

PAMPHILUS: So do I.

DAVUS: That's the way it goes in this world; you find out about my bad luck before I find out about your good luck.

PAMPHILUS: My Glycerium has found her parents.

DAVUS: That's fine.

CHARINUS (aside): Well!

PAMPHILUS: Her father is one of our best friends!

DAVUS: Who is he?

PAMPHILUS: Chremes!

DAVUS: Nice story you've got there.

PAMPHILUS: And I don't have to wait at all to marry her.

CHARINUS (aside): He's not letting himself daydream, is he?

PAMPHILUS: Besides, about the baby, Davus—

DAVUS: Stop, stop! You're the darling of the gods!

CHARINUS (aside): I'm saved, if what he says is true. I'll speak to him.

PAMPHILUS: Who's that? Oh, Charinus! You've come just at the right moment.

CHARINUS: Congratulations!

PAMPHILUS: You've heard the news?

CHARINUS: Yes, the whole story. Come on, now; you're in luck; give me a hand. Chremes is on your side now; I'm sure he'll do anything you want.

PAMPHILUS: I know it. But why should I delay things by waiting for him to come out? Come on in with me. He's in here with Glycerium now. Davus, you go on home. Hurry and bring over some people to escort her away from here. What are you standing there for? What are you waiting for? (*Exit* PAMPHILUS *and* CHARINUS.)

DAVUS: I'm on my way. (*To audience*) Don't wait for them to come out again. Charinus will get engaged in the house, and all the other loose ends will be tucked in there.

CANTOR: Your applause, please.

TERENCE

PHORMIO

INTRODUCTORY NOTE

Phormio was first produced in 161 B.C. It is based on Apollodorus' *Epidikazomenos* ("The Litigant"); as the Greek title suggests, it revolves around a lawsuit—or better, around a fictitious lawsuit, which never actually took place. It is certainly the wittiest, the cleverest, and the most lighthearted of all of Terence's plays; there is hardly a serious moment in it, and the psychological problems that so much interested Terence elsewhere seem either absent from the play or so subtly submerged in it that we generally fail to find them.

If we were to look among the plays of Plautus and Terence for that one which most nearly typifies them all, our choice would probably fall on *Phormio*. It contains all the elements that we regard as characteristic of Roman comedy: love intrigue; mild social satire; rapid, witty dialogue; and restrained but still delightful humor. The stock characters are all there: the lovelorn and not very enterprising young man; the stubborn and self-willed but still kindly father; the clever slave; the shrewish and garrulous wife; even the pimp and the "parasite"—that out-of-pocket member of a decayed aristocracy who lived precariously by cadging invitations to dinner from his more fortunate friends. The play is, in fact, named after its "parasite"—or "man-about-town," as I have chosen to style him—for Phormio belongs to this profession, if profession we may call it. Although technically not the protagonist of the play (this role should probably be assigned to Antipho, the first of the two young men), Phormio is nonetheless the mainspring of the action; the schemes, bold and clever, by which the plot is first complicated and then resolved, must be credited to him, and he is easily the most interesting personality of the lot.

The scene is laid on a street in Athens; the set shows three house fronts. The Prologue has nothing to do with the story but is concerned only with a literary quarrel, the nature of which is now somewhat obscure, between Terence and one of his chief dramatic rivals.

CHARACTERS

DAVUS, a slave
GETA, a slave
ANTIPHO, a young man, son of DEMIPHO
PHAEDRIA, a young man, son of CHREMES
DEMIPHO, an old man, father of ANTIPHO
PHORMIO, a man-about-town
HEGIO ⎫
CRATINUS ⎬ friends of DEMIPHO
CRITO ⎭
DORIO, a pimp
CHREMES, an old man, brother of DEMIPHO and father of
    PHAEDRIA
SOPHRONA, an old nurse
NAUSISTRATA, wife of CHREMES

THE SCENE: *A street in Athens. Upstage, the fronts of three houses, one belonging to* DEMIPHO, *the second to* CHREMES, *and the third to* DORIO, *with narrow passageways between them.*

PHORMIO

The present Dean of Playwrights has been trying by main
force to drag our young author away from his vocation and
compel him to go into retirement. He hasn't succeeded, so
now he's attempting, by being harshly critical, to scare him
away from writing. He keeps telling people that the plays
our young man has so far produced are thinly conceived and
carelessly written. "Why!" says he, "not once does he show us
the heart-sick hero watching his tender doe running away with
the dogs at her heels, and her pleading and begging him to
save her!" If the good Dean just realized that the success of
his own most recent play was occasioned more by the actor's
skill than by the author's, he'd be much less free with his
cutting remarks.

Now maybe some of you are saying or thinking that if the
good Dean hadn't started this knifing match, our young man
wouldn't have been able to think up any prologues for his
plays, because he wouldn't have anybody to hold up to scorn.
Well, here's your answer: The search for popular acclaim is
open to anybody who is interested in literary pursuits. The
Dean has been doing his best to drive our author out to starve;
all the young man has been trying to do is reply to his attacks;
he had no intention of starting anything. If the Dean had
tried to devise compliments, he'd have had compliments in
return. As it is, he should realize that he's getting exactly
what he gave.

But now I'd like you to hear my real message. We're bringing you a new play, one that the Greeks call *The Litigant*.
Our author has given it the name *Phormio*, because the chief
role will be that of Phormio, the man-about-town. He's going

to be the mainspring of the action—that is, if you people will show our author a proper consideration. Please give him a little of your time and attention; please be courteous and don't start any disturbances. We'd not care to repeat the experience we had on an earlier occasion, when boos and catcalls drove our company off the stage. Thanks to the kindness of the manager, we've regained our place here; your sympathy and courtesy will help us keep it.

ACT ONE

SCENE I

(Enter DAVUS, *stage left.)*

DAVUS: My good friend and fellow countryman, Geta, came to see me yesterday. There was a little matter of some money I'd owed him for quite a while—still had a bit to pay. Wanted me to finish it up. I got what I needed, and here it is. Yes, I hear his master's son has gotten married; I suppose Geta has to find some kind of gift for the bride. It just isn't fair, the way people who haven't anything are always giving gifts to people who have plenty! Look at the poor fellow! Penny by penny he saved a little something out of his allowance—starved his immortal soul to do it! Now she'll appropriate the whole thing and never even think how hard it was for him to get it. Then on top of that they'll strike Geta for another gift when she has a baby, and then another when the baby has his first birthday, and another when he is initiated into the Mysteries. Of course, it's his mother who gets it all; the baby is just an excuse for collecting it. But wait—is that Geta? *(Enter* GETA *from* DEMIPHO's *house.)*

SCENE II

GETA: If some redheaded fellow comes looking for me . . .
DAVUS: Here he is; you can stop.
GETA: Oh! I was hoping I'd run into you, Davus.

DAVUS (*hands him the money*): Here you are; take it. That's it. You'll find it's exactly what I owe you.

GETA: Thanks very much. I appreciate your going to all that trouble.

DAVUS: You should, especially the way things are now. If anybody actually pays a debt a man had better appreciate it. But what's the matter with you? Why so glum?

GETA: Who, me? You've no idea how uneasy I am or what a tight spot I'm in.

DAVUS: What's wrong?

GETA: You'll find out—that is, if you can hold your tongue.

DAVUS: Stupid! I paid back your money, didn't I? Why should you be afraid to lend me a word or two? What good would it do me to renege on that?

GETA: Well, all right; listen.

DAVUS: At your service, sir!

GETA: You know my master's older brother, Chremes, don't you, Davus?

DAVUS: Certainly.

GETA: Well, do you know his son, Phaedria?

DAVUS: As well as I do you.

GETA: It happened that both the old gentlemen went abroad at the same time; Chremes had to go to Lemnos, and my master, Demipho, to Cilicia—went to see an old friend over there. He'd been bombarding Demipho with letters, promising him a chance to make a mint.

DAVUS: What? Why, he's got more than he knows how to use already!

GETA: Yes, well, never mind. That's the way he is.

DAVUS: Hah! I should've been born rich!

GETA: When the two of them left here they appointed me to keep an eye on their sons.

DAVUS: Oh, Geta! You drew a rough assignment!

GETA: Yes, I found that out. How well I know it! I think that was the day my guardian angel got angry and deserted me. At first I tried saying no to the boys—but why make a long story of it? Being loyal to my master nearly cost me my hide.

DAVUS: I thought that's what would happen. What's the use of fighting when you're beaten before you start?

GETA: I decided just to do what I was told, anything they wanted.

DAVUS: Now that was smart!

GETA: My boy, Antipho, kept out of trouble to begin with, but the other, Phaedria, right away found himself a pretty young thing, a lute girl, and fell madly in love with her. She belonged to a pimp, a reprobate and liar, and Phaedria hadn't a penny to pay him—Demipho and Chremes had taken care of that. All that was left for him to do was to feast his eyes, trot around after her, and escort her to her training school and back again. We had nothing to do, so we gave our time to Phaedria. Now right across from this school where she had her lessons was a barbershop. We used to wait there until it was time for her to go home. One day while we were sitting there, some young fellow came in with tears streaming down his face. That struck us as odd, so we asked him what was the matter. "I've never realized until just now," he said, "what an awful, terrible thing it is to be poor. Just a minute ago I saw a girl, right around the corner here; the poor thing was crying over her mother, who'd died. The body was there beside her, and there wasn't a soul with a kind word for her—nobody she knew, no neighbor, nobody there to give her a hand with the funeral except one poor old woman. It just broke my heart to see her. And she's a really lovely girl, too." Why make a long story of it? He made us all feel sympathetic. Well, Antipho said, "How about going to have a look at her?" Phaedria said, "Good idea. Let's go. Will you show us the way, please?" We trotted off, arrived there, had a look. The girl was a real beauty and, what would make you say so all the more, she wasn't dressed up at all. Her hair was wild; she wore no shoes; she was really a mess—tears all over her face, clothes dirty and ragged. Why, if the fact that she was a wonderful person hadn't shone right through her looks, she wouldn't have had any looks at all! The one young fellow—the one who was in love with the lute girl—said, "Oh, she's attractive enough." But the other . . .

DAVUS: I know, I know. He fell in love with her.

GETA: You don't know the half of it. Wait till you hear the rest. The next day he went straight off to the old lady and begged her to let him have the girl. She said certainly not; what he was suggesting just wasn't right. The girl was an Athenian citizen, a respectable girl from a respectable family. If he wanted to marry her, there were legal ways of arranging that. On any other terms, nothing doing! Antipho didn't know which way to turn. He wanted to marry her, but at the same time he felt uneasy about doing it behind his father's back.

DAVUS: Well, once his father got home, wouldn't he have said it was all right?

GETA: Who, Demipho? He'd let Antipho marry a girl without a dowry, from some family nobody ever heard of? Not a chance!

DAVUS: What happened, then?

GETA: What do you think? There's a fellow around here who lives by his wits—Phormio's his name. Got plenty of nerve, damn him anyway!

DAVUS: What did he do?

GETA: He figured out an idea—wait till you hear it. "There's a law," he says, "that requires orphan girls to marry their next of kin, and the same law requires the next of kin to marry them. I'll say that you're the girl's cousin, and ask for a court order against you. I'll pretend that I'm a friend of her father's. We'll all go to court. Who her father was, and her mother, and how she's related to you—I'll make all that up. It will be simple and easy enough. You won't deny anything I say, so of course I'll win the case. When your father gets home, I'll have a lawsuit on my hands. What of that? We'll have the girl."

DAVUS: That's a good one! Amazing!

GETA: Antipho agreed to it. They did it—went to court and got the order; Antipho married her.

DAVUS: Wha-a-a-t!?

GETA: You heard me.

DAVUS: Oh, Geta, Geta, Geta! What's going to happen to you?

GETA: Blessed if I know. I'm sure of one thing: Whatever happens, I can take it.

DAVUS: Good! Spoken like a man!

GETA: I'm relying on myself—nobody else.

DAVUS: That's the right idea!

GETA: I suppose I could go to some friend of the family for help. He'd put in a word for me—you know how it goes: "Let him off this time, won't you please? If he ever does anything like this again, I won't have a word to say for him." He just forgets to add: "The minute I leave, kill him if you feel like it."

DAVUS: What about our young friend—the one who was running after the lute girl? How's he getting along?

GETA: Oh, so-so. Rather slim pickings.

DAVUS: Hasn't too much ready cash, maybe?

GETA: Much? Nothing! Just "hopes."

DAVUS: Is his father home yet?

GETA: Not yet.

DAVUS: Well, when are you expecting your master?

GETA: I don't know for sure. But I just heard that a letter has come from him and been left at the customs office. I'm going after it.

DAVUS: Anything else you need me for, Geta?

GETA: No. Good-by. Good luck to you. (*Exit* DAVUS. GETA *goes to the door of* DEMIPHO's *house and knocks.*) Hey, boy! Come out here, somebody! (*A slave opens the door;* GETA *hands him the money.*) Here, take this and give it to Dorcium. (*Exit* GETA, *stage right.*)

SCENE III

(*Enter* ANTIPHO *and* PHAEDRIA *from* DEMIPHO's *house.*)

ANTIPHO: To think that it's come to this, Phaedria. Here's my father, who just wants me to be happy, but when I think of his coming home I'm scared to death! And if I hadn't been so foolish, I'd be looking forward to seeing him, as I ought to.

PHAEDRIA: Why, what's wrong?

ANTIPHO: You're asking me that, after the foolish thing

we did? You had a share in it, too, you know. Oh, how I wish Phormio hadn't thought of it and hadn't gotten me all excited and urged me to do it. That's where all my troubles began. I'd have lost Phanium, of course. I'd have felt pretty bad about it for a few days, but I wouldn't be in this terrible state of mind, day after day after day . . .

PHAEDRIA: Yes?

ANTIPHO: . . . sitting around and wondering how soon my father's going to come back and break up my marriage.

PHAEDRIA: Most people worry because they lack something to love; your trouble is that you've got too much. Your cup of love is running over, Antipho. Why, look here; your life is the kind people hope and pray for! So help me, if I had the chance to keep my girl as long as you've kept yours, I'd give my life for it. Just look at the whole picture—what a poor man like me has, and what a rich man like you has. Not to mention the fact that without spending any money at all you've gotten a nice girl, a respectable girl, that you have exactly what you wanted—a wife. You don't have to worry about gossip; you don't have to hide a thing; perfectly happy, if you just had sense enough to appreciate your blessings. Suppose you had to deal with that pimp, as I do—then you'd know. Well, that's the way we all are; we're never satisfied with what we have.

ANTIPHO: No, you're all wrong, Phaedria; you're the one who's lucky. You can start from scratch and decide what you want to do—keep your girl or let her go. I've had the bad luck to get into a spot where I can neither keep mine nor let her go. But what's this? (*Enter* GETA, *stage right.*) Is that Geta I see coming this way? He seems to be in a hurry! Yes, it's Geta, all right. I'm scared! I wonder what he's going to tell me now?

SCENE IV

GETA (*to himself*): It's all over with you, Geta, if you don't think up something pretty quick. You just weren't ready! It happened too fast! What a pile of trouble you're heading for! I can't figure out how to get around it or get out of it, and if I don't plan pretty carefully it will be the end either for me or for Antipho. Can't keep that idiotic scheme of ours hidden any longer.

ANTIPHO (*to* PHAEDRIA): What's he so excited about?

GETA (*to himself*): And I've got just about half a minute to do the job. The master is home.

ANTIPHO (*to* PHAEDRIA): What's the matter with Geta? What's wrong?

GETA (*to himself*): And when he hears what's happened, he'll burst—and then what'll I do? Talk it over with him? That would just set him off. Keep my mouth shut? That would be sticking pins in him. Say I'm sorry? Pure waste of time. This is really terrible! I'm scared enough for myself, but Antipho's the one who's really breaking my heart. He's the one I feel sorry for; he's the one I'm worrying about; he's the one who's keeping me here. If it weren't for him, I'd have taken care of myself all right, and I'd have gotten back at the old man for shouting at me. I'd have packed up a few things and run out of here in a hurry.

ANTIPHO (*to* PHAEDRIA): What's all this talk about packing things up and running away?

GETA (*to himself*): But where will I find Antipho? Which way had I better go to look for him?

PHAEDRIA (*to* ANTIPHO): That was your name he just mentioned.

ANTIPHO (*to* PHAEDRIA): He's got some bad news for me; I'm sure of it.

PHAEDRIA (*to* ANTIPHO): Now, now, don't lose your head.

GETA (*to himself*): I'll go home; that's probably where he is. (*Starts toward* DEMIPHO's *house*)

PHAEDRIA (*to* ANTIPHO): Let's call him back.

ANTIPHO: Stop where you are!

GETA: Now that sounds like an order, whoever you are.

ANTIPHO: Geta!

GETA (*turns around*): Oh! The very man I was looking for!

ANTIPHO: For heaven's sake, tell me the news, will you? And make it short, if you know how.

GETA: Yes, sir!

ANTIPHO: Well, come on!

GETA: Just a minute ago, down on the waterfront . . .

ANTIPHO: My . . . ?

GETA: That's right.

ANTIPHO: Oh, ye gods!

PHAEDRIA: Oh-oh!

ANTIPHO: What am I going to do?

PHAEDRIA (to GETA): What did you say?

GETA: I said I saw his father, your uncle.

ANTIPHO: Now what? This has all happened so fast! It's the end! What am I going to do about it? If things have gotten to the point that I'm to be dragged away from you, Phanium, then I just don't want to go on living.

GETA: All right, Antipho, if that's the way things are, it's all the more important for you to keep your head. The gods help those who help themselves, you know.

ANTIPHO: I'm scared silly!

GETA: Now, look, Antipho. You just can't be like that, now of all times, because if your father gets an idea you're worried he'll be sure you've done something you shouldn't have.

PHAEDRIA: That's right.

ANTIPHO: I can't be any different.

GETA: What would you do if you had something now that was really hard?

ANTIPHO: Since I can't bear this, I'd be even less able to bear that.

GETA (to PHAEDRIA): This is no good, Phaedria. Let's go. Why are we wasting our time here? Why don't I just run along?

PHAEDRIA: Yes! I'll come with you. (They start off.)

ANTIPHO: No, look, please! I'll try. (He straightens up, tries to look brave.) How's this? All right?

GETA: Ridiculous!

ANTIPHO: Look at me now. There. All right?

GETA: No.

ANTIPHO: How about this?

GETA: We-e-ll, that's better.

ANTIPHO: How's this?

GETA: Good! That will do. Now hold it, just like that. And whatever he gives you, you give it right back. He's furious; he's going to give you a tongue-lashing; don't let him bowl you over.

ANTIPHO: Y-y-yes, I know.

GETA: They made you do it; you didn't want to.

PHAEDRIA: There was a law, and a court order.

GETA: Understand? But who do I see at the end of the street? It's the master himself!

ANTIPHO: No, I can't—I can't stick it. (*He starts off, stage left.*)

GETA: Here, what are you doing? Where are you going, Antipho? Don't go away! Here!

ANTIPHO: No, I know perfectly well what I'm good for, and I know exactly what I did. I leave it to you. Phanium and my life are in your hands! (*Exit* ANTIPHO.)

PHAEDRIA: Well, Geta, what happens now?

GETA: You're going to get yours ears pinned back, and I'm going to get a beating, unless I'm very much mistaken. But the advice we were giving Antipho just now—we'd better take it ourselves, Phaedria.

PHAEDRIA: What do you mean, "we'd better"? Just tell me what to do.

GETA: You remember all those things you said in the beginning—things we were going to say to clear ourselves of blame? That was a good case we made—smooth as silk—bound to win—the very best.

PHAEDRIA: Yes, I remember.

GETA: Well, that's what we must have now— or, if it's possible, something even better and smarter.

PHAEDRIA: I'll do my best.

GETA: Now you go first; I'll just slip back in here, where I can step in for you if you get into trouble.

PHAEDRIA: All right. (PHAEDRIA *and* GETA *withdraw into the alley between two of the houses.*)

ACT TWO

SCENE I

(*Enter* DEMIPHO, *stage right.*)

DEMIPHO (*to himself*): What is this? Has Antipho married without my consent? Didn't he have any respect for my authority and—never mind my authority—wasn't he even worried for fear I wouldn't approve? No sense of propriety at all! The audacity! And you, Geta—you put him up to it!

GETA (*aside*): Hah! Finally got around to me, did you?

DEMIPHO: What are they going to say to me? What explanation are they going to find? I really wonder!

GETA (*aside*): I'll find one; don't worry.

DEMIPHO: Is he going to tell me he didn't want to do it but the court ordered it? Yes, yes; of course, of course.

GETA (*aside*): That's right; good for you!

DEMIPHO: But when he knew the facts, to let the case go by default without saying a word—did the court order that, too?

PHAEDRIA (*aside, to* GETA): That's a hard one!

GETA (*aside, to* PHAEDRIA): I'll take care of it; forget it.

DEMIPHO: I don't know what to do! This is all so unexpected! Why, I can hardly believe it! I'm so furious I can't get my mind organized at all. Well, this makes one thing clear: When everything's going perfectly smoothly, that's when people ought to consider what they'll do if trouble comes—your life might be in danger, you might lose your money, you might have to leave home. And when a man comes back from a trip he ought always to expect that his son may be in trouble or his wife may have died or his daughter may be ill

—these things happen to everybody; they're perfectly possible. Then he won't be surprised at anything, and if anything unexpected happens it's bound to be good.

GETA (*aside, to* PHAEDRIA): Oh, Phaedria, you'd never believe how much smarter I am than my master. I've figured out all the unpleasant things that are going to happen to me when he gets home: I'll have to push the grindstone in the mill; I'll have to take a whipping; I'll have to wear the ball and chain; I'll be put to work on the farm. Not one of these things will surprise me. If anything unexpected happens to me, I know it will be good. But why don't you go and meet Demipho now—be especially nice to him to start with. (PHAEDRIA *steps out of the alley*.)

DEMIPHO: I see my brother's son Phaedria coming my way.

PHAEDRIA: Why, Uncle Demipho, hello.

DEMIPHO: Hello. Where's Antipho?

PHAEDRIA: I'm so glad you're . . .

DEMIPHO: Yes, yes. Answer my question.

PHAEDRIA: Oh, he's fine. He's around. Things look all right to you here?

DEMIPHO: I wish they did.

PHAEDRIA: Why, what's the matter?

DEMIPHO: *You* ask me *that*, Phaedria? That was a fine wedding you people arranged while I was away.

PHAEDRIA: Oh! Ha-ha-ha! Is that why you're angry at him?

GETA (*aside*): The boy's a real actor!

DEMIPHO: Angry? Of course I'm angry. What did you expect? I'd just like to lay eyes on that boy. I'd just like him to know that what he did has turned me—that good-natured father of his—into a holy terror.

PHAEDRIA: But look, sir, he didn't do anything that should make you angry.

DEMIPHO: Yes, sir! There you are! All alike! All exactly the same. Know one and you know them all.

PHAEDRIA: Oh, no, that's not true.

DEMIPHO: A's in trouble, B steps up to defend him; B's in trouble, A's ready to help. A mutual benefit association!

GETA (*aside*): The old boy doesn't know it, but he's drawn a good picture of what they did.

DEMIPHO: Because if this weren't so you wouldn't be on Antipho's side, Phaedria.

PHAEDRIA: Now look, sir, if Antipho has really done something he shouldn't, and has been a bit careless about his money or his reputation, then I haven't a word to say for him. He should get what he deserves. But if somebody had a grudge against him and knew how to make trouble, too— if somebody like that laid a trap for us young fellows and caught us in it—is that our fault or the court's fault? Why, the courts hate the rich and love the poor. They're always taking from the one and giving to the other.

GETA (*aside*): If I didn't know the facts I'd think he was telling the truth.

DEMIPHO: Yes, but what court is going to see your side of the case when you say nothing in your own defense, the way Antipho did?

PHAEDRIA: Why, he did just what you'd expect any decent, respectable boy to do; when they got him on the stand, he couldn't speak his piece at all—not a word! He was so scared and embarrassed he was tongue-tied.

GETA (*aside*): Phaedria's doing very well, but I think I'd better step in now. (*Steps out of alley. To* DEMIPHO) Why, hello, sir! Glad to see you back safe!

DEMIPHO: Oh, there you are, my good and faithful servant, pillar of the family! You're the one I told to take care of my son when I went away!

GETA: I hear that you've been complaining about us ever since you got here, and most of all about me. That's not fair at all, sir. What did you expect me to do for you in this kind of thing? The law doesn't allow a slave to argue a case in court or even to appear as a witness.

DEMIPHO: I'll grant you everything; I'll grant you that business about Antipho being inexperienced and scared and a mere boy; I'll let it pass about you being a slave. But even if that girl is ten times a relative, he didn't have to marry her. No.

As the law provides, you people could have given her a dowry and let her find somebody else to marry. What was the idea of having him marry a penniless girl instead?

GETA: It wasn't the *idea*, it was the *money* we didn't have.

DEMIPHO: He could have found it somewhere.

GETA: Somewhere? Yes, that's easy to say.

DEMIPHO: Well, if there wasn't any other way, he could have borrowed it.

GETA: Now that's a fine suggestion! As if anybody would have lent it to him at his age!

DEMIPHO: No, no, it's not going to be this way. I won't have it. You think I'd let him keep that girl as his wife even for one single day? This calls for stern measures. I want you to point out that fellow to me or show me where he lives.

GETA: You mean Phormio?

DEMIPHO: I mean the man that got the court order for that woman.

GETA: I'll get him here right away.

DEMIPHO: Where's Antipho now?

GETA: Out.

DEMIPHO: Phaedria, you run along and find him and bring him here to me.

PHAEDRIA: I'm on my way, sir—straight there. (*Exit* PHAE-DRIA.)

GETA (*aside*): Yes, straight to Pamphila's house. (*Exit* GETA.)

DEMIPHO: I'll stop in at home and say my thanksgivings to the gods of the house; then I'll go on downtown and get some friends together to help me with this. I don't want to get caught off guard when Phormio gets here. (*Exit into his house.*)

SCENE II

(*Enter* PHORMIO *and* GETA.)

PHORMIO: So when his father got home, Antipho was scared and ran away, right?

GETA: That's right.

PHORMIO: Left Phanium here all alone?

GETA: Yes.

PHORMIO: And his father furious?

GETA: Yes, sir!

PHORMIO: Well, Phormio, my boy, you're the man; it's up to you. You made your porridge; now you'll have to eat it. Get ready!

GETA: Please, I . . .

PHORMIO (to himself): Now if he asks me . . .

GETA: You're our only hope.

PHORMIO (to himself): Oh-oh! Suppose he says . . .

GETA: It was your idea.

PHORMIO (aside): Yes. That's it!

GETA: You've got to help us.

PHORMIO: All right! Bring on your master. I've got my plan all thought out.

GETA: What are you going to do?

PHORMIO: Well, what do you want? You want Phanium to stay, don't you, and me to slip Antipho out from under the trouble he's in and get his father to turn all his resentment on me. Isn't that right?

GETA: You've got courage and you're a real friend. But Phormio, I worry for fear that courage of yours is going to land you on the chain gang one of these days.

PHORMIO: Oh, no, it won't. I've run that risk; I know my way around now. How many people do you think I've already taken for everything they had, foreigners and citizens, both? The more I learned, the oftener I did it. Now tell me, did you ever hear of anybody suing me for damages?

GETA: No. Why not?

PHORMIO: Because nobody stretches nets to catch hawks or falcons; they're harmful birds. They stretch nets for the harmless ones, because there's some profit in them. In the others, you're just wasting your time. Most people have something here or something there that you can make them give up; people know I haven't anything. You'll say, "They'll get you bound over to them as a bondslave." Oh, no, they won't!

They don't want to feed a man with an appetite like mine!
I'd say they were pretty smart if they felt disinclined to do me
a favor in return for my bilking them.

GETA: Well, Antipho will never be able to thank you as
you deserve.

PHORMIO: No, no! Nobody like me can ever thank a rich
friend as *he* deserves! Why, just think, you don't have to
part with a penny, but here you come all fresh and clean from
the baths, not a worry in the world, while he fumes and frets
over expenses. Just to see that you have a good time, he pays
the bill. You're supposed to be happy; you're to get first choice
of the food and drinks. They put a wonder-dinner in front of
you.

GETA: What do you mean, "wonder-dinner"?

PHORMIO: Why, a dinner where you wonder what to take
first. Now when you see how nice all this is, and how much
it costs, wouldn't you say that the man who provides it is a
real ministering angel?

GETA: Here comes Demipho. Watch your step. The first
attack is the hardest. If you beat that back, you can lead him
around by the nose any way you like.

SCENE III

(*Enter* DEMIPHO, *stage left, accompanied by* HEGIO, CRA-
TINUS, *and* CRITO.)

DEMIPHO: Have you ever heard of anyone being dealt with
more disgracefully than I have been? Please, I need your help.

GETA (*aside, to* PHORMIO): He's furious!

PHORMIO (*aside, to* GETA): Furious? You just watch; I'll stir
him up! (*Aloud*) Great gods! Is Demipho claiming that Phanium isn't his relative? What? Phanium? Demipho's saying she's
not his relative?

GETA: That's right.

PHORMIO: Says he doesn't even know who her father was,
too?

GETA: That's right.

DEMIPHO (*to* HEGIO, CRATINUS, *and* CRITO): There he is! I think that's the man I was telling you about. Come on.

PHORMIO (*to* GETA): Yes, I know why. She was left penniless, the poor thing, so now he "doesn't know" her father and considers her beneath his notice. That's what the love of money does for you!

GETA: You accuse my master of dishonesty and you'll be in for trouble!

DEMIPHO (*to* HEGIO, CRATINUS, *and* CRITO): The audacity of the man! Is *he* bringing accusations against *me*?

PHORMIO (*to* GETA): After all, I can't blame the boy if he didn't know Phanium's father. He was an older man, you see, and he had no money. He worked hard all his life and hardly ever came to town. He had a farm that my father let him work. Many and many a time, when he'd gotten along in years, he used to tell me how Demipho, his own cousin, had pushed him aside. And what a wonderful fellow he was, too—the finest I've ever known!

GETA: Here's hoping you'll see yourself the kind of man you say he was.

PHORMIO: Forget it, will you? Why, if I hadn't thought he was like that I'd never have gotten into a fight with your people just to help Phanium. Pretends he doesn't know her, for heaven's sake! Is that the way a gentleman should act?

GETA (*pretending to threaten* PHORMIO): You'd better stop talking that way about my master behind his back, you . . . !

PHORMIO: It's exactly what he deserves.

GETA: Oh, is that so, you old . . . !

DEMIPHO: Geta!

GETA (*pretending not to hear*): You blackmailer, you shyster!

DEMIPHO: Geta!

PHORMIO (*whispers to* GETA): Answer him.

GETA: Who's that? Oh! . . . oh!

DEMIPHO: Be quiet, Geta.

GETA (*to* DEMIPHO): Why, while you were gone, sir, he's

been saying the most insulting things about you—things he ought to say about himself instead! Hasn't stopped once!

DEMIPHO (to GETA): That will do. (To PHORMIO) My good young friend, if you don't mind too much, if it's quite all right with you, I'd like to ask you a question. Who is this man you say was a friend of yours? Inform me, please. And just how did he claim he was related to me?

PHORMIO: Hah! Going on a fishing expedition, are you? As if you didn't know.

DEMIPHO: Didn't know?

PHORMIO: Yes.

DEMIPHO: I say I didn't know him. You say I did. Suppose you refresh my memory.

PHORMIO: Come now, come now; your own cousin, and you didn't know him?

DEMIPHO: You're killing me. Tell me his name.

PHORMIO: His name? Certainly . . .

DEMIPHO: Well, why don't you say something?

PHORMIO (aside, to GETA): Damn it, I've forgotten his name!

DEMIPHO: What's that?

PHORMIO (aside, to GETA): Geta, if you remember the name we used, tell me. (To DEMIPHO) No, I'm not going to tell you. You're pretending you don't know it, just to check on me.

DEMIPHO: Me? Checking on you?

GETA (aside, to PHORMIO): It was Stilpo.

PHORMIO (aloud): Well, after all, what do I care? The name was Stilpo.

DEMIPHO: Who? What was the name?

PHORMIO: Stilpo. You knew him all right.

DEMIPHO: I did not know him. I never had any relative by that name.

PHORMIO: Is that so? Aren't you ashamed—right in front of these gentlemen, too! But if he'd left a nice big estate . . .

DEMIPHO: Why, you . . . !

PHORMIO: . . . you'd remember, all right. You'd have stepped right up and recited your pedigrees all the way back to grandfather and great-grandfather.

DEMIPHO: Yes, exactly. The minute I got home I'd have told

how she was related to me. Now you do it. Come on, how is
she related to me?

GETA (to DEMIPHO): Good, sir! That's the stuff!

PHORMIO: I gave a perfectly clear explanation where I was
required to—in court. If I said anything then that wasn't so,
why didn't your son refute it?

DEMIPHO: My son? You talk about my son? I haven't the
words to tell you how stupid he is.

PHORMIO: Well, you—you're so smart. Let's see you go to
court and get them to reopen a case that's already been settled.
Apparently you're a privileged character around here and have
a special right to get a closed case reopened.

DEMIPHO: Well, even though I'm the injured party, just the
same rather than get tangled up in lawsuits or have to listen to
you—just as if she were my relative—the law says this about
providing a dowry—you take her away—I'll give you five hundred drachmas.

PHORMIO: Ha-ha-ha! You're a nice one!

DEMIPHO: What's the matter? What's wrong with that?
Don't I even get the rights that the law gives everybody?

PHORMIO: Now, please, see here, sir. Does the law say that
you're to treat her as if she were a common prostitute—after
you've used her, pay her off and tell her to run along? Is *that*
the law? Or was the law set up to prevent any woman who is
a citizen from being forced into a life of shame because she
has no money—and that's why she is required to marry her
next of kin, so that she can spend her life properly married
to one man? And now you say this isn't to be.

DEMIPHO: That's right, marry her next of kin. But where
do we come in? What's that got to do with us?

PHORMIO: Oho, now! You know what they say: "Case is
closed; what's done can't be undone."

DEMIPHO: Done, is it? Not for me, it isn't. I'm keeping right
at this until I get it cleared up.

PHORMIO: You're wasting your time.

DEMIPHO: That's *my* business.

PHORMIO: After all, Demipho, we have no quarrel with you.

The court order applied to your son, not to you. You're well past the age for getting married, you know.

DEMIPHO: I want you to consider that my son agrees with every single word I've been saying here. He'd better—or I'll lock both him and his wife out of the house!

GETA (*aside*): He's raging!

PHORMIO: It would be better to do that to yourself.

DEMIPHO: Oh, that's how it is, is it? Going to pick a quarrel with everything I say, are you?

PHORMIO (*aside, to* GETA): He's afraid of us, even if he's trying hard not to show it.

GETA (*aside, to* PHORMIO): Everything's going fine for you so far.

PHORMIO (*to* DEMIPHO): Look, there's no getting out of this. Why don't you just accept it? The kind of man you are, you and I really ought to be friends.

DEMIPHO: *Me?* Be friends with *you?* I wish I'd never seen or heard of you.

PHORMIO: Why don't you come to terms with the girl? You'd have somebody to take care of you in those "later years." You're not getting any younger, you know.

DEMIPHO: She can take care of you. You take her.

PHORMIO: Ah-ah! Temper, temper!

DEMIPHO: Now, you listen here. I've had all the talk I want. If you don't hurry up and get that woman out of my house, I'll throw her out. And that's that, Phormio.

PHORMIO: If you lay one finger on her, or do anything to her that shouldn't be done to a decent, respectable girl, I'll hale you into court so fast it will make you dizzy. And that's that, Demipho. (*To* GETA) If you need me for anything, I'll be at home. (*Exit* PHORMIO, *stage left.*)

GETA: I understand you.

SCENE IV

DEMIPHO: I'm dreadfully worried and upset about my son. What a tangle he's got us both into, getting married to that girl! And I haven't even seen him! I'd like at least to know what he has to say about all this and how he feels about it. (*To* GETA) Run along, will you, and see if he's come home yet.

GETA: Yes, sir. (*Exit* GETA.)

DEMIPHO (*to* HEGIO, CRATINUS, *and* CRITO): Well, you see what the situation is. What am I going to do? What do you think, Hegio?

HEGIO: Who, me? I pass to Cratinus, if you don't mind.

DEMIPHO: Well, Cratinus?

CRATINUS: You mean me?

DEMIPHO: Yes, you.

CRATINUS: I'd want you to do only what's best for you. Here's my opinion: Your son took a legal action while you were out of town, and it's only fair that it should be rendered null and void. You'll have no trouble about it. That's all I have to say.

DEMIPHO: How about you now, Hegio?

HEGIO: Oh, I think that what Cratinus said was very much to the point. But you know how it is; there are as many opinions as there are people; no one man thinks the same as another. I don't see how the marriage can be annulled. It was entirely in accord with the law. I doubt if it's quite right to try to annul it.

DEMIPHO: Well, Crito?

CRITO: I think the question needs much more discussion. It's no small matter.

CRATINUS: Do you need us any longer?

DEMIPHO: No. You've been a big help. (*Exeunt* CRATINUS, HEGIO, *and* CRITO.) I'm a lot less certain than I was before. (*Enter* GETA.)

GETA: They say Antipho isn't home yet.

DEMIPHO: I think I'd better wait for my brother. He'll have something to say about this, and I'll do what he thinks best. I'll go down to the waterfront and see if I can find out when he's expected back. (*Exit* DEMIPHO, *stage right.*)

GETA: I'm going to go look for Antipho, so he'll know what's been going on here. (*Enter* ANTIPHO, *stage left.*) Oh, I see him. There he is. Came right when I wanted him!

ACT THREE

SCENE I

ANTIPHO (*to himself*): Oh, Antipho, Antipho! What an attitude to take! You really deserve anything they say about you! Running out like that and expecting other people to take care of the girl you love! Did you think that other people were going to take more interest in your affairs than you yourself? No matter how the rest of it was, you might have taken some thought for her, your own wife. She trusted you! You wouldn't want that to get her into trouble, would you? The poor thing! You're her only hope!

GETA: Well, sir! We've had a thing or two to say about you while you were away. Running out like that!

ANTIPHO: I was hoping I'd find you.

GETA: Just the same, we didn't quit on you—not a bit!

ANTIPHO: Please tell me. How are things going for me? Has my father got any idea of the truth?

GETA: No, not yet.

ANTIPHO: Well, how does it look? Any hope?

GETA: I really can't say.

ANTIPHO: O-o-oh!

GETA: Anyway, Phaedria was right in there fighting for you all along.

ANTIPHO: That doesn't surprise me.

GETA: And Phormio, too. Same as he always does, he really gave it everything.

ANTIPHO: What did he do?

GETA: What he had to say completely shut your father up— and was he furious!

ANTIPHO: Good for Phormio!

GETA: And I did what I could, too.

ANTIPHO: Oh, Geta, you're all real friends.

GETA: For the moment things stand like this: Everything's

peaceful, and your father is going to wait for your uncle to get back.

ANTIPHO: Why wait for him?

GETA: The way he put it, he wants to follow your uncle's advice in the matter.

ANTIPHO: That makes me frightened to see my uncle come home safely now, Geta! Because from what you tell me, whether I live or die is all up to him.

GETA: Here comes Phaedria, see? (*Enter* PHAEDRIA *from* DORIO's *house.*)

ANTIPHO: Where? Where?

GETA: Over there, see? Just coming out from his daily exercises.

SCENE II

PHAEDRIA (*speaks back through the door*): Dorio! (*Enter* DORIO.) Dorio, please listen!

DORIO: Can't hear a word you say. (*He starts off.*)

PHAEDRIA: Wait a minute!

DORIO: Let me go, will you?

PHAEDRIA: Listen to me.

DORIO: Why? I'm getting tired of hearing the same thing over and over again.

PHAEDRIA: But this time I'll say something that will interest you.

DORIO: Well, all right. Go on, I'm listening.

PHAEDRIA: Can't I get you to wait just three more days? (DORIO *starts off again.*) Where are you going?

DORIO: I wondered if you had anything new to offer.

ANTIPHO (*aside, to* GETA): I'm afraid that pimp may . . .

GETA (*aside, to* ANTIPHO): What? Sew himself up tight? So am I.

PHAEDRIA (*to* DORIO): Don't you trust me even now?

DORIO: Talk, talk, talk!

PHAEDRIA: Look, I'm giving you my word!

DORIO: Words, words, words!

PHAEDRIA: You'll say the favor was well worth it!

DORIO: Nonsense!

PHAEDRIA: No, believe me, you'll be glad you did it. I swear that's the truth!

DORIO: Waste of time!

PHAEDRIA: Dorio! Dear old friend . . . !

DORIO: Go on, break my heart!

PHAEDRIA: How can you be so hardhearted? Haven't you any feelings at all? Don't you know how to feel sorry for somebody? Isn't there anything I could say that would make you listen?

DORIO: How can you be so stupid? Haven't you any sense of decency, Phaedria? Don't you know any better than to try to trick me with all those fine words? Try to get the use of my girl for nothing?

ANTIPHO (aside, to GETA): Poor fellow!

PHAEDRIA: Yes, you're right. You win.

GETA (aside, to ANTIPHO): Both of them, right in character.

PHAEDRIA: And as if Antipho weren't wrapped up in troubles of his own—that's when I get into this predicament!

ANTIPHO (aloud): Hey, Phaedria, what's the matter?

PHAEDRIA: Oh, Antipho! You don't know how lucky you are.

ANTIPHO: Who, me?

PHAEDRIA: Yes, you. The girl you love is safe at home. You've never had to battle it out with a dirty so-and-so like him.

ANTIPHO: Safe at home? Oh, no! As they say, I've got a wolf by the ears!

DORIO: That's exactly the spot I'm in, too.

ANTIPHO: Here, now! Don't start acting like a decent human being! (To PHAEDRIA) He hasn't done anything, has he?

PHAEDRIA: Who, him? Only what an absolutely heartless man would do. He's sold my Pamphila.

ANTIPHO: What? Sold her?

PHAEDRIA: Yes. Sold her.

DORIO: Yes, dreadful, isn't it? I only paid my own good hard cash for her!

PHAEDRIA: And I can't get him to wait for me, can't get him to change his agreement with the buyer, for just three days, until I can get the money my friends promised me. (*To* DORIO) If I don't pay you then, you don't need to wait one hour longer.

DORIO: Pound away!

ANTIPHO (*to* DORIO): That's not a very long time he's asking for, Dorio. Let him have it. He'll pay you twice over for the favor you've done him.

DORIO: Just a lot of hot air!

ANTIPHO: Are you going to let Pamphila be taken away from her home town here? And besides, can you stand to see the two of them separated?

DORIO: Nor I, nor you.

PHAEDRIA: Damn you, damn you, anyway!

DORIO: I've been putting up with you for a good many months against my better judgment—always promising, never paying, feeling sorry for yourself. Now, on the other hand, I've found somebody who pays and doesn't weep on my shoulder. Make way for your betters.

ANTIPHO (*to* PHAEDRIA): Wait a minute! If I remember rightly, you agreed originally on a time limit for paying him, didn't you?

PHAEDRIA: Yes, we did.

DORIO: I'm not denying it, am I?

ANTIPHO: Well, is the time up?

DORIO: No, but this is the last day.

ANTIPHO: You ought to be ashamed—going back on your word like that!

DORIO: Not I—not when there's money in it.

GETA: You dirty cheat!

PHAEDRIA: Dorio, after all, is that the right way to do things?

DORIO: I'm me, see? If you like me, deal with me.

ANTIPHO: Are you going to cheat Phaedria like that?

DORIO: I, cheat Phaedria? Oh, no, Antipho; he's cheating me. He knew I was like this, but I thought he was different. He fooled me; I'm exactly the way I always was. Well, however that may be, I'll do this much: The captain said he'd pay me the money tomorrow morning; if you get there before he does, Phaedria, I'll follow my usual rule of first come, first served. I'll be going now. (*Exit* DORIO.)

SCENE III

PHAEDRIA: Now what do I do? Great gods! Where am I going to find the money for him, just like that? I haven't got a penny to my name. And if I could just have persuaded him to give me three more days, I had a promise of all the money.

ANTIPHO: Geta, are we going to let the poor man go through all this just after he finished really putting himself out for me, as you told me? No, he needs our help. Don't you think we ought to try to pay him back for the favor he did?

GETA: Yes, I do. You're absolutely right.

ANTIPHO: Well, come on, then. Nobody but you can save him.

GETA: What am I supposed to do?

ANTIPHO: Find the money.

GETA: Fine, fine! Have any idea where?

ANTIPHO: Well, my father is home.

GETA: Yes, I know. So then what?

ANTIPHO: Go on! A word to the wise is sufficient!

GETA: Oh, that's it, is it?

ANTIPHO: Yes.

GETA: Now that's a really fine suggestion! Get out of here, will you? Don't I win enough glory if I manage to keep out of trouble over your getting married to Phanium? Are you telling me on top of that to trade trouble for death just to help Phaedria?

ANTIPHO (*to* PHAEDRIA): What he says is true enough.

PHAEDRIA: What, Geta? Aren't we friends any more?

GETA: Oh, I wouldn't say that. But isn't it bad enough that

the master is furious with all of us without our stirring him up still more? Then there won't be any way out for us.

PHAEDRIA: Is some other man going to take Pamphila away some place that I don't know about, where I'll never see her again? Well, all right, then; while I'm still here and while you still can, talk to me, Antipho; take a good look at me.

ANTIPHO: What for? What in the world are you going to do?

PHAEDRIA: No matter where they take her, I swear I'll follow her or die in the attempt.

GETA: Well, blessings on you! But take it easy, will you?

ANTIPHO (*to* GETA): Look, isn't there something you can do to help him?

GETA: Something? What, for instance?

ANTIPHO: Try to figure out something, will you? We wouldn't want him to do anything rash. We'd feel bad about that later, Geta.

GETA (*to himself*): Now, let me see . . . (*Aloud*) He's safe, I think. But I'm afraid there's going to be trouble.

ANTIPHO: Don't worry about that. Whatever happens, good or bad, we're in it with you.

GETA: Tell me, how much money do you need, Phaedria?

PHAEDRIA: Three thousand drachmas.

GETA: Three thousand? She's rather expensive, isn't she, Phaedria?

PHAEDRIA: For her, it's a bargain, I tell you!

GETA: All right. I'll find it and see that you get it.

PHAEDRIA: You're a real friend!

GETA: Get out of here, will you?

PHAEDRIA: I need it right away, you know.

GETA: You'll get it right away. But I'll have to persuade Phormio to help me with my scheme.

PHAEDRIA: He's available. You don't have to worry. Put any load on him that you like; he'll walk away with it. He's a real friend in need, he is.

GETA: What are we waiting for, then? Let's go and find him.

ANTIPHO: Anything else you need me for?

GETA: No, not a thing. Why don't you go on home and see

what you can do to cheer up poor Phanium? I'm sure she's scared half to death. Run along, will you?

ANTIPHO: Nothing I'd rather do! (*Exit into* DEMIPHO's *house.*)

PHAEDRIA: How are you going to do all this?

GETA: I'll tell you as we go. Just come away from here. (*Exeunt, stage left.*)

ACT FOUR

SCENE I

(*Enter* DEMIPHO *and* CHREMES, *stage right.*)

DEMIPHO: Well, Chremes, the matter that took you to Lemnos—did you bring your daughter back with you?

CHREMES: No, I didn't.

DEMIPHO: You didn't? Why not?

CHREMES: In the first place, her mother had decided that I had stayed away much too long. Besides, the girl was growing up; they couldn't wait forever for me to come back. So she packed up the whole household and came over here to look for me. At least that's what I was told.

DEMIPHO: Well, for heaven's sake, why did you stay there so long after you'd learned that?

CHREMES: I got sick and couldn't leave.

DEMIPHO: How did that happen? What was the matter with you?

CHREMES: The matter? Oh, I'm getting old—and being old is a sickness in itself. But they got here safely, all right. I found that out from the captain of the boat they came on.

DEMIPHO: You heard what happened to my son while I was away, didn't you, Chremes?

CHREMES: Yes, and it's made me uncertain what to do next. You see, if I arrange a marriage for my daughter with somebody outside the family, I'll have to explain all the details—

where she came from, and who her mother is. With you, I knew I could trust you as well as I could myself; with an outsider, supposing I could get him to agree to the match, he'd hold his tongue just so long as we were on good terms. But if we had a falling-out, he'd know entirely too much, and I'm afraid my wife might find out what I've been doing. If that happens, the only thing left for me will be to shake myself free and be on my way. In my house, I'm all I can call my own.

DEMIPHO: I understand that perfectly, and I'm worried about the difficulty you're in. We'll, I'm not going to give up. I'll keep on working at this until I accomplish what I promised you.

SCENE II

(Enter GETA, stage left.)

GETA *(to himself)*: I've never seen a smarter man than Phormio. I came to the fellow to tell him we needed money and how we could get it. I'd hardly given him half the plan when he caught on. He was delighted, congratulated me, wanted to know where Demipho was, said he was happy to have this chance to show that he was as good a friend of Phaedria as he was of Antipho. I told him to go downtown and wait for me there—said I'd bring the master down there to meet him. Oh-oh! There he is! Who's that behind him? Great gods! Phaedria's father is home! Well, why are you afraid, you idiot? Why? Because you've got two to put over the jumps instead of one? A lot better that way, I think; it gives me an extra string to my bow. I'll tackle Demipho first, as I planned. If he pays, that will be fine. But if I get nothing from him, then I'll go after our traveler here.

SCENE III

(Enter ANTIPHO from DEMIPHO's house.)

ANTIPHO *(to himself)*: I wonder how soon Geta is coming back? Oh-oh! There's my uncle right there with my father!

I'm afraid of what he'll get my father to do, now that he's home. (*He steps to one side.*)

GETA (*to himself*): I'll go and say hello to them. (*Aloud*) Why, hello, Chremes, sir!

CHREMES: Hello, Geta.

GETA: Awfully glad to see you back safe.

CHREMES: Thanks.

GETA: Well, how are things? See a lot of changes here, now that you're home, I suppose?

CHREMES: Yes, quite a few.

GETA: Did you hear what happened to Antipho?

CHREMES: Yes, I heard, all right.

GETA (*to* DEMIPHO): Did you tell him, sir? It's a terrible thing, Chremes! To be deceived like that!

CHREMES: Yes. Demipho and I were just talking about it.

GETA: Yes. Well, I've been thinking it over, too, very carefully, and I think I've found a way out.

CHREMES: What, Geta?

DEMIPHO: What way out?

GETA: After I left you, sir, I just happened to run into Phormio . . .

CHREMES: Who's Phormio?

DEMIPHO (*nudges* CHREMES; *whispers*): You know. The fellow who . . . that girl . . .

CHREMES: Oh, I see.

GETA: I decided to try to find out how he felt. I got him off to one side. "Now, look, Phormio," I said, "why don't we settle this matter between us in a friendly way—you know!— instead of with a lot of hard feelings? My master's a decent, respectable person; he doesn't want to get involved with the law. Why, every last one of his friends has been telling him— every one of them—to put Phanium out, just like that!"

ANTIPHO (*aside*): What is he up to? What does all this mean?

GETA: "You talk about the law?" I said to him. "You think we'll get into trouble with the law if he puts her out? Oh, no! That's been tried before. Believe me, you'll sweat if you start anything with that man. You ought to hear him when he argues a case in court! But anyway, suppose he does lose; it isn't a matter of life and death with him, just of a little money." I saw that this was making him weaken, so I said, "There's nobody else around now. Look, how much would you want, in cash, on the understanding that Demipho would forget about lawsuits, Phanium would leave, and you would stop bothering us?"

ANTIPHO (*aside*): Has he gone crazy?

GETA: "I'm quite sure, you see," I said to him, "that if you name any reasonable amount, he's a decent sort of fellow, and it won't take three minutes to settle the whole thing."

DEMIPHO: Who told you to say anything like that?

CHREMES: No, no! There couldn't be a better way of getting where we want.

ANTIPHO (*aside*): Oh, great gods!

DEMIPHO: Well, go on; tell us the rest.

GETA: At first the man was just plain crazy.

CHREMES: Come on, how much did he want?

GETA: How much? Much too much!

CHREMES: *How* much? Tell us!

GETA: Well, he thought if somebody'd give him maybe six thousand drachmas . . .

DEMIPHO: Six thousand! I'll give him hell first! The insolence of the man!

GETA: My words exactly! "Now, look, please," I said, "what if he were arranging a match for his own daughter? He might as well have had one; they've found him one, and she wants her dowry." Well, to cut it short and leave out all the foolishness, this is what he finally proposed. "Now," he said, "right from the start I was perfectly willing to marry my friend's daughter, because that was the right thing to do. I kept thinking all the time that it wouldn't be good for a poor girl like her to go making a slave of herself to some rich man. But to be quite frank with you, I needed the little bit of money a wife would bring me to pay my debts. And even now, if Demipho is willing to pay me as much as I'm getting from the girl I'm engaged to, there's nobody I'd rather marry than Phanium."

ANTIPHO (*aside*): Is he just stupid, or is he being malicious?

Does he know what he's doing or doesn't he? I don't understand.

DEMIPHO: Yes, but what if he's in debt up to his neck?

GETA: Well, he said, "There's a farm, mortgaged for a thousand drachmas."

DEMIPHO: All right, all right. He can marry her. I'll pay.

GETA: "Then there's a bit of a house, too; a thousand more."

DEMIPHO: Here, now, that's too much.

CHREMES: Never mind! I'll take care of that thousand.

GETA: "Then I'll have to buy a slave girl of some sort for my wife, and we'll need a few pieces of furniture. And there are the wedding expenses. Lump all that together," he says, "for another thousand."

DEMIPHO: He can file a dozen suits against me if he wants to; I won't pay one penny! Why, that . . . ! Does he think he can make a fool of me?

CHREMES: No, please! I'll pay. Just never mind. You just see to it that your son marries my . . . the girl we want him to.

ANTIPHO (aside): Ye gods, Geta! You and your schemes! You've really left me stranded.

CHREMES: It's for my sake we're getting rid of Phanium; it's only fair that I should pay the costs.

GETA: "Let me know as soon as you can," he says, "if they're going to have Phanium marry me, so I can break my engagement to this other girl. I'd like to know for sure, because her parents have already arranged to pay me her dowry."

CHREMES: He'll get his money right away. Tell him to break the other engagement. He can marry Phanium.

DEMIPHO: Yes, and I wish him all the worst of it.

CHREMES: Isn't it fortunate that I brought that money back with me—the income from my wife's properties on Lemnos? I'll take it from that, and tell my wife you needed it. (Exeunt DEMIPHO and CHREMES into CHREMES' house.)

SCENE IV

ANTIPHO: Geta!

GETA: Oh! Yes?

ANTIPHO: *What* have you done?

GETA: Done? Why, I just tricked the old gentlemen out of their money.

ANTIPHO: And that's all, is it?

GETA: All? Why, I don't know. That's all I was told to do.

ANTIPHO: You worthless . . . ! You dare be insolent with me?

GETA: Insolent? What do you mean?

ANTIPHO: What do I mean? I mean what you just did. Why didn't you just hand me a rope to start with? Why, you . . . ! I hope all the powers in heaven and hell will pursue you! (*To audience*) Look, everybody! Here he is! If you have a job you want done in fine style, just hand it to him! (*To* GETA) What was less to the point than stirring up that old trouble and dragging in my wife's name? Now you've made my father think he can push her out the door. Now, look; if Phormio takes the dowry, he'll have to marry Phanium. Then what happens?

GETA: Why, he's not going to marry her!

ANTIPHO: Oh, yes, of course. And then when they want their money back he'll trot off to jail, just for me.

GETA: There's no story, Antipho, that can't be spoiled by the way you tell it. You're leaving out all the good and telling all the bad. Now listen to the other side. Naturally if Phormio takes the dowry money he'll have to marry Phanium, just as you say. I grant you that. But still, he'll be given some time to get ready for the wedding—sending out invitations, making arrangements. It'll take a little while. In the meantime Phaedria's friends will get us the money they promised, and Phormio will pay your father and uncle back out of that.

ANTIPHO: Yes, but what will he use for an excuse? What will he tell them?

GETA: Tell them? What do you think? "The things that have happened since my engagement! Bad luck signs everywhere! A strange dog, dead black, walked into the house! A snake dropped off the roof and fell into the cistern! A hen crowed! Every seer in town has advised against it! It's nearly the new year, too; I don't want to start new business before the turn of the year!" That last one will get them. See, that's how it will go.

ANTIPHO: Well, I hope so.

GETA: It will go, all right. Just leave it to me. (*Enter DE-MIPHO and CHREMES from CHREMES' house.*) Oh, here comes your father. You go along and tell Phaedria we've got the money. (*Exit ANTIPHO, stage left.*)

SCENE V

DEMIPHO (*to CHREMES*): Calm down, I tell you. I'll see that he doesn't pull any tricks on us. (*Holds up purse with money*) See this? I won't be careless with it. I won't let him get his hands on it except in front of witnesses; I'll make it perfectly clear who I'm paying it to and what I'm paying it for.

GETA (*aside*): Cautious, isn't he? But it's a waste of time.

CHREMES: Yes, that's the only thing to do. Hurry up, will you, before he has a chance to change his mind. If that other girl starts putting the pressure on, you know, he just might walk out on us.

GETA (*aside*): That's a good idea! Thanks!

DEMIPHO (*to GETA*): All right, Geta. Let's go find him.

GETA: Yes, sir! At your service!

CHREMES (*to DEMIPHO*): When you get back, will you drop in on my wife? Ask her to have a talk with Phanium before she leaves—tell her that we're having her marry Phormio, and that she mustn't get upset; he was closer to her father and will make her a much better husband; tell her we haven't neglected our duty, for we've paid Phormio every penny of the dowry he wanted.

DEMIPHO: What is the point of all that?

CHREMES: There's plenty of point, Demipho. It isn't enough just to discharge your obligations; you want it to look right, too. I'd like Phanium to do all this willingly, so she won't go around saying we just showed her the door.

DEMIPHO: I can take care of that myself.

CHREMES: Yes, but woman-to-woman is better, you know.

DEMIPHO: Well, all right, I'll ask her. (*Exeunt* DEMIPHO *and* GETA, *stage left.*)

CHREMES: Now I wonder where I could find those women-folk of mine?

ACT FIVE

SCENE I

(CHREMES *on stage. Enter* SOPHRONA, *from* DEMIPHO'S *house.*)

SOPHRONA (*to herself*): What am I going to do? Where can I find a friend? Oh, dear, dear! Where can I get some advice? Where can I find some help? I'm afraid my mistress is going to get into some terrible trouble because of what I advised her to do, the way the young man's father is taking this. They tell me he's really wild!

CHREMES (*aside*): Who's that old woman coming out of my brother's house? She looks scared to death.

SOPHRONA (*to herself*): We were so poor. That's why I felt I had to do it, even though I knew the match probably wouldn't last. That's why I advised it, so she'd be taken care of at least for the time being.

CHREMES (*aside*): Well, for heaven's sake! Unless I'm losing my mind or my eyes are deceiving me, that's my daughter's old nurse I see there.

SOPHRONA (*to herself*): And I can't find a single trace of him . . .

CHREMES (*aside*): Now what do I do?

SOPHRONA (*to herself*): . . . that father of hers.

CHREMES (*aside*): Do I speak to her, or do I wait until I get a better idea what she's talking about?

SOPHRONA (*to herself*): If I could just find him now, I wouldn't have anything to worry about.

CHREMES (*aside*): It's Sophrona, all right. I'll go and speak to her.

SOPHRONA: Who's that? Who's talking here?

CHREMES: Sophrona!

SOPHRONA: That's my name! Who's calling me?

CHREMES: Look behind you. Here I am.

SOPHRONA: Well, for heaven's sake, is that Stilpo?

CHREMES: *No!*

SOPHRONA: What? You're not?

CHREMES: Come over this way, a little farther from the house! Please, Sophrona, don't ever call me by that name again!

SOPHRONA: Why? For heaven's sake, aren't you . . . the one you always said you were?

CHREMES: Ssh!

SOPHRONA: What's the matter with that house? What are you afraid of there?

CHREMES: I've got a wife in there—a wife with a terrible temper. Now about that name; it's not my right name, but I used it with you people because I wasn't sure how discreet you might be. I was afraid you might go blurting it out in public and then my wife might somehow find out.

SOPHRONA: Well, my goodness! That's why we could never find you here! We had a dreadful time!

CHREMES: Look, tell me: What have you to do with the people in that house? Where are my daughter and her mother?

SOPHRONA (*bursts into tears*): Oh, dear, dear, dear!

CHREMES: Goodness! What's the matter? Are they still alive?

SOPHRONA: Your daughter is. But her mother was just so brokenhearted . . . she . . . passed on. Poor thing!

CHREMES: Oh, that's too bad.

SOPHRONA: And then there I was—old, all by myself, no money, didn't know anybody. I did the best I could. I let your daughter marry the young man here—the one that lives in this house.

CHREMES: You mean Antipho?

SOPHRONA: Why, yes, Antipho. That's the one.

CHREMES: What? Has he got two wives?

SOPHRONA: Good gracious, no! She's the only one.

CHREMES: Well, what about the girl that was supposed to be his cousin?

SOPHRONA: Why—why she's the one!

CHREMES: *Wha-a-at?*

SOPHRONA: It was all planned. He was in love with her, and this way he could marry her even though she didn't have a dowry.

CHREMES: Well, I'll be blessed! So many times things happen purely by chance that you wouldn't even dare to hope for. Here I come home and find my daughter happily married just as I'd wanted, to the very man I wanted. My brother and I were working with might and main to bring about something Antipho had already done all by himself without causing us any trouble at all—although it's made a lot for him.

SOPHRONA: But now look. Something will have to be done. Antipho's father is home, and they say he's simply furious.

CHREMES: There's no danger at all. But Sophrona, don't you dare let anybody know that she's my daughter.

SOPHRONA: Nobody will hear it from me.

CHREMES: Come in with me. I'll tell you the rest in there. (*Exeunt into* DEMIPHO's *house.*)

SCENE II

(*Enter* DEMIPHO *and* GETA, *stage left.*)

DEMIPHO: It's our own fault. We make it worth while for people to be dishonest by being so anxious ourselves to have everybody say we're honest and kindhearted. Don't run so fast that you miss home, as they say. Wasn't it bad enough to have him trick us in the way he did? No, we've got to toss some money his way, too, so he can have something to live on while he dreams up more deviltry.

GETA: That's absolutely right, sir.

DEMIPHO: The ones who win the prizes now are the ones who "make the worse appear the better cause."

GETA: That's certainly true.

DEMIPHO: That was perfectly stupid, the way we handled the deal with Phormio.

GETA: Yes. I just hope that will be the end of it and he'll marry the girl.

DEMIPHO: What? You mean to say there's still some doubt about it?

GETA: Well, really, sir, I don't know. The way Phormio is, he might change his mind.

DEMIPHO: What? Change his mind?

GETA: I don't know that he will. But I'm saying, *if* he *should.*

DEMIPHO: I'm going to follow my brother's suggestion and ask his wife to come over and talk with Phanium. Geta, you go in and tell her Nausistrata's coming. (*Exit* DEMIPHO *into* CHREMES' *house.*)

GETA: We've got Phaedria his money. No trouble at all. We've arranged things so that, at least for the present, Phanium won't have to leave. Now what? What do you mean, "Now what?" You're stuck in the same old mud hole, Geta —robbing one purse to fill the other. The trouble we actually had has been put off for a day or so, but things are getting worse all the time. You'd better watch out. I'll go home now and make it clear to Phanium that she isn't to worry about Phormio or anything he says. (*Exit* GETA *into* DEMIPHO's *house.*)

SCENE III

(*Enter* DEMIPHO *and* NAUSISTRATA *from* CHREMES' *house.*)

DEMIPHO: Come on, then, Nausistrata; just be yourself. Get her to calm down and do this willingly. She has to, anyway.

NAUSISTRATA: I'll take care of it.

DEMIPHO: Help me now with a little of your time, in the way that you just came to my rescue with your money.

NAUSISTRATA: I was glad to do that. You know, it's my husband's fault that I can't be as much help as I'd like.

DEMIPHO: How do you mean?

NAUSISTRATA: Heavens! That property of my father's is all perfectly sound, but Chremes manages it very badly. Father always got twelve thousand drachmas a year out of it. Oh! The difference in men!

DEMIPHO: Twelve thousand! You don't say!

NAUSISTRATA: Yes, and business wasn't nearly so good then as it is now. Even so—twelve thousand.

DEMIPHO: My, my!

NAUSISTRATA: What do you think of that?

DEMIPHO: Of course, of course.

NAUSISTRATA: Oh, I wish I were a man! I'd show him . . .

DEMIPHO: I'm sure you would.

NAUSISTRATA: . . . show him how . . .

DEMIPHO: Please, don't tire yourself. Save your strength for Phanium. She's young and strong; don't want her to tire you out.

NAUSISTRATA: I'll do as you told me. But there's my husband, see? Coming out of your house! (*Enter* CHREMES.)

CHREMES: Oh, Demipho! Have you paid that fellow the money yet?

DEMIPHO: Yes, sir! Took care of it right away.

CHREMES: I could wish you hadn't—oh-oh! There's my wife. Almost said too much.

DEMIPHO: Why do you wish I hadn't, Chremes?

CHREMES: Never mind. It's all right.

DEMIPHO: Well, how about it? Did you tell the young lady why we were bringing Nausistrata to see her?

CHREMES: Yes, I explained everything.

DEMIPHO: You did, did you? What did she say?

CHREMES: We can't send her away.

DEMIPHO: Why can't we?

CHREMES: Why—why—they love each other. Dearly.

DEMIPHO: What difference does that make to us?

CHREMES: A lot. And anyway, I've found out she is related to us.

DEMIPHO: What? You must be out of your mind.

CHREMES: No; it's true. I'm not just imagining things. I finally remembered.

DEMIPHO: Have you taken leave of your senses?

NAUSISTRATA: My gracious! You better not do anything to hurt her if she's related to you.

DEMIPHO: She isn't.

CHREMES: Don't say that. She gave her father's name wrong. That's why you were led astray.

DEMIPHO: Didn't she know her own father?

CHREMES: Of course she did.

DEMIPHO: Why did she get his name wrong, then?

CHREMES: Aren't you ever going to stop arguing with me? Aren't you ever going to understand?

DEMIPHO: Understand? When you aren't saying anything that makes sense?

CHREMES: You're killing me!

NAUSISTRATA (to DEMIPHO): I wonder what this is all about?

DEMIPHO: I'm sure I don't know.

CHREMES: You want to know? So help me heaven, there isn't a living soul who's closer to her than you and I.

DEMIPHO: For heaven's sake, let's go in and see her. I'd like to get this straightened out in front of us all.

CHREMES: Oh! No, no!

DEMIPHO: Why not?

CHREMES: Is that all the faith you have in me?

DEMIPHO: You want me to trust you? You don't want me to ask any more questions? Well, all right. What about that girl—"our friend's" daughter? What's going to happen about her?

CHREMES: That's all taken care of.

DEMIPHO: Shall we just tell Nausistrata here that we don't need her?

CHREMES: I think so.

DEMIPHO: And Phanium is to stay?

CHREMES: Yes.

DEMIPHO: Well, I guess you can go home, Nausistrata.

NAUSISTRATA: Good! I must say I think it's much better for all of us than the way you'd planned. She should stay. The minute I laid eyes on her I thought to myself, "She's a very sweet girl." (*Exit* NAUSISTRATA.)

DEMIPHO: What's this all about?

CHREMES: Has she shut the door?

DEMIPHO: Yes, she has.

CHREMES: Ye gods! Is this our lucky day! I've found out it's my daughter your son married!

DEMIPHO: Now wait. How could that be?

CHREMES: This isn't a very safe place to talk about it.

DEMIPHO: Well, come on in, then.

CHREMES: Listen, I don't want our sons to find out about this. (*Exeunt* DEMIPHO *and* CHREMES *into* DEMIPHO's *house.*)

SCENE IV

(*Enter* ANTIPHO, *stage left.*)

ANTIPHO: However things may be for me, I'm delighted that my cousin has what he wanted. That's the wise way: Want only those things that can easily be set straight if they don't go right. Now, Phaedria—as soon as he got his money he was free of all his worries. But I don't see any way to get out of the trouble I'm in. No—if things are kept under cover, I'll be on pins and needles; if they get out, I'll be in disgrace. I wouldn't even be coming home now if they hadn't given me some hope of keeping Phanium. Now where can I find Geta? He can tell me the best time to approach my father.

SCENE V

(*Enter* PHORMIO, *stage left.*)

PHORMIO: I got the money, paid the pimp, took the girl away, arranged things so Phaedria can have her all to himself—we've set her free. Now I have just one job left to do:

Persuade the old gentlemen to allow me a few days for a bachelor party. Yes, I'm going to take a few days off now.

ANTIPHO: Why! Its Phormio. How are things?

PHORMIO: What things?

ANTIPHO: What's Phaedria going to do? How is he planning to spend his honeymoon?

PHORMIO: Oh, it's his turn to play Antipho now.

ANTIPHO: What do you mean?

PHORMIO: Run away from father. He asked you to play Phaedria—turnabout, see?—and speak his piece for him. He's coming to my house for a party. I'm going to tell Demipho and Chremes that I'm making a little business trip to Sunium to buy that "bit of a slave girl" Geta was talking about a while ago. Then if they don't see me they won't think I'm squandering the money they gave me. But the door squeaked over at your house!

ANTIPHO: Look, will you, please? Who's coming out?

PHORMIO: It's Geta.

SCENE VI

(Enter GETA.)

GETA: Oh, you Luck! You lucky, lucky Luck! Talk about your blessings! All at once you've opened up and filled the day with them for my master Antipho!

ANTIPHO *(to PHORMIO)*: What in the world does he mean?

GETA: And for us, his friends—you've cleared away every worry we had! But what am I waiting for? Why don't I load my coat on my back and move along—go find the boy and let him know what's happened?

ANTIPHO *(to PHORMIO)*: Can you understand what he's talking about?

PHORMIO *(to ANTIPHO)*: No. Can you?

ANTIPHO *(to PHORMIO)*: Not at all.

PHORMIO *(to ANTIPHO)*: Neither can I.

GETA: I'll go over to the pimp's. There's where they are. *(Starts toward DORIO's house)*

ANTIPHO: Hey, Geta! (GETA *pays no attention.*)

GETA: There you go! Something new and different, isn't it? Just get started somewhere and you get called back.

ANTIPHO: Geta!

GETA: He's keeping it up! Go ahead, be nasty; you won't make me stop.

ANTIPHO: Wait, won't you?

GETA: Go to the devil.

ANTIPHO: That's where you'll go if you don't stop.

GETA: Huh! Must be somebody from home; he's getting rough with me. (*Turns around*) Well, bless me! If it isn't the very man I'm looking for! The boy himself! Come here quickly!

ANTIPHO: What's going on?

GETA: Of all the men in the world, you, my boy, are the top prize-winner. No argument about it, you're destiny's darling, Antipho!

ANTIPHO: I'd like that. But would you mind telling me why I should think so?

GETA: Will you be satisfied if I drown you with joy?

ANTIPHO: You're killing me!

PHORMIO: Listen, never mind the future commitments. Just tell us the news.

GETA: Oh, Phormio! Were you here, too?

PHORMIO: Yes, I was here. You're stalling.

GETA: All right! Here we go! After we delivered the money to you downtown, Phormio, we went straight home; and then master sent me in, Antipho, to see your wife.

ANTIPHO: Why?

GETA: I'll leave out the prologue; it isn't important. I was just going into the room where the women were when a slave came running up—it was Midas. He grabbed me from behind and nearly pulled me over backward. I turned around and asked him why he was stopping me. He said that nobody was allowed to go in and see "little mistress." "Sophrona," he says "just brought the master's brother, Chremes, in here," and he was in there with the ladies now. As soon as I heard that I went up to the door on tiptoe very quietly; I stopped, held my breath, put my ear to the keyhole, listened. I was trying to hear what they were saying, understand?

PHORMIO: Good boy, Geta!

GETA: And then I heard something perfectly wonderful! Yes, sir! I almost shouted for joy!

ANTIPHO: What did you hear?

GETA: Now, what do you think?

ANTIPHO: I haven't the slightest idea.

GETA: Oh, it was perfectly marvelous! They've found out that your uncle is the father of your wife—yes, of Phanium!

ANTIPHO: What? What are you trying to tell me?

GETA: He had an arrangement with her mother on Lemnos some years ago. Nobody knew about it.

PHORMIO: Nonsense! How would she not know who her own father was?

GETA: Oh, there's some explanation for it, Phormio. You can be sure of that. Look—you don't suppose that I could catch everything they were saying to each other in the room, do you?

ANTIPHO: Why, yes, you know, I heard some story like that, too.

GETA: No, no; I'll tell you something that will really make you believe it. In a little while your uncle came out, and a few minutes later he came back with your father and they both went in. The two of them said that you were to be allowed to keep Phanium. Finally they sent me to find you and bring you in.

ANTIPHO: Well, for heaven's sake, take me! What are you waiting for?

GETA: This way!

ANTIPHO: Well, Phormio, good-by! (*Exeunt* ANTIPHO *and* GETA *into* DEMIPHO's *house.*)

PHORMIO: Good-by, Antipho. Well, well, this is very nice. I'm delighted.

SCENE VII

PHORMIO: What wonderful luck for them! So sudden, too! This is my chance to strip the old gentlemen of their money and to dispose of Phaedria's worries so he won't have to go begging from his friends. Yes, sir! He got that money and now he's going to keep it. What's happened has given me an idea how to make sure of that. Now I'll have to change my style and try a new approach. I'll just go back here between the houses, and then I'll step out to meet Demipho and Chremes when they come out. That business trip I pretended I was going on—I'll drop that. (*He steps back between* DEMIPHO's *and* CHREMES' *houses.*)

SCENE VIII

(*Enter* DEMIPHO *and* CHREMES *from* DEMIPHO's *house.*)

DEMIPHO: I'm really very grateful and very happy, Chremes, since all this has turned out so well for us. Now we must find Phormio just as soon as we can and get our money back from him before he knocks too big a hole in it.

PHORMIO (*steps out*): I wonder if Demipho is at home? I'll just go and see, so that . . .

DEMIPHO: Hello, Phormio. We were on our way to your house.

PHORMIO: For the very same reason, perhaps?

DEMIPHO: Yes sir!

PHORMIO: That's what I thought. Well—why *were* you going?

DEMIPHO: Oh, nothing very important.

PHORMIO: Were you worrying for fear I wouldn't do what I said I'd do? Now, see here: I may be a poor man—and I am—but just the same there's one thing I've always been very careful about: I never break my word.

CHREMES (*to* DEMIPHO): See, I told you. He's an honest fellow.

DEMIPHO: He certainly is.

PHORMIO: And that's what I was on my way to tell you, Demipho: I'm all ready. Whenever you wish, we can have the wedding. You see, I put off everything else I had to do. It

seemed the only right thing, since I could see that you were
anxious to have it that way.

DEMIPHO: Well, now, as a matter of fact Chremes here has
been urging me to call off the wedding. "What are people going
to say," he says, "if you do a thing like that? There was a time
when it would have looked perfectly all right to give Phanium
to Phormio, but we didn't do it then. Now she's being pushed
off on him, as you might say. That won't look right." Practically the same considerations that you were urging on me right
here not so long ago.

PHORMIO: So you didn't mean what you said to me? That's
pretty highhanded!

DEMIPHO: How so?

PHORMIO: How so? Why, because I can't marry that other
girl now. How can I go back and face her now, after I told
her our engagement was broken?

CHREMES (*whispers to* DEMIPHO): "Well, you see, I found out
that Antipho won't hear of divorcing Phanium"; tell him that.

DEMIPHO: Well, you see, I found out that my son simply
won't hear of divorcing Phanium. Would you mind, now? Just
come to the bank and have that money put back to my account, Phormio.

PHORMIO: What? Why, I've already used it to pay my debts!

DEMIPHO: What are we going to do, then?

PHORMIO: If you want me to marry Phanium as we agreed,
I'll marry her. But if you've changed your mind and want
her to stay with you people, then the dowry money remains
with me, Demipho. It isn't fair that I should have to stand a
loss just to do you a favor. After all, it was to save your reputation that I broke off with the other girl, and she would have
brought me exactly the same dowry.

DEMIPHO: Why, what do you mean? You miserable shyster,
are you condescending to me? Do you think we still don't
know who you are and how you operate?

PHORMIO: I don't think I like that.

DEMIPHO: Are you trying to tell us you'd marry Phanium if
we gave you the chance?

PHORMIO: Try me, and see what happens.

DEMIPHO: Yes! So my son could go right on sleeping with her at your house—that was your little scheme!

PHORMIO: I *beg* your pardon! *What* were you saying?

DEMIPHO: Now, see here: You give that money back.

PHORMIO: Nothing doing. You give me my bride.

DEMIPHO: Go on! Sue me!

PHORMIO: Well, all right . . . if you insist on being unpleasant . . . (*He starts to walk away.*)

DEMIPHO: What are you going to do?

PHORMIO: Who, me? Maybe you people think that I only take an interest in girls who have no dowries. Oh, no! I like the ones *with* dowries, too.

CHREMES: What's that to us?

PHORMIO: Oh, nothing. I used to know a certain lady here whose husband had another . . .

CHREMES: What?

DEMIPHO: What's all this?

PHORMIO: . . . had another wife on Lemnos . . .

CHREMES: Oh, great gods!

PHORMIO: . . . and he had a daughter by her, and brought her up without telling anybody about it . . .

CHREMES: This is the end for me!

PHORMIO: . . . and now I think I'll go and tell that lady all about this.

CHREMES: For heaven's sake, don't do that!

PHORMIO: Oh! Are *you* the husband in the case?

DEMIPHO: A-a-h, he's only being funny.

CHREMES (*to* PHORMIO): Look, you just run along. It's all right.

PHORMIO: Oh, no, you don't!

CHREMES: Well, what do you want? The money—you've got it—we make you a present of it.

PHORMIO: Ve-e-ry interesting! Look here, you two: What do you mean by leading me on like this? Acting like a couple of silly children! "I won't—I will," "I will—I won't." "Take it

—give it back." "I said—I didn't say." "It's a deal—it's not a deal."

CHREMES (*to* DEMIPHO): Where did he get word of this? How did he find out about it?

DEMIPHO (*to* CHREMES): I haven't the slightest idea. I know perfectly well I didn't tell anybody.

CHREMES (*to* DEMIPHO): It has me completely mystified, so help me!

PHORMIO (*aside*): I gave them something to think about!

DEMIPHO (*to* CHREMES): What! Is he going to get all that money away from us and stand there and laugh at us? I'll see him in hell first. Come on, now, be a man and keep your wits about you. It's perfectly clear that your little "arrangement" is public property and you can't keep your wife from finding out about it. She's bound to hear it from somebody, Chremes, and it would be much better for you if we told her ourselves. Once that's done we'll be able to take care of this rascal any way we like.

PHORMIO (*aside*): Oh-oh! If I don't watch out, I'll be in for it. They're coming my way with blood in their eye.

CHREMES (*to* DEMIPHO): Yes, but I'm worried. I don't know if I can make my peace with Nausistrata.

DEMIPHO (*to* CHREMES): Don't let that bother you. I'll see that she forgives you. There's one good argument I can use, Chremes: The woman who was Phanium's mother has passed away.

PHORMIO: So that's how it's to be, is it? Pretty smart, the two of you! Well, Demipho, you didn't do Chremes any good when you began needling me. (*To* CHREMES) Aha, you! Did anything you pleased over there on Lemnos, did you? Didn't worry your head about this fine lady here? No! Had to go and pull a dirty trick like that on her! I never heard of such a thing! And now you're going to go tell her you're sorry, and all will be forgiven, is that it? By heaven, what I'm going to tell her will put her in such a flaming rage that you won't be able to cool her down if you produce tears by the bucketful!

DEMIPHO: Tears, is it? I'll "tears" you, you . . . ! Did you ever see anything like it? The gall of the man! He ought to be arrested and transported to the middle of the desert!

CHREMES: Well, he's got me stopped. I don't know what to say to him now.

DEMIPHO: Hmph! I do. Let's file suit against him.

PHORMIO: File suit? This way, please . . . (*He starts off.*)

CHREMES: Go after him! Hang onto him until I get the slaves out here. (*Starts toward house*)

DEMIPHO (*grabs* PHORMIO): Look, I can't manage alone. Come here, quickly! (CHREMES *runs up and also grabs* PHORMIO.)

PHORMIO (*to* DEMIPHO): All right! One charge of assault and battery against you.

DEMIPHO: You just tell that to the judge.

PHORMIO (*to* CHREMES): Second charge against you, Chremes.

CHREMES: Take him in the house! (*They start to drag him toward* DEMIPHO'S *house.*)

PHORMIO: Oh, that's it, is it? Well, I guess I'll have to use my voice. Nausistrata! Come out here!

CHREMES: Hold your filthy tongue! (*To* DEMIPHO) Say, this fellow is strong!

PHORMIO: Nausistrata! Nausistrata!

DEMIPHO: Shut up, will you?

PHORMIO: Shut up? No, sir!

DEMIPHO: If he won't come along, punch him in the stomach.

PHORMIO: Sure, sure! Poke my eye out, too. I've got you fellows where I want you, all right!

SCENE IX

(*Enter* NAUSISTRATA *from* CHREMES' *house.*)

NAUSISTRATA: Who's calling me? Well, for heaven's sake, what's all this noise about, Chremes?

PHORMIO: Well, Chremes, why don't you say something?

NAUSISTRATA: Who is this gentleman? Aren't you going to answer me?

PHORMIO: Answer you? Him? He doesn't know where his home is!

CHREMES: Don't you believe a word he says, my dear.

PHORMIO: Go on, touch him. If he isn't as cold as ice, strangle me.

CHREMES: I-i-i-t's n-n-n-nothing!

NAUSISTRATA: What's the matter, then? What is this man talking about?

PHORMIO: You'll find out. Just listen.

CHREMES: Are you going to believe what he says?

NAUSISTRATA: For goodness' sake, how am I going to believe what he says when he hasn't said anything?

PHORMIO: Poor fellow! He's scared out of his wits.

NAUSISTRATA: There must be something to it if you're that scared.

CHREMES: Who, m-m-me? S-s-scared?

PHORMIO: That's exactly right. You're not a bit scared, and what I have to say isn't important at all, so you tell her.

DEMIPHO (*to* PHORMIO): Damn you! (*To* CHREMES) Is he going to do your talking for you?

PHORMIO (*to* DEMIPHO): Yes, you really worked hard for your brother!

NAUSISTRATA: Chremes, dear, aren't you going to tell me?

CHREMES: Yes, . . . but . . .

NAUSISTRATA: What do you mean, "yes, . . . but"?

CHREMES: It's nothing important.

PHORMIO: Not to you, maybe. But it's important for her to know. Over on Lemnos . . .

DEMIPHO: Here! What are you saying?

CHREMES: Be quiet, will you?

PHORMIO: . . . without your knowing anything about it . . .

CHREMES: Oh, great gods!

PHORMIO: . . . he married another woman.

NAUSISTRATA: Why, Chremes! You didn't!

PHORMIO: Yes, he did.

NAUSISTRATA: Oh, dear, dear, dear!

PHORMIO: And what's more, he had a daughter by her, and you never knew a thing about it.

CHREMES: Now what do we do?

NAUSISTRATA: Well, I never! What a dreadful . . . ! Of all the mean . . . !

PHORMIO: That's what happened.

NAUSISTRATA: Have you ever heard of anything worse? You men! But when it comes to your wives, you're "too tired"! Demipho, I appeal to you; I'm sick of talking to *him*. Was this why he had to make all those trips to Lemnos and stay there so long? Are these those "poor business conditions" that kept my income down?

DEMIPHO: Now, Nausistrata, I don't deny that Chremes deserves blame, but it's the sort of thing we all ought to forgive.

PHORMIO (*aside*): He's dead. "Rest in peace, Chremes!"

DEMIPHO: It wasn't, you know, because he'd lost interest in you or didn't love you any more. He had too much to drink once, about fifteen years ago, and forced some poor young woman, and the girl here was the result. He never had anything to do with her after that. The woman is dead; she's passed away, and she was the one thing that would have caused difficulties here. So please be reasonable—just as you always are —about this.

NAUSISTRATA: Be reasonable? Well! I'd like to be sure that this will be the end of it! But why should I think so? Am I supposed to believe that as he gets older he'll behave himself better? He was no youngster in those days, if years have anything to do with keeping men on the straight and narrow path. Look at me, Demipho. Am I getting any prettier or any younger? What reason can you offer me for expecting, or even hoping, that he will ever be any different?

PHORMIO (*aside*): Chremes' funeral is about to begin! Come one, come all! That's how I operate. Come on, now; does anybody feel like making trouble for Phormio? I'll fix him! I'll lay him out just the way I did our friend here. (*To* NAUSISTRATA) Forgive him now, will you? He's had his punishment, as far as I'm concerned. (*To audience*) She has something to shout in his ear as long as he lives.

NAUSISTRATA: Yes, and I should have. Why, Demipho, do I need to tell you all the things, one after another, that I've done for him?

DEMIPHO: I know that story as well as you do.

NAUSISTRATA: Do you think I deserved to have anything like this happen to me?

DEMIPHO: Most certainly not. But listen, please: What's done can't be undone by faultfinding. Forgive him. He's asking you to; he's confessed; he's said he's sorry. What more do you want?

PHORMIO (*aside*): Oh-oh! Before she forgives him, I'll take care of my own interests, and Phaedria's too. (*To* NAUSISTRATA) I beg your pardon, Nausistrata! Don't be in too much of a hurry to answer him. Listen to me.

NAUSISTRATA: What is it?

PHORMIO: I got three thousand drachmas out of your husband by a little scheme of mine, and I gave it to your son. He took it and paid it to a pimp for a girl he was in love with.

CHREMES: What? What's that?

NAUSISTRATA: Well! Does that seem so awful to you, Chremes, if your son, who's a young man, has one mistress, while you have two wives? Completely shameless, that's what you are! How will you have the audacity to say anything to him about it? Just answer me that.

DEMIPHO: He'll do anything you want.

NAUSISTRATA: No, no, I want you all to know exactly how I feel. I'm not going to forgive him; I'm not going to promise anything; I'm not going to say one word more until I see my son. I'll leave everything for him to decide, and I'll do whatever he says.

PHORMIO: You're a wise woman, Nausistrata.

NAUSISTRATA: Does that suit you?

PHORMIO: Suit me? It certainly does! I'm coming out of this very well—much better than I expected.

NAUSISTRATA: Who are you? What's your name?

PHORMIO: Who am I? I'm Phormio, a true friend to your whole family, madam, and a very special friend of Phaedria.

NAUSISTRATA: Phormio, is it? Well, my heavens! From now on, if there's anything I can do for you, I'll be only to happy to do it.

PHORMIO: You're very kind.

NAUSISTRATA: Goodness! You deserve it.

PHORMIO: Would you like to start by doing something right now that would make me happy—and give your husband a dreadful headache?

NAUSISTRATA: I'd love to.

PHORMIO: Well, then, invite me to dinner.

NAUSISTRATA: Please do come. But where is Phaedria, our arbiter?

PHORMIO: I'll have him here right away.

CANTOR: Goodbye, all—and give us a good hand!

TERENCE

THE BROTHERS
(Adelphoe)

INTRODUCTORY NOTE

Generally regarded as the last of the extant comedies of Terence, *The Brothers* (*Adelphoe*) was first produced in 160 B.C. It is based on Menander's *Adelphoi*, but, as the Prologue tells us, it also contains one scene taken from the *Synapothneskontes* ("Companions in Death") of Diphilus. It is a well-paced but rather sober play, with more bitter irony than humor.

Like several of Terence's plays, *The Brothers* is preoccupied with the father-son relationship, with particular emphasis on the proper way in which to bring up boys. One father, Micio, believes in the gentle, guiding influence of love, tolerance, and understanding; the other, Demea, holds to the old-fashioned rule of precept, discipline, and punishment. In the end, the conflict is left unresolved. The "kind" father, Micio, is subjected to unkindness and ridicule; the "good" son, Aeschinus, turns out to be thoughtless, vain, and disloyal, almost making a mockery of Micio for his years of love and sympathy. The "stern" father, Demea, on the other hand, never proves his point; his son, the shallow and self-willed Ctesipho, remains coarse and foolish to the end. If Demea triumphs at all, he does so only by appearing to show that Micio's method is no better than his own. Neither scholars nor critics have ever been able to agree on the lesson of the play, which may well be that nobody knows what the right way is.

The scene is a street in Athens. There are two house fronts, upstage, with doors opening on the street. The Prologue says little about the play itself; it consists primarily of a gentle and tactful refutation of the charge that Terence did not write his own plays but presented the work of Laelius and Scipio as his own.

CHARACTERS

MICIO, an elderly gentleman
DEMEA, his older brother
SANNIO, a pimp
AESCHINUS, elder son of DEMEA, adoptive son of MICIO
SYRUS, an elderly man, slave of MICIO
CTESIPHO, younger son of DEMEA
SOSTRATA, a poor but respectable widow
CANTHARA, an old woman, slave of SOSTRATA
GETA, an old man, slave of SOSTRATA
HEGIO, cousin of SOSTRATA's deceased husband
DROMO, a boy, slave of MICIO

   Also:
BACCHIS, a slave girl
PARMENO, slave of MICIO
PAMPHILA, daughter of SOSTRATA
STEPHANIO, slave of MICIO

THE SCENE: *A street in Athens. Upstage, the fronts of two houses, with doors opening onto the street. Stage left, the house of* MICIO; *stage right, the house of* SOSTRATA.

THE BROTHERS

Prologue

As soon as our playwright observed that his work was being
subjected to unfriendly scrutiny, and that his critics were
being particularly harsh toward the play we are to stage today* . . . he will take the stand on his own behalf, and you
shall judge for yourselves whether you think what he did deserves commendation or censure. There is a play by Diphilus
called *Companions in Death;* Plautus translated it, title and
all, into Latin. Now in the Greek original there is a scene in
which a young man forcibly takes a slave girl away from a
pimp. The incident occurs near the beginning of the play, and
Plautus chose to omit it from his Latin version. Our author
took this particular scene and inserted it into his play, *The
Brothers,* translating it practically word for word. And this,
his latest production, is the play we are going to do for you.
We'll leave it to you to decide whether our playwright is
guilty of plagiarism or simply picked up and used a scene that
Plautus had passed over because he found it uninteresting.

And another matter: A number of people who wish our
author none too well are claiming that certain gentlemen of
distinction have been helping him with his plays—in fact,
writing line for line with him. They think that this is a
serious accusation, but our author considers it the greatest
compliment to be counted a friend of men who are much be-
loved by all of you and by all our nation. Every one of us has
had occasion to accept their help, and without reserve, in
time of war, and in affairs of business or state.

And now to conclude: Don't expect me to tell you the plot
of our play. The two old gentlemen who will appear in the
opening scene will reveal part of it; the rest will come out as

the action goes on. Please give us a fair hearing* . . . and encourage our author to write still other plays.

ACT ONE

SCENE I

(Enter MICIO *from his house. He turns and calls back through the door.)*

MICIO: Storax! *(He shrugs and turns away.)* Aeschinus isn't home yet from that party last night, and not one of those confounded slaves, either. They were supposed to go and get him. Yes, sir, it's really true, what people say: If you turn up missing or are late getting home, you'd be a lot better off with the sort of things an angry wife says or imagines about you than with what your loving parents think up. A wife, if you're late, thinks you've gotten involved with some woman or are drinking with your friends and amusing yourself; you have all the fun, and she gets all the grief. But look at me now; my son hasn't come home, and what am I thinking? What is worrying me? Maybe he's caught pneumonia or tripped and fallen and broken a leg. Why! A man's a fool to take on anything that's more important to him than himself! And at that, Aeschinus isn't my own son, but my brother's, and *his* ideas have been different from mine ever since we were boys. I've been living an easygoing, pleasant life here in town, and—what many people would call good luck—I've never married. My brother did exactly the opposite; he stayed on the farm. He always saved his money and worked hard. He married and had two sons, and one of them—the older—I adopted for myself. I took him when he was a baby, brought him up, and have always loved him like my own flesh and blood. He's my pride and joy—the only thing in life I really care about. And I do everything I can, too, to make him feel the same way about me. I give and forgive; I don't feel that

*Some lines are lost from the Latin text.

I have to exert my full authority over him. Then, too, there are things that most young fellows try to keep from their fathers—the "boys-will-be-boys" kind of thing—but I've taught my son to tell me everything. Because if a boy gets in the habit of lying or deceiving his father, he'll be all the more likely to try it with other people. I think it's better to discipline children by developing their sense of decency and their gentlemanly instincts, than by making them fear authority. My brother doesn't agree with me in this; in fact, he doesn't like it at all. He keeps coming to me and scolding at me: "What *are* you doing, Micio? What do you mean by ruining our young man? Why is he getting involved with these women and these drinking parties? Why do you give him money for things like that? Why do you buy him those expensive clothes? You must be out of your mind!" Well, now, Demea himself is much too strict, quite unreasonably so. In my opinion he's completely wrong in thinking that paternal authority based on force will carry more weight than authority that grows out of love. Here's what I think, and I'm convinced I'm right: The man who behaves well because he's afraid of being punished does so only as long as he thinks he may be caught. If he thinks he can go undiscovered, he reverts to his natural tendencies. The man whose devotion you've won by kindness acts out of conviction. He's anxious to give as much as he's received, and he's always the same, whether or not you're there. A father's job is to train his son to do the right things as a matter of course rather than through fear—in fact, that's the difference between a father and a master. A man who can't do this had better admit that he doesn't know how to handle children. (*Enter* DEMEA, *stage right*.) But isn't this the very man I was talking about? Yes, it is. He looks a bit upset. I suppose he'll give me an argument, as usual. Oh, hello, Demea! Glad to see you!

SCENE II

DEMEA: Well, it's about time. I've been looking for you.
MICIO: What's the matter with you?

DEMEA: What? We've got Aeschinus on our hands, haven't we? And you want to know what's the matter?

MICIO (*aside*): Didn't I say this would happen? (*To* DEMEA) Why? What has he done?

DEMEA: What has he *done*? Why, the boy has no sense of decency, no respect for anybody. He seems to think he's above the law. I'll say nothing of what he's done before—but *now* what has he thought up?

MICIO: Well, what has he?

DEMEA: Breaking down doors, forcing his way into other men's houses, beating the owner and his people practically to death, dragging away a girl he'd taken a fancy to—that's what. The whole town is furious! I don't know how many people have stopped me and told me that. Everybody's talking about it! And good heavens! If he needs an example, why doesn't he look at his brother? *He* keeps his mind on his work; *he* stays on the farm; *he* saves his money; *he* never touches liquor. *He's* never behaved like Aeschinus! I'm talking about Aeschinus now, but everything I say applies to you, too, Micio; you're the one who's spoiling him.

MICIO: Demea, you just haven't had much experience, and nobody is more unfair than people like that; unless they've done something themselves, they think it can't be right.

DEMEA: What do you mean by that?

MICIO: I mean that you simply don't understand these matters. It's no disgrace, believe me, for a young fellow to play around with the girls, or drink—it just isn't. No, not even to break down a door or two. I know; you and I never did that sort of thing, but that was because we couldn't afford it. Are you congratulating yourself now for something you did because you hadn't the money to do anything else? That's hardly fair, for if we'd had the means, we would have done things like that, too. And if you were half a man, you'd let your son do them now, while he's still young enough to get away with it. Or would you rather he'd wait until you're safely laid away and then do them anyway, when he's too old and ought to know better?

DEMEA: Great gods! Why, you'll drive me crazy! It's no disgrace for a young man to do such things?

MICIO: Oh, come now! Don't keep after me about it. You allowed me to adopt your son, and that makes him mine. If he does anything wrong, Demea, it's my business; I'm the one who is chiefly concerned. He has his dinner parties, his drinking parties; he reeks of perfume; it's all on me. He's got a girl; I'll give him the money for her, as long as it's convenient. If some day it isn't, she'll probably lock him out. He broke down a door, did he? I'll have it repaired. He tore somebody's clothes? I'll have them mended. I've got—thank heaven! —the money to do it, and so far expenses haven't run too high. So look, now: Either stop criticizing me or ask some disinterested person to judge between us. I'll prove that you're more mistaken than I am.

DEMEA: Oh, my! Learn to be a father from these people who know it all!

MICIO: You're his father by blood; I'm his father at heart.

DEMEA: You and your heart! What good did that ever . . .

MICIO: Now, look; if you're going to talk like that, I'm leaving. (*He starts to walk away.*)

DEMEA: That's how it's to be, is it?

MICIO: But do I have to hear you on this same subject again and again and again?

DEMEA: Well, I'm worried.

MICIO: And so am I. But, Demea, let's divide the worrying fairly between us; you worry about Ctesipho, and I'll worry about Aeschinus. When you worry about them both you're practically asking me to give Aeschinus back to you.

DEMEA: But, Micio . . .

MICIO: No, I really mean it.

DEMEA: Well, why argue? If that's the way you want it, let him throw money around and lose his last penny and ruin himself. It's none of my business. And if I say one more . . .

MICIO: Demea, Demea! Are you losing your temper again?

DEMEA: Don't you believe me? I'm not asking you to give me back my son, am I? Of course I'm upset. After all, I am

his father! If I'm in the way . . . no, that's enough. You want
me to concern myself with just the one boy? All right, I will,
and I thank God that he's the kind I want him to be. That
boy of yours will find out one of these days . . . no, I won't
say anything more against him. (*Exit* DEMEA, *stage right.*)

MICIO: What he said isn't entirely beside the point, but
it isn't all to the point, either. It's true; I'm worried about
what has happened, but I didn't want him to know. That's
the way he is, you know; I try to calm him down, talk things
over, or warn him to be careful, and he can't even take that
like a normal human being. But if I add to his bad temper
or actually encourage him in it, I'll end up as ill-tempered
as he is. Just the same, Aeschinus has been asking a good deal
of us. Is there a girl in town he hasn't had an affair with or
given money to? And then to top it off, he told me a few days
ago—I thought he was getting tired of the whole business—
that he wanted to get married. That made me really hope
that he had just about finished sowing his wild oats, and I
was delighted. And now, it's starting all over again! Well . . .
but still, whatever has happened, I'd like to know about it.
I'll go downtown and see if I can find the boy there. (*Exit,
stage left.*)

ACT TWO

SCENE I

(*Enter, stage left,* AESCHINUS, SANNIO, PARMENO, *and* BAC-
CHIS. AESCHINUS *has* SANNIO's *arm twisted behind him;* PAR-
MENO *is escorting* BACCHIS.)

SANNIO: Help, somebody! This is awful! I'm a decent, law-
abiding citizen! Help! Help! What'll I do?

AESCHINUS: Take it easy, now. (*To* BACCHIS) Just wait right
there. Why are you looking over your shoulder? You're perfectly safe. He won't touch you as long as I'm here.

SANNIO: I don't care what you say. I'm going to take her . . .

AESCHINUS (*gives* SANNIO's *arm a twist*): He may be tough, but he won't risk another beating today.

SANNIO: Now, see here, Aeschinus, don't pretend you don't know what I am. I'm a pimp.

AESCHINUS: Yes, I know.

SANNIO: Yes, a pimp, but not a man in the world more surely means what he says than I do. If you come around later apologizing, and telling me you're sorry you did this to me, I won't give *that* for it. Believe me, I'll have my rights. You won't compensate with talk for the way you've mistreated me. I know what you fellows say: "I'm terribly sorry! I swear a thing like this should never have happened to a man like you." Well, it *did* happen.

AESCHINUS (*to* PARMENO): Go ahead, now! Hurry! Unlock the door! (PARMENO *moves to the door of* MICIO's *house.*)

SANNIO: So you couldn't care less—is that it?

AESCHINUS (*to* BACCHIS): All right, my dear; you go in.

SANNIO (*grabs* BACCHIS): Oh, no, you don't!

AESCHINUS (*pulls him back*): Come back here! Parmeno, you were too far away. Stand right by this man. There! That's it! Now! Keep your eye on me all the time. The minute I give the signal, you punch him right on the chin!

SANNIO (*to* PARMENO): I'd like to see you try that.

AESCHINUS (*to* PARMENO): There! Now hold it! (*To* SANNIO) Let the lady go. (SANNIO *pays no attention.* AESCHINUS *nods at* PARMENO, *who punches* SANNIO.)

SANNIO: Of all the dirty, low-down . . . ! (*He pulls* BACCHIS *closer.*)

AESCHINUS: You'll get another, if you don't look out. (PARMENO *punches* SANNIO *again.*)

SANNIO: Here, here! That hurt!

AESCHINUS (*to* PARMENO): I didn't give you a signal, but feel free to make that kind of mistake. (*To* BACCHIS) All right. Go on in. (*She pulls loose from* SANNIO *and exits into* MICIO's *house.*)

SANNIO: What's going on here, anyway? Do you think this town is your private property, Aeschinus?

AESCHINUS: If I did, you'd have gotten the sort of decorations you deserve.

SANNIO: Have you ever had any business with me?

AESCHINUS: No, never.

SANNIO: Have you any idea what sort of man I am?

AESCHINUS: No, and I'm not interested.

SANNIO: Did I ever touch anything of yours?

AESCHINUS: If you had, that would have been your unlucky day.

SANNIO: What gives you more rights than me? What gives you the right to take my girl? I paid good money for her. Answer me that!

AESCHINUS: You'd be wiser not to start a disturbance out here in public. If you insist on being unpleasant, I'll drag you in the house and wrap you in so much rope it'll kill you.

SANNIO: Rope? On me? A law-abiding citizen?

AESCHINUS: That's right.

SANNIO: Why, you dirty . . . ! And they try to tell me that everybody's free and equal here!

AESCHINUS: If you've got the yelling out of your system, Sannio, listen to me for a minute.

SANNIO: I've been yelling at you, or you've been yelling at me—which?

AESCHINUS: Oh, forget that. Let's get down to business.

SANNIO: Business? What business?

AESCHINUS: I have a proposition that will interest you. Want to hear it?

SANNIO: Certainly, if it's anything like a fair one.

AESCHINUS: Hah! A pimp, and he insists that he will listen only to what is fair!

SANNIO: I'm a pimp, that's right—enemy-in-chief to all the young men. I'm a liar; I'm strictly a bad lot. But still I never did you any harm.

AESCHINUS: Missed me, did you? Well, I'm the only one.

SANNIO: Look, Aeschinus, you said something about a proposition. Let's get back to that.

AESCHINUS: You paid two thousand drachmas for that girl Bacchis, didn't you? (And I hope it brings you bad luck!) I'll give you the same for her.

SANNIO: Oh? Well, suppose I don't want to sell her? Will you force me?

AESCHINUS: No.

SANNIO: Well! That's a relief!

AESCHINUS: The way I see it, you have no right to sell her anyway. She's a free woman. I'm filing a claim for her freedom. Now which would you prefer—to get your money, or to start thinking what to say to the judge? You think about it, Sannio. I'll be back. (*Exit into* MICIO's *house.*)

SANNIO: Great gods! I'm not a bit surprised that people have been driven insane by sheer mistreatment! He dragged me out of my house; he beat me up; he took my girl without so much as consulting me. I ache all over; he must have hit me more than five hundred times. And my compensation is an offer to buy the girl at cost. My, my! Such kindness and consideration. Well, I suppose it's all right. He has been so very thoughtful. Wait, now; it might be a good idea at that, if he'll pay me in cash. Cash? Am I dreaming? The minute I agree to sell her for a certain price, he'll close the deal and title will pass to him. As for payment—just forget it! "Oh, right away! Come back tomorrow!" Well, I could even stand that, if he really would pay, even if it isn't a fair price. But I might as well face the facts; when you're in a trade like mine, you're sure to be cheated by these young fellows and then have to keep quiet about it. Pay? Who's going to pay? I'm wasting my time trying to balance the books on that one.

SCENE II

(*Enter* SYRUS, *from* MICIO's *house. He speaks back through the door to* AESCHINUS, *within.*)

SYRUS: Just forget it; I'll talk to him. I'll make him eager to accept your offer. He'll even say we've been very kind to him. (*Turns to the front*) What's this I hear, Sannio? Have you and my master been having some sort of disagreement?

SANNIO: Disagreement? That was a pretty one-sided contest we had. I've never seen one more so; I took the beating and he gave it, and now we're both worn out.

SYRUS: It was all your fault.

SANNIO: My fault? What could I do?

SYRUS: You should have been kinder to the boy.

SANNIO: I don't see how I could have been; I deliberately led with my chin the whole time.

SYRUS: Well, all right. Do you want to hear what I have to say? There are times when we make the most money by forgetting about money. Why, you fool! You've been afraid that if you gave up a little something and were kind to the boy, you wouldn't make a profit.

SANNIO: I lay out no cash on the future.

SYRUS: You'll never make any money that way. Look, Sannio, haven't you ever heard of the come-on game?

SANNIO: No doubt your way is better. But I guess I'm just not that smart. I'd rather take what I can get, right here and now.

SYRUS: Oh, come now! I know what you're thinking. What's two thousand drachmas to you, if you could do Aeschinus a favor? And one thing; people have been telling me that you're about to make a trip to Cyprus.

SANNIO: What's that?

SYRUS: Yes! They say that you've bought up a lot of stock, and that you have already arranged your passage. This is what's really important to you right now, I'm sure. But then, I suppose that when you return you could pick up the deal with Aeschinus again.

SANNIO: I'm not putting one foot outside Athens! (*Aside*) That's bad! They knew I was going; that's why they started all this.

SYRUS: (aside): He's worried! I gave him something to think about!

SANNIO (aside): Damnation! He caught me at the worst possible moment! I've bought a lot of women, and a lot of other things too, that I want to take to Cyprus. If I don't get there for the fair, I'll lose everything. If I drop my deal with Aeschinus now, and try to pick it up again when I return, that's no good. The whole thing will have gotten cold: "What? A bit late, aren't you? Why did you let things go? Where have you been?" Why, I'll be money ahead if I let the girl go, rather than postponing my trip as long as that, or trying to catch up on things later.

SYRUS: Well, have you figured out how much you're going to make?

SANNIO: Was this the right sort of thing for Aeschinus to do? Use force? Literally tear the girl away from me?

SYRUS (aside): He's weakening. (To SANNIO) This is all I have to offer; see how you like it. Rather than taking your chances on an all-or-nothing proposition, why not split the difference? Aeschinus can scrape together a thousand drachmas somewhere.

SANNIO: What? Do I have to wonder whether I'll even get back what I spent to begin with? Hasn't the boy any sense of decency? He's loosened every tooth I have and raised lumps all over my head! On top of that, is he going to cheat me? No, sir; I'll stay here.

SYRUS: Suit yourself. Well, I guess I'll run along now. (Starts off.)

SANNIO: No, no! Please, please, Syrus! No matter what's happened, I don't want to make a fuss about it. I'd rather he'd pay me what's coming to me—at least what I paid for the girl, Syrus. Until now, I know, you've never had any favors from me, but you'll see that I don't forget, and that I know my friends.

SYRUS: I'll keep that in mind. But look, here comes Ctesipho. He's really pleased with his girl.

SANNIO: What about my proposition?
SYRUS: Just be patient.

SCENE III

(*Enter* CTESIPHO, *stage right.*)

CTESIPHO: When you need a favor, it's a joy to get it from anybody. But what's really nice is to get it from somebody you'd naturally expect it from. Oh, Aeschinus, Aeschinus! Good old brother! What can I say about you? Of this much I'm sure: No matter how extravagantly I praised you, I could never do justice to a man like you. One thing I know I have that nobody else in the world has—a brother who's really a prince.

SYRUS: Say, Ctesipho—

CTESIPHO: Oh, hello, Syrus. Where's Aeschinus?

SYRUS (*points to* MICIO's *house*): Right in there, at home. He's expecting you.

CTESIPHO: My!

SYRUS: What do you mean, "My"?

CTESIPHO: What do you think? Aeschinus has saved my life! He's wonderful! He put helping me ahead of everything else. The ugly talk, the bad reputation, the hard work, the questionable conduct—all of that really belonged to me, but he took it over. You can't do more than . . . listen! Didn't I hear a door opening?

SYRUS: Relax, relax! It's Aeschinus coming out.

SCENE IV

(*Enter* AESCHINUS *from* MICIO's *house.*)

AESCHINUS: Where is the old so-and-so?

SANNIO (*aside*): He's looking for me. He doesn't have the money, does he? Damn! Can't see a sign of it.

AESCHINUS (*to* CTESIPHO): Oh, fine! I was looking for you.

(CTESIPHO *throws his arms around* AESCHINUS.) Why, what's this for, Ctesipho? You're in the clear. Come on, be happy!

CTESIPHO: Happy? Why wouldn't I be happy! After all, I've got you for a brother! Really, Aeschinus, I'm uneasy about going on like this right to your face. You might think I was trying to play up to you instead of to express my gratitude.

AESCHINUS: Don't be silly, Ctesipho. As if you and I didn't know each other! The only thing that bothers me is that I found out so late. Things had almost gotten to the point where nobody in the world could have helped you, even if they'd wanted to.

CTESIPHO: I was ashamed to tell you.

AESCHINUS: Now, look; that's just foolishness, not shame. A little matter of a girl, and you almost left home because of it! That's terrible! I hope nothing like that will ever happen.

CTESIPHO: I'm sorry.

AESCHINUS (*to* SYRUS): How is Sannio feeling about us, anyway?

SYRUS: Gentle as a lamb.

AESCHINUS (*to* CTESIPHO): I'm going downtown and take care of Sannio, here. You go in to Bacchis, Ctesipho.

SANNIO: Syrus, hurry him up.

SYRUS (*to* AESCHINUS): Let's go. Sannio is in a hurry to leave for Cyprus.

SANNIO: Not as much of a hurry as you'd like. I can wait. I have plenty of time.

SYRUS (*to* SANNIO): You're going to have your money. Don't get excited.

SANNIO: Yes, but I want *all* of it.

SYRUS: You'll get all of it. Just keep quiet and come along.

SANNIO: Here I come. (*Exeunt* SANNIO *and* AESCHINUS, *stage left.* SYRUS *starts to follow them.*)

CTESIPHO: Say, Syrus!

SYRUS (*turning back*): What do you want?

CTESIPHO: Please, please, you two, pay off that old reprobate as quickly as you can! If he becomes any more annoyed, my father may somehow hear of this business, and then I'll certainly be finished.

SYRUS: That won't happen, don't you worry. Just go in and enjoy yourself with the lady. Oh, yes; while you're at it, prepare things and we'll all have a party. I'll finish this job and come right back. On the way, I'll pick up something to eat.

CTESIPHO: You do that. Things have turned out very well, so let's celebrate. (*Exit* SYRUS, *stage left; exit* CTESIPHO *into* MICIO's *house*.)

ACT THREE

SCENE I

(*Enter* SOSTRATA *and* CANTHARA *from* SOSTRATA's *house*.)

SOSTRATA: Oh, Canthara, Canthara! What will happen now?

CANTHARA: What will happen? Why, things will go just fine, I'm sure.

SOSTRATA: But, my dear! Her pains are starting! She had the first little ones just now!

CANTHARA: Are you getting worried at this point, as if you'd never seen a baby born and never had one yourself?

SOSTRATA: Yes, but oh, dear! I haven't anybody! We're all alone. And Geta isn't here either; there's nobody to send for the midwife, nobody to get Aeschinus!

CANTHARA: Aeschinus? He'll be here. He never lets a day go by without coming.

SOSTRATA: It's all so terrible! He's the only one who can help!

CANTHARA: The way things are, it couldn't have turned out better, ma'am. If she had to get into trouble, at least it's Aeschinus who is involved—such a nice young man, intelligent and kind, and from such a good family.

SOSTRATA: Well, yes, I guess you're right. I only hope we don't lose him.

Scene II

(Enter GETA, *stage left.)*

GETA: Now we're in trouble! If all the people in the world put their heads together and tried to find a solution to this problem, they couldn't come up with a thing that would help. That's the kind of trouble we have—my mistress, her daughter, and me. It's just terrible! All at once everything is closing in on us, and leaving no way out. We have no influence, no money; the law won't help us; nobody cares about us; nobody even knows us. What an age to be living in! Nothing is sacred today! And that man—not a shred of decency in him!

SOSTRATA: Oh, dear! What's this I see? Why is Geta so scared? Why is he in such a hurry?

GETA: Nothing stopped him; nothing changed his mind— not his word of honor, not his oath, not even ordinary human feeling! No, not even that she was about to have a baby, the poor girl. And he was the one who played that dirty trick on her—forced her, got her into trouble.

SOSTRATA: I can't quite hear what he's saying.

CANTHARA: Well, let's get over closer to him then, Sostrata.

GETA: Great gods! I can hardly control myself, I'm so furious! There's nothing I'd like better than to meet up with the whole bunch of them, so I could pour it all over them before I get a chance to cool off. First thing I'd do is wring the neck of the old bird that fathered that dirty devil. Then that Syrus—he put him up to it!—how I'd tear him apart! I'd grab him by the middle and hoist him up and bring his head down —hard!—on the ground—scatter his brains all over the street. Then that young whippersnapper—I'd snatch out his eyeballs and throw him head first the hill! And the rest of the lot—I'd push and I'd pull and I'd pound them; I'd lay them all flat on the ground! But what am I doing? I must hurry and tell my mistress the bad news. *(Starts toward* SOSTRATA's *house.)*

SOSTRATA: Let's call him back. Geta!

GETA: For heaven's sake, whoever you are, leave me alone!

SOSTRATA: But it's Sostrata!

GETA: Sostrata? Where's Sostrata? Oh! You're the one I'm looking for! I've been hoping to find you. I'm awfully glad you came my way. Oh, ma'am . . .

SOSTRATA: What's the matter? Why are you shaking?

GETA: Oh, God!

CANTHARA: Why the panic, Geta? Pull yourself together.

GETA: It's all . . .

SOSTRATA: What do you mean, "It's all"? What's "all"?

GETA: It's all over for us. We're finished.

SOSTRATA: Will you please tell me what you mean?

GETA: Well . . .

SOSTRATA: Well, *what*, Geta?

GETA: Aeschinus . . .

SOSTRATA: Well, what about him?

GETA: He's walked out on all of us.

SOSTRATA: Oh, good heavens! Why?

GETA: He's fallen in love with another girl.

SOSTRATA (*bursts into tears*): Oh, dear; oh, dear!

GETA: Yes, and he isn't even trying to keep it quiet. He took her right out of the pimp's house, in broad daylight.

SOSTRATA: You're absolutely sure about this?

GETA: Absolutely. I saw it with my own eyes, Sostrata.

SOSTRATA: Oh, this is awful! What can you believe? Whom can you trust? Is this Aeschinus—our Aeschinus? The one who meant everything to us? The one who was our only hope, our only strength? The one who swore, over and over again, that he couldn't live one single day without my Pamphila? The one who said so many times that he'd take the baby and put it in his father's arms and beg him to let him marry my daughter?

GETA: Please, ma'am, stop crying, and let's figure out what we have to do. Are we going to sit and take this, or are we going to tell somebody about it?

CANTHARA: For heaven's sake, are you crazy? Do you think we can afford to let this be known?

GETA: Well, I must say I don't like the idea. In the first

place, it's perfectly clear that he's walked out on us, so if we let people know about Pamphila's condition, he'll say he had nothing to do with it. I'm sure of that. And that won't help either your reputation or your daughter's health. And even suppose that he does admit his responsibility; he's involved with another girl, and so having Pamphila marry him is strictly no good. No, no matter what, we've got to keep this quiet.

SOSTRATA: No, sir; no, sir! I will not!

GETA: What are you going to do?

SOSTRATA: I'm going to tell.

CANTHARA: Oh, Sostrata, ma'am, watch what you're doing!

SOSTRATA: Things couldn't be worse than they are right now. First, she has no dowry; secondly, what was her "second dowry" she has lost; we can't offer her in marriage as a virgin. So there's nothing else left to do. It Aeschinus denies responsibility, I've got evidence (*she pulls a ring out of her dress*); here's a ring he lost. Finally, I know my hands are clean; no money has passed between us, or anything else unbecoming to either Pamphila or me, Geta. So I'm going to take it to court.

GETA: Well, all right. I give up. You've convinced me.

SOSTRATA: You hurry along now and find Hegio—he's her nearest relative. Tell him the whole story, from beginning to end. You know he was very close to Simulus, my poor husband, and has always been a good friend to us.

GETA: Right! He's the only one who gives us any consideration at all.

SOSTRATA: And you, Canthara; quickly, now! Run and get the midwife, so she'll be here when we need her. (*Exeunt* GETA *and* CANTHARA, *stage left; exit* SOSTRATA *into her house.*)

SCENE III

(*Enter* DEMEA, *stage right.*)

DEMEA: Confound it! I've just heard that my son, Ctesipho, took part in that kidnaping with Aeschinus. Believe me, it will be the last straw if he takes his brother, who's still a fairly decent person, and gets *him* into trouble. Where am I going to find him? I suppose Aeschinus has him hidden in some dive. He talked him into it, the young rascal! I'm sure of that. (*Enter* SYRUS, *stage left, followed by* DROMO *and* STEPHANIO *with baskets of food.*) But look! Here comes Syrus. I'll soon find out from him where Ctesipho is. Wait a minute; he's on their side. If he thinks I'm looking for him, he'll never tell me anything! I won't let him know that's what I want.

SYRUS (*to* DROMO *and* STEPHANIO): I've just told the whole story to Micio, and I've never seen anybody more delighted.

DEMEA (*aside*): Great gods! The man's an idiot!

SYRUS (*to* DROMO *and* STEPHANIO): He complimented Aeschinus, and thanked me for giving the boys that advice.

DEMEA (*aside*): I'll burst!

SYRUS (*to* DROMO *and* STEPHANIO): He gave us the money on the spot, and added an extra fifty drachmas for "expenses" —and I laid that out very nicely, I can tell you.

DEMEA (*aside*): Here's your man, if you want a job done well.

SYRUS: Why, Demea, sir! I didn't realize you were here. How are you?

DEMEA: How am I? Why, I'm simply dumbfounded at the way you people carry on.

SYRUS: Yes, silly, isn't it? In fact, utterly ridiculous! (*Turns to* DROMO) Look, Dromo; clean all the fish, but take that big eel and let him splash around in water for a bit. When I get there, we'll skin him, but not until then, hear? (DROMO *nods, exits into* MICIO's *house.*)

DEMEA: Of all the disgraceful conduct!

SYRUS (*to* DEMEA): Well, I certainly don't approve of it, and I keep telling them so, too. (*To* STEPHANIO) Stephanio, take the salt mackerel and put them to soak—do a good job, now! (*Exit* STEPHANIO.)

DEMEA: Good heavens! Is Micio making this his aim in life—does he think he's doing something fine if he ruins my son? It's perfectly terrible! Yes, I can see the day coming when my boy won't have a penny to his name and will have to run off somewhere and join the army.

SYRUS: You're so right, sir. A smart man doesn't watch just what's in front of his face; he keeps an eye on the future, too.

DEMEA: Tell me, is that slave girl at your house?

SYRUS: Yes, sir, right in there!

DEMEA: What? Is he going to keep her in his own home?

SYRUS: I guess so. He's crazy enough.

DEMEA: Why, I never heard of such a thing!

SYRUS: Micio is much too easygoing; his good nature is positively immoral.

DEMEA: Yes, and he's my brother, too! He makes me ashamed! He makes me sick!

SYRUS: There's a great difference, Demea—a tremendous difference—between you and your brother, and I'm not just saying this because you're here. Add it up any way you like, you're pure good sense, but *he*—good heavens! You wouldn't let Ctesipho do anything like this, now, would you, sir?

DEMEA: Let him? Why, six months before he'd even thought of the idea, I'd have known about it.

SYRUS: *You're* telling *me* how carefully you watch him?

DEMEA: Well, I'd like him to stay the way he is, if you don't mind.

SYRUS: Of course, sir. "As the twig is bent . . . ," you know.

DEMEA: What about him? Have you seen him today?

SYRUS: Ctesipho, you mean? (*Aside*) Here's where I chase Demea back to the farm. (*To* DEMEA) Why, I think he's been at work on the farm for some time now.

DEMEA: Are you quite sure that's where he is?

SYRUS: Yes, of course. I went out there with him myself.

DEMEA: That's fine. I was afraid he might be hanging around here.

SYRUS: And my-oh-my! Was he furious!

DEMEA: Furious? Why?

SYRUS: He and Aeschinus got into quite an argument downtown because of that slave girl.

DEMEA: You don't say?

SYRUS: Yes, sir! He went after Aeschinus tooth and nail. Micio happened to be just handing out the money when all at once up came Ctesipho. He burst right in with "Aeschinus, Aeschinus! To think that you'd do a disgraceful thing like this! Do a thing that's such a reflection on our family!"

DEMEA: I'm so happy I could cry!

SYRUS: "See here," he said, "it's not money you're throwing away; it's your whole life."

DEMEA: Oh, God bless him! He's a chip off the old block.

SYRUS: Yes, he *is!*

DEMEA: Why, Syrus, the boy is brimful of principles like that.

SYRUS: My, my! (*With a little bow to* DEMEA) He has somebody at home to learn from.

DEMEA: And learn he does, all the time. I never miss a chance to teach him good habits. You know what I say? I tell him to look at everybody's lives as if they were mirrors. I tell him to take other people as examples, like "Do this. . . ."

SYRUS: Fine, fine!

DEMEA: "Keep clear of that. . . ."

SYRUS: Excellent!

DEMEA: "People approve of this. . . ."

SYRUS: That's right!

DEMEA: "This, now, they disapprove. . . ."

SYRUS: Splendid!

DEMEA: And then I go on. . . .

SYRUS: I'm sorry, sir, but I haven't time to hear any more right now. I bought some very nice fish; I want to be sure they aren't ruined. For us slaves that would be disgraceful, just as it would be for you, if you failed to do the things you've just been talking about. As far as I can, I give lessons to the other slaves, exactly the way you do. "This is too salty," I say. "This is too brown." "Didn't do a very good job of cleaning this one." "There, that's right; next time remember to do it that way!" I'm always giving them all the advice I can, considering that I really know very little. You know what I say, Demea? I tell them to look at the pots and pans as if they were mirrors and then I suggest what needs doing. I know what we fellows do is unimportant, but after all, what do you expect? You have to take people as you find them. Well—anything else I can do for you?

DEMEA: Yes, show better sense, you people.

SYRUS: Are you going back to the farm now?

DEMEA: Yes, straight back.

SYRUS: Splendid! What is there for you to do here, where nobody pays any attention to your good advice? (*Exit* SYRUS *into* MICIO's *house.*)

DEMEA: Well, I might as well be going. The boy I came after has gone back to the farm. He's my only concern; he's my real interest. That other one—since my brother wants it that way, let him look after him. But who's that I see down at the end of the street? Is that my old friend, Hegio? If I'm seeing straight, it's Hegio, all right. Yes, sir. He's been a friend of the family since I was a boy. Yes, indeed! There's a great shortage these days of people like that—good, old-fashioned, honest people. It will be a long time before he starts any trouble in our town. I feel good all over when I see that there are still a few of his kind left. Yes—makes you glad to be alive! I'll wait here and pass the time of day with him.

Scene IV

(*Enter* HEGIO *and* GETA, *stage left.*)

HEGIO: For heaven's sakes, Geta! That's simply outrageous! What *are* you telling me?

GETA: Exactly what happened.

HEGIO: From a family like that, such a disgraceful piece of conduct! Oh, Aeschinus! What you did there you never learned from your father!

DEMEA (*aside*): Obviously he's heard about that slave girl, and he's hurt and offended, even though he's not one of the family. Yes, and the boy's own father doesn't care a bit. Oh, how I wish Micio were around somewhere and could hear this!

HEGIO: If they don't do what they're duty-bound to do, they won't escape that easily.

GETA: Hegio, you're our only hope. You're the only friend we have; you're our protector; you're the head of our household. When old Simulus was dying, he told us to rely on you. If you desert us, we're finished.

HEGIO: Don't talk like that. I'll do no such thing. I know perfectly well that it wouldn't be right.

DEMEA (aside): I'll go and speak to him. (To HEGIO) How do you do, Hegio! So nice to see you.

HEGIO: Oh! The very man I was looking for! Hello, Demea.

DEMEA: What did you want?

HEGIO: It's about your older son, Aeschinus, the one you let your brother adopt. He's done something that no decent, well-bred young man ought to do.

DEMEA: Why, what did he do?

HEGIO: You knew our friend Simulus, didn't you—a man about my age?

DEMEA: Of course.

HEGIO: He had an innocent young daughter. Aeschinus attacked her.

DEMEA: He *did?*

HEGIO: Wait a bit. You haven't heard the worst yet, Demea.

DEMEA: Why, could there be anything worse?

HEGIO: Indeed there could. Because, you see, that sort of thing just has to be borne one way or another. Nighttime, passion, wine, youth—all that's pretty persuasive, and boys will be boys. When he found out what had happened he came on his own to the girl's mother. He shed tears; he begged and beseeched them to pardon him; he gave his word of honor and took an oath that he'd marry her. They accepted his apology, hushed the matter up, and trusted his promises. As a result of the attack, the girl became pregnant, and it's the ninth month now. And that fine young gentleman—God save us!—has gone and bought himself a slave girl to live with. He's walked out on the one he attacked.

DEMEA: You're perfectly sure of what you're telling me?

HEGIO: The girl's mother is here to be seen, the girl herself, the fact that she's pregnant. Besides, there's Geta here—as slaves go, not a bad fellow and certainly a hard worker. He's kept them from starving and has taken care of the whole household without any help from anybody. Take him along, tie him up, ask him for the facts.

GETA: No, more than that, Demea; torture me, if it's not the truth. And anyway, Aeschinus won't deny it. Just call him out here.

DEMEA: This is most embarrassing. I don't know what to do or say.

PAMPHILA (within): Oh, great gods! The pain! The pain! Juno Lucina, help me! Save me! Oh-h-h!

HEGIO: Why, what . . . ? Geta, she isn't having her baby, is she?

GETA: Yes, she is, Hegio.

HEGIO: You see, Demea, she's making an appeal to your sense of honor, hoping that you'll do on your own what the law would force you to do anyway. And that would be my first wish, too, because it's what I'd expect of you. But if you're otherwise inclined, Demea, I'll stand up for Sostrata and for her late husband with all the strength I have. He was a cousin of mine; from the time we were small boys we were brought up together. We did our army service together; we practically lived together, all the time. When times were hard, we stuck it out together. And so I'll give it everything I have; I'll go to court; yes, I'll kill myself at it before I'll abandon them. What have you to say to that?

DEMEA: I think I'd better get hold of my brother, Hegio.

HEGIO: All right, Demea, but here's something I'd like you to keep in mind. You people can do practically anything; you have lots of influence, lots of money; you've had an easy time; you're a family of prominence and position. And that all puts you under the greatest obligation to be fair and do what's right—that is, if you want people to continue thinking of you as a decent, respectable family. (*He starts toward* SOSTRATA's *house.*)

DEMEA: Don't go yet. We'll discharge our obligations, all of them.

HEGIO: That's no more than right. Geta, take me in to Sostrata. (*Exeunt* HEGIO *and* GETA *into* SOSTRATA's *house.*)

DEMEA: They can't say I didn't warn them that this would happen. I just wish this were going to be the end of it! But Micio is entirely too easygoing. Some day it's going to end up in something really serious. I'll go and see if I can find him; I'd like to throw this right in his face. (*Exit stage left.*)

SCENE V

(*Enter* HEGIO *from* SOSTRATA's *house.*)

HEGIO: (*speaks back through door*): Now just keep your spirits up, Sostrata, and do what you can to make Pamphila feel better. I'm going downtown to find Micio, if he's around, and tell him exactly what's happened. If he's going to do the right thing, I want him to get at it, but if he's otherwise disposed, I want him to tell me, so that I'll know as soon as possible what plans I'll have to make. (*Exit stage left.*)

ACT FOUR

SCENE I

(*Enter* CTESIPHO *and* SYRUS *from* MICIO's *house.*)

CTESIPHO: You say my father's gone back to the farm?

SYRUS: Yes, some time ago.

CTESIPHO: Just say it again, will you?

SYRUS: He's out there now. I expect this very minute he's working at some job.

CTESIPHO: If only I could be sure! I don't wish him any bad luck, but I hope he gets so tired that he won't be able to get out of bed for three days.

SYRUS: I hope so, too—or something better than that, if possible.

CTESIPHO: Yes, because now that I've made a start on it, I'm terribly anxious to spend this whole day enjoying myself. That blasted farm! The chief reason I hate it so much is that it's so close. If it were farther away, it would be night-time before he could get back here again. As it is, when he doesn't see me there, he'll be here on the run, I'm sure of it. He'll want to know where I've been: "I haven't seen you all day long!" What will I tell him?

SYRUS: Haven't you any ideas?

CTESIPHO: Never a one.

SYRUS: So much the worse for you. Haven't you people any friends or acquaintances or business associates here?

CTESIPHO: Of course we have. What of it?

SYRUS: How about having some business with one of them?

CTESIPHO: When I didn't have any? I'd never get away with it.

SYRUS: Of course you would.

CTESIPHO: Maybe, for the daytime. But if I spend the night here, what excuse will I give, Syrus?

SYRUS: Too bad, isn't it, that it's not customary to do business with your friends at night. Well, just take it easy. I have a good idea how your father's mind works. When he's about to boil over, I'll make him gentle as a lamb.

CTESIPHO: How?

SYRUS: He loves to hear people say nice things about you. When I see him, I'll praise you to high heaven. I'll tell him what a sterling fellow you are.

CTESIPHO: Sterling? Me?

SYRUS: Yes, you. In half a minute I'll make him so happy he'll cry like a baby. (*Enter* DEMEA, *stage left*.) Aha! There we are!

CTESIPHO: "There we are" what?

SYRUS: Speak of the devil . . .

CTESIPHO: My father, is it?

SYRUS: In person!

CTESIPHO: Syrus, what are we going to do?

SYRUS: You just run into the house. I'll take care of him.

CTESIPHO: If he asks about me, you haven't laid eyes . . . understand?

SYRUS: Calm down, can't you? (*Exit* CTESIPHO *into* MICIO'S *house.*)

SCENE II

(DEMEA *to stage center.*)

DEMEA: This has certainly been my unlucky day! I can't find my brother anywhere. And on top of that, while I was looking for him I ran into a hired man from the farm, and he told me Ctesipho wasn't out there. Now I don't know what to do.

CTESIPHO (*opens door a crack, whispers*): Syrus!

SYRUS (*whispers*): What do you want?

CTESIPHO (*whispers*): Is he looking for me?

SYRUS (*whispers*): Yes!

CTESIPHO (*whispers*): Oh, ye gods!

SYRUS (*motions to him to go away, whispers*): Just relax, won't you?

DEMEA: Of all the rotten luck! I can't understand it, except that I'm sure I was cut out for just one thing—to have everything go completely wrong. If there's any bad news, I'm the first to get wind of it; no matter what it is, I hear about it first, and then I have to be the first to report it—and then nobody cares but me!

SYRUS (*aside*): That's a laugh! He says he's the first to know; he's the only one who doesn't know anything!

DEMEA: Well, here I am back again. I'll go see if my brother is home yet.

CTESIPHO (*opens door again, whispers*): Syrus! For heaven's sake, don't let him come charging in here!

SYRUS (*whispers*): Will you be quiet? I won't let him.

CTESIPHO (*whispers*): Well, I certainly am not going to leave it all to you! I'm going to find some back room and lock myself in there with Bacchis. That'll be safest.

SYRUS (*whispers*): Good! Just the same, I'll get him out of here. (CTESIPHO *closes door.*)

DEMEA: Well, look who's here—that villain Syrus!

SYRUS (*pretends to be just coming ouf of* MICIO'S *house; to himself*): By heaven, even if a man wanted to, he couldn't stand such behavior. I'd like to know how many masters I have. What a life!

DEMEA: What's he carrying on about? What does he mean? Say there, my good man, is Micio at home?

SYRUS: "Good man," my eye! What are you talking about? I'm through.

DEMEA: What's wrong with you?

SYRUS: Fine question! Ctesipho nearly beat the stuffing out of me and that slave girl.

DEMEA: What? What are you trying to tell me?

SYRUS: Look at my lip, split wide open!

DEMEA: Why?

SYRUS: He accused me of putting Aeschinus up to buying that girl.

DEMEA: Weren't you telling me a while ago that you'd just gone out to the farm with him?

SYRUS: Yes, I did. But he came right back, mad as blazes. He really laid it on! Absolutely shameless! Beating up an old man like me! Why, when he was a little boy I used to carry him around in these arms of mine!

DEMEA: Wonderful! Ctesipho, you take after your father! Yes, sir, today I call you a man!

SYRUS: You approve of him? Well, sir, he'll keep his hands to himself after this, if he's smart.

DEMEA: Good boy!

SYRUS: Yes, very good boy—because he beat a helpless woman and me, a poor old slave, who didn't dare hit back. Yes, indeed—a *very* good boy!

DEMEA: A fine job—couldn't have been better! He knows exactly what I do—that you started all this. Tell me, is Micio at home?

SYRUS: No, he isn't.

DEMEA: I wonder where I might find him?

SYRUS: I know where he is, but I'm not going to tell you.

DEMEA: What? What's that you say?

SYRUS: You heard me.

DEMEA: I'll take your head off, that's what I'll do!

SYRUS: Well, there's this fellow—I don't know his name, but I know where his place is.

DEMEA: Tell me where it is, then.

SYRUS: You know the arcade near the butcher shop down this way? (*Points*)

DEMEA: Yes, of course.

SYRUS: Go right past it, and then straight up the street. When you get to the top, you'll see a hill in front of you. Take a run down that. Then at the bottom there's a little shrine on *this* side (*gestures*), and not far from it there's an alleyway.

DEMEA: What alleyway?

SYRUS: *That* one—you know!—where the big wild-fig tree is.

DEMEA: Oh, I know.

SYRUS: Go down that.

DEMEA: Wait a minute. That alley's a dead end.

SYRUS: Oh, yes, of course! How stupid can I be? I was mixed up. Better go back to the arcade again. Yes, it's a lot shorter that way, and you're less likely to get lost. You know Cratinus, the one with all the money—his house?

DEMEA: Yes.

SYRUS: Just after you pass it, turn left and keep right on up the street. When you get to Diana's temple, turn right. Just before you get to the city gate, there's a fountain, and right by it there's a little pastry shop and across from it a carpenter shop. That's where Micio is.

DEMEA: What's he doing there?

SYRUS: He ordered some garden chairs made—solid oak.

DEMEA: Hah! So you people can carouse out in the garden, too! Just fine! But why don't I go along and find him? (*Exit* DEMEA, *stage left.*)

SYRUS: Yes, for heaven's sake, do. I'll give you some exercise today, you old crape-hanger. Blast Aeschinus! What's keeping him? The fish will be spoiled. And Ctesipho's all wrapped up in his girl. Well, I'll look out for myself. I'm going to move along and pick off all the best bits, and have a few drinks, too, just to kill time. (*Exit into* MICIO's *house.*)

SCENE III

(*Enter* MICIO *and* HEGIO, *stage left.*)

MICIO: I see absolutely no reason, Hegio, why you should be showering me with praises. I'm only doing my duty. We are responsible for the harm that was done, and I'm just straightening it out. Or do you imagine that I am one of those people who get insulted if you complain of some wrong they themselves did, in fact, commit? And because I didn't react like that, you think you have to thank me?

HEGIO: No, no! Not at all! The thought never entered my head! I never misjudged you. But, Micio, would you mind going with me to see the girl's mother? Would you tell the lady just what you've been telling me—that it's Aeschinus' *brother* that's the cause of her worries, that the slave girl belongs to *him?*

MICIO: If you think that's what I should do, or that it would be helpful, let's go.

HEGIO: Thanks. That way you'll put her mind at rest. The poor thing has been going to pieces. And you'll have done everything we have a right to expect. But if you'd rather not, why, I'll tell her about it myself.

MICIO: No, no. I'll go with you.

HEGIO: Thanks. People who've had a hard life are all inclined to be sensitive. They take offense at almost anything. They're helpless, you see, and this makes them imagine that people are trying to take advantage of them. That's why it will be more effective if you go and explain things to her yourself.

MICIO: That's thoughtful of you, and quite right.

HEGIO: Well, come in with me, then.

MICIO: Certainly. (*Exeunt into* SOSTRATA's *house.*)

SCENE IV

(*Enter* AESCHINUS, *stage left.*)

AESCHINUS: I'm in a terrible state! All of a sudden, all this trouble coming my way. I don't know what to do with myself; I don't know what move to make! I'm feeling weak in the knees; my mind is a complete blank; I can't think straight at all! How in the world am I going to get out of this trouble? People are so suspicious of me—though of course it's no wonder. Sostrata thinks that I bought the girl for myself. Canthara tipped me off to that. It so happened that she had been sent to fetch the midwife; I saw her and went to her and asked her about Pamphila—was the baby coming? Was that why she was going for the midwife? She fairly screamed at me, "You just get out of here, Aeschinus! Go on, now! We've listened to your fine talk long enough. We've had all we need of your broken promises." "What?" I said. "What in heaven's name are you talking about?" "No," she said, "it's good-by to you. You can have that girl. You seem to like her." I saw right away: that's what they were thinking! But just the same I controlled myself. I wasn't going to tell that old gossip about my brother and have it spread all over town. Now what am I going to do? Shall I tell them that the girl is Ctesipho's? The last thing we want is for that to get out. But never mind; we could arrange it so that wouldn't happen. What I'm really afraid of is that they won't believe me. The whole thing looks pretty convincing: I was the one who went in and got her; it was I who paid for her; it's my house they took her to. I'll have to admit all this was my doing. Why didn't I tell my father about Pamphila, no matter what happened? I'd have persuaded him to let me marry her. Well, so far I've been dragging my feet. Time to wake up, my boy! Now let's see; the first thing is to go to Sostrata's house and explain myself. Here we go! (*Goes to door, raises hand to knock*) Oh, God! I get the cold shivers every time I start to knock on this door! (*Knocks*) Hello. Anybody home? It's Aeschinus. Come on, somebody, open up! Somebody's coming, but I don't know who. I'll step off to one side.

Scene V

(*Enter* Micio *from* Sostrata's *house. He talks back through the open door.*)

Micio: You people do as I told you, Sostrata. I'll go find Aeschinus and let him know what we've decided. (*Closes door, turns.*) Now who knocked at the door?

Aeschinus (*aside*): Ye gods, it's my father! This is the end!

Micio: Aeschinus!

Aeschinus (*aside*): What has he been doing here?

Micio: Aeschinus, was it you who knocked on this door? (*Aside*) He's tongue-tied. Why don't I have a little fun with him? Good idea, since he never did bring himself to tell me about this. (*To* Aeschinus) Are you going to answer me or not?

Aeschinus: Who? Me? That door? Not so far as I know.

Micio: Is that so? Well, I was wondering what business you'd be having here. (*Aside*) He blushed. Everything's fine.

Aeschinus: Well, if you don't mind, father: What business do *you* have here?

Micio: I? None at all. A friend of mine met me downtown a while ago and brought me here to advise him about a matter.

Aeschinus: What matter?

Micio: Oh, it's like this: A couple of women live here; they're practically penniless—but then I don't suppose you know them; in fact, I'm sure you don't. They moved in here only a little while ago.

Aeschinus: Yes, and so?

MICIO: It's a young girl and her mother.

AESCHINUS: Go on.

MICIO: The girl's father is dead. This friend of mine is her nearest relative, and according to law she's required to marry him.

AESCHINUS: Oh, no! No!

MICIO: What's the matter?

AESCHINUS: Nothing at all. It's all right. Go on.

MICIO: He came here to take her away with him. He lives in Miletus, you see.

AESCHINUS: What? He's going to take the girl away with him?

MICIO: That's right.

AESCHINUS: All the way to Miletus, for heaven's sake?

MICIO: Yes.

AESCHINUS: Oh, I feel sick! What about the girl and her mother? What do they have to say?

MICIO: What do you think? Why, not a word. The mother did mention that the girl had had a baby by some other man —she didn't tell us his name. He had first claim, she said, and so she really shouldn't marry my friend.

AESCHINUS: Well, don't you think that's a perfectly fair objection?

MICIO: No, I don't.

AESCHINUS: You *don't?* Why . . . ! Is he actually going to take her away, father?

MICIO: And why shouldn't he?

AESCHINUS: The two of you have been completely unfeeling! You've shown no human understanding! Yes, father, I'd go so far as to say that—speaking quite frankly—you haven't even acted like gentlemen.

MICIO: Why do you say that?

AESCHINUS: You ask why? How do you think *he's* going to feel—I mean the poor fellow who made love to her first? He's getting a bad break. For all I know, he may still be madly in love with her, and now he'll have to stand by and see her snatched away, taken off where he'll never lay eyes on her again. That's a terrible thing to do, Father.

MICIO: Why do you say that? Who promised her to anybody? Who gave her away? Whom did she ever marry? Who's sponsoring the whole business, anyway? Why did that fellow take somebody else's girl?

AESCHINUS: Was she just supposed to sit there, a grown-up girl like her, and wait until this relative appeared? That's what you should have said, father. That's the position you should have taken.

MICIO: Nonsense! Was I to argue against the man who had asked me to come and help him? But what has all this got to do with us, Aeschinus? Why should those people concern us? Let's run along. What's the matter? Why the tears?

AESCHINUS: Father, please! Listen!

MICIO (*puts his arm around* AESCHINUS): Now, now, my boy! I've heard the whole story. I know all about it. Why, I love you; that's why I'm so much concerned about your behavior.

AESCHINUS: As I'd want to deserve your love all your life long, father, I'm sorry—just terribly sorry—to have done a thing like this. I can hardly face you.

MICIO: I believe you; I really do. After all, I know your heart's in the right place. But I'm afraid you've been very, very indiscreet. Really, now, what sort of community do you think you're living in? The girl you got into trouble was one you had no right to touch. That was the first thing you did wrong—and it was very wrong. But it was normal and human; it's been done again and again by lots of perfectly respectable young men. But after it happened, tell me: Did you think at all about what was to be done, or how it was to be done? How it might get to me if you were ashamed to tell me about it yourself? And while you've been sitting around doing nothing, nine months have gone by. You've been untrue to yourself, to the poor girl, and to your baby—just about as much as you could be. Why! Did you think that you could calmly go to sleep and let heaven take care of your problems for you,

and that without lifting a finger you'd wake up some morning and find yourself married to her? I wouldn't care to have
you so casual in other matters. Well, cheer up! You shall
marry her.

AESCHINUS (*wryly*): Oh, yes.

MICIO: No, no, I tell you; cheer up!

AESCHINUS: Father, please! You're not making fun of me,
now?

MICIO: *I?* Making fun of *you?* Why would I?

AESCHINUS: I don't know. I'm so anxious to have all this
be true, and that makes me uneasy.

MICIO: Run along home now and pray heaven to bless
your wedding.

AESCHINUS: What? Wedding? Right now?

MICIO: Right now.

AESCHINUS: This minute?

MICIO: This very minute.

AESCHINUS: Heaven help me, father, if I don't love you more
than anything else in the world.

MICIO: What? More than *her?*

AESCHINUS: Well, just as much.

MICIO: That's a concession!

AESCHINUS: Say, where's that fellow from Miletus?

MICIO: He got lost; he's gone—took ship. But what are you
waiting for?

AESCHINUS: Go on, father! Why don't you pray for that
blessing, rather than I? You're so much better a man than I
am, I'm sure the gods would be more willing to listen to you.

MICIO: I'll go in and get everything ready. You do as I
told you, if you're wise. (*Exit* MICIO *into his house.*)

AESCHINUS: What *is* this? Is this what's meant by being a
father, or being a son? If he were a brother or a friend, how
could he be more understanding? How can I help loving
him? How can I help holding him to my heart? He's been
so kind to me! I'm so afraid I might happen by mistake to
do something he wouldn't like. I'd never do such a thing

knowingly. But what am I waiting for? I'll go in, so I won't be delaying my own wedding. (*Exit into* MICIO's *house.*)

SCENE VI

(*Enter* DEMEA, *stage left.*)

DEMEA: I've worn myself out walking—damn you, Syrus— you and your directions! I've tramped all over this town— to the city gate, to the fountain—where not? And there wasn't any carpenter shop there, and not a soul said he'd seen my brother. Now, by heaven, I'm going to sit right here at his house until he comes home. (*He sits on* MICIO's *doorstep.*)

SCENE VII

(*Enter* MICIO *from his house.*)

MICIO: I'll go and tell Sostrata and her daughter that we're all ready.

DEMEA: Aha! There he is! I've been looking for you for a long time, Micio.

MICIO: Why?

DEMEA: I have some bad news for you—positively monstrous —about that fine young man.

MICIO (*aside*): Oh, my! Here we go!

DEMEA: It's unheard-of! It's positively criminal!

MICIO: Now, now, now!

DEMEA: You just don't know that boy.

MICIO: Oh, yes, I do.

DEMEA: You idiot! You're fondly imagining that I'm talking about that slave girl. Oh, no; this is something he's done to a perfectly respectable young lady.

MICIO: Yes, I know.

DEMEA: Oh, you know, do you? Aren't you going to do anything about it?

MICIO: Why should I do anything?

DEMEA: You mean to say you aren't giving him a tongue-lashing? Aren't you angry enough to burst?

MICIO: No. Of course, I'd rather . . .

DEMEA: They've had a baby!

MICIO: Yes, isn't that nice?

DEMEA: But the girl hasn't a penny!

MICIO: So I've heard.

DEMEA: He'll have to marry her without a dowry!

MICIO: Naturally.

DEMEA: Well, what happens now?

MICIO: Why, what the circumstances require, of course. We're going to bring the girl from her house to ours.

DEMEA: Good heavens! Just like that? Is that right?

MICIO: What else is there to do?

DEMEA: What else? If you're not actually upset by what has happened, a decent person would at least pretend to be.

MICIO: No, no; the engagement has been announced; all arrangements have been made; they're going to be married. I've solved all their worries. That's even more what a decent person would do.

DEMEA: But look, Micio, are you satisfied with what's happened?

MICIO: I wouldn't be, if I could change things. But since I can't, I'm relaxing. That's the way life is, like a game of dice. If you don't get the number you want, you make the best of the one you get.

DEMEA: You and your "make the best"! Some skill you have! It's lost you two thousand drachmas for that slave girl —and you'll have to get rid of her somehow. If you can't sell her, you'll have to give her away.

MICIO: I certainly will not give her away, and I'm not a bit interested in selling her.

DEMEA: What are you going to do, then?

MICIO: She's going to stay with us.

DEMEA: Good heavens! A common prostitute and a respectable married woman in the same house?

MICIO: Why not?

DEMEA: Are you sure you're feeling all right?

MICIO: Why, yes, I think so.

DEMEA: So help me heaven, as crazy as you are, I bet you're going to keep her there to entertain *you!*

MICIO: Well, why not?

DEMEA: And our young bride will take lessons from her!

MICIO: Naturally.

DEMEA: And you'll take the two of them and have a charming little dance together.

MICIO: Good idea!

DEMEA: Good idea?

MICIO: Yes. Might take you for a fourth, if we need you.

DEMEA: Oh, my God! Such talk! Aren't you ashamed?

MICIO: Oh, come now, Demea, stop being so unpleasant. Your son is getting married! You ought to be cheerful and happy. I'll go and stir up the people over here. (*Starts toward* SOSTRATA'S *house*) I'll be back. (*Exit into* SOSTRATA'S *house.*)

DEMEA: Good heavens! What a way to live! What a way to behave! What sheer insanity! We're to have a bride without a dowry and a whore to share the house—a house where all they do is spend money. The young man is a complete rascal and the old one a complete fool. If the gods themselves wished, they couldn't save this family—not at all! (*Exit stage right.*)

ACT FIVE

SCENE I

(*Enter* SYRUS, *drunk, from* MICIO'S *house. Enter* DEMEA, *stage right.*)

SYRUS: Syrus, old fellow, you've had a lovely time, and done a fine job of carrying out your duties; run along now. Well, I took on a load of everything there was in the house, and now I think I'll take a little walk.

DEMEA (*to audience*): Just look at that, will you? Fine example of discipline!

SYRUS: Oho! Oho! Look who's here! The old gentleman himself! How are things? What are you scowling about?

DEMEA: Disgraceful!

SYRUS: Oh, is that so? A bit free with words, aren't you, Professor?

DEMEA: If you were my slave . . .

SYRUS: Why, you'd be a rich man, Demea; you'd have had a fortune all stored away.

DEMEA: I'd have made an example of you for the whole lot, that's sure.

SYRUS: Why? What did I do?

DEMEA: What did you *do*? Everything is in wild confusion; a perfectly terrible thing has been done, which is still far from settled, and you've been drinking, you devil, as if this were a time to celebrate.

SYRUS: Ye gods! I wish I hadn't come out here.

SCENE II

(*Enter* DROMO *from* MICIO's *house.*)

DROMO: Hey, Syrus! Ctesipho wants you to come back in.

SYRUS: No! No! Get out (*Exit* DROMO *into* MICIO's *house.*)

DEMEA: What's that? Ctesipho? What did he say?

SYRUS: Oh, nothing.

DEMEA: Now look here, you rascal; is Ctesipho in there?

SYRUS: Why, no, no!

DEMEA: Why did that fellow mention his name, then?

SYRUS: Oh, that's another man, some cheap scrounger—you know him?

DEMEA: I'll soon find out. (*Starts toward* MICIO's *house;* SYRUS *grabs him.*)

SYRUS: What are you doing? Where are you going?

DEMEA: Take your hands off me, you devil! Or do you want your head cracked? (*Exit into* MICIO's *house.*)

SYRUS: Well, there he goes! There's one guest who will be

less than welcome, especially to Ctesipho. Now what shall I do? I guess until things quiet down, I'll find a corner somewhere and sleep off this little old drunk. Yes, that's a good idea. (*Exit into* MICIO's *house.*)

SCENE III

(*Enter* MICIO *from* SOSTRATA's *house, speaks back through door.*)

MICIO: We've gotten everything ready, as I told you, Sostrata. Anytime you wish . . . (DEMEA *throws open door of* MICIO's *house, rushes out.*) Who slammed the door over at my house?

DEMEA: Oh, my God! What shall I do? *What shall I do?* What can I say? How can I say it? God's heaven and earth and deep blue sea!

MICIO: Well, there it is! He has learned the whole story; that's what he's shouting about. Let's go! The boys have a fight on their hands; it's up to me to help them.

DEMEA: Aha! There you are! You're the rot that corrupted our boys, both of them!

MICIO: Come now, control that temper; get hold of yourself.

DEMEA: I *have* controlled it; I *have* gotten hold of myself; I won't say one more harsh word. Let's have a look at the facts. Didn't we agree, the two of us (and wasn't it your idea, too?) that you'd keep hands off my son, and I off yours? Answer me that.

MICIO: We did; I'm not denying it.

DEMEA: Then why is my son at your house now, getting drunk? Why have you taken him in? Why did you buy him a girl, Micio? It isn't wrong, is it, that I should have the same rights over you as you have over me? I'm keeping my hands off your son; now you just keep yours off mine.

MICIO: That's not quite fair, what you say.

DEMEA: It's not?

MICIO: No. Why, you know the old saying, "Between friends, there's no such thing as private property."

DEMEA: Very funny! So that's your nice, bright, new excuse, is it?

MICIO: Listen a minute, Demea, if you don't mind. In the first place, if what's bothering you is the money the boys are spending, just think this over: In the beginning, you were bringing them up strictly in accord with your own means, because you thought that your property would be just about enough for the two of them. At that time, of course, you assumed that some day I would get married. Well, why don't you just keep to your original plan? Save money, make money, be economical; leave them as much as you possibly can. That will be to your eternal glory; stay with it. As for my money, no one ever expected them to get it anyway, so let them spend it. It won't cost you or them a penny. Anything that comes from me is pure profit, don't you see? If you could just bring yourself to think of this realistically, Demea, you'd save me, yourself, and the boys a lot of worry.

DEMEA: I don't care about the money—but the way those two are carrying on . . .

MICIO: Wait a minute. I know; I was just getting to that. In any individual, Demea, there are lots of signs that tell us what he's really like. As a result, when two people perform the same act, it's often quite possible to say that one of them can be permitted to do it and the other can't, not because the act is different but because the people are. Now, in our two boys I see lots of reasons for being confident that they'll turn out as we want them to. I see common sense, intelligence, a sense of propriety, mutual affection—anybody would know that they are fine, well-bred boys. Any time you want to tighten the reins on them, you can. But I suppose you're afraid that they may be a bit careless with money. Demea, old fellow—in all other respects we get wiser as we get older; there's just one bad trait old age brings to us; we worry entirely too much about money. Time will make the boys quite sharp enough about that.

DEMEA: I just hope, Micio, that all this sweet reasonableness and good nature of yours won't land us in serious trouble.

MICIO: Don't even say it; of course it won't. Come now, forget your worries. Do things my way today. Get that frown off your face.

DEMEA: Well, all right. This is the time for it. I guess I'll have to. But tomorrow morning, my son and I are heading for the farm, the minute it gets light.

MICIO: Even earlier than that! It's all right with me. Just be happy today.

DEMEA: And I'm going to drag your slave girl right along with me.

MICIO: The battle's over! You do that and you'll really have your son nailed down. Just see to it that you keep the girl.

DEMEA: I'll keep her, all right. She'll be covered with soot and smoke and flour, because I'm going to set her to cooking and grinding grain. On top of that, I'll send her out at noontime to gather straw; I'll make her as hard and dry and black as a piece of charcoal.

MICIO: Good. Now you're showing sense. And I have one further suggestion: Make the boy go to bed with her even when he doesn't feel like it.

DEMEA: Making jokes, are you? Must be nice to have such a sense of humor. Now to *my* way of thinking . . .

MICIO: Now, now! Not some more?

DEMEA: Very well, very well. I'll stop.

MICIO: Come in the house and let's spend the day as it ought to be spent. (*Exeunt into* MICIO's *house.*)

SCENE IV

(*Enter* DEMEA *from* MICIO's *house; he is wearing a garland, slightly askew, and is obviously drunk.*)

DEMEA: You never add things up so well in this life that something unexpected doesn't turn up and set you wondering —some money matter, some event, some personal problem. As a result, you find you don't know what you thought you knew, and things that seemed fine turn out to be worthless when they're put to the test. That's what has happened to me just now. I've been a stern, hard-working man all my life; and here I am, almost at the end of the road, giving up on it. And why? I've found that in actual fact nothing is more profitable than good humor and kindness. Anybody can easily see that this is the case by comparing me and my brother. He has always taken life easy and enjoyed himself; he's kind and gentle, never hurts anyone's feelings, has a smile for everybody, lives as he pleases, spends his money as he pleases. And everyone loves him and has a good word for him. Now I've been the old farmer, tough, serious-minded, penny-pinching, impatient, determined to get ahead. I married—and what a misery that turned out to be! I had two sons—more worries. Well, well! I was anxious to get together as much property as I could for those boys, and so I wore myself out, year after year, trying to make money. Now my life is nearly over, and what return do they give me for all my hard work? Their cordial dislike! And my brother, without lifting a finger, is collecting all the benefits of a father. They love him; they can't stand me. They tell him everything, they enjoy his company, they're both at his house; I'm left all alone. They wish him a long life; as for me, they're just waiting for me to die. I went to all that effort to bring them up, and he's taken them over at practically no cost. I get all the trouble; he gets all the fun. Well, now, let's try an experiment, to see if I'm any good at soft talk and kind treatment. After all, Micio suggested it. I very much want my boys to love me and think highly of me; if you get that by being generous and indulgent, I'm not going to take second place. Money may run short, but that isn't going to bother me at all; I'm the oldest in the family.

Scene V

(*Enter* SYRUS *from* MICIO's *house.*)

SYRUS: Oh, Demea, sir, your brother asks you not to go too far away.

DEMEA: Who's that? Oh, Syrus, my friend, hello! How are you? How're you doing?

SYRUS (*startled*): Uh—all right.

DEMEA: That's fine. (*Aside*) I've already said three things I wouldn't normally say: "My friend," "How are you," and "How are you doing." (*To* SYRUS) You're turning out to be a very well-bred fellow, and I'd be glad to do something nice for you.

SYRUS: Well—uh—thanks!

DEMEA: No, Syrus; I really mean it. You'll find out one of these days.

SCENE VI

(*Enter* GETA, *from* SOSTRATA'S *house; he speaks back through door.*)

GETA: I'll go and see, ma'am, how soon they want Pamphila brought over. (*Turns away*) Oh, look, there's Demea. How do you do, sir?

DEMEA: Oh, you—what's your name?

GETA: Geta.

DEMEA: Geta, I've been thinking it over, and I've decided that you're a very fine fellow. You see, to my mind, a slave has really passed his test if his master is his first concern. I've observed that that's true of you, Geta, and so, if the opportunity were to arise, I'd be glad to do something nice for you. (*Aside*) I'm practicing being good-natured, and it's going very well!

GETA: It's kind of you to say that.

DEMEA (*aside*): I'm making a start! One by one, I'm getting the rank and file on my side!

SCENE VII

(*Enter* AESCHINUS *from* MICIO'S *house.*)

AESCHINUS (*to himself*): They're practically killing me with all their fussing about a fancy wedding. They're taking the whole day to get ready for it!

DEMEA: How do you do, Aeschinus!

AESCHINUS: Oh! Why, father, were you here?

DEMEA: That's right. Yes, sir—your own father, soul and body, and I love you more than anything else in the world. But why aren't you bringing the bride over to your house?

AESCHINUS: I wish I could, but I'm waiting for a fluteplayer and some singers for the weddingsong.

DEMEA: Say—do you want to lend an ear to an old man?

AESCHINUS: About what?

DEMEA: Forget all that folderol—weddingsong, wedding-party, torches, fluteplayers—and have the wall there in the garden torn down, as quickly as you can. Bring her through that way. Make one house of it! Bring the mother and the slaves, all of them, over to our house.

AESCHINUS: Good idea! Father, you're wonderful!

DEMEA (aside): Oho! I'm "wonderful" now! They'll break a hole in my brother's house and bring in a whole company! It will cost him a pretty penny, but what do I care? I'm "wonderful," and people are beginning to like me. Go on, now, and tell that old Sybarite to pay out his two thousand drachmas! (To SYRUS) Syrus, what are you waiting for? Get busy!

SYRUS: Busy? Busy at what?

DEMEA: Tear that wall down! (To GETA) And you, run along now and bring over the girl and her mother.

GETA: God bless you, Demea, for being so kind and thoughtful to all of us.

DEMEA: I'm sure you deserve it. (To AESCHINUS) What do you say to that?

AESCHINUS: Why—why—why, I agree, of course.

DEMEA: It's much better than dragging the poor girl through the street. She's just had her baby and can't be feeling too well.

AESCHINUS: I've never seen anything better, father.

DEMEA: That's the way I am. But look, here's Micio coming out.

SCENE VIII

(*Enter* MICIO *from his house; he speaks back through door.*)

MICIO: My brother told you to? Where is he? (*Turns away*) Did you tell them to do that, Demea?

DEMEA: I certainly did. I told them to use this and every other way to make us as much as possible into one single household—to love each other, help each other, and all join together.

AESCHINUS (*to* MICIO): Please let it be that way, father.

MICIO: Well—uh—I have no objection.

DEMEA: Objection? Why, it's the only right thing to do! Now, to begin with: Aeschinus' wife has a mother.

MICIO: Yes. What about her?

DEMEA: She's a very nice lady.

MICIO: So they say.

DEMEA: Getting along in years.

MICIO: I know.

DEMEA: It's been a long time since she passed the child-bearing stage, and she has no one to look out for her. She's alone in the world.

MICIO (*aside*): What does he mean?

DEMEA: It would be nice if you'd marry her. You ought to try to arrange it.

MICIO: What? I? Marry her?

DEMEA: Yes, you.

MICIO: You mean *me*?

DEMEA: You. That's what I said.

MICIO: You're being silly.

DEMEA (*to* AESCHINUS): If *you* were half a man, he'd do it.

AESCHINUS (*to* MICIO): Please, father!

MICIO (*to* AESCHINUS): What do you mean by listening to him, you young fool?

DEMEA: It's no use, Micio. There's nothing else to do.

MICIO: You're out of your mind!

AESCHINUS (*to* MICIO): Please let me persuade you, father. (*Puts his arm around him*)

MICIO (*to* AESCHINUS): You're crazy. Let go of me!

DEMEA: Come on, do it to please your son.

MICIO: Are you in your right mind? I? Be a bridegroom at this point? At sixty-five? And marry a broken-down old hag? Is that what you're suggesting to me?

AESCHINUS: Yes, do it! I promised them you would.

MICIO: *You* promised them? Listen, boy, be generous at your own expense!

DEMEA: Come now; what if he should ask for something even bigger than that?

MICIO: Bigger? As if there could be anything bigger!

DEMEA: Do it for the boy!

AESCHINUS: Don't be angry!

DEMEA: Do it! Say you will!

MICIO: Stop it, will you!

AESCHINUS: No, not unless you say yes.

MICIO: This is really putting on the pressure!

DEMEA: Come on, Micio! Be nice!

MICIO: To my way of thinking this is immoral, idiotic, ridiculous, and utterly foreign to my way of living, but if you're so very anxious to have it, I'll do it.

AESCHINUS: Oh, good! Thanks!

DEMEA: I always knew you were a fine fellow. But . . .

MICIO: But what?

DEMEA: I'll tell you after I have what I want.

MICIO: Why? What else is there to do now?

DEMEA: Well, there's Hegio. He's a close relative of Sostrata and Pamphila, and he's related to you and me by marriage. He hasn't a penny to his name. It would be nice for us to do him a favor.

MICIO: What sort of favor?

DEMEA: You own a little piece of land not far from town —the one you always rent out. Let's give him a life interest in it.

MICIO: You call that a *little* piece of land?

DEMEA: Little—big; even so, you ought to do it. He's like a father to the girl; he's a nice man; he's a good friend. It's a suitable return to him. And anyway, Micio, I'm going to repeat what you were saying a while ago, so wisely and so well: "It's a very common failing among men to become too interested in money when we get old." This is a real blot, and you and I ought to avoid it. That's right! We really must do it.

AESCHINUS: Please, father?

MICIO: Well, all right. Hegio shall have the land, since Aeschinus wants it that way.

AESCHINUS: Good, good!

DEMEA (to MICIO): Now you really are my brother, body and soul. (Aside) I'm cutting his throat with his own knife!

SCENE IX

(Enter SYRUS from MICIO's house.)

SYRUS: I've done as you told me, Demea.

DEMEA: Good boy! Why—say, do you know what I think? I feel it's only right and proper that Syrus be set free.

MICIO: Who, Syrus? Free? For what earthly reason?

DEMEA: Lots of reasons.

SYRUS: Oh, Demea, sir! You're a fine man! Those boys of yours, you know; I've been taking good care of them all their lives. I've been their teacher and adviser—taught them carefully, day after day, everything I could.

DEMEA: That is fairly obvious. I might even elaborate a bit —taught them to run up bills at the market, to hire party-girls, to give wild parties—takes a real man to do that.

SYRUS: God bless you, sir!

DEMEA: And just to finish the list: Syrus pitched in and made the arrangements for buying that slave girl today. That ought to be worth something to him. It will encourage the other slaves to mend their ways. Last but not least: Aeschinus is in favor of it.

MICIO (to AESCHINUS): You really want Syrus freed?

AESCHINUS: Yes, very much.

MICIO: Very well, if that's what you want. All right, Syrus; come over here to me. (SYRUS *kneels in front of* MICIO, *who places his hand on his shoulder.*) I declare you a free man.

SYRUS: Oh, thank you, sir—thank you all, and most specially thank you, Demea!

DEMEA (*shakes* SYRUS' *hand*): Congratulations!

AESCHINUS (*does the same*): From me, too.

SYRUS: Thank you. There's just one thing I need to make me completely happy, and that would be to see my wife, Phrygia, free along with me.

DEMEA: Yes, of course—a fine woman!

SYRUS (*to* MICIO): You know, sir, she gave your grandson, Aeschinus' son, his first nursing this morning.

DEMEA: Well, now, seriously, if she gave him his first nursing, there's no doubt at all that she should be set free.

MICIO: What? Just for that?

DEMEA: Yes, for that. Anyway, I'll pay you what she's worth.

SYRUS: Oh, Demea! God bless you, God bless you, sir!

MICIO: Syrus, you've done very well for yourself today.

DEMEA: One more thing, Micio. Why don't you do the job right; give Syrus here a little something to start him off— just a loan. He'll pay it back promptly.

MICIO: No, sir, not a penny!

AESCHINUS: He's reliable, Father.

SYRUS (*to* MICIO): Oh, I'll pay it back, yes, sir! Just let me have it.

AESCHINUS: Please, father?

MICIO: Well, I'll think about it.

DEMEA (*to* SYRUS): He'll do it.

SYRUS (*to* MICIO): You're very kind, sir!

AESCHINUS (*to* MICIO): Oh, father, you 're just wonderful!

MICIO (*to* DEMEA): Say, what's going on here? Why have you changed your ways so suddenly? What has happened to you? Why are you so generous all of a sudden?

DEMEA: I'll tell you: I wanted to prove something to you. These fellows think you're such a prince; well, that's not for

any honest or proper reason, Micio. It's because you let them
do anything they wish, let them get away with anything, and
give them lots of money. Now, Aeschinus, if you find my way
of life distasteful, because I don't tolerate everything indis-
criminately, right or wrong, I haven't a word to say. Waste
and spend; do anything you like. On the other hand, there
are things you feel you simply *must* have, regardless of cost,
things you don't really think through. Now, if you'd like me
to pull you up short and straighten you out and give you a
hand when it's appropriate, here I am, glad to do it for you.

AESCHINUS (*to* DEMEA): We put ourselves in your hands,
father. You really know what's best. But what about Ctesipho?
What's going to happen to him?

DEMEA: Leave him alone. He can keep the girl—but she's
to be his last!

MICIO: Good for you, Demea.

CANTOR: Give us a hand, please.

MEDEA

INTRODUCTORY NOTE

Jason was the son of Aeson, king of Iolcus in Thessaly. When his uncle Pelias seized the throne, Jason, then an infant, was spirited away and brought up by the centaur Chiron. Upon reaching manhood he returned to demand the kingdom, and Pelias agreed to surrender it if Jason would fetch the Golden Fleece, which was in the possession of King Aeetes of Colchis and guarded by an ever-watchful dragon. For this enterprise Argus, with Athena's help, built the world's first ship, the Argo, which was manned by fifty heroes, including such personages as Hercules, Orpheus, Castor and Pollux, Theseus, and their like. The most famous of the many perils of the voyage was the passage through the Symplegades, mountains which guarded the entrance to the Black Sea by clashing together; after the Argo eluded them these mountains were fixed apart. At Colchis King Aeetes agreed to surrender the Fleece if Jason would plough a field with a team of fire-breathing bulls and sow it with dragon's teeth which would spring into armed soldiers. Aphrodite caused Aeetes' daughter Medea to fall in love with Jason, and she provided magic means by which he mastered the bulls and the earthborn soldiery; then she lulled the watchful dragon to sleep and sailed off with Jason and the Golden Fleece. To retard pursuit she killed her brother Absyrtus and strewed his dismembered body over the sea. At Iolcus, Medea deceived Pelias' daughters into attempting to rejuvenate their father by cutting him in pieces and boiling him; the consequent hostility of Pelias' son Acastus forced Jason and Medea to flee to Corinth. Here they lived for some years and had two sons; but in order to secure his position Jason resolved to dismiss Medea and marry King Creon's daughter, Creusa. In her resentment at this betrayal Medea murdered their two sons, and herself escaped in a chariot drawn by two flying dragons.

The story of the Argo and the Golden Fleece is one of Europe's oldest. Homer (*Odyssey* XII.70) speaks of it as a familiar thing; Pindar deals with it in one of his longest and finest odes (the *Fourth Pythian*); and it is the subject of the best epic in Greek next to Homer's, the *Argonautica* of Apollonius of Rhodes. The central interest of the *Argonautica*, and the first full treatment of romantic love in European literature, is the episode of Jason and Medea, which served Vergil as a model for the Dido episode in the *Aeneid*. But far the most familiar ancient treatment of the love and hate of Jason and Medea is the *Medea* of Euripides, which is the model for Seneca's play.

Euripides' theme, like Seneca's, is the reaction of a passionate woman when her husband deserts her for a younger bride. Euripides no more approves of Medea's vengeance than does Seneca or any sane man, but Euripides is also concerned to criticize social conventions which were ultimately responsible for the tragedy—masculine smugness toward women and Greek smugness toward foreigners. When Medea reproaches Jason with ingratitude he replies that his gratitude, if any is due, must go to Aphrodite; Medea could do no other than fall in love with him and serve him. On the contrary, she should be grateful to him for taking her from a barbarian land and bringing her to civilized and law-abiding Greece.

To these or other social implications of the story Seneca is indifferent. Even on the matter of kingship, regarding which Seneca, as a Stoic and tutor to a tyrant, is regularly concerned to emphasize the role of the king as servant rather than master, the implications of this play are equivocal. Medea scores tyranny and advocates moderation, but she does so not out of conviction but only to temporize, and it is Creon's very yielding that makes the horrible outcome possible. If the play has an ethical content it is that strong passions (the Stoics called them perturbations) are harmful and make life unlivable. Each of Seneca's plays, indeed, shows the awful consequences of some passion, and in *Medea* the passion is love. But even without Stoic moralizing the display of colossal passion can be edifying. The spectacle of emotional intensity, as of extraordinary prowess in other departments, enlarges the spectator's perception of human potentialities and vicariously enhances his own stature.

CHARACTERS

MEDEA, daughter of King Aeetes of Colchis, wife of JASON

JASON, prince of Iolcus, sometime commander of the Argo-
nauts

CREON, king of Corinth, father of JASON's bride Creusa

NURSE, confidante of MEDEA

MESSENGER

TWO SONS (mutes) of MEDEA and JASON

CHORUS OF CORINTHIANS

GUARDS, SERVANTS, CORINTHIAN CROWD

SCENE: *The front of* JASON's *house in Corinth*

MEDEA

I

(*Enter* MEDEA.)

MEDEA: Ye Jupiter and Juno, patrons of wedlock; thou
Lucina, keeper of the conjugal couch; thou Minerva, who
didst teach Tiphys to bridle a novel craft that would master
the seas; thou Neptune, savage lord of Ocean's depths; thou
Sun, who dost apportion bright light to the globe; thou
triform Hecate, whose radiance serves as accomplice to silent
sacraments—yet deities by whom Jason swore to me, yea, and
ye deities whom Medea hath better right to invoke: Thou
Chaos of endless night; ye realms opposed to the upper
world's; ye impious ghosts; thou Pluto, lord of the gloomy
demesne; thou Proserpina, ravished with more honorable intentions than was I—all you I invoke, but not for blessing.
Attend, ye goddesses who avenge crime, attend, your unkempt
hair foul serpents, your bloody hands grasping the ominous
torch; attend now in such dread presence as once ye showed
when ye stood posted at my bridals. Make your gifts death
for the new bride, death for the father-in-law and the royal
stock.

But for the husband I have a worse gift to beg: Let him
live. Let him wander through cities he knows not, a needy
vagabond, a trembling alien, hated and homeless. Let him
beg at a stranger's threshold, now a recognized cadger. May
he wish I were his wife. May his children—I can think of
no worse imprecation—be like their father, yes, and like their
mother. Born is my vengeance, already born; I have given
birth.

But idle are the plaints I broadcast, mere words. Shall I
not march against the enemy? I shall wrest the wedding torches
from their hands, the very light from heaven. Can Sun,

founder of my race, look on? Can he let himself be looked at as he sits upon his chariot and drives his customary course in untainted air? Will he not return to his rising and retrace the day's course? Grant me to ride through the air in my father's chariot, do grant it; hand me the reins, sire, assign me to steer that fire-bearing car with blazing traces. Corinth with the obstruction of its twin shores shall be burned down, and its two seas joined.

Only this remains, that I myself serve as matron of honor and carry the flambeau into the bridal chamber!—and after sacrificial prayers slaughter the victims on the appointed altars. Through the vitals find a path for punishment, my soul, if you still have feeling; if a spark of your old energy is left, banish womanish timidity and put on the temper of stranger-hating Caucasus. Whatever crime Phasis and Pontus have seen, Corinth's Isthmus shall see. Savage and unexampled enormities, horrifying to heaven and earth alike, my mind within me is churning up, wounds and murder and death that slithers along the limbs. Too trivial are the deeds I recall— those things I did as a girl. 'Tis time for deeper passion; now I am a mother, more impressive crimes are expected. Gird yourself in fury, with all your frenzy ready yourself for de- struction! Let the tale of your divorce be as memorable as that of your marriage: How did you leave your husband?—by the methods by which you won him. Away with laggard lethargy; the bond concluded by crime must by crime be severed.

(MEDEA *withdraws to one side as the* CHORUS *enters in pro-*
cession, chanting the epithalamium for the marriage of JASON
and CREUSA.)

CHORUS: With divine benison attend ye the marriage of princes, ye heavenly gods and ye that govern the sea; and in manner ordained show your good will, ye people.

First, to the scepter-bearing Thunderers a bull of gleaming white shall raise his lofty neck. To Lucina a heifer of snowy body, untried by the yoke, shall be offered. Venus, who re- strains rough Mars' bloody hands, who offers terms to warring peoples and holds plenty in her rich horn, will be presented, for her gentleness, with a tenderer victim. And thou, Hymen, patron of legitimate marriage, who dost disperse night's darkness with the torch in thine auspicious right hand, come thou forward with languorous step wine-drenched, thy brows bound with a chain of roses. And thou, star of the evening, twilight's herald, whose slow coming makes lovers impatient, whom eager matrons and brides long for, quickly as may be spread thy clear rays.

Our maiden's comeliness surpasses far the beauty of Athenian brides, and those of unwalled Sparta who exercise like boys on the ridges of Taygetus, and those on the banks of Theban Aonia or Elis' sacred Alpheus.

If our Jason, Aeson's scion, would display his beauty, then would the wicked lightning's offspring yield to him, even Bacchus, who harnesses tigers to his chariot. Yield, too, would Apollo, who shakes the tripod, severe Diana's brother; Pollux, adept in boxing, would yield, along with his brother Castor. So, I pray you heaven-dwellers, so may our lady transcend all wives, the husband far surpass all husbands.

When our lady takes her stand in the maidens' choir, her sole beauty outshines them all, as when comeliness fades from the stars when the sun rises, or the dense crowds of Pleiades hide when Phoebe completes her wonted orb with her circling horns of borrowed light. As snowy whiteness blushes when tinged with scarlet, so the dewy shepherd beholds the shining beam of fresh dawn.

Delivered from the wedlock of uncouth Phasis, schooled fearfully and with unwilling hand to fondle the bosom of an incontinent mate, now, happy groom, take unto yourself an Aeolian maid; only now can you marry with the blessings of the bride's kin.

Come, lads, banter is seasonable: Take your fun. From this side and then from that discharge your barbed verses; license to chaff nobles comes rarely.

Flawless Hymen, noble offspring of thyrsus-bearing Bacchus, now is your time to kindle the torch of splintered pine: Wave the ritual blaze with drunken fingers. Let the Fescennine patter pour out its festive banter, let the crowd chaff and jest. In silence and darkness depart the woman who surreptitiously marries a foreign husband.

II

(*As the* CHORUS *retires backstage* MEDEA *steps forward.*)

MEDEA: Lost! The wedding chant has beaten on my ears. Even I can hardly believe, even now, so total a calamity. Could Jason do this? He robbed me of father, country, kingdom; can he cruelly desert me, all alone and in a foreign place? Is he scornful of my services when he has seen fire and ocean vanquished by my crime? Or does he believe that all my uncanniness is used up? Without resolution or decision or rational wit, I am tossed about in all directions. In what quarter can I take vengeance? I wish *he* had a brother! But he has a wife; against her shall my sword be driven. But is this satisfaction for my abuses? If cities Pelasgian or cities barbarian have learned any enormity of which your hands are ignorant, now is the time to study them. Your own crimes should urge you on; recall them all: The glorious symbol of royalty stolen away; the impious girl's little brother dismembered with a sword, his death thrust upon his father, and his body scattered over the sea; the limbs of aged Pelias boiled in a brass cauldron. How often have I perpetrated bloody murder! Yet no crime have I committed in anger; it was ill-starred love that impelled me.

But what could Jason do, subject as he was to another's decision and authority? He should have bared his breast to the sword—more kindly, mad grief, speak more kindly! Let Jason live, if possible, my own as in the past, but if not, let him live nevertheless, and remember me, and cherish the life I gave him. The whole fault is Creon's; with capricious lordliness he dissolves marriages, tears mothers from children, and severs loyalties cemented by the most intimate of pledges. It is he that must be attacked; he alone shall pay the score he owes. His house I shall heap high with ashes. As his roofs are blackened with flame they shall be conspicuous at Malea, which enforces long delay on shipping.

(*As* MEDEA's *tirade reaches a crescendo, enter the* NURSE, *hurriedly.*)

NURSE: Silence, please! Muffle your complaints, confide them to secret sorrow. One who is mute under hard blows, and keeps patient and collected, can requite them; wrath concealed can inflict injury, but hatred professed forfeits opportunity for vengeance.

MEDEA: Light is the grief which can take counsel and dissemble; great ills cannot take cover. I choose open hostility.

NURSE: Halt this passionate offensive, my darling; passive defense will scarcely save you.

MEDEA: Fortune fears the brave, the cowardly crushes.

NURSE: Valor is admirable when it has a place.

MEDEA: It is impossible that valor should ever have no place.

NURSE: No hope points a path in your prostrate position.

MEDEA: Who has nothing to hope should despair of nothing.

NURSE: The Colchians have deserted you, your husband is gone, of all your resources nothing is left.

MEDEA: Medea is left. Here you see sea and land, steel and fire and gods and thunderbolts.

NURSE: A king is to fear.

MEDEA: My father was a king.

NURSE: Are you not afraid of soldiery?

MEDEA: No! though they sprouted from earth.

NURSE: You will die!

MEDEA: So I desire.

NURSE: Flee!

MEDEA: I have regretted flight.

NURSE: Medea—

MEDEA: —will I prove myself.

NURSE: You are a mother.

MEDEA: You see by whom.

NURSE: Then do you hesitate to fly?

MEDEA: I shall fly, but first take my vengeance.

NURSE: The avenger will track you.

MEDEA: Perhaps I shall contrive to delay him.

NURSE: Restrain your words, have done with threats, mad woman, bate your temper. One must adjust oneself to the situation.

MEDEA: Fortune can cancel my resources, not my spirit.— But who is that knocking at my palace door? It is Creon himself, swollen with Pelasgian lordship.

(*As* CREON *enters* MEDEA *moves to the rear. Exit* NURSE.)

CREON: Has Medea, Colchian Aeetes' cankerous growth, not yet carried herself off from my kingdom? She is working some mischief; I know her guile, I know her power. Whom will that woman spare, whom will she leave in peace? For my part, I was ready to eradicate that dangerous plague with the sword, but my son-in-law begged her off. I have granted her life, but she must free my realm from fear and go elsewhere for her safety.

Beetling she strides toward me; her expression is menacing as she approaches nearer to address me. Keep her off, slaves!— far off from touch or access; bid her be silent. It is time she learned to accept a king's edict. (*To* MEDEA) Go, fly headlong! Take your monstrous, savage, repulsive self away at once!

MEDEA: What is the charge? What offense brings sentence of exile?

CREON: An innocent woman asks why she is expelled!

MEDEA: If you are judge, examine the case; if king, issue your orders.

CREON: Just or unjust, a king's orders you must accept.

MEDEA: Unjust rule is never lasting.

CREON: Go, complain to the Colchians.

MEDEA: I go, but he who carried me from Colchis should take me back.

CREON: Speech comes late when the decree is fixed.

MEDEA: Whosoever passes sentence with one party unheard —even though the sentence be just, not just was the judge.

CREON: Did you hear Pelias before he received his doom? But speak on; for your excellent case a place shall be made.

MEDEA: How difficult it is to sway an excited temper from anger, how royal the man whose proud hands have touched the scepter regards it to persist in a course he has begun, I have learned in my own experience of royalty. Yes, though I am overwhelmed with wretched ruin, expelled, a beggar, forlorn, forsaken, afflicted on every side, once I shone brilliant in my father's high birth and traced glorious lineage from my grandfather, the Sun. Whatever lands the Phasis waters with its placid bends, whatever Scythian Pontus sees at its back, where the seas grow sweet with the waters of the marshes, whatever lands live in fear of the manless troop armed with shields bounded by Thermodon's banks—all this broad domain my father holds under his sway. Nobly born, blessed, royalty and power made my life a shining splendor. Then did nobles sue for my hand—now I must be the suitor. Rapid is fortune and fickle. Headlong it has swept me from royalty and delivered me to exile.

Trust kingship when the slightest accident plays havoc with its mighty state! But there is a glorious and incalculable possession in the power of kings which time can never snatch away: To protect the downtrodden, to shelter suppliants on a hearth they can trust. This alone have I brought with me from my Colchian realm, that myself I saved that magnificent and illustrious flower of Greece, bulwark of the Achaean race, progeny of gods. Orpheus is my gift, who enchants stones by his song and draws the forests to hear; my gift, too, are Castor and Pollux, and Boreas' scions, and Lynceus, whose sharp sight perceives things beyond Pontus, and all the Minyans. Of the leader of leaders I say nothing; for him there is no debt, him I charge to no one's account. The others I brought back for you; Jason, for myself.

Proceed now and pile your indictments high; I shall confess all. The sole charge to which I am liable is the return of the Argo. Suppose my choice had been maidenly modesty and my own father; then all the Pelasgian land would have collapsed along with its leaders, and first of all would this son-in-law of yours have succumbed to the fiery breath of that fierce bull. Fortune may overwhelm my case as it will; I am not sorry I saved that numerous band of glorious princes. It is in your power to fix the reward I receive for all my transgressions. Condemn the defendant, if you like, but give me back the source of my sin. I am guilty, Creon, I confess it; but so you knew me to be when I touched your knees as a suppliant and begged the solemn protection of your hand. Again I beg for some little corner, some repose, for my miseries, some humble hovel to hide in. If the decision is to drive me from this city, let me have some faraway cranny in your kingdom.

CREON: I think I gave sufficient evidence that I am not a man who is overbearing in wielding the scepter or who tramples upon misery with proud foot when I chose for my son-in-law an exile helpless and haunted by pressing fear, inasmuch as Acastus, who holds the Thessalian realm, is demanding his person for capital punishment. Acastus' complaint is that his aged father, palsied and heavy with years, was murdered, and that the limbs of the aged victim were dismembered when his dutiful sisters, deceived by your cheat, ventured on an undutiful enormity. Jason can defend his case if you separate yours from it. No blood has tainted his innocence, his hand plied no sword, he has detached himself from complicity and kept himself undefiled. It is you, you, who are the architect of odious crime. You have a woman's irresponsibility for reckless daring and the strength of a man, with no thought of reputation; begone, purge my realm, take your lethal herbs with you, free my citizens from terror, settle in some other land and there trouble the gods!

MEDEA: Is it flight you enforce? Then for flight give me back my ship, give me back my shipmate. Why do you order me to flee alone? I was not alone when I came. If it is fear of war that impels you, eject us both from your realm; why do you differentiate between a pair equally guilty? It is for him

Pelias fell, not for me. Add to your indictment elopement and theft, a deserted father and a butchered brother—all the crimes which the bridegroom teaches his new wives; the sin is not mine. Many times have I been made guilty, but never for myself.

CREON: You should have been far away by now. Why do you purposely delay matters with speechmaking?

MEDEA: I am going; this is my last humble petition: Let the mother's guilt not drag her innocent children down.

CREON: Go, I will take them into my fatherly embrace as if they were mine.

MEDEA: By the blessed bed of this royal marriage, by your hopes for the future, by the continuance of kingdoms, which is subject to the vicissitudes of variable fortune, I pray you: Bestow the largesse of a brief stay upon the refugee mother, until I imprint what may be my dying kiss upon my sons.

CREON: It is for a trick you want time.

MEDEA: What trick is there to fear when the time is so slight?

CREON: For the wicked no time is too scant to work harm.

MEDEA: Will you deny a poor creature a tiny respite for her tears?

CREON: Though inveterate fear opposes your plea, one day shall be given you to prepare for exile.

MEDEA: Generous, even if you curtail it a bit; I, too, am impatient.

CREON: But you will pay with your head if you have not cleared the Isthmus before Phoebus raises bright day.

But the marriage rites summon me, the festive day of Hymen calls me to prayer.

(*Exeunt* CREON *and* MEDEA *severally.*)

CHORUS: Too bold the man who first ploughed the treacherous sea with frail bark, who saw his familiar mainland receding behind him and entrusted his life to the fickle winds; slicing through the unbroken surface in his uncertain course he dared put his faith in a thin board which drew too tenuous a line between the paths of life and death.

No one as yet knew the constellations or understood the use of the stars which spangle the ether. Not yet could craft avoid the rainy Hyades; unnamed as yet were the lights of the Olenian Goat, or the Attic Wain which creeping old Bootes follows and guides, or yet the North Wind, or yet the West.

'Twas Tiphys who ventured to spread sail over the vast main and to write new laws for winds: Now to stretch canvas to belly out full, now to haul the sheet forward to catch cross winds from the south, now to set the yards safely in the middle of the mast, now to make them fast to the very top, when the too eager sailor is greedy for every gust and the ruddy spinnaker flutters aloft.

Stainless the ages our fathers saw, when trickery was far distant. Every man trod his own shore free of ambition and waxed old on his ancestral heath; rich on a pittance, he knew no wealth but what his native soil produced. Worlds well and lawfully dissevered that Thessalian timber forced into one; it bade ocean endure lashes and the hitherto isolated sea to be reckoned among human fears.

Upon that willful boat a severe penalty was inflicted after it had made its way through far-off perils when two mountains, barriers of the abyss, were driven together from this side and that by a sudden thrust, and roared as with heaven's thunder, and the trapped sea splattered their peaks and the very clouds. Bold Tiphys blanched and his faltering hand relaxed its hold upon all the reins; Orpheus fell mute, his lyre stunned to silence; and Argo itself lost its god-given voice. And what panic was there when the maid of Sicilian Pelorus, Scylla, girt about her waist with rabid hounds, opened all her gaping maws at once! Who would not quake in every limb when so many simultaneous barks issued from a single monstrosity? What turmoil when the Sirens, those deadly plagues, mesmerized the Ausonian sea with their melodious chant, when Thracian Orpheus responded to their song on his Muse-given lyre and almost forced the Siren, whose habit it was to hold ships back, herself to follow! And what was the prize of this voyage? The Golden Fleece and Medea, an evil worse than the sea and an appropriate cargo for the first of ships.

Today the sea has capitulated and submits to human terms. There is no need for a famed Argo fashioned by Pallas' hand and manned by princely oars; any skiff may wander at will over the deep. All boundaries have been abolished, cities fix their walls in new lands, nothing is left where it had always been, the whole world may be freely traversed. Indian quaffs cold Araxes, Persians drink Elbe and Rhine. An age shall come in latter years when Ocean shall relax nature's bars, when the whole wide surface of earth shall be open and Tethys shall uncover new worlds; Thule shall no longer be land's end.

III

(*Enter* MEDEA, *her movements showing her distraction, followed by the* NURSE, *whom she ignores and who proceeds to describe her movements.*)

NURSE: Darling, where to abroad in such haste? Stop, control your emotion, bridle your impetuosity.

Like a maenad crazily bounding when she is possessed by the god and beside herself, on the snowy peak of Pindus or Nysa's ridges, so is Medea coursing from this side to that, her movements undirected and signs of frantic fury in her face. Her cheeks are hectic, her breath a deep panting, she shouts, she floods her eyes with a gush of tears, she beams with ecstasy, she passes through the gamut of every passion. She is frustrated, she threatens, she seethes, she complains, she groans. How will her mind's weight veer, how will her threats be directed, where will that surging wave break? Her fury spills over its bounds. It is no slight or ordinary crime she is brewing; she will outdo herself. I recognize the symptoms of her old intensity; something big is afoot, something monstrous, huge, godless.

(MEDEA's *paroxysm subsides and she pauses to speak.*)

It is the visage of a madwoman I see; may the gods disprove my fear!

MEDEA: If you ask, poor creature, what limit you should place on your hatred, copy your love. Can such as I tolerate this wedding without vengeance? Can this day, campaigned for with such ado and with such ado granted, drag idly by? So long as earth's core shall bear heaven in balance, so long as the bright universe shall unroll its sure alternations, as sands are numberless and day follows sun and stars night, so long as the pole rotates the waterless Bears and rivers fall into the sea, my passion to exact punishment shall never falter, but ever wax greater. What savagery of wild beasts, what Scylla, what Charybdis, sucking up Ausonian sea and Sicilian, what Aetna resting heavily on heaving Titan shall boil with threats so dire? No rushing torrent, no storm-tossed sea, no Pontus whipped to fury by the north wind or fire sustained by its violent gale could match my drive and my intensity. I shall overturn everything, flatten everything to ruins.

Was Jason afraid of Creon and the saber-rattling Thessalian chief? True love can fear no one. But suppose that he gave in under duress and yielded his hand; at least he could have come for a last conversation with his wife. Even this he was afraid to do, for all his fierceness. Surely a son-in-law could procure a postponement for the harsh sentence—one single day was given me for two children. But I do not complain of the shortness of time; it shall stretch far. This day shall bring to pass a deed, aye, it shall bring to pass a deed which no other day can overlook. I will assail the gods, I will make the universe totter.

NURSE: Master your heart, mistress, which your woes have set in turmoil; mollify your spirit.

MEDEA: I can be quiet only if I see everything overwhelmed along with my ruin. As you go down it is a satisfaction to drag others with you.

(*Exit* MEDEA.)

NURSE: See how much we have to fear if you persist. No one can attack the powerful and remain safe.

(*Exit* NURSE; *enter* JASON.)

JASON: Ah, fate always hard and fortune harsh, malignant alike when she rages and when she forbears. How often does the god find us remedies worse than our perils! If I should choose to keep faith with my wife's deserts, I should have to yield my head to death; but if I should choose not to die, I must, poor wretch, prove faithless. Yet it is not fear that has vanquished faith, but the apprehension of a conscientious father, for surely the children would follow their parents to death. Hallowed justice, if thy seat is in heaven, I invoke thy divinity to witness: The sons have prevailed over the father. Nay, I do believe that fierce as she is in heart and impatient of the yoke, she would herself be more concerned for her children than for her marriage. Angry though, she be, I am determined to ply her with prayer. (*Enter* MEDEA.) And look, at sight of me she bridles, shows her fury, makes her hate plain to see; all her passion is in her face.

MEDEA: I am on the run, Jason, on the run. That is nothing new, to scurry from shelter to shelter; it is the cause of my running that is new; it was *for* you I used to run. You force me to fly from your house—I leave it, I go away; but where are you sending me? Shall I make my goal Phasis and the Colchians, my father's kingdom and the fields drenched with my brother's blood? What country do you direct me to? What seas do you point out to me? Shall it be the jaws of the Pontic strait through which I carried back that noble band of princes when I followed an adulterer through the Symplegades? Shall I make for little Iolcus or Tempe in Thessaly? Every road I opened up for you I closed for myself. Where would you have me go? You decree expulsion for the refugee, but assign no place of exile. But I am on my way; a king's son-in-law has issued his orders, and I accept them. Heap cruel tortures upon me! I have deserved them. Let regal wrath crush your concubine with bloody torments, load her hands with chains, bury her in the rocky dungeon of eternal night; my sufferings will be less than I deserve.

Ingrate! Let your mind dwell on the fiery puffing of that bull; on the blazing crew in Aeetes' arms-sprouting field amidst the wild terror of that untamed race; on the weapons of the instantaneously ripened enemy, when, at my bidding, the soldiery born of earth fell at each other's hands. Recall, too, the spoil of the ram of Phrixus; the sleepless dragon compelled to close his eyes in unprecedented slumber; the brother done to death, and the compounding of the crime when he was dismembered; the daughters who minced the limbs of the old man, deceived by my trick into thinking he would be resurrected. By the hopes of your children, your secure home, by the monsters vanquished, by these hands which I have never spared in your service, by the perils we have passed through, by heaven and sea, the witnesses of my marriage, pity me. You are happy; give the suppliant her turn. Gaining kingdoms for others, I abandoned my own. Of all the wealth the Scythians accumulate, raided from as far afield as the sun-scorched folk of India and so abundant that our palaces are too full to hold more treasure and we decorate the woodland with gold—of all this I took nothing away with me except my brother's limbs, and those, too, I squandered for you. For you my country is lost, my father, my brother, my chastity; that was the dowry I brought when I married you; now that I am rejected, give me back my own.

JASON: When Creon was resolved to do away with you, it was my tears that prevailed upon him to grant you banishment.

MEDEA: And I thought it was a punishment; I see now that exile is a favor.

JASON: Escape while you can still leave, get yourself away. The anger of kings always falls heavily.

MEDEA: So you urge me in Creusa's interest; you are trying to rid her of a paramour she loathes.

JASON: Is Medea taking exception to love?

MEDEA: And to murder, and to guile.

JASON: But what act of mine can you really take exception to?

MEDEA: Every act I committed.

JASON: That is all that is wanting, that I, too, should be guilty of your crimes!

MEDEA: They are yours, they are yours, indeed! The one who profits by a crime is guilty of it. Though the world should insist your wife is infamous, you alone must defend her, you alone declare her innocent. In your sight she should be guiltless if her guilt is for your sake.

JASON: Life is thankless when one is ashamed of having received it.

MEDEA: One should not cling to it when one is ashamed of having received it.

JASON: Nay, try to master your angry and excited heart, be reconciled for the children's sake.

MEDEA: I resign them, disclaim them, disown them! Shall Creusa bear brothers to *my* children?

JASON: A queen to the sons of aliens, a lady of position to the afflicted.

MEDEA: Never may so black a day befall the unhappy as shall adulterate a noble stock with a vile, the issue of Phoebus with the issue of Sisyphus.

JASON: Why, wretched woman, are you dragging us both down to destruction? Go away, please!

MEDEA: Creon listened to a suppliant.

JASON: Tell me what I can do.

MEDEA: For me? Crime.

JASON: On this side a king and on that—

MEDEA: —Medea, a greater terror. The two of us should compete, with Jason as the prize.

JASON: I give up, I am worn down by my troubles. But you had better be wary of tempting chance too often.

MEDEA: Fortune has always stood inferior to me.

JASON: Acastus is on the offensive.

MEDEA: Creon is a nearer enemy. Flee them both, Jason. Medea is not forcing you to take arms against your father-in-law or to pollute yourself with the murder of your kinsman Acastus; flee with me, free of guilt.

JASON: But who will defend us if twin wars assail us, if Creon and Acastus join forces?

MEDEA: Add the Colchians, too, add Aeetes to be their general, combine Scythians with Pelasgians; I will overwhelm them all.

JASON: I am terribly afraid of lofty scepters.

MEDEA: Are you sure you do not covet them?

JASON: Our long colloquy will arouse suspicion; cut it short.

MEDEA: Now, supreme Jupiter, thunder in all heaven, stretch forth your right hand, prepare your avenging flames, cleave the clouds and set the whole world a-tremble. Poise your weapons, with hand indifferent, against me or him; whichever of us falls, a criminal will perish. Against us your bolt cannot mis-strike.

JASON: Do begin to think rationally and speak sanely. If any consolation from my father-in-law's house can ease your flight, ask for it.

MEDEA: You know that my spirit is able and accustomed to despise royal riches. All that I ask is that I may have my children as companions in my exile, so that I can pour my tears into their bosom. *You* can expect new sons.

JASON: I confess I should like to comply with your request, but paternal obligation forbids. Not even king or father-in-law could compel me to agree to their leaving. They are my reason for living, the solace of a heart burned black with cares. Sooner would I be deprived of breath, of limbs, of light.

MEDEA (*aside*): Has he such love for his children? Fine! I have him, the place to wound him is uncovered. (*To* JASON) At least allow me to give them my last injunctions, allow me a final embrace; even that will be appreciated. This is my last plea: I beg you, if my despair and grief have overflowed, do not let what I have said stick in your mind. I would have you retain a better memory of myself; ascribe the other to my passion, and blot it out.

JASON: All that I have put out of my mind. And I, too, pray that you govern your hot temper and cultivate placidity. Calm mollifies misery.

(*Exit* JASON.)

MEDEA: He has gone. Is this how it is? Do you walk away forgetful of me and all I have done? Have I become a cipher to you? I shall never be a cipher. To work! Summon all your powers and skills. The profit of your crimes is to count noth-

ing a crime. For guile there is no chance; fear has alerted
them. Attack where no one could fear. Oh, now, be bold, venture what Medea is capable of, and what she is not capable of.

(Enter NURSE.)

You, my loyal nurse, companion of my sorrow and my
changing fortunes, help my poor schemes. I have a robe, a
divine heirloom which is the glory of our house and kingdom,
bestowed on Aeetes by the Sun as a pledge of his fatherhood.
There is also a necklace woven of shining gold, and a gold
band for binding the hair set with brilliant gems. These things
my sons shall take as a gift to the bride, but first they must be
smeared and steeped with baneful art. Invoke Hecate and
prepare the lethal rites. Have altars set up, and let their flames
crackle inside the house.

(Exeunt.)

CHORUS: No force of fire or of whistling wind or of hurtling
spear is so violent as a wife's blazing hatred when she is
robbed of her marriage—not when cloud-laden South Wind
brings wintry rain and the Danube in spate sweeps bridges
apart and wanders unchanneled; not when Rhone pounds
the sea or when invigorated Sun melts the snows into torrents
as Haemus dissolves in mid-Spring. Blind is love's fire when
goaded by anger; it scorns guidance, will not tolerate check-
reins, has no fear of death; it strains to advance upon ready
swords.

Spare him, ye gods; we pray your indulgence for the man
who subdued the sea. Let him live unhurt, though the lord
of the deep resents the conquest of the realm second to heav-
en's. The youth who made bold to drive the Sun's immortal
chariot disregarded the limits his father had set, and was
himself victim of the sparks he so madly scattered over
heaven's vault. High is the price of the pioneer path; walk
where former generations have found it safe, nor breach, willful man, the hallowed covenants of the universe.

All who laid hand to the noble beams of that audacious
ship and despoiled Pelion of its sacred woodland's thick shade,

all who passed between the wandering rocks and traversed the sea's many perils, who tied hawser to barbaric shore to ravish and bring back the prize of foreign gold, expiated the violated rights of the sea by some dire doom.

Challenged, the sea exacts its penalty. First of all, Tiphys, who tamed the deep, left his rudder to a novice pilot. Dying on a foreign strand, far from his ancestral kingdom, he lies covered in a contemptible grave, among alien shades. Aulis remembered the king it had lost, and its windless harbor holds the Greek fleet, which chafes at standing still.

Orpheus born of the melodious Muse, whose plectrum evoked chords at which torrents halted and winds fell silent, at whose music the birds left off their song and with the whole woodland attending followed the singer—Orpheus lies mangled over the Thracian plains while his head floats down mournful Hebrus. He reached Tartarus and the Styx he already knew, but this time never to return.

Hercules laid North Wind's sons in the dust and slew Neptune's scion whose habit had been to transform himself into numberless shapes. But Hercules himself, after he had brought peace to land and sea, after he had forced open the realm of cruel Dis, laid him down on blazing Oeta while he was yet alive, and to the pitiless flames gave his limbs eroded by his wife's gift, mingled of the gore of Nessus and the Hydra.

Ancaeus was laid low by the fierce charge of the bristly boar, whereat, Meleager, you impiously slew your mother's brother and yourself died at your angry mother's hand. All these deserved the punishment which tender Hylas incurred, the lad Hercules could not find because he had been ravished away amidst waters which held no dread. Then proceed, my stalwarts, to plough the sea whose waters are full of dread!

Idmon, though clairvoyant of others' fate, was dispatched by a serpent in the sands of Libya. Mopsus, truthful to others but to himself false, succumbed far from his Thebes. If Mopsus prophesied truly, Thetis' husband Peleus shall be a roaming exile. Nauplius shall fall headlong into the deep as he seeks to wreck the Argives with spurious beacons, and his son Palamedes shall pay with his life for his father's voyage in the Argo. Ajax died by lightning and the sea. Alcestis ransomed her husband and paid her life for Admetus'. Pelias himself, by whose orders the prize of the golden spoil was fetched back on that first ship, was boiled in a hot cauldron, in whose narrow waters he, too, was a wanderer, and so burned to death. Enough, ye gods, have you avenged the sea: Spare him who was ordered to his deed.

IV

(Enter NURSE.*)*

NURSE: My spirit quakes and shudders; great calamity looms near. Her passion grows prodigious; it stokes its own fires and keeps its violence undiminished. Often have I seen her in a frenzy, assailing the gods and pulling heaven down; but this is bigger. Medea is preparing some bigger monstrosity. With step distraught she strode forth to gain her deadly shrine. There she is pouring forth all her stock; phials she herself had feared she now broaches. She is unwrapping her whole baneful pharmacopeia, specifics arcane, occult, uncanny. With her left hand she conjures her baleful witchery and invokes her pestilential powers—all that the burning sands of Libya bring forth and all that frozen Taurus, stiff with Arctic cold, holds imprisoned in everlasting snow, and everything that is monstrous. Drawn by her magic chants the scaly throng leave their lurking and stand at attention. Here a savage serpent drags its huge length along, darts out its forked tongue, and asks to whom it shall deal death; when it hears the chant it yields its own will, twines its swelling mass into piled folds, and shapes them into coils. "Puny the evils and paltry the weapons which lowly earth begets," says she; "from heaven will I seek my drugs. Now is the time, now, to transcend common trickery. Hither descends serpent Draco, who stretches over heaven like a torrent, whose enormous knots the two Bears feel—the Greater used by Pelasgians, the Lesser by Sidonians; let Ophiuchus at last relax his tight grip and pour

his virus forth. Come, Python, to my chant, who dared assail
Apollo and Diana. Let Hydra, which renewed its heads as
Hercules lopped them off, and every snake that Hercules
scotched, come back. Even you, wakeful dragon, first lulled
by my incantations, leave the Colchians and come to serve
me."

After she had conjured up the whole tribe of snakes, she
heaped together the virulence of her noxious herbs. Whatever
impassable Eryx produces on its rocky heights; whatever the
ridges of Caucasus, swathed in endless winter and spattered
with Prometheus' blood, bring forth; tinctures which the rich
Arabs apply to their arrows, or the Mede, whose prowess is
in his quiver, or the nimble Parthians, the extracts which
Suebian ladies collect under the wintry sky in the Hyrcanian
forests; whatever earth produces in the nesting season of spring
or when stiff winter has shaken off the woodland's crowning
glory and has congealed all things with flaky frost; every shrub
whose burgeoning bloom is lethal or which generates noxious
juices in its twisted roots—all these she is manipulating. These
poisons Haemonian Athos contributed, those towering Pindus;
that surrendered its tender foliage to the ruthless sickle on
the ridges of Pangaeus; these Tigris checked its deep eddies
to nurture, those the Danube, those the gem-bearing Hydaspes
whose warm waters course through stretches of desert, and
the Baetis, after which the Spanish province is named, whose
slow waters batter the western seas. This plant suffered the
knife while Phoebus was readying the day, that growth was
culled in deepest night, and this was harvested with fingernail
and incantation.

These death-dealing herbs she grasps, squeezes over them
the venom of serpents, and adds obscene birds to the brew—
the heart of a hoot owl, and the vitals cut out of a living
screech owl. Other properties that artificer of wickedness arranges in separate heaps; some hold within them the tearing
violence of fire, others the frigid stiffness of inert cold. To her
witch's brew she adds mutterings no less formidable.—But

look, hear the mad beat of her footsteps, the sound of her chant. At her opening lines the whole world shudders.

(*Enter* MEDEA, *chanting.*)

MEDEA: I conjure the mob of the silent, and you, deities of the dead, and blind Chaos, and the opaque dwelling of shadowy Dis, and the enclaves of foul Death fixed to the banks of Tartarus. Leave you torments, ghosts, and hie you to the new marriage. Halt the wheel that whirls Ixion's limbs and let him touch ground; let Tantalus quaff Pirene's waters unfrustrated; come you, too, Danaids, mocked by the vain task of fetching water in perforated pitchers: This day requires the service of your hands. Let only Sisyphus, father of my husband's father-in-law, stay back for a heavier punishment; let the slippery stone carry him with it as it rolls back down the rocks.

Summoned now by my sacraments, thou luminary of night, come clothed in thy most baneful visage, thy three forms all threatening.

For thee, after the manner of my race, I have loosed my hair from its band and paced the mystic grove with bare feet. I have evoked water from dry clouds; I have driven the seas back to their depths; Ocean has bestowed his mighty waves deep within, his tides defeated. Heaven's law, too, have I confounded: The world has seen sun and stars together, and the Bears have touched the sea forbidden them. The order of seasons I have rearranged: By my witchcraft earth has blossomed in summer, and at my bidding Ceres has seen harvest in winter. Violent Phasis has turned its waters back to their source, and Hister, divided into many mouths, has constricted his truculent billows and fallen spiritless in all his banks. Waves have crashed and the sea has raged and swelled, though the winds were still. The home of the ancient woodland lost its shadows when daylight returned at my imperious voice. Phoebus has halted in mid-course, and at my incantation the Hyades totter and collapse.

It is time, Phoebe, to attend to thy rites. (*She holds her*

offerings up in turn as she presents them to Hecate.) For you
these wreaths woven with bloody hand, each knotted with
nine serpents; for you these members which the fractious
serpent Typhoeus bore when he shook Jove's throne. In this
is the blood of Nessus which the perfidious ferryman presented to Alcmena when he gasped his last. These ashes are
the residue of the pyre on Oeta which consumed Hercules
and the venom that afflicted him. Here you see the brand
Althaea burned when she proved a dutiful sister but undutiful mother. These feathers the Harpy abandoned in her track-
less covert when she fled from Zetes. With them are the quills
of the Stymphalian bird, whom the darts of Hercules, steeped
in the Lernaean Hydra's venom, wounded.

You have rumbled, my altars; I perceive my tripods are
stirred by my divine patroness.

Trivia's nimble car I see, not as when she drives it with
full face lighted all through the night, but with the livid and
gloomy aspect she bears when she is assailed by Thessalian
witchcraft and skirts heaven with a nearer rein. Such a gloomy
night do thou now diffuse through the heavens with thy pallid
torch; terrify the peoples with a new horror, and make them
sound costly Corinthian bronzes, Dictynna, to relieve thine
eclipse. To thee we offer our solemn rites on bloody turf: For
thee a torch snatched from a burning funeral pyre heaves its
blaze up in the night; for thee I toss my head and writhe
my neck and utter incantations; for thee a fillet flattened in
the funereal fashion binds my loosened locks; for thee I
brandish this mournful branch from the Stygian pool; for
thee I bare my bosom like a maenad and strike my arms with
ritual blade. Let my blood drip upon the altars; inure yourself, my hand, to draw sword and endure shedding dear blood
—I have struck, I have supplied the hallowed liquid.

But if you complain that you are too often summoned by
my petitions, forgive me, I pray; the reason for my too frequent invocation of your aid, Hecate, is always one and the
same—Jason.

(*She takes up various flasks and caskets as she addresses them.*)

Do you tinge Creusa's robe, so that as soon as she puts it on the creeping flame shall burn her inmost marrow. In this golden casket lies hidden a fire given me by Prometheus, who expiates its theft from heaven with the new growth of his vitals; he taught me how to keep its force safe stored. Mulciber also gave me fire, concealed in powdered sulphur; and from my kinsman Phaethon I received bolts of living flame. I have gifts from Chimaera's fiery middle section, and I have flames snatched from the scorched gorge of that bull; these I have mixed with Medusa's gall, and so enjoined them to keep their evil power in silence.

Sharpen my poisons with thy stings, Hecate, and preserve the seeds of fire which I am hiding in my presents. Let them deceive sight and endure touch till their heat penetrates heart and veins. Let her limbs ooze and her bones smoke; let her blazing hair outshine the new bride's wedding torches.

My prayers have been received. Thrice has bold Hecate uttered her bark, and her luminous torch has spurted its mystic flames.

All my power has now been exercised. Call my sons here to carry these costly gifts to the bride.

(MEDEA'S SONS *are led in.*)

Go, my sons, go. The mother that bore you is unlucky; placate your mistress and stepmother with presents and humble prayer. March, now, and quickly come home again, to give me the pleasure of a last embrace.

(*Exeunt,* MEDEA *into the house, the children toward* CREON'S *palace.*)

CHORUS: Whither is savage love sweeping this bloody maenad headlong? What crime is she preparing in her unbridled frenzy? Her expression is rigid with stark passion, her head she weaves with gesture fierce and proud, and threatens even the king; who would believe her an exile?

Her cheeks burn red, then ruddiness makes way for pallor; her aspect is changeable, she keeps no complexion long. She dashes to this side and that, just as a tigress bereft of her cubs scours the jungles of the Ganges in frenzied arcs.

The curbing of neither anger nor love does Medea understand; and now that anger and love are joined in their suit, what will the issue be? When will that unspeakable Colchian rid Pelasgian fields of her presence and liberate king and kingdom from terror? Do give your team their head, Phoebus, spare the reins; let welcome darkness shroud the light, let night's herald Hesperus sink this terrifying day!

V

(*Enter* MESSENGER *at a run.*)

MESSENGER: Ruin, total ruin! Our royalty is annihilated. Daughter and father are one low heap of ashes.

CHORUS: How were they trapped?

MESSENGER: As kings regularly are, by gifts.

CHORUS: But what trap could those gifts entail?

MESSENGER: I, too, wonder, and though the evil deed is accomplished, I can scarcely believe it could have been. The disaster is endless; through every part of the palace the fire rages as if it were under orders. Now the whole structure has collapsed, and the city is feared for.

CHORUS: Water can quench flames.

MESSENGER: This is another strange aspect of that disaster: Water *feeds* the flames. The more it is fought, the harder the fire burns; of itself it seizes upon its adversary.

(MEDEA *and* NURSE *enter as the* MESSENGER *completes his speech; exit* MESSENGER.)

NURSE: Out of the Peloponnese at the double quick, Medea! Go anywhere, but make haste!

MEDEA: *I* retreat? Even if I had already fled I would have come back for this. It is a novel wedding I witness. (*Soliloquizing*) Why, my soul, do you falter? Exploit your successful sally. How small a fraction of your revenge elates you! You are still in love, madwoman, if you are satisfied with Jason celibate. Find some species of punishment wholly unexampled; this is how to make yourself ready: Away with every scruple, out every trace of conscience! Paltry the punishment which innocent hands inflict. Put your weight into your passion, goad your lethargy, from deep down in your heart force up your *élan* of old. Give the name of piety to what you have perpetrated up to this point. Put forth your efforts to make them realize how trifling and of what common brand were the crimes I obliged him with. Those were merely school exercises for my passion; could prentice hands achieve a masterpiece, could a girl's temper? Now I am Medea; my genius has matured with evils.

A fine thing that I wrenched off my brother's head, it is a fine thing! A fine thing that I minced his body and robbed my father of that mystic symbol; a fine thing that I instigated the daughters to arm themselves for the destruction of their old father. Find fresh scope, my passion; there is no crime for which your hand is not sufficiently schooled.

What then is your objective, my anger, with what weapons will you ply your treacherous foe? The fierce spirit within me has determined upon a measure, but does not yet dare acknowledge it to itself. I have been foolish in my breathless haste—my enemy should have had a few children by his bedfellow. But your children by him have Creusa for mother. On that mode of punishment I am resolved, and rightly resolved. I must prepare my temper, I realize, for the ultimate crime. Children once mine, you must pay the price for your father's wickedness.

Horror has knocked at my heart, my limbs are numb with cold, my breast is a-tremble. Anger has yielded place; the wife in me is banished, the mother wholly returned. Shall I slaughter my own children, my own flesh and blood? Forfend it, mad passion! Far be a crime so unprecedented, an enormity so accursed, even from me! What sin have the children to atone? That Jason is their father is a sin, but that Medea is their mother, a greater sin. They are not mine, let them die.

Shall they indeed perish? They are mine. They are without
crime or fault, they are innocent—true enough, but so was
my brother. Why, soul of mine, do you teeter? Why are my
cheeks flooded with tears, why do I waver and let anger now
jerk me this way, and love, now that? I am buffeted by a
riptide, as when rushing winds wage ruthless war and from
both sides opposing waves lash the seas and the cornered surface seethes; just so does my heart oscillate; anger routs affection and affection anger. Yield, anger, to affection.

Here, dear children, sole solace of a house overthrown, come
here and fuse your limbs with mine in close embrace. Your
father may have you unharmed, provided your mother, too,
may have you. But exile and flight press hard; any moment
they will be torn from my bosom, weeping and sighing amidst
their kisses as they are snatched away. They are lost to their
mother; let them be lost to their father. Again my passion
waxes and my hatred boils; the old Erinys reaches for my
unwilling hand. Where you lead, wrath, I follow. Would that
proud Niobe's brood had issued from my womb, that I had
given birth to twice seven sons! I have been too sterile for
vengeance, but two I did bear, enough for a brother and a
father.

(*Enter* MEDEA'S SONS.)

That unruly crowd of Furies—where are they rushing,
whom are they seeking, for whom preparing their flaming
strokes? Against whom is that hellish band stretching forth
their bloody torches? A whip cracks and a monstrous snake
hisses. Whom is Megaera attacking with her menacing beam?
Whose ghost is that approaching? Its limbs are scattered and
it is hard to recognize; it is my brother, and he is demanding
vengeance. I shall pay, the whole account. Thrust your torches
into my eyes, mangle, burn; see, my breast is bared to the
Furies.

Tell the avenging deities to leave me, Brother, tell them
to return content to the ghosts below. Leave me to myself,

Brother, use this hand of mine; it holds a drawn sword. With this victim I placate your ghost. (*She kills one son.*)

What is that sudden tumult? Arms are brandished, they are seeking me to destroy me. I shall mount the lofty roof of our palace; my slaughter is incomplete. (*To the living son*) You come along with me; (*to the murdered son*) your corpse also I will carry away with me. Now to work, my soul; your prowess must not be wasted in obscurity; demonstrate your handiwork for popular approval.

(*Exit* MEDEA, *carrying the body of one son and leading the other by the hand; presently she appears on the roof. Enter* JASON *at the head of an excited crowd.*)

JASON: Here, quickly, every loyal subject who grieves over royalty's ruin! Let us seize the author of this horrible crime herself! This way, aim your weapons this way, stout soldiers, turn the house upside down!

MEDEA (*from the rooftop*): Now, now have I recovered my scepter, my brother, my father; again the Colchians hold the prize of the gilded ram; my royal state is restored, my virginity returned. O divinities complaisant, at last, O festive day, O joyous wedding! Onward, the crime is consummated, but not yet vengeance. Finish the task while your hands are at it. Why delay now, my soul? Why hesitate when you have the power? But now wrath has subsided. I am sorry for my deed, ashamed of it. What, poor wretch, have I done? Poor wretch? Though I am sorry, I did it; a delicious pleasure steals over me, without my will, and look, it is growing: All that was missing was yonder man to be spectator. What I have done so far I count as nothing; any crime I committed without his seeing it is wasted.

JASON: Look, there she is, leaning over the steep part of the roof! Bring fire, someone, quickly! Let her burn and fall in her own flames!

MEDEA: For your sons, Jason, you must heap a funeral pyre and build a tomb. Your wife and father-in-law have already received the rites of the dead; it is I who buried them. This son has met his fate; this other shall be delivered to like destruction as you look on.

JASON: By every deity, by our shared flights and shared bed, which my faith has not violated, spare the boy. If there is any crime it is mine. I devote myself to death; immolate my guilty head.

MEDEA: Nay, *here* will I drive my sword, where you like it least, where it will hurt you most. Go now, proud man, find maids to marry, and abandon mothers.

JASON: One is enough to punish me.

MEDEA: If this hand of mine could be satisfied with one death it would have sought none; even though I slay two, the number is too petty for my passion. If any pledge of yours is lurking in my womb, even now, I shall rummage my vitals with a sword and with iron drag it forth.

JASON: Presently carry out what you have begun, I will not beseech you further; only give me a respite for my punishment.

MEDEA: Enjoy your deliberate revenge, my grief, do not hurry. This day is mine, and I am using the time allotted me.

JASON: 'Tis me you loathe; kill me.

MEDEA: You bid me be merciful; (*she kills the boy*) very well, it is finished. I have nothing more to offer you for atonement, my passion.

> (*A car drawn by dragons appears at* MEDEA's *side.*)

Lift your swollen eyes this way, ingrate Jason. Do you recognize your wife? This is how I am accustomed to flee. A path is opened in the sky and twin serpents submit their scaly necks to the yoke. Take your sons back now, Father. (*She throws the bodies down to him.*) On my winged chariot I shall ride through the air.

JASON: Ride through the lofty spaces of high heaven, and wherever you go bear witness that there are no gods.

FINIS

SENECA

OEDIPUS

INTRODUCTORY NOTE

Greek tragedy draws preponderantly upon two cycles of myth, the Argive (involving Agamemnon, Menelaus, Clytemnestra, Orestes, Electra, and their kin), and the Theban (involving Oedipus, Jocasta, Creon, Eteocles, Polynices, Antigone, Ismene). These every educated Roman could be expected to know; Sophocles' *Oedipus,* which was the most admired of all Greek plays, he would certainly know. This antecedent knowledge Seneca could exploit, and so eliminate or abbreviate material that would otherwise be essential in order to elaborate his own treatment. This is what the audience is expected to know before the play begins:

Laius and Jocasta, king and queen of Thebes, had received an oracle that Laius would be killed by his own son. When a son (later called Oedipus) was born to them, a shepherd was instructed to expose him on Mount Cithaeron. Instead, the shepherd gave the infant to a retainer of King Polybus of Corinth, who was childless, and Polybus and his queen Merope brought him up as their own. When Oedipus was grown, a half-drunken man reviled him for his questionable birth, and the reproach so rankled that Oedipus went to Delphi to confirm the facts as he believed them. At Delphi the oracle told him simply that he would murder his father and marry his mother. Still convinced that his parents were Polybus and Merope, Oedipus determined to avoid his doom by never returning to Corinth, and from Delphi he proceeded toward Thebes instead. At the fork of the roads an older man riding in a carriage rudely thrust him from the path, and Oedipus retaliated by killing the old man; the old man was Laius, his true father. Thebes was plagued by the mysterious Sphinx, and at his coming Oedipus destroyed her by solving her riddle. The grateful Thebans made him king in place of Laius, and he married Laius' widow Jocasta, who was his own true mother. After some years Thebes was visited by a deadly plague, and Creon, Jocasta's brother, was sent to Delphi to ascertain how the city might be relieved. It is at this point that our play begins. At dawn Oedipus, waiting for Creon to return, soliloquizes on the devastation of the scourge and creates a boding sense of worse to come.

CHARACTERS

OEDIPUS, king of Thebes
JOCASTA, wife (and mother) of OEDIPUS
CREON, brother of JOCASTA
TIRESIAS, blind Theban seer
MANTO, his daughter
OLD MAN, messenger from Corinth
PHORBAS, shepherd of Theban royal house
MESSENGER, witness of OEDIPUS' self-blinding
CHORUS OF THEBAN ELDERS
GUARDS
SLAVES

SCENE: *Before the royal palace of Thebes.*

OEDIPUS

I

(Enter OEDIPUS.*)*

OEDIPUS: Night is now banished and the sun is returning, hesitantly. The glow of its rising is dulled by a discolored cloud; sad and sorrowful is the light its flame will bring when it looks forth upon homes desolated by ravening plague. Day will reveal the carnage night has wrought.

Who can take pleasure in kingship? Specious blessing, what a host of evils your amiable exterior conceals! Always it is the lofty crags that are buffeted by the winds, the promontory between stretches of sea whose rocks are lashed even when the ocean is calm; just so is lofty kingship vulnerable to fate. How lucky I was to escape my father Polybus' scepter! Carefree, liberated, a vagabond exile, I stumbled upon kingship in Thebes—heaven and the gods will bear me out. What I fear is beyond utterance—that my own hand shall slay my father. This the Delphic bays warned me, and they point to another and greater crime. Can any wickedness be blacker than murdering a father? A forlorn piety makes me ashamed to utter my doom—it is with the father's chamber that Phoebus threatens the son, with an accursed bed made incestuous by an unholy union. This is the dread that banished me from my father's kingdom. It is not for a crime that I am an exile from my home: I have safeguarded your laws, Nature, out of distrust of myself. Though you think the enormities you dread can never come to pass, you must fear them nevertheless. I tremble at everything, and I do not trust myself to myself.

At this very moment the fates are preparing some stroke against me. What else am I to think when the pestilence which is ravaging Thebes so far and wide is sparing me alone? What

is the disaster for which I am reserved? Amidst the ruins of a
city, deaths upon lamentable deaths, the wreckage of a people,
I stand untouched—Phoebus' prisoner for certain. Could you
expect that crimes so black would be rewarded with a healthy
kingdom? I have infected the very air.

No gentle breeze soothes our hot, panting breasts with its
cool breath, no soft zephyrs stir, but the sun intensifies the
searing flame of the Dog Star, pressing close upon the chine
of the Nemean lion. Rivers are without moisture, grass without color. Dirce is dry, Ismenus a trickle whose impoverished
flow scarcely dampens its exposed bed. Phoebus' sister glides
through the sky without brightness; the day is overcast and the
sad world pallid. Never a star twinkles in a serene night, but a
heavy black fog broods over the earth. The citadels of the
heaven-dwellers and their lofty mansions are muffled to a like-
ness of hell. Grain full-grown yields no harvest; tall stalks
sway with yellow ears, but they are parched and sere, and
the shriveled corn dies. No group is immune to ruin; every
age and sex perishes. Young and old, children and fathers,
are leveled by the lethal plague. A single torch consumes husband and wife, and there are no bitter tears, no funereal
keening. The grim persistence of affliction has dried all eyes;
tears have perished, as in such extremity they must. Here a
stricken father carries his son to the final burning, there a
crazed mother, and hurries back to fetch another to the same
pyre. In the midst of grief, new grief arises; in the midst of
funerals their own obsequies fall. Then they burn their own
corpses with others' flames; fire is stolen, for the wretched have
no shame. No separate mounds cover the hallowed bones. It
is enough to have burned them—but how small a part is reduced to ashes! There is no ground left for tombs; no wood in
the forests for funeral pyres. Prayers nor any skill can relieve
the stricken. Those who would heal fall; death drags the
helper down.

I grovel at the altar and stretch prayerful hands to beg a
speedy fate. Let me outstrip the fall of my kingdom, let me not
be the last to succumb, let mine not be the final funeral of

my realm! Deities too cruel, O heavy fate! Am I alone among all this people to be deprived of death, now so ready to strike? Spurn the land your fatal touch has polluted, leave behind tears and funerals and the poisonous infection the ominous guest brings! Begone, even to your parents!

(*Enter* JOCASTA *as* OEDIPUS *completes his soliloquy.*)

JOCASTA: What is the use of aggravating troubles by lamenting them, husband? This, I suggest, is the kingly way: Confront adversity; the darker the situation, the more the weight of empire totters, the firmer must you stand your ground. To turn your back to fortune is not manly.

OEDIPUS: None can charge me with the reproach of cowardice; my valor knows no ignoble fear. If swords were drawn upon me, if Mars' bristling might should assault me, I would boldly encounter fierce giants hand to hand. I did not run from the Sphinx when she wove her words in enigmatic measures; I was steadfast before the bloody gaping jaws of that unmentionable witch and the ground white with scattered bones. Even when she perched poised for the pounce on her high rock and readied her wings and lashed her tail like a savage lion, I still demanded her riddle. Her shriek was horrible, her jaws crashed, and her talons, impatient for my vitals, tore the rock. But that fell bird's knotty words, her boding riddle interlaced with guile, I solved.

JOCASTA: Then why, foolish man, do you now pray for death? You could have died then. Your achievement was rewarded by your scepter; killing the Sphinx brought you that prize.

OEDIPUS: It is that tricky monster's ashes—that is what is fighting me; for her death she is ruining Thebes. Our only salvation is for Phoebus to show us a path of deliverance.

(*Enter* CHORUS OF THEBAN ELDERS.)

CHORUS: You are fallen, highborn stock of Cadmus, you and all your city. Your land is bereft of its dwellers, pitiable Thebes. Culled is your soldiery, Bacchus, which accompanied you to farthest India, which dared ride the eastern prairies

and plant your banner where the world begins. They saw the
Arabs, rich with forests of cinnamon; they saw the Parthian
horsemen who shoot as they flee; they trod the shores of the
Red Sea where Phoebus shows his rising and spreads out his
light, and with his nearer blaze tints the unclad Indians.

But we, the offspring of that invincible brood, are perish-
ing. A harsh fate is sweeping us to our downfall. Funeral
cortege follows funeral cortege; the long procession of the sor-
rowing column hastens on to the shades. But the sad ranks
must mark time; seven gates wide open are not enough for
the throng making for the cemetery. The dreary remains halt;
one funeral presses hard on another.

First to be affected were the torpid sheep; the rich grass the
flocks cropped doomed them. The priest stands ready at the
victim's neck, but as his raised hand is poised for the sure
stroke, the bull with gilded horns falls inert. At the shock of
his great weight the neck gapes open. But no blood stains the
priest's knife; ugly pus streams from the wound. The steed
is dispirited and collapses on the track, throwing the jockey
from his sinking flank. Abandoned cattle die in the fields; the
bull languishes as his herd dies. The herdsman fails his
diminished stock, for he is himself dying amidst his emaciated
cattle. The deer are not afraid of the rapacious wolves, the
angry roar of the lion is silenced, the shaggy bear has lost her
ferocity, the lurking serpent its bane—it is drained dry, its
venom hardens, it dies.

Forests no longer shade the dark mountains with their
comely foliage. Vines no longer stoop their branches with full
clusters. Everything is tainted with the evil which afflicts us.

The troop of Furies with their hellish torch have crashed
through the bars of abysmal Erebus. Phlegethon has changed
his course and mingled Styx with Theban streams. Black
death has opened his greedy jaws wide and spread his wings
full. The ancient ferryman who plies that swollen river with
his capacious boat, hardy though he is, can scarcely lift his
arms to wield his pole; his endless passengers have wearied

him. They say that the dog of Tenara has broken his iron chains and is haunting our territory, that the earth has rumbled, that ghosts of superhuman stature go wandering through our woodland, that the Theban grove has twice shuddered and shaken off its snow, that Dirce was twice discolored with blood, that the dogs of Amphion bayed in the silent night.

Ah, the grim symptoms of this strange death, which are worse than death! A torpid languor seizes the numb limbs, the wan face is hectic, the head is blotched with sores. Then the burning vapor scorches the very citadel of the body and distends the cheeks with an effusion of blood. Eyes grow rigid as the accursed fire feeds on the members. Ears ring, black gore bursts the stretched veins and drips from the nostrils. Rasping sobs convulse the inmost vitals.

Now they seek relief by holding cool stones in a tight embrace. Where watchers have died and the patients are unrestrained, they make for springs and feed their thirst with draughts of water. A crowd lies prostrate at the altars and prays for death. To this prayer alone the gods are complaisant. Men crowd the shrines to pray, not that the gods be placated, but that they be satiated.

II

(CREON, *returning from Delphi, approaches.*)

OEDIPUS: Who is that striding toward the palace? Can it be the noble and doughty Creon, or is it a hallucination of my sick brain?

CHORUS: It is Creon, whose presence we craved.

(*Enter* CREON.)

OEDIPUS: I quake with horror: Which way will the fates veer? My troubled heart sways with a double apprehension, for the joyous and the grim tidings lie unsorted. My mind hesitates; I am eager to know, but afraid. Brother-in-law, if you bring any help to the weary, tell it quickly.

CREON: The responses are ambiguous and perplexing.

OEDIPUS: An ambiguous deliverance is none at all for men in trouble.

CREON: It is the custom of the Delphic god to veil revelations in enigmas.

OEDIPUS: Even if it is ambiguous, speak. Oedipus alone has the gift of understanding enigmas.

CREON: The god enjoins that the murder of our king be expiated by exile, that Laius be avenged. Until this is done, heaven's light shall never shine clear nor vouchsafe us secure draughts of pure air.

OEDIPUS: And who murdered the noble king? Say whom Phoebus mentions, and he shall be punished.

CREON: I pray it may be safe for me to recount things awful to see and hear. Numbness settles on my limbs; my chilled blood congeals.

When I entered Phoebus' holy temple with reverent step and dutifully lowered my hands in prayer to the deity, the twin peaks of snowy Parnassus gave forth a terrifying crash; the overhanging laurels of Phoebus quivered and stirred the temple, and suddenly the sacred waters of the Castalian fount stood still. The prophetess of Leto's son began to spread her bristling locks in ecstasy and to be possessed by Phoebus. She had not yet reached the pit when with a reverberating roar a voice louder than human sounded forth:

"Kindlier stars will return to Cadmean Thebes if you leave Ismenian Dirce behind, fugitive guest, guilty of a king's murder, known to Apollo from infancy. You will not long retain the satisfactions of your wicked murder; you will wage war with yourself. Bequeath war also to your children, foully reverting to your maternal source."

OEDIPUS: What I now prepare to do at the god's behest should long since have been done for the ashes of the late king, so that no one should treacherously violate the sacred scepter. It behooves a king to guard the safety of kings. No one investigates the murder of a man he feared alive.

CREON: A greater fear supplanted our concern for the victim.

OEDIPUS: Can any fear prevent a pious duty?

CREON: The Sphinx did, with the grim threats of her unspeakable chant.

OEDIPUS: Then the crime shall be expiated now, at heaven's command.

Whoever of the gods looks upon this realm with kindness; you, Jupiter, who ordain the laws of the swift heavens; and you, Phoebus, shining glory of the unclouded world who guide the twelve signs with changing course, who unroll the slow ages with swift wheel; and you, his sister Phoebe, wanderer by night, whose course is opposite to your brother's; and you, Neptune, powerful over the winds, who drive your cerulean car over the deep main; and you, Pluto, who assign lightless abodes—be present all: The murderer of Laius let no peaceful dwelling, no loyal household gods, no hospitable exile tolerate. May he agonize over his indecent mating and unholy progeny. May he slay his father with his own right hand, may he perpetrate (could any curse be deadlier?) the crime I avoided. There shall be no room for pardon. I swear by the realm I rule as an alien and the realm I forsook; by my private gods; by you, Father Neptune, whose twin flood washes either shore of my native Corinth with choppy waves. I invoke Apollo himself to witness, who inspires the prophetic lips of Cirrha's priestess. So may my father Polybus pass a gentle old age and end his life secure on his lofty throne, so may my mother Merope know no wedlock other than her husband's, as no favoritism shall snatch the culprit from my grasp.

But tell me, where was the unspeakable crime committed? Was it in open battle or by treachery that he died?

CREON: He was walking toward the leafy groves of sacred Castalia on a road hedged with thickets, where it forks out into the plain. One path cuts through Phocis, favored of Bacchus, out of whose fields lofty Parnassus with its two peaks towers heavenward by a gentle slope. Another leads to the Isthmus of Corinth. A third track winds through the low-lying Olenian fields, touching the wandering waters and dividing the cool shoals of the Elean river. Here, suspecting no hostility, a band of armed robbers sprang upon him and perpetrated the crime unseen.

(TIRESIAS *approaches, led by* MANTO.)

Most opportunely, Tiresias has been pricked by Phoebus' oracle. Though his palsied knees are slow, he is hurrying; Manto is with him to draw the blind man on.

(*Enter* TIRESIAS, *led by* MANTO.)

OEDIPUS: Holy priest, intelligence next to Phoebus', expound the responses, say whom the avengers demand.

TIRESIAS: You must not wonder, lofty spirit, that my tongue is slow to speak, that it asks for delay. From the blind, much of the truth is hidden. But where my country, where Phoebus calls, I shall follow. The fates must be searched out; if my blood were fresh and warm I would receive the god directly in my heart. Drive to the altar a white bull, and a heifer whose neck the curved yoke has never pressed. And you, Daughter, guide your sightless father and report the aspects of the prophetic rite.

(*The victims are brought.*)

MANTO: An unblemished victim stands before the sacred altars.

TIRESIAS: Invoke the gods to our rite in due form and strew the altars with an offering of oriental incense.

MANTO: I have now heaped incense on the god's sacred hearth.

TIRESIAS: What of the flame? Has it caught its generous feast?

MANTO: It flared with a sudden light, and suddenly died.

TIRESIAS: Did the fire stand erect, clear and sharp? Did it rise heavenward perpendicularly with peak sharply outlined, and then spread branches into the air at the top? Or did it grope uncertainly sideways and then collapse, discolored with puffs of smoke?

MANTO: It was a changeable flame, with more than one aspect. It was like showery Iris who weaves various colors into her rainbow when it arches over a great stretch of heaven to advertise the clouds. You could not be sure which color was there and which missing. There was a flickering blue, mixed with yellow spots, and again a red; at the end it trailed off into black.

But look! The quarrelsome fire is separating into two factions, schism divides the embers of a single sacrament—Father, I shudder to see! The libation of wine changes to blood, a heavy smoke circles the king's head, settles very thick around his face, shuts the blotched light out with its dense fumes. Say what it means, Father!

TIRESIAS: What can I say? My mind is in turmoil, shocked and hesitant. How should I speak? Dire evils are afoot, but hard to divine. Usually the gods' wrath is manifested with unmistakable signs: What can they be willing, yet again unwilling, to publish? What grim passion are they veiling? Something the gods are ashamed of. Bring the bulls here, quickly, sprinkle their necks with salt meal. Are they placid under the ritual handling?

MANTO: The bull raised his head high when he was placed to face east; he was afraid of daylight and shrank in terror from the sun and its rays.

TIRESIAS: Is one stroke enough to bring them to earth?

MANTO: The heifer threw herself on the knife and collapsed with one wound; the bull, though he was struck twice, is lunging uncertainly this way and that, and in exhaustion panting forth his unresisting life.

TIRESIAS: Does the blood gush from a narrow wound, or is there a slow flow over a broad gash?

MANTO: In one a stream is flowing from the breast through the aperture itself; in the other, the deadly wounds are barely spotted with a sprinkle, while the gush turns backward, through the mouth and eyes.

TIRESIAS: These ominous sacrifices portend great enormities. But prognoses from the viscera are sure; describe them.

MANTO: Father, what is this? The vibration of the entrails is not faint, as is usually the case; they are shaking both my hands, and fresh blood is spurting from the veins. The heart is diseased and shrunken and deeply hidden; its veins are livid. The rotten liver is missing a great part of its fiber, and oozing black gall. Look—this is always a bad sign for monarchy— two heads rise with equal swelling, and each severed head is covered with a thin membrane; there is no hiding secrets. The hostile side is raised and rugged, with seven taut veins, but an oblique line intercepts them and prevents their turning back. The arrangement is altered; nothing is in its proper place, everything is pushed back. The lung, all bloody and with no room for air, is on the right; the heart does not occupy the left; there is no caul pliantly drawn over the bulging folds of the viscera. Nature is reversed, the womb does not follow its law. Let us see why the entrails are so taut. What monstrosity is this? A fetus in a virgin heifer!— and not in the usual position; it occupies a strange part of its parent. It moans as it moves its limbs; its feeble joints twitch with stiff convulsions.

The disfigured carcasses are trying to walk! A disemboweled trunk is rising and attacking the priests with its horns! The viscera dodge out of my hands! That deep lowing which troubles your ears is not the bellowing of any frightened cattle hereabouts; it is the fire on the altar, the terrified hearth, that is rumbling.

OEDIPUS: What do the omens of this terrifying rite signify? Tell all: I am not afraid to hear the worst. Men are steadied when the situation is desperate.

TIRESIAS: The desperate situation you seek to remedy you will find enviable.

OEDIPUS: Tell me the one thing heaven wishes me to know: Who has polluted his hands with a king's murder?

TIRESIAS: That name neither birds which cleave high heaven on light wings, nor vitals plucked from living victims, can conjure up. Another procedure must be tried. Laius himself must be evoked from the steppes of perpetual night; he must be released from Erebus to point out his murderers. Earth must be unbarred, the implacable divinity of Dis must be petitioned, the denizens of hellish Styx must be drawn up to light. To whom will you assign the liturgy? Because you exercise kingship, it is wrong for you to look upon the shades.

OEDIPUS: Creon, this task must be yours, for you are next in succession to me.

TIRESIAS: While we are loosing the barriers of abysmal Styx, let the folk chant the praises of Bacchus.

(*Exeunt* CREON, TIRESIAS, MANTO.)

CHORUS: Loosen your hair, bacchants, twine it with quivering ivy, grasp the Nysean thyrsus in your soft hands!

Bacchus, shining glory of heaven, vouchsafe your presence at the prayers which your own illustrious Thebes with suppliant hands offers you; benignly turn your virginal face toward us; with your starry visage disperse the clouds, the grim threats of Erebus, rapacious fate. For you it is seemly to garland your locks with spring flowers, to cover your head with Tyrian snood, to wreathe your smooth brow with berry-laden ivy, to shake your loosened locks with abandon, to draw them orderly again with a knot. So you did when in fear of your stepmother Juno you feigned limbs not your own, in the role of a girl with golden hair and a yellow girdle to tie your dress. Thereafter such soft attire was your pleasure—loose folds and flowing drape. As you sat in your golden chariot and covered your lions with sweeping robes, all the vast steppes of the Orient beheld you, those that drink the Ganges and those that break the ice of Araxes.

Old Silenus follows you on a humble donkey, his knobby temples bound with ivy garlands. Sportive initiates lead your mystic revels. In your suite a troop of Bassarids pounds the earth in Edonian dance, on Mount Pangaeus or the peak of Thracian Pindus. Now amidst Cadmean matrons comes a wild maenad, companion of Ogygian Bacchus; her loins are girt with a sacred fawnskin, her hand brandishes a light thyrsus. Filled with your ecstasy, bacchant matrons loose their hair, rend Pentheus' limbs, and when they are lulled after their frenzy they look upon their unspeakable deed without recognition.

Cadmean Ino, brilliant Bacchus' foster mother, holds the realm of the sea, encircled by choirs of Nereids; rule over the waves of great ocean is in the hands of Palaemon, a boy newly arrived, no common divinity, kinsman of Bacchus. A Tyrrhenian band captured you, lad, and Nereus flattened the swollen sea and changed the blue strait to a meadow. On it the plane tree grows green with spring foliage, and the laurel grove dear to Phoebus, and the chatter of birds is heard through the branches. The oar sprouts with lush ivy, and grapevines twine at the masthead. At the prow an Idaean lion roars, and a Ganges tiger crouches at the stern. The terrified pirates take to the sea, and as they swim their appearance is transformed. First the brigands' arms fall away, breast strikes belly and is fused with it, a little hand hangs at the side; with curving back they meet the waves, a crescent tail cleaves the sea; and now curved dolphins follow the retreating sails.

Lydian Pactolus has carried you on its rich waves as it follows its golden course along its torrid banks. The Massagete who mixes blood with milk for his drink has unstrung his vanquished bow and Getic arrows. The realm of ax-wielding Lycurgus has felt Bacchus, the fierce lands of the Zalaces have felt him, and the nomads whom a near Boreas strikes, and the tribes washed by the cold stream of Maeotis, and those whom the Arcadian stars—Charles's Wain—look straight down upon. He has mastered the scattered Gelonians; he has taken their weapons from the warrior Amazons. With faces downcast those troops of Thermodon came down to earth; they laid their light arrows aside and became maenads. Sacred Cithaeron has billowed with the blood of Pentheus slaughtered; Proteus' daughters took to the woods; and Argos, though his stepmother was there, worshiped Bacchus.

Naxos, surrounded by the Aegean, gave him deserted Ariadne for a bride, bestowing upon her a better husband than the one she lost. From the dry pumice rich wine flowed, babbling brooks cut through the grass, earth drank deep of the liquors—white fountains of snowy milk and Lesbian wine flavored with fragrant thyme. The new bride is escorted to high heaven; Phoebus, his hair spread over his shoulders, intones the ritual chant, and twin Cupids wave their torches. Jupiter lays his fiery weapon aside; at Bacchus' coming he abhors his thunderbolt.

As long as shining stars shall run their courses in hoary heaven, as long as ocean shall circle earth within its waves, as long as full moon shall recover the light it lost, as long as Lucifer shall herald the dawn, as long as the lofty Bears shall remain alien to the sea, so long shall we worship the bright countenance of handsome Bacchus.

III

(Enter CREON.*)*

OEDIPUS: Your very face heralds disaster: Tell me, with whose head are we to placate the gods?

CREON: You bid me speak; fear dictates silence.

OEDIPUS: If the losses of Thebes do not move you, be moved by your kindred's loss of rule.

CREON: You will wish you had not known what you are so bent on knowing.

OEDIPUS: Ignorance cannot mend mischief. Are you cloaking the signpost to the general welfare?

CREON: Where the remedy is foul, better not be cured.

OEDIPUS: Tell me what you have heard, or else a hard sentence will teach you the power of an angry king.

CREON: Kings hate to hear what they order said.

OEDIPUS: You will be dispatched to hell, a cheap atonement for us all, unless you speak up and disclose the oracle's secret.

CREON: Allow me silence; could a man ask a smaller favor of a king?

OEDIPUS: The favor of silence often hurts kingship more than speech.

CREON: Where silence is not allowed, what is?

OEDIPUS: A man who is silent when he is bidden to speak weakens authority.

CREON: The words you force I pray that you will hear without indignation.

OEDIPUS: Is anyone ever punished for speech that is enforced?

CREON: Far from the city there is a grove black with ilex, a moist valley around the spring of Dirce. Above the tall forest a cypress thrusts its head, and its green trunk unites the whole grove. Gnarled and decayed branches spread from an ancient oak. The side of the oak has been lopped off by corrosive time; the cypress' roots are torn, and its falling trunk hangs propped on another tree. There is laurel with bitter berries, slender lindens, Paphian myrtle, an alder that supplies oars for the boundless sea, and a pine towering to the sun and confronting the zephyrs with a knotless trunk. In the middle a huge tree presses down upon the lesser forest with its heavy shade from the mighty circle of its branches; alone it guards the grove. Under it flows a gloomy spring which never knows light or warmth and is always freezing cold; a marshy fen surrounds the sluggish pool.

No need to wait for night when the hoary priest arrived; the place supplied darkness. A ditch is dug and brands snatched from funeral pyres thrown in it. The seer swathes his body in a funereal pall and waves a branch. His lugubrious shawl sweeps over the old man's feet as he paces forward in his dismal attire. His snowy hair is bound with death-bringing yew. Black-fleeced sheep and pitchy cattle are dragged backward. The flame consumes its feast, and the living animals writhe in the deadly fire. Then he calls upon the shades, and upon the ruler of the shades, and upon the dog that bars Lethe's mere. He drones a magic litany, and with fierce and frenzied expression intones a formula either to cajole or compel the insubstantial ghosts. Upon the coals he pours a libation of blood, and burns holocausts, and drenches the pit with quantities of gore. Over this he makes libation of snowy milk, pours wine with his left hand, again chants, and with eyes fixed on the ground invokes the shades in an emotional and sonorous voice.

Hecate's pack barked; thrice the hollow valley gave forth a lugubrious moan, the ground quaked, the earth throbbed. "I am heard," said the seer; "the words I uttered are correct. Blind Chaos is bursting open, Dis's people will be afforded a path to the upper world." The whole forest subsided, and its foliage bristled; oaks were riven, the whole grove was shaken with horror, the earth shrank back and groaned deeply; perhaps Acheron was indignant that his deep abyss was assailed, or perhaps Earth itself resounded as she broke her fastenings to make way for the dead, or it was three-headed Cerberus rattling his heavy chains in his fury.

Suddenly earth yawned wide and a measureless cleft was before me. I myself saw the sluggish pools among the shadows, I myself saw the pallid deities and truest night. The blood froze in my veins and stood still. There sprang forward a savage troop, the whole viper brood of brothers sown with the dragon's teeth, and stood armed. Then fierce Erinys shrieked and blind Fury and Horror and all the beings which eternal darkness fashions and hides: Grief, tearing her hair; Disease, scarcely supporting her weary head; Age, a burden to itself; tremulous Fear; and greedy Pestilence, the bane of the Ogygian folk. We were unmanned. Even Manto was stunned, though she knew the old man's rites and practices. But her father was undaunted; bold by his sightlessness he summons the bloodless mob of cruel Dis.

Immediately they flit forth like cloud puffs and suck in the air of the open sky. Eryx does not shed so many leaves, nor does Hybla sprout so many blooms in the heart of spring when the bees mass about them in thick swarms; not so many waves break in the Ionian Sea; not so many birds flee the threatening cold of Strymon and by long flight change Arctic snows for the warm Nile; far more numerous were the ghosts the seer's summons evoked. Greedily the shivering souls seek the shelter of the shadowy forest. First to emerge from the ground was Zethus, grasping a fierce bull by the horns; then Amphion, holding in his left hand the lyre which moved the rocks by its sweet notes. Niobe, now safe in her pride, holds her scornful head high amidst her brood and counts their ghosts over. Another and worse mother is there, frenzied Agave, followed by the rout that mangled their king; and after the bacchants comes mangled Pentheus, still sternly tenacious of his threats.

One figure, repeatedly called, finally raises his head; shamefaced, cringing back from the rest, hiding himself. The priest persists, and redoubles his Stygian prayers until he brings the hidden face out into the open—Laius himself! I shudder to name him. There he stood, an awful sight, his limbs splotched with blood, his unkempt hair matted with filth, and with crazed lips he spoke:

"Murderous house of Cadmus, always reveling in blood of kin, shake the thyrsus, mangle your sons with frenzied hand, for Thebes' heinous crime of mother love is worse. It is not by the wrath of heaven but by your own crime, my country, that you are ravished. It is not the pestilential South Wind with its noxious blast that does you hurt, nor yet the dry breath of earth unsatisfied by heaven's rain; it is your bloodstained king who has usurped his father's scepter and untouchable bed—a detestable offspring! Yet worse than the son is the mother, her accursed womb again teeming. He plied his own source and begot unholy issue upon his own mother. His own brothers he fathered, a thing wild beasts avoid—a tangle of evil, a monster more baffling than his own Sphinx. You, you who hold the scepter in your bloody hand, you and your whole city shall I assault, a father unavenged; and with me I shall bring Erinys to be attendant on your nuptials, I shall bring her cracking her whip. I shall overturn your incestuous house, I will crumble your home with unholy war.

"Well, then, quickly eject the king from your borders; drive him into whatever exile. His step is deadly; let him leave this soil. It shall recover its greenery and its spring flowers, the pure air will provide life-giving breath, its comeliness will return to the forest. Ruin, Pestilence, Death, Suffering, Wasting, and Grief, his proper entourage, will depart with him. He himself will wish to flee our seats with rapid strides, but I will impede his going and hold him back with an affliction that will retard his pace. He will grope uncertainly for the road, tapping his path with an old man's staff. Do you deprive him of earth; I, his father, will take bright sky from him."

OEDIPUS: My bones, my limbs, are charged with an icy tremor. All I feared to do I am accused of having done. But Merope, still married to Polybus, disproves incest; and Polybus, safe and sound, proves my hands clean. My parents absolve me of both murder and incest. What room is left for guilt? Thebes mourned Laius' death long before I set foot on Boeotian ground. Is the old man deceived, or is the god afflicting Thebes? Now, now I understand: The seer has contrived the story, using the gods as a subterfuge, and has promised my scepter to you.

CREON: Could I wish my sister driven from the throne? Even if the sacred ties of family did not hold me firm in my present station, too high a lot with its inevitable anxieties would frighten me off. You may now lay the burden down and be safe; now you may safely take a humbler station.

OEDIPUS: Are you urging me voluntarily to lay down the heavy burdens of my kingship?

CREON: I would urge anyone free to take either course to do so; but you are now obliged to accept the humbler lot.

OEDIPUS: Praise of moderation and talk of ease and sleep is the surest road for a man covetous of kingship. Ambition frequently disguises itself as indifference.

CREON: Is not my long loyalty sufficient refutation?

OEDIPUS: To the disloyal, loyalty is a wedge for mischief.

CREON: I am free from royal burdens and yet enjoy royal prerogatives. Concourses of citizens make my house flourish;

no day rises but what my relationship to the throne enriches my house. Apparel, sumptuous feasts, deliverance, are granted to many through my influence. In such a happy situation what more could I desire?

OEDIPUS: Whatever remains desirable; prosperity sets no limits.

CREON: Shall I be executed without trial?

OEDIPUS: Did you weigh arguments on my life? Did Tiresias hear my case? Nevertheless, you find me guilty. You have set the example; I follow it.

CREON: What if I am innocent?

OEDIPUS: Kings fear doubts as if they were certainties.

CREON: If you dread fears that are empty, you deserve fears that are real.

OEDIPUS: Free a culprit and he hates you; wherever there is doubt, execute.

CREON: That makes unpopularity.

OEDIPUS: A man afraid of unpopularity cannot be king; it is fear that protects kingship.

CREON: A cruel and imperious ruler is in terror of those he terrorizes; fear recoils upon its author.

OEDIPUS (*to guards*): Shut that criminal in a rock cave and guard him. I go home to the palace.

(*Exeunt* OEDIPUS, *and* CREON *under guard.*)

CHORUS: It is not you, Oedipus, who are the cause of our perils, the source of the fates' assault on the Labdacids; it is an inveterate anger of the gods that persecutes us. The Castalian grove provided shade for Cadmus from Sidon, and Dirce bathed the Tyrian immigrants when great Agenor's son Cadmus, tired of tracking Jove's stolen Europa through the world, halted trembling under our trees and worshiped the kidnaper. Phoebus bade him be companion to a straying heifer which had never strained at a plow or the curved yoke of a lumbering cart, and so he abandoned his chase and gave Boeotia its name from that inauspicious heifer.[1]

---

[1] βοῦς (*bous*).

From that time forward our country has always produced strange monsters. Now it is a serpent towering up from the lowest valley to overtop the pines and hiss above the ancient oaks; high above the Chaonian trees he erects his blue head, though the larger part of him is still recumbent. Now the earth, pregnant with an impious issue, pours forth armed men; the curved horn sounds the battle call, and the trumpet blares its strident notes. Their first use of the agile tongue and of lips hitherto voiceless was for a battle cry. These kindred companies, this offspring worthy the seed whence it sprung, measured life by a single day; they were born after the passing of the morning star, and died before the rising of the evening. The new arrival [2] trembled at these monstrosities and feared hostility from the new-sprung people, until the savage warriors fell and their mother earth saw the darlings she had just borne returned to her bosom. May this have ended impious civil war in Thebes, may Hercules' city know no other fratricidal battles!

What of the fate of Cadmus' grandson Actaeon when the branched antlers of a brisk stag strangely covered his brow and his own dogs hunted their master? Headlong swift Actaeon fled hills and forests, and as he dodged nimbly through rocks and thickets he feared the feathered lures fluttering in the breeze and avoided the nets he himself had set. At last he saw his horns and animal face in the waters of a still pool. There Diana, goddess too severely modest, had bathed her virginal limbs.

IV

(Enter OEDIPUS.)

OEDIPUS: Anxiety revolves in my mind, fears recur. Powers celestial and infernal declare that Laius died by my crime; but this my mind, which knows itself better than the gods know it, denies, and asserts its innocence. Through a dim

2 Cadmus.

track memory recalls that a man I met did fall by a blow of my club and was dispatched to Dis; it was an old man; he started the attack by thrusting the younger aside in his arrogance. But that was far from Thebes, in Phocis where three roads meet.

(Enter JOCASTA.*)*

My sympathetic wife, please unravel my bafflement. How old was Laius at his death? Did he die in his prime or when his vigor was broken?

JOCASTA: Between age and youth, but nearer age.

OEDIPUS: Was his royal person surrounded by numerous attendants?

JOCASTA: The greater part strayed at the crossroads; loyal diligence kept a few by his car.

OEDIPUS: Did any of his companions share the king's fate?

JOCASTA: His loyalty and courage made one man do so.

OEDIPUS: I know the man; the number is right and so is the place. But the time: When was it?

JOCASTA: It was ten harvests back.

(Enter OLD MAN, *from Corinth.)*

OLD MAN: The people of Corinth summon you to your father's throne. Polybus has gone to his eternal rest.

OEDIPUS: How Fortune lunges at me from every quarter! But tell me, what caused my father's death?

OLD MAN: It was gentle sleep that loosed his aged spirit.

OEDIPUS: My father lies dead, not murdered. I solemnly assert that I may now piously raise to heaven pure hands that have no fear of crime. Yet the more fearful part of my doom persists.

OLD MAN: Your father's kingdom will dispel all fears.

OEDIPUS: I would return to that kingdom; it is my mother that frightens me.

OLD MAN: Are you afraid of your mother? She is in anxious suspense for your homecoming.

OEDIPUS: It is filial duty that keeps me away.

OLD MAN: Will you leave her bereft?

OEDIPUS: Precisely that is what makes me afraid.

OLD MAN: Tell me this undersurface fear that weighs on your mind. I am accustomed to preserve loyal silence in the affairs of kings.

OEDIPUS: A warning from Delphi makes me afraid I might cohabit with my mother.

OLD MAN: Stop shuddering at shadows, lay aside your ugly apprehensions. Merope was not your real mother.

OEDIPUS: Why would she choose a supposititious son?

OLD MAN: Kings' children bind restive loyalty.

OEDIPUS: Tell me how you learned the secrets of the bed-chamber.

OLD MAN: It was these hands of mine that gave you to your mother when you were a baby.

OEDIPUS: You gave me to my mother: Who gave me to you?

OLD MAN: A shepherd, under snow-capped Cithaeron.

OEDIPUS: How did you happen to be in that forest?

OLD MAN: I used to herd cattle there.

OEDIPUS: Tell me what physical marks I bear; that is certain identification.

OLD MAN: Your feet had been pierced with metal; it was from their lameness and swelling that you got your name Oedipus.[3]

OEDIPUS: I ask you: Who was the man that made a present of my body?

OLD MAN: He was keeper of the royal flocks and had a crowd of subordinates to tend them.

OEDIPUS: Tell me his name.

OLD MAN: An old man's memory is indistinct; it fades and fails in the passage of time.

OEDIPUS: Could you recognize the man by the cast of his face?

OLD MAN: Perhaps I could; sometimes a trifling mark brings back a memory which time has dimmed.

3 "Swell-foot."

OEDIPUS: The shepherds and their flocks must be brought to the sacred altars. Go quickly, slaves, fetch the man in charge of the herds.

(Exeunt slaves.)

OLD MAN: Whether logic or luck has hidden these things, let lie forever what has lain so long. The truth a man digs up sometimes hurts him.

OEDIPUS: Is any greater hurt than ours conceivable?

OLD MAN: The hurt you are so diligently seeking is, you must realize, very great. The public safety and the king's are in collision, each with equal pressure. Keep yourself neutral, disturb nothing, and let the fates unfold themselves.

OEDIPUS: A happy condition should not be disturbed; but when a situation is desperate it is safe to act.

OLD MAN: Are you seeking something nobler than royal birth? Take care you won't be sorry for the parentage you discover.

OEDIPUS: Even if my parentage is sorry, I must confirm it; I am determined to know the truth.

(Enter PHORBAS.)

There is Phorbas, old and decrepit, who used to have charge of the royal herds. (*To* OLD MAN) Do you recognize his name or face?

OLD MAN: His figure looks familiar; his face I cannot say I know, nor yet that it is strange. (*To* PHORBAS) When Laius was king, did you drive rich herds on Cithaeron's ranges?

PHORBAS: Cithaeron is always lush with fresh pasturage; in the summer I kept my flocks there.

OLD MAN: Do you know me?

PHORBAS: My memory is vague and uncertain.

OEDIPUS: Did you ever give this man a baby boy? Speak up. You hesitate? Why have your cheeks changed color? Why are you fumbling for words? Truth is impatient of delay.

PHORBAS: You start a train which has been shrouded by the long years.

OEDIPUS: Confess, or torture will extort the truth.

PHORBAS: A useless thing I gave him; the baby could never live to enjoy light and air.

OLD MAN: Away with the omen! He is alive, and I pray he may long be.

OEDIPUS: Why do you say the baby you gave did not survive?

PHORBAS: His limbs were cramped together by a thin iron rod driven through both feet, and the wound had swollen with a noisome infection which inflamed the little body.

OEDIPUS: (aside): Why seek further? Now the fates gather close. (To PHORBAS) Tell me who that baby was.

PHORBAS: Loyalty forbids.

OEDIPUS: Fire, someone! Flame will shake loyalty loose.

PHORBAS: Is the way to truth so bloody? Pardon, I beseech you.

OEDIPUS: If you think me cruel and savage, vengeance is ready to your hand: Speak the truth. Who was he? Who was the father that begot him, the mother who bore him?

PHORBAS: He was born of your wife.

OEDIPUS: Yawn open, earth, and you, master of the shadows, ruler of the shades, to deepest Tartarus sweep away the reversed roles of begetter and begotten! Pile stones upon my accursed head, citizens, hew me down with weapons. Let fathers, let sons, attack me with steel, let husbands and brothers take arms against me, let the sickened people snatch brands from the funeral pyre to hurl at me. I walk abroad an indictment to the age, an abomination to the gods, the ruin of sacred law, worthy of death the first day I drew awkward breath.

Now make your spirit stern, dare a deed worthy your wickedness. Onward, go, hurry to the palace, bestow upon your mother a house enlarged with children.

(Exit OEDIPUS.)

CHORUS: If I could fashion fate at my discretion, I would trim my sails to gentle breezes, lest a wind too fresh shake and bend the rigging. Let my barque be borne serenely by the moderate and even flow of a light breeze; let life bear me forward in the safety of the middle course.

Young Icarus in fear of the Cretan king made for the stars
in his folly; trusting in his contrived wings, he demanded too
much of them and strove to surpass real birds. His name alone
survives in the sea's. But Daedalus old and wise steered a
middle course; he halted in the midst of the clouds to wait
for his winged son (so a bird fleeing a threatening hawk
gathers her brood that fear has scattered), until the boy
thrashed about in the sea, his hands hampered by the fetters
of his foolhardy flight. Whatever is excessive hangs precarious.

(Enter MESSENGER, from the palace.)

But what is this? There is a sound at the doors, a woebegone servant of the king is beating his head with his fist.
Give the news you bring.

V

MESSENGER: When Oedipus knew he was overtaken by the
fate that had been foretold, knew his cursed identity, he
damned himself as guilty. With fell purpose he made for the
palace he hated, and strode into its interior with rapid pace.
He was like a lion raging in the African wold, its brow
menacing, its tawny mane shaking. His face beetled with
passion, his eyes glared, his groans rumbled from the depths,
cold sweat poured over his limbs, his mouth foamed with
twisted threats, submerged anguish overflowed in volume.
In his savage loneliness he is planning some enormity, as
monstrous as his own fate. "Why delay punishment?" he says.
"Someone stab this sinful heart with a sword, overwhelm me
with burning fire or with stones. Will no tigress or fierce bird
pounce upon my vitals? Cursed Cithaeron, you who contain
all wickedness, from your forests send your wild beasts against
me, send your mad dogs, bring Agave herself back. Soul of
mine, why do you fear death? Death alone delivers the innocent from fortune."

This said, he lays an impious hand on the hilt and draws
his sword. "Is this the way? Will so brief a punishment atone

for great crimes; will you pay for them all with a single stroke? You will die; for your father that is enough; but what compensation will you give for your mother, for the children you sinfully brought into the world, for your grieving country which is expiating your crimes by its own utter ruin? Adequate payment is impossible. For Oedipus alone has Nature reversed established laws and contrived unexampled births; let that same Nature devise unexampled punishment for me. Life after life and death after death should be your lot, repeated rebirths in which repeatedly to undergo unexampled punishment. Use your wit, wretch; choose something that cannot recur and make it last, some death long drawn out. Find a path where you will wander separate from the dead but dissociated from the living. Die, but not, like your father, wholly. Do you falter, soul of mine?"

Suddenly, see, a profuse shower floods his face; his cheeks flow with tears. "Is it enough to weep? Will this thin liquid be all my eyes can pour forth? They should be scourged from their sockets, follow their tears! Gods of marriage, is it enough? These eyes must be pried out!" His speech is frenzied; he raves. His cheeks are hectic, their angry flame is menacing; his eyes can scarcely keep within their sockets. His expression is wild, reckless, passionate, ferocious—a madman's. He groans, he shrieks horribly, he thrusts his hands into his face. But his glaring eyes protrude to meet them, they are glued to their matching hands, strain forward to touch them, rush upon their own laceration. Greedily he scrapes his sockets with hooked fingers, wrenches his eyeballs from their very roots, heaves them out. His hands stick in the empty sockets and his nails furrow the deep recesses now empty of their eyes. His savagery is now futile, his rage pointless.

Now light's trial is over. He raises his head, and when his hollow orbs sweep the spread of heaven he senses night. The shreds which hang from the crude digging he breaks off, and triumphantly he shouts to all the gods, "Spare my country, I pray; look, I have settled the score, I have paid the penalty I owed. At last I have found a night worthy of my spousals."

A repulsive shower drenches his face; his mutilated head spews gushing blood from ruptured veins.

CHORUS: The fates drive us; to the fates we must yield. No anxious care can change the spindle's ordained skein. Whatever mortal kind undergoes, whatever we do, comes from on high; Lachesis preserves her distaff's decree, and no hand may reverse it. All things proceed in the path laid out; our first day appoints our last. Even god may not turn the course of issues which are functions of their causes. For each man the course ordained proceeds to its end, and no prayer can change it. Many find fear itself the evil; they encounter their fate in the act of avoiding it.

There is a sound of doors opening. The man himself, sightless and with none to guide, makes his toilsome way.

(*Enter* OEDIPUS.)

OEDIPUS: Good; it is done. I have paid my father his due. Darkness is a relief. What god, at last placated, has swathed my head in black? Who has remitted my crimes? I have escaped accusing daylight. You are not obliged to your right hand, parricide; the light has fled from you. This is the proper face for Oedipus.

CHORUS: Look, there is Jocasta, wild and distraught, dashing forward with a frantic gait; she is like Agave, smitten with frenzy, who wrenched her son's head off and realized what she had done. She hesitates to speak to the broken wretch; she yearns to, but is afraid. Now shame yields to woe, but still her first words stick in her throat.

JOCASTA: What shall I call you? My son? Do you stick at it? But you are my son. Are you ashamed to be? Speak, my son, though you had rather not; why do you turn your head, your empty face, away?

OEDIPUS: Who is it that forbids me to enjoy my darkness? Who gives me back my eyes? It is my mother's voice, yes, my mother's. My effort was in vain. To meet again is anathema. Wastes of seas must separate our wickednesses, some hidden land strip one from the other; if beneath this world there hangs another, facing different stars and an alien sun, let it receive one of us.

JOCASTA: Your dereliction was fated, and fate cannot make guilt.

OEDIPUS: Spare your words, Mother, and spare my ears: I beg of you, by this shell of my mutilated body, by the unblessed pledges of my blood, by all that is right and all that is wrong in our relationship.

JOCASTA: (aside): Why so numb, my soul? You are accomplice in crime; why refuse to share the punishment? Every decency of human usage you have confounded and destroyed, incestuous woman. Die, take sword and banish your accursed spirit. If the father of the gods himself should shake the world and hurl his jagged lightning with angry hand, my punishment could never equal my offense. Come, Oedipus, if you are a parricide, accommodate your mother; only that is wanting to complete your work. I must seize the sword. By this blade perished my husband—but why not call him by his true name?—my father-in-law. Shall I plunge the weapon into my bosom, or press it deep into my bared throat? But do you not know where the wound belongs? Strike here, my right hand, strike this womb which had room for both husband and son.

(JOCASTA dies.)

CHORUS: She lies dead. Her lifeless hand covers the wound; the gushing blood forces the sword out.

OEDIPUS: You, oracular god who presides over truth, you I reproach. My father only I owed the fates; doubly a parricide, more guilty than I feared, I have murdered my mother also, for it is my sin that killed her. Lying Phoebus, I have outdone the impious fates.

With timorous step follow the blurred path, with hanging gait drag your feet, guide them through thick blackness with groping hand. Now mend your pace, take strides albeit treacherous, onward, away, march—but halt; you might stumble over your mother.

All who are weary in body and heavy with sickness, you whose listless hearts strain to bear half-living, look, I fly, I depart; lift up your heads. After me heaven's atmosphere will be gentler. The prostrate sufferers who struggle for faint life may now easily draw vital draughts of air. Go, do your service to the departed; with myself I rid the country of its lethal infection. Come with me, you turbulent fates, Disease, you palsied monster, Emaciation, black Plague, rabid Anguish, with me, come. These are my proper guides!

FINIS

SENECA

THYESTES

Introductory Note

The cycle of Greek stories which was most prolific in themes for tragedy was that involving the legendary dynasty of Argos in the Peloponnese, of which Agamemnon and Menelaus, Clytemnestra and Helen, Orestes and Electra, are the most familiar figures. The line begins with Tantalus, king of Lydia, son of Jupiter and a nymph, and father of Pelops and Niobe. At a banquet Tantalus attempted to serve to the gods the flesh of his son Pelops (who was subsequently restored to life); in consequence, he was condemned to be eternally *tantalized* in Hades. The ghost of Tantalus opens the Prologue to the present play. Tantalus' son Pelops (who gave his name to the Peloponnese, which means "Pelops' isle") won the hand of Hippodamia by unfairly defeating her father Oenomaus in a bride-race; Oenomaus was wrecked when his charioteer Myrtilus, who had been bribed by Pelops, secretly removed the linchpins from his chariot. Pelops' sons were Atreus (father of Agamemnon and Menelaus) and Thyestes; they killed their half brother Chrysippus, and Pelops banished them with the curse that they and their posterity would die by each other's hands. At Pelops' death it was agreed that the brothers would rule alternately, but Atreus retained possession of the throne. Thyestes seduced Atreus' wife Aerope and with her help stole from Atreus' stalls the golden-fleeced ram which betokened kingship for its possessor. Atreus banished Thyestes, but the affront rankled, and he resolved on the horrible vengeance which is the subject of the present play. Besides the three sons (Tantalus, Plisthenes, and one unnamed) whom Atreus slew, Thyestes begot another, Aegisthus, by an incestuous union with his daughter. It was this Aegisthus who seduced Clytemnestra, wife of Atreus' son Agamemnon, and caused the murder of Agamemnon himself; the story is told in the Agamemnon plays of Aeschylus and of Seneca. Subsequently,

431

Agamemnon's son Orestes avenged his father by murdering
Aegisthus and his own mother Clytemnestra, and was pursued
by the avenging Furies. The court of the Areopagus, newly
instituted by Athena, absolved Orestes and put an end to the
curse on the house of Atreus.

No story in classical mythology is more widely known. Seg-
ments of it were treated by all ancient tragedians, and echoes
of their interpretations still reverberate in our own literature
and in the terminology of psychology. Yet no Greek model for
Seneca's *Thyestes* has survived, and although the feast of Thyestes is known to us from frequent allusions, Seneca's play
is our only full literary treatment of it. But this uniqueness
is not the only claim the *Thyestes* can make upon our attention. It offers a complete and concise introduction to Seneca's
regular approach and manner, and although the action is
even more frankly repulsive than usual, given Seneca's pre-
mises and purposes its horror is attractive rather than otherwise. The protagonists are after all not intended to typify
ordinary humanity; a passion so intense that it affects the
courses of sun, moon, and stars sets them apart from other
men, and they engage our interest not as fellow adventurers
through the encounters of life but as spectacular prodigies.
The lesser persons—the doomed boys, the Henchman, the
Messenger, the Chorus—do appeal by reason of their ordinary
humanity, and provide a gauge for assessing the more monstrous figures. The spectacle, therefore, although it is horrible,
is not morally shocking, because the perpetrators are outside
ordinary standards; the demonstration of passion so intense
may even be edifying, in the sense that it enlarges our con-
ception of human potentiality. It is clearly and intentionally
edifying in showing the evil results of a spirit of vengeance
and in its repeated praise of a life of simplicity which is
immune to such horrors. Nor do we have the immorality of
evil triumphing over good. As Atreus says, Thyestes could not
have been overreached unless he himself meant to overreach,
and the character of Thyestes, as traditionally received and as
established in the play, deprives him of any sympathy.

Characters

Atreus, king of Argos, son of Pelops and grandson of Tantalus

Thyestes, brother of Atreus, who has banished him for se-
ducing his wife and attempting to seize his throne

Tantalus (named for his great-grandfather), eldest son of
Thyestes; the other two sons, of whom only Plisthenes
is named, are silent characters

Ghost of Tantalus, who was founder of the dynasty and
its criminality

Fury, charged with avenging injury to kin

Henchman of Atreus

Messenger

Chorus, Mycenaean elders

Scene: *The palace at Argos and its approaches.*

THYESTES

I

(*The* GHOST OF TANTALUS *arises; the* FURY *looks on.*)

GHOST OF TANTALUS: Who is dragging me up from the home of the damned as I snatch at elusive victuals with greedy lips? What god, damn it, would again show Tantalus the houses of the living? Have they found something worse than parching thirst in the midst of water, than hunger always openmouthed? It can't be that Sisyphus' slippery stone will come my shoulders' way, or that Ixion's whirling wheel will pull my limbs apart, or that Tityus' torment—he lies in a vast cavern feeding black birds with his scooped-out vitals, and at night he fills out what he lost by day to furnish a full crib for new-come monsters—can it be that I shall have that assignment? What is the new torture I am being transferred to? Whoever you are, strict judge of the shades who assigns the dead their new punishments, if you can pile on a penalty at which the turnkey of our terrible dungeon would shudder, at which gloomy Acheron would quake, for fear of which even I would tremble, go find it. From my stock there is arising a brood that will outdo its own ancestry; it will dare crimes none has dared before, and make me seem innocuous. Any vacant space in the accursed region my line shall fill; as long as Pelops' house stands, Minos will be kept busy.

FURY: On, detestable ghost, scourge your impious house to madness. Set up competition in every category of crime, let them draw swords by turn, let there be no limit to passion, no shame, let blind fury goad their minds, let the fathers' insanity persist and the long chain of guilt march onward with their children, let none have space to abhor old crime for the new that will always emerge, not singly but manifold, and let crime be multiplied even while it is punished. Proud brothers shall lose their realms, shall recall the exiled; the wavering fortune of a violent dynasty shall totter in uncertainty, the powerful shall become wretched and the wretched powerful, and chance shall heave the kingdom with unremitting tides. Expelled for crime, they shall return to crime when god restores them to their land, and shall be as loathsome to all men as to themselves. Nothing shall passion hold forbidden: Brother shall dread brother, father son, son father; children shall scurvily perish and yet more scurvily be born; a murderous wife shall doom her husband; they shall carry war across the sea, and every land shall be manured with the blood they shed; over the grand leaders of nations triumphant Lust shall exult. In this shameful house adultery shall be negligible; a brother's duty and loyalty and every law shall be annihilated. Heaven itself shall not be exempt from your wickedness—why do the stars glitter in the firmament, why do their fires maintain the brilliance they owe the world? Night shall be transformed, daylight shall depart from heaven. Confound the household deities, fetch hatred, slaughter, death, fill the whole house with Tantalus!

Deck the tall column, make the doors green with festive laurel, light up a blaze worthy of your advent, repeat Philomela's crime, but with more victims. Why is the uncle's hand idle? Thyestes is not yet bewailing his son; when will Atreus get to work? The cauldrons must be set seething over the fire, the severed members must be passed in, blood must stain the ancestral hearth, the banquet table must be laid—you have had part in such criminal feasts before. We have made you free for this day, have released you from starvation for the sake of that board; satisfy your craving, wine mixed with gore will be drunk before your eyes. I have found a meal which even you would shun—stop, where are you off to in such a rush?

GHOST OF TANTALUS: To my pools and streams and receding waters, to the laden trees which dodge my very lips. Let me go back to my dungeon's black pallet. If you think me not wretched enough, let me change my river: Leave me in the middle of your channel, Phlegethon, circle me with a flood of flame.

Hear Tantalus' voice, you who are sentenced to undergo punishments decreed by the Fates' law, you who lie trembling under an eroded cave in fear of the mountain about to crash down on you, you who shudder at the fierce maws of gluttonous lions and the grim bands of Furies in which you are entangled, you now half-burned who are fending off the torches thrust at you—believe me, I have had experience: You must *love* your punishments. When can *I* manage to get away from the upper world?

FURY: First confound your house, bring with you battle and lust for steel, the king's bane, rouse savage breasts to berserk rage.

GHOST OF TANTALUS: I should suffer punishments, not be one. I am dispatched like some toxic fume from the riven earth, like some plague to strew grim destruction among people; I must direct my own grandchildren to a repulsive enormity. Ah, great father of the gods, and mine too, however embarrassing, though my impertinent tongue be requited with some torment I will not keep silent. I warn you all: Do not violate your hands with accursed murder, do not spatter the altars with insane wickedness. I shall stand fast and fend off the crime—(*To the* FURY) Why are you brandishing your lash at my face, why do you glare at me and menace me with snakes? Why are you stirring the hunger in my inmost marrow? My heart is on fire with blazing thirst and the flame is licking through my scorched vitals. I yield.

FURY: This same mania take and distribute over the whole house. They must be overborne the selfsame way, they must thirst viciously for each other's blood. The house senses your advent and shudders throughout at your tainted touch. You have played your part to the full. Off with you now to the infernal caves and your familiar river; now the earth is irked and chafed by your tread. Do you see how the water is drawn backward and deserts its springs, how the river banks are empty, how a fiery wind carries the occasional clouds away? Every tree grows pallid, and the vanishing fruit leaves the branches naked. Where the Isthmus which divides neighboring seas with a thin strip of land roared with the near breakers on this side and that, the sounds now reach the shore from a remote distance. Lerna has retreated, the Phoronean artery has hidden, sacred Alpheus does not issue its waters, Cithaeron's ridges are nowhere hoar, their snow laid away, and the noble Argives fear a recurrence of Phaethon's drought. Look, even Titan is hesitant about bidding his horses advance and using his reins to make the day proceed to its doom.

(Exeunt.)

CHORUS: If any god loves Achaean Argos and Pisa's houses famous for chariots, if any loves Corinth's Isthmian realm, its twin harbors and cleft sea, if any loves Taygetus' conspicuous snows which Sarmatian Boreas lays upon its lofty ridges in the wintry season and summer melts with its sail-filling Etesians. if any is concerned for Alpheus' cool and crystal stream where Olympia's renowned stadium stands—let him incline his benign divinity to ward off these recurrent alternations of crime; let not a bad grandfather be followed by a worse grandson or lesser lines choose weightier crimes. May the accursed progeny of dry Tantalus be exhausted at last and put away its savage impulses. Enough of sins; right has not asserted itself, nor has common wrong. Myrtilus who deceived his lord was betrayed and succumbed; he was swept away by his own brand of loyalty and made a sea notorious by the new name he gave it—no tale is more familiar to Ionian shipping. When his little son ran to his father's kiss he was caught up on the sword's point and fell an untimely victim to the hearth; it was your hand that butchered him, Tantalus, to spread a feast for the gods you entertained. Eternal hunger is requital for such viands, eternal thirst.

There stands Tantalus foredone with empty gullet. Over his guilty head hang provisions abundant but more elusive than Phineus' harpies. On either side of him a tree is weighed down by its laden branches which bow and quiver with their

fruit and tease his gaping jaws. Greedy he is and impatient
of delay, yet he gives over touching it, cheated in so many attempts, and turns his eyes away and clenches his lips and
fetters his tongue behind the bars of his teeth. But then the
whole grove droops its riches nearer and the complaisant fruit
above mocks him from its inert leaves and rekindles his
hunger, which constrains him to work his unavailing hands.
When he has put them forth and has been excited by a near
miss, the whole harvest of the movable forest is snatched upward. Then severer pangs of thirst attack, and when his blood
has been heated to a blaze by its flaming brands the wretch
stands snapping at the waves before him, but the fugitive
liquid turns away and leaves its bed bare, frustrating his attempts at pursuit. From the eddying whirl he drinks deep—
of dust.

II

(*Enter* ATREUS.)

ATREUS (*soliloquizing*): Spiritless, nerveless, spineless, and
(what I consider a tyrant's worst reproach in high issues)
vengeanceless, are you passing your time in idle plaints after
so many injuries? After a brother's betrayal and the rupture
of every obligation, are you merely an indignant Atreus? The
whole world should be clashing arms by now, navies should be
scouring both the twin seas, city and countryside should be
blazing flames and drawn swords sparkle on every side. All
the Argolid plain shall reverberate to the tramp of our cavalry;
neither forests nor citadels perched on lofty mountain peaks
shall afford the enemy shelter; its people shall leave Mycenae
en masse to sound war's clarion. Any that protect or shelter
that hated head shall die a grievous death. Upon myself, too, I
would have this stately mansion of renowned Pelops crash
down, provided it crashed down on my brother also. Up, my
soul, wreak a deed no posterity can approve but none ignore.
Unholy, ruthless, gory must my venture be, a deed my brother
would wish were his. Crimes cannot be avenged without out-

doing them. But what could be savage enough to surpass him? Is he humble? Does he accept a limit to his prosperity? Is he inactive with exhaustion? I know the man's untamable spirit; bent it cannot be, but it can be broken. Before he makes himself strong, therefore, before he readies his resources, I must take the offensive; his attack must not find me quiescent. He will either destroy or perish; the crime is the prize for the man who seizes the initiative.

HENCHMAN (*who has entered in time to hear the end of* ATREUS' *soliloquy*): Does your people's disapproval not give you pause?

ATREUS: This is the greatest prerogative of royalty: People must praise as well as tolerate their master's doings.

HENCHMAN: Where fear constrains praise, fear makes enemies. The man who aims at the glory of true favor will prefer praise of the heart to praise of the voice.

ATREUS: True praise falls even to a humble lot, false only to the powerful. Men must like what they dislike.

HENCHMAN: The king should like what is honorable, and all men will like the same.

ATREUS: Sovereignty is precarious where the ruler is limited to the honorable.

HENCHMAN: Where there is no shame, no concern for right, no scruple, loyalty, faith, sovereignty's base is unsteady.

ATREUS: Scruple, loyalty, faith are citizen virtues; kings may go as they please.

HENCHMAN: Count it wrong to hurt even a bad brother.

ATREUS: Any hurt that is wrong to do to a brother is right to do to him. What did his criminality leave intact, when did he forbear to sin? My wife he reft from me by adultery, my kingdom by theft. The ancient symbol of our rule he procured by guile, and by guile confounded our house. In Pelops' stately barns there is a noble flock, and a mystic ram is the leader of the affluent company. Over all his body hangs a fleece of molten gold, and the gilded scepters carried by the successors to the Tantalid throne are from his back. Who holds the ram holds the throne, and to him the fortune of the great dynasty yields. The hallowed ram grazes on safe pasturage in a secluded meadow hedged with stone; a rocky wall protects his grazing. This ram treacherous Thyestes carried away; he made the partner of my bed his accomplice in the brazen and monstrous iniquity. Hence has flowed the whole accursed stream of mutual destruction. I have roamed my realm as a trembling exile, none of my kin is secure from ambush, my wife is debauched, the pledge of [alternate] rule is shattered, my house is sick, my offspring questionable—the only certainty is that my brother is my enemy. Why stand gaping? It is high time to begin; put on your courage. Tantalus and Pelops—these are your patterns; my hands must do as theirs have done.

Tell me, how shall I butcher the blackguard?

HENCHMAN: A sword stroke will make him spit his hateful soul out.

ATREUS: It is punishment's conclusion you speak of; my wish is the punishment itself. An easygoing tyrant can put men to death; in my reign death must be a favor to beg.

HENCHMAN: Is kinship's obligation not a consideration?

ATREUS: Out, kinship's obligation, if ever you were housed in my demesne! Come, Furies' troop and Erinyes,[1] and Megaera brandishing her twin torches! The rage in my heart is not hot enough; I must be filled with ampler fiendishness.

HENCHMAN: What monstrosity is your mad passion shaping?

ATREUS: Nothing passion's ordinary measure can hold. I shall leave no crime unperpetrated; none is enough.

HENCHMAN: The sword?

ATREUS: Not enough.

HENCHMAN: Fire, then?

ATREUS: Still not enough.

HENCHMAN: Then what weapon will your hot anger use?

ATREUS: Thyestes himself.

HENCHMAN: This is worse than anger.

ATREUS: I agree. A frenzied tumult pounds at my bosom and churns its depths. I am swept away; where, I do not know; but

---

[1] Fomenters of strife among kindred.

I am swept away. The ground rumbles from its lowest abysses, the clear sky thunders, the palace creaks at every joint as if it were shattering, the Lares stir and turn their faces aside—it must be done; the crime which makes you afraid, ye gods, must be done.

HENCHMAN: What pitch of passion are you building up to?

ATREUS: Burgeoning in my soul is a thing larger and broader than ordinary, a thing beyond the limits of human ways, and it is goading my reluctant hands; what the thing is I do not know, but it is very big. So be it. On with it, my soul. It is a deed worthy of Thyestes—and worthy of Atreus. Each shall commit it. The Odrysian house once saw a feast unspeakable—it was an enormity, I confess, but it was resorted to, and my passion must find something greater. Inspire me with your example, mother Procne and sister Philomela; our cases are alike; stand by me and direct my hand. The greedy father shall eagerly rend his sons and devour his own limbs. It is well, it is ample. This is the mode of punishment I choose.

But where is he? Why is Atreus so long dallying in innocence? Already the whole picture of slaughter comes into focus before my eyes, there is the father's loss heaped on the platter before him—my soul, why recoil, why fall back before the act? You must go through with it, on! The most repulsive part of the crime will be his doing.

HENCHMAN: But how will he be lured to step into the trap? He sees danger everywhere.

ATREUS: He could not be overreached if he did not mean to overreach. It is his hope to acquire my kingdom, and in this hope he will confront Jove brandishing his thunderbolt, in this hope he will brave the menace of the raging whirlpool and venture into the perilous shoal of Libyan Syrtes, in this hope he will undergo what he deems the worst trial of all— he will look upon his brother.

HENCHMAN: Who will give him assurance of peace? Whom will he trust so far?

ATREUS: Wicked hopes are gullible. But I will give my sons

a commission to their uncle: The banished vagabond is to
leave his hostels, exchange wretchedness for a throne, and rule
Argos in shared sovereignty. If Thyestes proves adamant and
spurns my urging, it will sway his sons, who are inexperienced
and tired of their heavy troubles and easy to gull. However
stubborn the man, the combination of inveterate lust for kingship on this side and grim need and grievous hardship on
that will force submission.

HENCHMAN: Time has made his sufferings tolerable by now.

ATREUS: You are mistaken. The sense of injury grows day
by day. It is easy to show patience under misfortune's stroke
but to continue patient is hard.

HENCHMAN: Choose other agents for your grim plan.

ATREUS: The young are readier to heed bad lessons.

HENCHMAN: They will apply to their father what you teach
them with reference to their uncle. Wickedness often turns
upon its teacher.

ATREUS: If no one should teach them the ways of deceit and
crime, the throne would. Are you afraid they will turn bad?
They were born so. What you call savage and harsh, the policy
you think cruel and impious, is quite likely being practiced
on the other side as well.

HENCHMAN: Will your sons know it is a cheat that is being
staged?

ATREUS: At such an inexperienced age discretion is not to
be expected; they might reveal the plot. The lesson of silence
comes with the manifold troubles of life.

HENCHMAN: So you will deceive the agents of your deceit?

ATREUS: To keep them free of blame and fault. What need
is there to implicate my sons? My hatred will unfold itself
through my own responsibility.

You are shirking, my soul, you are retreating. If you are
considerate of your sons you will be considerate of his also.
Agamemnon must be the witting accomplice of my crime,
Menelaus must knowingly assist his father. Clarification of
their questionable paternity can be fetched from this crime:

If they balk at this war and refuse to give play to hatred, if they call him uncle, then he is their father. On with the test.

But a nervous expression can reveal a great deal and grand schemes invite unintentional betrayal; they must *not* know the importance of the project they serve. And *you* must cover my undertaking.

HENCHMAN: I need no admonition; loyalty and fear will lock it in my heart, but mainly loyalty.

(Exeunt.)

CHORUS: What fury scourges you to shed blood by turn, to approach the scepter through crime? You do not realize, in your craving for palaces, wherein kingship consists. It is not wealth nor the purple robe nor the royal tiara nor the shiny gold doors which make a king. A king is a man who has put aside fear and the distemper of a brooding heart; who is not moved by overweening ambition or the mercurial favor of the unthinking mob, by the yield of the western mines or the billows of gold carried on Tagus' clear channel, or the harvests trodden in Libya's torrid threshing floors; who does not quake at the downward path of the streaking thunderbolt, nor at Eurus as he harries the sea, nor at the rabid swelling of the gusty Adriatic in its savage strait; who is not awed by the soldier's lance or his naked steel; who maintains his position unimpinged and from his vantage sees all things beneath him; who willingly goes to meet his fate and makes no complaint of death.

Though monarchs combine—those who lord it over the sparse Scythians, those who hold broad dominion over the shoals of the ruddy shore and the spacious blood-red sea with its translucent gems, and those whose Caspian heights baffle the rugged Sarmatians; though the bold treader upon the frozen Danube enter the lists and the Chinese (wherever they may live) who are ennobled by their silks—it is still the sound mind which possesses true kingship. He has no need of horses nor of armor nor of the spiritless missiles which the Parthian volleys from afar as he feigns flight, no need of artillery whirling boulders from a distance to raze cities to the ground. A king is a man who fears nothing, a king is a man who craves nothing; such kingship each man bestows upon himself.

Whoso will may stand on royalty's slippery pinnacle in his power; I would be steeped in sweet repose. Sheltered in obscurity, let me enjoy easy tranquility, let my life flow quietly on unnoticed by the citizenry. And when my days have thus passed without commotion, I shall die an elderly plebeian. Death weighs heavily on the man who is known to many, but not to himself, when he dies.

III

(THYESTES *with his sons is seen approaching.*)

THYESTES: There is my city's sky line that I yearned for, the stateliness of Argos, and the most blessed sight of all to a wretched exile, a stretch of my native soil and my ancestral gods—if gods there are. There are the majestic Cyclopean towers, too handsome for human workmanship, the stadium thronged with young men, where more than once I won the prized palm with my father's chariot. Argos will come to meet me, the populace will turn out in crowds—and Atreus? Back to your sylvan retreats; the thick woodland, and the life mingled with and like the animals', is preferable. The bright glitter of kingship is not a thing to blind my eyes with its spurious sheen; when you examine the gift, scrutinize the giver also. Just now, when I was where people thought life harsh, I was stalwart and happy, and now I find myself afraid. My spirit sticks and craves to carry my body back, but I move forward with reluctant step.

TANTALUS (*aside*): How faltering (what can this be?) my father's step! He is in a daze, he turns his face back, his posture shows uncertainty.

THYESTES (*to himself*): Why waver, my soul, why torture logic so easy? Will you trust such unreliable elements as a brother and a throne? Will you fear deprivations you have already conquered and tamed, will you flee hardships well invested? Misery has proved a boon. Turn your step back while you may, pull yourself away.

TANTALUS: What can make you turn back from your country, Father, now you have seen it? Why draw back your pouch when blessings are falling in it? Your brother has banished his anger and comes back to you, has restored your share of the kingdom, has rejoined the severed limbs of your house, has given you back to yourself.

THYESTES: You ask the cause of my fear; I do not myself know. I see nothing to be afraid of, but I am afraid nevertheless. I decide to go on, but my knees falter and my limbs give way, and I am carried against my will in a direction other than the one I aim for. It is like a vessel propelled by oar and sail which a tide counter to oar and sail sweeps backward.

TANTALUS: Overcome whatever it is that obstructs and impedes your purpose. See what rich rewards await your return. Father, you can be king.

THYESTES: Because I can die.

TANTALUS: Sovereign power—

THYESTES: Is nothing if you desire nothing.

TANTALUS: You can leave it to your children.

THYESTES: Kingship has no space for two.

TANTALUS: Will a man who can be happy prefer to be miserable?

THYESTES: The titles which make greatness attractive are spurious, believe me, and fear of straitness is vain. When I stood towering I was never without dread and feared the very sword at my side. How good it is to stand in no man's light, to take carefree food lying on the ground! Crime has no entry to the cottage, and the victuals on a frugal board are safe; poison is quaffed in cups of gold. I speak from experience: Adversity is better than prosperity. My house is not perched threateningly atop a high hill to overawe the humble citizenry, my high ceilings do not shine with polished ivory, no sentinel guards my sleep. I do not go fishing with whole fleets, I do not drive the sea back with piled breakwaters. I do not feed my shameless belly with the tribute of nations, no estates are harvested for my account beyond the Getae or among the Parthians. I am not adored with incense, nor are my altars decked out while Jove is neglected. My rooftop is not planted with a nodding forest nor do a variety of artificially heated pools give off clouds of steam. My days are not given to sleep nor my nights joined in unbroken orgies. No one is afraid of me, and my house is safe without weapons; deep peace attends my modest estate. To be content without kingship is ample kingdom.

TANTALUS: But sovereignty must not be refused if a god offers it; you do not have to struggle for it; your brother is asking you to rule.

THYESTES: Asking? That is frightening. There is a trick somewhere.

TANTALUS: The sense of kinship often returns where it has been supplanted, and normal affection recovers the force it has lost.

THYESTES: His brother cherish affection for Thyestes? Sooner will the sea wash the heavenly Bears and the rapacious waves of the Sicilian strait stand still, harvests grow to ripeness on the Ionian Sea and black night illuminate the earth; sooner shall water unite with fire, life with death, and wind enter a solemn compact with the sea.

TANTALUS: What kind of cheat are you afraid of?

THYESTES: Every kind. I can set no limits to my fear; his power is as enormous as his hatred.

TANTALUS: What power has he over you?

THYESTES: For myself I am no longer afraid. It is you who make Atreus frightening to me.

TANTALUS: Are you afraid of being overreached when you are so cautious?

THYESTES: Caution is too late in the midst of hostility. But on we go. In this one point I assert my fatherhood: I will follow, not lead you.

TANTALUS: God will watch over our well-considered course. Move forward without misgivings.

(*Enter* ATREUS, *at first unnoticed by* THYESTES *and his sons.*)

ATREUS: My spread net has caught the game and holds it fast. I see himself, and the whelps of the odious breed along with the sire. Now my hatred has a fair pitch. Thyestes has walked into my hands at last. I can scarcely curb my temper, my spirit is restive on the leash. It is like a sharp-set Umbrian hound; as it tracks the game and snuffs the trail with muzzle to the ground it is held on a long leash, and when the faint scent tells it the boar is far off, it minds and scours the ground without baying; but when the game is near it strains at the collar with all its might and chides its dawdling master with sobs and wrenches away from his hold. When passion sniffs blood it brooks no cover, but covered it shall be. See how his hair, thick with filth, covers his woebegone face, how his dirty beard straggles. Now I shall exhibit my "faith."

(*To* THYESTES) I am delighted to see my brother. Give me the embrace I have longed for. Any anger there has been must be done with. From this day forth ties of blood and kin shall be fostered and accursed hatred be purged from our hearts.

THYESTES: I might have extenuated my record if you had not shown such magnanimity. But I confess, Atreus, I confess to everything you have believed of me. Black indeed has your affection made my case. Unequivocally guilty is the man whom so good a brother has found guilty. Tears are my only plea; you are the first to see me a suppliant. These hands which have never touched a man's foot now beseech you. Put all anger aside, erase its growth from your mind and away with it. As hostages for my good faith, brother, take these innocent boys.

ATREUS: Up from my knees; use your hands to embrace me. And you, too—a fine lot of boys, an old man's bulwark—come, cling to my neck. Take off your common clothes (spare my eyes!) and put on a costume like mine. Gladly assume your fraternal share of sovereignty. I shall have the higher praise for not hurting my brother but restoring his hereditary dignity to him; holding sovereignty is accident; giving it, virtue.

THYESTES: May the gods give you due requital for your

great deserts. My squalor refuses the royal tiara, my unblessed hand shrinks from the scepter. Allow me an inconspicuous existence in the crowd.

ATREUS: This kingdom has room for two.

THYESTES: Whatever you have I will consider mine, Brother.

ATREUS: Who can reject the gifts of fortune's tide?

THYESTES: One who has experienced how easily they ebb.

ATREUS: Will you frobid your brother to win great glory?

THYESTES: Your glory is achieved, mine is to seek. It is my firm resolve to reject kingship.

ATREUS: I shall abandon mine unless you accept your share.

THYESTES: I accept it. I shall bear the title of king imposed upon me, but laws and army and I too shall be at your discretion.

ATREUS (*crowning* THYESTES): Wear these links I set upon your worshipful head. I go to offer the appointed sacrifice to the gods.

(*Exeunt.*)

CHORUS: Could anyone believe this? Fierce, hot-headed, truculent, willful Atreus stood mesmerized at the sight of his brother. There is no power stronger than the true bond of kinship. Hostile brawling between strangers persists, but where true love has held in bond it will hold again. When wrath, pricked to fury by momentous issues, has ruptured amity and sounded war's clarion, when the trappings of agile squadrons resound, when the brandished sword glitters on this side and on that as the raging war god showers strokes in his lust for fresh blood, then will kinship suppress the sword and lead the chafing adversaries to join hands in peace.

What god has transformed this intense melee to sudden quiet? A moment ago armed civil strife roared through Mycenae; pale mothers clutched their sons, and the wife trembled for her mailed husband as his reluctant hand grasped a sword rusty with the disuse of peace. One man struggled to repair dilapidated walls, another to reinforce towers crumbling with neglect, another to make the gates fast with iron bars, and on the bastions the fearful sentry bivouacked through the anxious night: War's terror is worse than war. But now the sword's savage menace has collapsed, now the trumpet's ominous tocsin is mute, now the skirling of the hoarse horns is silent; deep peace has been called back to the happy city. Just so, when the waves well up from the abyss under the north wind's lashing of the Bruttian strait, when Scylla reverberates in her battered cavern and sailors ashore tremble at the sea which rapacious Charybdis sucks up and spews forth, when savage Cyclops squatting on Aetna's seething crag fears his father Neptune with his flooding wash may quench the roaring fires in his everlasting smithy, when Ithaca's tremors make ragged Laertes fear his realm will be submerged, then when the wind's violence subsides, the sea lies smoother than any pool. Now the waters which merchantmen feared to negotiate are flattened out into a spacious playground for yachts, and the full sails strewn over it make a pretty sight. Where but lately the Cyclades dislodged by the raging blast were afraid of drowning, it is now possible to count the fish deep down.

No lot is lasting; pain and pleasure give way to each other —pleasure more quickly. An hour lightly exchanges the lowest and the highest. The man crowned with diadem, before whom nations tremble on bended knee, at whose nod the Mede lays down his arms, and the Indian at the equator, and the Dahae, whose cavalry is a threat to the Parthians—uneasy is that man's hold of the scepter; he is apprehensive of revolutionary change, afraid of quick reverses and time's uncertainties.

You to whom the ruler of sea and land has vouchsafed high authority over death and life, lay aside your inflated and pompous bearing. All that a lesser being fears of you a greater master holds over you; your sovereignty is subject to a higher sovereignty. Whom the rising sun sees proud, the setting sun sees humble. No man should be confident in prosperity, none in adversity should despair of improvement. Clotho mingles one strand with the other, will allow no condition to stand fast, turns fate upward and downward. No man has had the

gods so propitious that he can promise himself the morrow.
God keeps our affairs moving in a rapid whirl.

IV

(A horrified MESSENGER *enters panting.)*

MESSENGER: Will some whirlwind carry me headlong through
the air and wrap me in a black cloud to thrust this unspeakable horror from my sight! What a house! Pelops even, and
Tantalus, would be ashamed.

CHORUS: What is the news you bring?

MESSENGER: What country is this? Is it Argos, is it Sparta
of the affectionate Twins, is it Corinth hugged by twin seas,
or is it the Ister which provides covert for the barbarous
Alans, the Hyrcanian jungle under its eternal snow, the
desert of the nomad Scyths? What place is this that knows
such indescribable monstrosity?

CHORUS: Speak out, unfold the mischief, whatever it is.

MESSENGER: If my mind can steady itself, if the terror that
freezes me loosens its clutch. The picture of the ghastly deed
sticks in my face. Take me somewhere far away, ye wild winds,
take me where daylight goes when it is snatched from us.

CHORUS: You do ill to keep us in suspense. Tell what makes
you shudder. Point out the man responsible. I do not ask *who*
but *which*. Speak up at once.

MESSENGER: On its high citadel, part of Pelops' palace faces
south. Its farthest wing rises as high as a mountain; it presses
down upon the city and affords a vantage for striking the
populace that is contumacious of its rulers. Here the huge
edifice which can house a multitude shines out; its gilded
beams are carried by noble columns of variegated color. Behind this familiar façade which is open to the public the
palatial establishment spreads in many directions. Deep in
the grounds is a mysterious area where an ancient grove is
enclosed in a recessed glade; this is the kingdom's holy of
holies. Here no tree offers pleasant shade or is ever tended by

pruning knife, but yew and cypress and a forest of inky ilex sway in gloom; a towering oak looks down upon the grove and dominates it. It is here that the Tantalids are used to inaugurate their rule and here to seek aid in adversity or danger. Votive offerings are affixed, noisy trumpets and broken chariots, spoils of the Myrtoan Sea, wheels cheated by the faked axle—the inventory of the clan's criminality hangs there. Here Pelops' Phrygian tiara is attached, here enemy spoil and an embroidered cape from a triumph over the barbarians.

Under the shade stands a dismal spring, whose sluggish water sticks in the black marsh; such is the ugly pool of ominous Styx by which the gods swear. It is rumored that in the blind night the gods of the dead groan from this place, clanking chains sound in the grove, and ghosts howl. Things terrifying even to hear are there seen. An age-old troop is released from ancient tombs and roams about, and monsters more horrible than any known cavort. More, the whole forest flickers with tongues of flame and the high balks glow without fire. Repeatedly the grove reverberates with threefold barking, repeatedly the palace is shaken with huge phantoms. Nor does day allay the terror; night is the grove's perquisite and even in broad daylight the eeriness of the dead holds sway. Here petitioners receive sure responses; fates are loosed from the inner shrine with a great bellow, and the cavern roars when the god frees his voice.

After raging Atreus entered this grove, dragging his brother's children—but who could do justice to the scene? Behind their backs he trusses the lads' noble hands and binds their sad heads with a purple fillet. Incense is not forgotten, nor sacramental wine, the salt meal to sprinkle on the victims, the knife. The complete order of service is followed; so great a deed must be ritually correct.

CHORUS: Who performs the service of the knife?

MESSENGER: He personally is the officiant, he personally pronounces the grim prayer and with violent lips chants the formula of death, he personally stands at the altars, he personally manipulates the chosen victims, arranges them, takes up the knife, he personally attends to the whole ritual—no detail is wanting. The grove begins to quake, and with the earth's tremors the whole palace teeters, like a man in doubt, uncertain in which direction to throw its weight. From the sky on the left a star skims by dragging a murky trail, the wine aspersed upon the fire is transformed to flowing blood, the crown slips from Atreus' head twice and thrice, and the ivories in the temples shed tears.

Everyone was disturbed by these portents, but Atreus, alone unmoved, perseveres and even overawes the gods who threaten him. And now, the preliminaries over, he stands by the altar with beetling, sidelong look. As a fasting tigress in the Ganges jungle wavers between two bullocks, greedy for both but undecided where she should first clamp her jaws—she directs her maw this way, then back to the other, and keeps her hunger on edge—so does flinty Atreus eye the bodies doomed to his unholy wrath. He hesitates over which to sacrifice first, which to immolate next. It makes no difference, but he still holds off and takes pleasure in arranging the sequence of his crime.

CHORUS: Still, whom *did* he attack first?

MESSENGER: The first place (you must not suppose he disregarded precedence of kinship) he dedicates to his grandfather's namesake: Tantalus is the first victim.

CHORUS: What was the boy's spirit when he was murdered, what was his expression?

MESSENGER: He stood indifferent and did not deign to offer pleas which must prove futile. The brute buried the sword in the wound, pressing so deep that his hand touched the neck. When the steel was withdrawn the corpse stood erect, and after hesitating long whether to fall on this side or that it fell upon its uncle. Then that brute dragged Plisthenes to the altar and thrust him by his brother. His head he amputated at a stroke, and when the neck was cut through the torso fell prone and the head rolled away, complaining with an unintelligible murmur.

CHORUS: After executing the double murder, what did he do next? Did he spare one boy or did he pile crime on crime?

MESSENGER: He was like a shaggy lion who springs triumphant upon the herd and wreaks widespread slaughter. The lion's maw drips gore, but though his hunger is quenched his fury is not assuaged; he charges the bulls on this side and that and threatens the calves though his fangs are now weary and slow. Precisely so did Atreus rage, his passion inflamed. He grasps the sword dripping with the double butchery, forgetting against whom he is raging, and with murderous hand drives the sword through the body; the sword that entered the boy's breast immediately protruded at his back. He falls, extinguishing the altar fires, and dies by the double gash.

CHORUS: Oh, savage crime!

MESSENGER: Are you horrified? If the crime stopped at this point it would be piety.

CHORUS: Is nature capable of atrocity beyond this?

MESSENGER: Do you suppose this was the consummation of the crime? It was only a stage.

CHORUS: What more could he do? Perhaps he cast the bodies out to be torn by wild animals and denied them cremation?

MESSENGER: If only he had denied them cremation! If only earth had not covered the departed or fire consumed them! He might even have dragged them out as ghastly provender for scavenging birds and beasts to feast on! In this case what is ordinarily counted an affliction is a thing to pray for—would that the father could see his sons unburied. Ah, crime which no age can believe, which posterity will deny! The entrails torn from the pulsing breast quiver, the lungs breathe, and the still-fluttering heart throbs. But Atreus manipulates the organs, inspects them for signs of the Fates, and observes the reticulation of their veins while the viscera are still warm.

The victims found acceptable, Atreus is at liberty for his brother's menu. He personally carves the severed body into portions; he separates the broad shoulders down to the trunk, disengages the arms, unfeelingly strips the flesh off, and hacks the bones. He keeps intact only the faces and the hands that had been stretched out to him in good faith. Some of the flesh is spitted on skewers and hung to drip over slow fires, some boiling water bobs up and down in a heated cauldron. The fire leaps over the meat set on it and is raked back into the throbbing hearth two or three times, where it smolders grudgingly in impatience at the enforced delay. The liver sputters on its skewer; it is hard to say whether the remains or the flames sighed louder. The fire goes off into pitchy smoke, and the somber, heavy cloud does not rise to the air in an upright column but settles on the very household gods in an ugly mist.

Ah, patient Phoebus, though you fled backward and submerged shattered daylight in midheaven, your setting was too late. The father tears gobbets off his sons and champs his own members with ghastly lips. His hair is spruce with perfumed ointment, and he is heavy with wine. Repeatedly his food sticks in his choking gullet. The sole saving grace in your disaster, Thyestes, is that you do not realize it. But this too will soon pass. Though Titan himself should reverse his chariot and steer it on a backward course, though thick night be ordered out at day's proper rising to swathe the loathsome act in unexampled darkness, it must nevertheless be visible; every iniquity will be published.

(*Exit* MESSENGER; *darkness settles over the scene.*)

CHORUS: Whither, father of earth and sky at whose rising all dark night's comeliness flees, whither do you turn your course, why do you extinguish daylight at high noon? Why so hasty, Phoebus, in hiding our sight of you? Vesper, evening's harbinger, has not yet summoned night's luminaries, its westward-turning wheel has not yet finished its course and been discharged, the third trumpet has not yet sounded day's decline, the ploughman with oxen still fresh is astonished that the supper hour has come so soon. What has driven you from your heavenly course? What has happened to dislodge your horses from their established track? Can it be that Dis's prison is opened and the vanquished Giants are again attempting war? Can it be that maimed Tityus has renewed the ancient

wrath in his foredone heart? Has Typhoeus thrown his mountain off and extricated his frame? Is a road being paved on
high by the Giants of Phlegra field and is Thracian Ossa piled
on Thessalian Pelion?

The customary alternations of the firmament have ceased;
there will be no setting, no rising. The dewy mother of morning light, Dawn, whose use is to hand the god his reins, is
astonished at her threshold's change of function; it was not
her part to wet the weary chariot down or to plunge the
sweaty and steaming horses in the sea. A novice in this un-
accustomed haven, Sun finds Dawn at his setting and bids
darkness fall though Night is yet unready. The stars do not
take their posts and no fires twinkle in heaven; Luna does not
push the thick shadows aside. But whatever this means, would
it were night! Our hearts are a-tremble, a-tremble, they are
smitten with a great fear that the universe may totter and
crash in fate's ruin, that shapeless Chaos may once more overwhelm gods and men, that Nature may once more cover up
lands and circling sea and the wandering stars that spangle
the firmament. No more shall their leader who guides time's
flow by the rising of his eternal torch provide signs of summer
and winter; no more shall Luna intercepting Phoebus' flame
dispel night's terrors and outstrip her brother's driving on the
arc of her shorter track. The whole troop of gods in a heap
shall descend into a single cleft. The Zodiac through which
the hallowed stars move, whose path bisects the Zones at an
angle, who guides the long years and is their standard-bearer,
shall fall, and in its fall see the falling constellations. The
Ram, who gives sails to warm Zephyr before spring has grown
benignant, shall fall headlong into the waves over which he
had ferried fearful Helle. The Bull who carries the Hyades
before him on his shiny horn will drag the Twins down with
him and the Crab's curving claws. Herculean Leo, seething
with torrid heat, will again fall from the sky. Virgo will fall
to the earth she abandoned, and in their fall Libra's just
balances will force fierce Scorpion down. Old Sagittarius, who
holds feathered shafts to his Haemonian bowstring, shall lose

those shafts when the bowstring breaks. Frigid Capricorn, who brings chill winter back, will fall and break your pitcher, Aquarius, whoever you are. With you shall fall the Fish, heaven's last constellation, and the Wain, which was never washed by the sea, the swathing whirlpool shall engulf. Slippery Serpent, which separates the Bears like a river, shall fall, as will chill Cynosura the Lesser, which is joined to Draco the Greater by hard frost. The slow wagoner Arctophylax will lose his steadfastness and crash.

Are we alone of mankind deemed worthy of being overwhelmed by an unhinged universe? Is it upon us the last day has come? Ah, hard lot to which we were created, whether we have lost the sun to our misery or driven it away! Away with complaint, begone fear! A man unwilling to die when the world dies with him is too greedy of life.

V

(Enter ATREUS.)

ATREUS: On the stars' level I stride, I overtop all men and touch high heaven with my proud head. Now the glory of the realm, now the throne of my ancestors is within my grasp. I need not importune the gods; I have attained the height of my prayers. It is well, it is abundantly well, it is enough even for me. But why should it be enough? I shall go further, though the father is now sated by his sons' deaths. To obviate shame daylight has retired; on, while the sky is blank. But I wish I could hold the fugitive deities back and drag them perforce to make them all spectators of my avenging banquet. Still, the father must see it, and that is enough. Though daylight would say me nay, I will disperse the darkness under which your miseries lie covered. Too long have you reclined at table with expression carefree and cheerful; you have been at your courses long enough, long enough at your wine. For a shock so great we need a sober Thyestes. (*To his footmen*) Unbar the temple doors, my trooping slaves, open the festive chamber wide. It will be agreeable to see his changing complexion when he views his children's heads, what words he will use in the shock of grief, how his stunned gasps will stiffen his body. This is the fruit of my effort. I do not wish to see him miserable but to see him becoming miserable.

(*The doors are opened.* THYESTES *is seen at his banquet, in festive dress, half drunk, and forcing himself to be gay, but oppressed by premonitions. He is not aware that he is being watched.*)

The broad chamber is brilliant with numerous flambeaux. Himself is stretched on a couch of purple and gold, bolstering his head, which is heavy with wine, on his left hand. He is belching. Ah, most exalted of celestials am I, and king of kings. I have surpassed my hopes. He is sated, he is quaffing neat wine from a capacious silver goblet. Do not spare the drink; there is still the gore of victims in plenty, and this the tint of the wine will hide. With this chalice the dinner shall be closed. The father shall drink the mingled blood of his sons; he would have drunk mine. Look, he is now breaking into song, mumbling festive ditties, but he is not master of his mind.

THYESTES: Heart dulled with long troubles, put your anxious cares aside now. Away with melancholy, away with timorousness, away with bare poverty, the quaking exile's companion, and shame, which is affliction's burden; the level from which you fall matters more than where you land. It is a great thing to plant your feet firmly on the plain when you fall from a high pinnacle; when crushed to earth by overwhelming disasters it is a great thing to tolerate the weight of crumbled kingship with pliant neck, to bear the shards heaped upon your shoulders with posture erect, unbroken in spirit and unvanquished by adversity. But disperse now the clouds of cruel fate, erase all the scars of the years of affliction. Resume a serene expression for your flourishing state, banish the old Thyestes from your soul.

But the downtrodden cannot shake off their special neurosis; they can never believe that their state is happy. Though prosperity return, the afflicted find it hard to feel easy. Why do you pull me short, forbid me to celebrate this glad day, bid me weep? There is no discernible reason for this upwelling sadness; why does it prevent me from tying this pretty nosegay around my hair? But it does forbid me, it does! The spring roses have slipped down from my head, my hair which was glossed down with nard stands on end in sudden horror, despite myself my tears rain down, and my speech is punctuated with sighs. Grief loves its familiar tears, an uncanny passion for weeping depresses the miserable. I feel impelled to utter boding lamentations, I feel impelled to rip off this robe steeped in Tyrian purple, I feel impelled to shriek. My mind forebodes approaching sorrow, it presages disaster to itself. A fierce tempest hangs over sailors when the waters heave with no wind to ruffle them. What sorrow or what upheaval are you conjuring up, fool? Show your brother a trusting heart. Your apprehensions, whatever they are, are either baseless or too late. I do not choose to be unhappy, but some indefinable terror is stirring within me, my eyes pour out sudden tears, and I do not know why. Is it grief, or fear? Or are tears a function of great pleasure?

ATREUS (*moving toward* THYESTES *with simulated affability*): This happy day, dear Brother, we must celebrate with hearty accord. It shall make my scepter strong and knot the bonds of assured peace.

THYESTES: I have eaten to repletion, and I have drunk. One extra touch can increase my pleasure, if it were given me to share this joyous occasion with my sons.

ATREUS: Believe that they are here, in their father's bosom. Here they are and here they shall remain; no part of your offspring shall be taken from you. Ask, and I shall give whatever you desire. Presently I shall fill the father full with his whole brood. You will have enough, don't be uneasy. At present they are joined with mine in observing the jolly rites of the children's table, but they shall be fetched up. Take this brimming goblet; it is symbolic of our family.

THYESTES: I accept the toast of this brotherly feast. I shall pour drops out to our ancestral gods and then drain the wine down. But what is this? My hands refuse to mind, the cup's weight multiplies and bears my right hand down. The lifted wine recoils from my mouth and spills over my open but cheated lips. The very table jumps from the quaking floor. The fire barely shows light; more, the very sky is leaden and, with luminaries gone, stands stunned between day and night. What is this? More and yet more the arch of stricken heaven is tottering, the impenetrable gloom of close-packed darkness is thickening, night is piled on night, every star has fled. Whatever it is, I pray it may spare my brother and my sons, that the whole storm break upon this vile head! Now give me back my children!

ATREUS: I shall, and nothing shall ever take them from you.

(*Exit* ATREUS.)

THYESTES: What is this agitation that is churning my entrails? What is throbbing inside me? I sense a restive burden. My bosom is groaning, but the groans are not mine. Come, my sons, your unhappy father is calling you, come! The pain will go away at sight of you—they are reproaching me, from where?

(*Enter* ATREUS, *bearing a covered charger.*)

ATREUS: Ready your fatherly embraces; they are here. (*Uncovers the charger, which holds the boys' heads*) Do you recognize your sons?

THYESTES: I recognize my brother. Do you consent to carry such enormity, Mother Earth? Will you not plunge this kingdom and king to the infernal darkness of Styx, will you not cleave a broad path for them down to empty Chaos? Will you not pull this palace down to the very ground and overturn Mycenae? Both of us should long since have been standing where Tantalus stands. Wrench your bars asunder on this side and on that, and if there is any place lower than Tartarus and our grandfather's niche sink your huge chasm down to that point, bury us deep, and cover us with the whole of Acheron. The dead shall ramble over our heads, and fiery Phlegethon cascade all his sands in a white-hot stream as he tears violently over our prison.—But Earth lies unmoved, an indifferent bulk; the gods are gone.

ATREUS: Do take these boys you have so long wanted, and welcome. Your brother is not detaining you. Enjoy them, kiss them, share your embraces out to all three.

THYESTES: Is this your treaty? This your grace, your fraternal pledge? Is this how you put an end to hatred? I do not ask that my sons be restored unhurt to their father. But as brother to brother, I ask a favor you can grant without abating crime or hatred—permission to bury them. Give back what you will see burned at once. A father asks you for nothing he will keep but for what he must lose.

ATREUS: All that is left of your sons you have, and you have all that is not left.

THYESTES: Are they lying afield to feed ravenous birds? Are they being kept for monsters? Are they provender for beasts?

ATREUS: You have yourself eaten your sons in your impious dinner.

THYESTES: This is what made the gods ashamed, this is what drove day back to its rising. What shall I say in my misery? What plaints can I utter? What words will be adequate? I see the amputated heads, the hands wrenched off, the feet broken away from the cracked legs—this is what the greedy father could not hold. Their vitals are writhing inside me, the crime locked in its doorless prison is struggling to find an avenue of escape. Give me, Brother, a sword—your sword holds so much of my blood—the steel shall pave an opening for my children. You refuse me the sword? Then I shall beat my bosom until its welts wail aloud—hold your hand, unhappy man, we must spare the shades. Who has seen such enormity? What Heniochian who lives on barbarous Caucasus' rocky crags, what Procrustes who terrorized the Cecropian country? Here I am, a father who crushes his sons and am by my sons crushed: Is there any limit to crime?

ATREUS: Crime should be limited when you commit it, not when you requite it. Even this requital is too little for me. I ought to have poured the hot blood down your throat directly from the gash and made you drink the gore of your living sons. My haste cheated my anger. I gashed them with thrusts of my sword, I cut them down at the altar, I placated the hearth fire with ritual slaughter, I dissected the limbs of their lifeless bodies, carved them into small gobbets, plunged some into boiling cauldrons and spitted some to drip over slow fires. I tore their limbs and sinews apart while they were still alive, I saw the organs sputter on their skewers, and I fed the fire with my own hands. The father could have done all this, and it would have been much better; my passion was spent in vain. He did tear his sons with impious teeth, but he did not know, and they did not know!

THYESTES: Hear, you seas shut in by shifting shores, hear too this crime, you gods, wherever you have fled; hear, you gods infernal; hear, Earth; Night, heavy with black Tartarean clouds, hearken to my voice—to you am I abandoned, you only see my misery, you too have lost your stars. I shall proffer no wicked prayers, I ask nothing for myself—what could do me any good? It is you gods my prayers have in view. Thou, sky's supreme ruler, powerful lord of the ethereal court, wrap the whole world in thy fearful clouds, loosen war among all the winds, thunder mightily in every quarter, not with the lesser bolt which strikes buildings and harmless houses, but with the bolt that shattered the threefold mass of mountains and the Giants who ranged tall as these mountains. These weapons do thou brandish, hurl thy flame. Redeem the daylight that was lost, sweep thy fires through the heavens, with thy lightning bolts supply the light that was reft away. Thou needest not ponder: Count both cases damnable, and if not, count mine damnable. Aim at me, pierce this heart of mine with thy flashing three-pronged bolt. If as a father I wish to give my sons burial, to commit them to the final flames, I must myself be cremated. But if nothing sways the gods, if no deity will bring weapons to bear on the impious, may night persist forever and cover measureless crime with unending darkness. I do not complain, Titan, if you continue as you are.

ATREUS: Now I can admire my handiwork, now the palm is

truly won. If you did not suffer as you do, my crime would have been wasted. Now I can believe that my sons are my own, now my marriage has recovered its chastity.

THYESTES: How were my children at fault?

ATREUS: By being yours.

THYESTES: And to their father you—

ATREUS: Of course I did, and because they were indubitably yours I am glad.

THYESTES: I invoke the gods who preside over blood kin.

ATREUS: And not those of wedlock?

THYESTES: Who weighs crime out for crime?

ATREUS: I know why you are complaining. You are sorry you lost the initiative in crime. You are downhearted not because you wolfed that unspeakable meal but because you did not serve it. It was your intention to arrange a similar menu for your unwitting brother, to ambush my children with their mother's help, and to lay them out in the same kind of death. Only one thing stood in your way—you thought they were yours.

THYESTES: The gods will exact vengeance; to them my prayers deliver you for punishment.

ATREUS: And I deliver you to your sons for punishment.

FINIS

The Library of Liberal Arts